Spring System Design in Practice

Build scalable web applications using microservices and design patterns in Spring and Spring Boot

Rodrigo Santiago

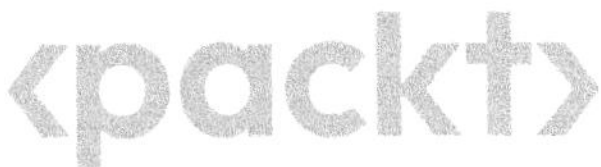

Spring System Design in Practice

Portfolio Director: Ashwin Nair

Relationship Lead: Aaron Lazar

Content Engineer: Kinnari Chohan

Project Manager: Ruvika Rao

Technical Editor: Aniket Shetty

Copy Editor: Safis Editing

Proofreader: Kinnari Chohan

Indexer: Rekha Nair

Production Designer: Vijay Kamble

Growth Lead: Anamika Singh

First published: April 2025

Production reference: 3061125

Published by Packt Publishing Ltd.

Grosvenor House

11 St Paul's Square

Birmingham

B3 1RB, UK

ISBN 978-1-80324-901-8

www.packtpub.com

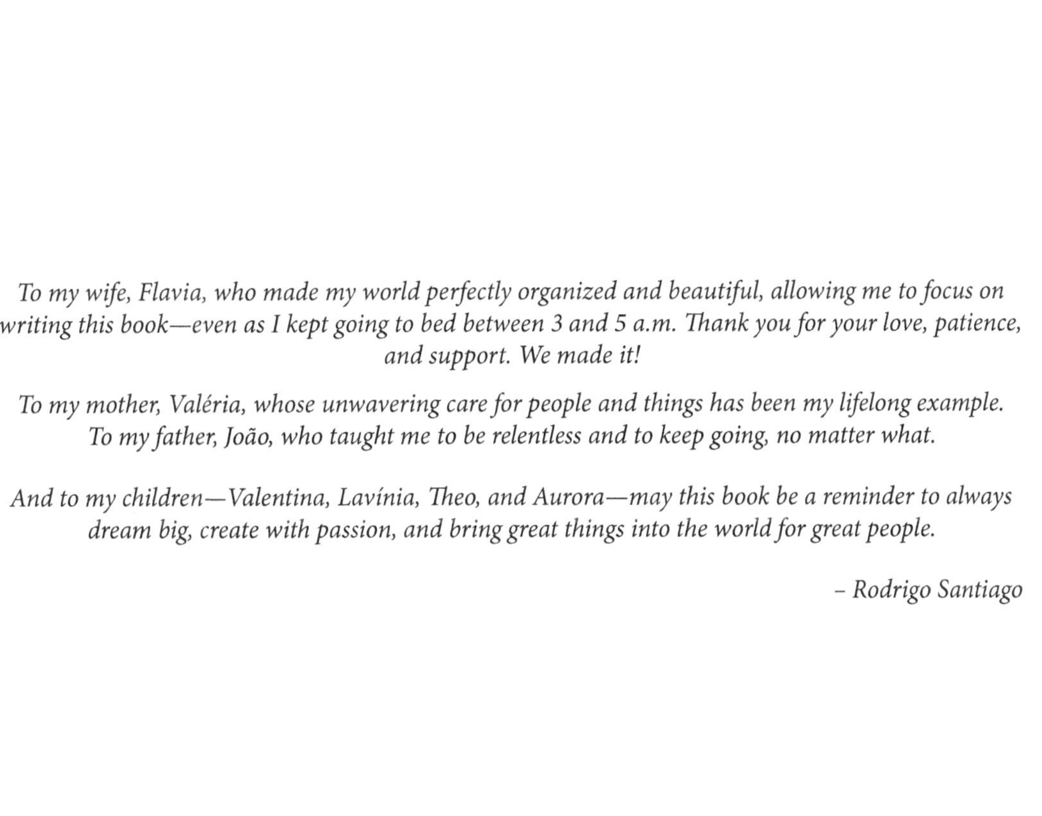

To my wife, Flavia, who made my world perfectly organized and beautiful, allowing me to focus on writing this book—even as I kept going to bed between 3 and 5 a.m. Thank you for your love, patience, and support. We made it!

To my mother, Valéria, whose unwavering care for people and things has been my lifelong example. To my father, João, who taught me to be relentless and to keep going, no matter what.

And to my children—Valentina, Lavínia, Theo, and Aurora—may this book be a reminder to always dream big, create with passion, and bring great things into the world for great people.

– Rodrigo Santiago

Foreword

In my 20 years of corporate world experience, I've read countless technical books – some inspiring, many forgettable. But few, if any, have captured the raw reality of software engineering within large, complex organizations quite like this one. *Spring System Design in Practice* doesn't just talk about system design – it lives in it, surprisingly.

As I turned each page, I went back to my own early years – navigating ambiguity while dealing with the complexity of the systems. It reminded me of the long nights spent trying to piece together scattered concepts and wondering how to bridge the gap between the development team and the business. If only I had a book like this 10 to 15 years ago… Alas, we can't go back in time – not yet, at least.

Rodrigo Santiago has created something truly special. His writing flows with the ease of a mentor explaining things across a whiteboard – grounded, clear, and refreshingly pragmatic. This book isn't a dry reference manual. It's a well-lit path through the chaos, guiding you through the architectural terrain of real-world systems with patience and precision.

What struck me most is how deeply relatable the scenarios are. Whether it's the trade-offs of microservice communication, the hidden costs of premature optimization, or the art of aligning development with actual business needs, every topic is framed through lessons that feel earned, not just researched.

For developers who feel overwhelmed by the jargon of modern system design, this book offers a sense of clarity. For seasoned engineers looking to sharpen their architectural lens, it serves as a reality check. And for aspiring architects, it's a roadmap and a reference rolled into one, full of hard-won insights and battle-tested patterns.

It also reminds us of something we often forget in fast-paced environments: good system design isn't about clever solutions, but clear thinking. It's about understanding before implementing – the "why" before the "how."

Spring System Design in Practice doesn't just show you what's possible with Spring – it shows you how to think holistically, build with confidence, and lead with insight.

Read it. Reflect on it. Then, go and build better systems – not just technically, but thoughtfully.

Shalini Goyal

Global Technology Leader, Ex-Amazon

Contributors

About the author

Rodrigo Santiago is a software developer with years of experience streamlining systems and improving products and processes. He has led projects that turned chaotic challenges into high-performance solutions, focusing on areas where small changes had a big impact. Known for his calm and positive approach under pressure, Rodrigo has successfully guided cross-functional teams to deliver results.

Rodrigo has worked in diverse industries, from legal tech to fintech, tackling system architecture and team dynamics. His expertise in system design, microservices, and event-driven architecture has enabled scalable solutions that meet both technical and business needs.

About the reviewer

Ibidapo Abdulazeez is a software engineer with over two years of experience building scalable solutions, particularly in the fintech and real estate sectors. Holding a master's degree in Computer Science, Abdulazeez is passionate about leveraging technology to address critical challenges in underdeveloped sectors.

With expertise in cloud computing, machine learning, and backend development using Spring, Abdulazeez has worked on projects such as credit card fraud detection systems and student loan accessibility APIs. Aspiring to pursue a PhD in Computer Science, Abdulazeez is committed to driving technological advancements and innovation in the field.

Table of Contents

Part 1: Foundations for System Design

1

What are the Product Requirements?   3

2

Sorting Complex Requirements into Features, Use Cases, and Stories   21

3

Defining Domains for Your Application   57

4

Defining Services for Your Domains   81

Part 2: Designing Great Spring Services

5

Writing Your Services – Introducing REST APIs with the Spring Framework   99

6

Translating Business Requirements into Well-Designed Spring APIs   159

7

Handling Data and Evolving Your Microservice   207

Part 3: Security, Performance, and Scalability

8

Securing Services with Spring Security and OAuth 2.0   261

9

High-Performance Secure Communication Between Spring Services   301

10

Building Asynchronous, Event-Driven Systems With NoSQL Databases   327

Part 4: Orchestrating Resilient Services

11

Launching Your Self-Organizing Microservice Cloud   359

12

Optimizing Your Services   393

13

Unlock Your Exclusive Benefits   413

Index   417

Other Books You May Enjoy   430

Preface

Welcome to this journey into the heart of Spring! If you've ever stared at a blank IDE, wondering where to even begin when building a robust, scalable service, you're not alone. The world of software development is full of grand ideas and ambitious goals, but turning those into well-structured, maintainable applications? That's both an art and a science. This book is here to help you bridge that gap.

We will start with the foundations because great software is built on clarity. We'll walk through dissecting requirements, distinguishing between functional and non-functional needs, and transforming them into domain objects and solid API contracts. It's like laying down the blueprint before building a skyscraper—you wouldn't want your application to topple at the first gust of real-world complexity.

Then, we'll roll up our sleeves and get into the real magic: building services with Spring. How should interfaces interact with implementations? What's a clean way to design services that will grow gracefully over time? We'll answer these questions and propose a practical blueprint for creating new APIs and communicating seamlessly with other systems. And since security is a non-negotiable in today's world, we'll dive into user authentication, token creation, and validation using asymmetric keys.

Of course, no journey is complete without a few obstacles. We'll face them head-on with testing—unit tests, integration tests, and end-to-end tests—ensuring that what we build is not just functional, but reliable. We'll also explore event-driven architectures, discuss best practices for handling data integrations with SQL and NoSQL databases, and even build a fully-fledged Spring Cloud application.

But what happens when things go wrong? Because, let's face it, they will. Services fail, networks break, and race conditions lurk in the shadows. That's why we'll also talk about designing for resilience: structuring configurations effectively, handling failures gracefully, and resolving concurrency issues like a seasoned architect.

Throughout this book, we'll keep things practical. This isn't an abstract tour of Spring 6's features; it's a hands-on guide to building applications that work in the real world—applications that scale, recover from failures, and integrate cleanly with the systems around them. We will work from a sample application that we call the HomeIt app, which connects landlords with tenants interested in renting properties.

So, grab your favorite beverage (coffee, tea, or whatever fuels your coding sessions), fire up your IDE, and let's build something great together. Welcome to the world of Spring!

> **Note on Spring Framework Updates**
>
> At the time of writing, milestone releases for Spring Framework 7 have begun rolling out, with the official release expected in November 2025. While Spring 7 introduces enhancements and changes, particularly around HTTP client interfaces, this book focuses primarily on software architecture and system design concepts that are largely framework-agnostic.
>
> The examples and practices discussed do not rely on specific features of Spring's HTTP client tooling (such as OpenFeign), and as such, remain valid and applicable despite the updates in Spring 7.
>
> We are committed to maintaining the accuracy and relevance of our content, and will continue to monitor major updates to ensure that readers are well informed.

Who this book is for

Whether you're taking your first steps into the world of Spring or you're an experienced system architect looking to refine your approach to scalable web services, this book has something for you.

If you're new to Spring, you might feel overwhelmed by its vast ecosystem. Where do you start? How do you structure your application? How do all these components fit together? We've been there. That's why this book walks you through the fundamentals—from dissecting requirements to designing APIs, writing services, integrating databases, and handling security. By the time you finish, you'll have built a fully functional, production-ready Spring application with confidence.

For system architects and experienced developers, this book provides a structured approach to designing scalable, resilient services. We'll cover best practices for API design, authentication with asymmetric keys, event-driven architectures, and fault tolerance. If you want to ensure your Spring applications can handle real-world complexity while staying maintainable and performant, this book will help you get there.

This book assumes you have some prior experience with an object-oriented programming language and a basic understanding of how to write Java code. You don't need to be an expert in software development processes—our goal is to provide a clear framework that will help you take high-level requirements and break them down into a resilient family of services that scale effectively.

So, whether you're just starting out or refining your craft, let's dive in and build great things together!

What this book covers

Chapter 1, What Are the Product Requirements?, explores how to capture product requirements in a structured, precise way that sets the foundation for well-defined problems and solutions. Every great system starts with a well-defined purpose. You'll learn how to identify key business needs and translate them into technical goals that guide development from the very beginning.

Chapter 2, Sorting Complex Requirements into Features, Use Cases, and Stories, untangles the complexity of software projects often starting as a tangled web of expectations by breaking down requirements into clear features, use cases, and user stories. This structured approach ensures that we capture what truly matters while keeping the development process manageable and focused.

Chapter 3, LayinDefining Domains for Your Application, explains how, before we write a single line of code, we need to understand the business domain. In this chapter, we'll use a key **domain-driven design (DDD)** technique to create visual representations of our system's core concepts, ensuring that our models align with real-world business logic.

Chapter 4, Defining Services for Your Domains, explains how functional requirements tell us what the system must do, but technical requirements define how it should operate. We'll cover the crucial technical constraints and expectations on the technical side, ensuring that our services are built for real-world demands with the right tools in place.

Chapter 5, Writing Your Services – Introducing REST APIs with the Spring Framework, introduces the core principles of RESTful APIs and walks you through creating your first Spring-powered service, complete with controllers, request handling, and responses. Now that we have a strong foundation from the previous chapters, it's time to start building!

Chapter 6, Translating Business Requirements into Well-Designed Spring APIs, teaches you how to build adaptable Spring services by defining clear interfaces, decoupling implementations, and seamlessly integrating different services with each other. We'll also cover key concepts of how Spring provides interfaces and implementations for connecting to external systems very efficiently.

Chapter 7, Handling Data and Evolving Your Microservice, explains how data is the lifeblood of any system, and how we handle it determines the flexibility of our services. In this chapter, we'll explore how to work with relational databases in Spring, how to prototype your service very quickly, and what the different approaches for creating custom queries versus out-of-the-box data connections are that make it easier to retrieve or save data.

Chapter 8, Securing Services with Spring Security and OAuth 2.0, provides a hands-on guide to implementing authentication and authorization using Spring Security and OAuth 2.0, ensuring that our services protect sensitive data while providing seamless user access. Security is non-negotiable in modern applications.

Chapter 9, High-Performance and Secure Communication Between Spring Services, explains why when multiple services need to communicate, performance and security become critical concerns. We'll dive into strategies for making inter-service communication efficient, secure, and scalable, covering how to create asynchronous services with WebFlux.

Chapter 10, Building Asynchronous, Event-Driven Systems with NoSQL Databases, introduces event-driven architectures, showing how to decouple services using messaging systems and NoSQL databases to build scalable, reactive applications, as not all interactions need to happen in real time.

Chapter 11, Launching Your Self-Organizing Microservice Cloud, explores how to launch a cloud-native Spring application, leveraging service discovery, API gateways, remote configurations, and other critical features that make your services connect to each other smoothly.

Chapter 12, Optimizing Your Services, focuses on critical performance tuning, caching, handling failures gracefully, and improving resilience. From circuit breakers to concurrency solutions and distributed transaction consistency checks, we'll ensure our services thrive under real-world conditions.

To get the most out of this book

Software/hardware covered in the book	Operating system requirements
Java (22 minimum, 25+ recommended)	Windows, Ubuntu
Spring 6+	
Gradle	
Intellij Community Edition (optional)	

If you are using the digital version of this book, we advise you to type the code yourself or access the code from the book's GitHub repository (a link is available in the next section). Doing so will help you avoid any potential errors related to the copying and pasting of code.

Download the example code files

You can download the example code files for this book from GitHub at `https://github.com/PacktPublishing/Spring-System-Design-in-Practice`. If there's an update to the code, it will be updated in the GitHub repository.

We also have other code bundles from our rich catalog of books and videos available at `https://github.com/PacktPublishing/`. Check them out!

Conventions used

There are a number of text conventions used throughout this book.

`Code in text`: Indicates code words in text, database table names, folder names, filenames, file extensions, pathnames, dummy URLs, user input, and Twitter handles. Here is an example: "Mount the downloaded `WebStorm-10*.dmg` disk image file as another disk in your system."

A block of code is set as follows:

```
html, body, #map {
  height: 100%;
  margin: 0;
```

```
    padding: 0
}
```

When we wish to draw your attention to a particular part of a code block, the relevant lines or items are set in bold:

```
[default]
exten => s,1,Dial(Zap/1|30)
exten => s,2,Voicemail(u100)
exten => s,102,Voicemail(b100)
exten => i,1,Voicemail(s0)
```

Any command-line input or output is written as follows:

```
$ mkdir css
$ cd css
```

Bold: Indicates a new term, an important word, or words that you see onscreen. For instance, words in menus or dialog boxes appear in **bold**. Here is an example: "Select **System info** from the **Administration** panel."

> **Tips or important notes**
> Appear like this.

Get in touch

Feedback from our readers is always welcome.

General feedback: If you have questions about any aspect of this book, email us at customercare@ packtpub.com and mention the book title in the subject of your message.

Errata: Although we have taken every care to ensure the accuracy of our content, mistakes do happen. If you have found a mistake in this book, we would be grateful if you would report this to us. Please visit www.packtpub.com/support/errata and fill in the form.

Piracy: If you come across any illegal copies of our works in any form on the internet, we would be grateful if you would provide us with the location address or website name. Please contact us at copyright@packt.com with a link to the material.

If you are interested in becoming an author: If there is a topic that you have expertise in and you are interested in either writing or contributing to a book, please visit authors.packtpub.com.

Share your thoughts

Once you've read *Spring System Design in Practice*, we'd love to hear your thoughts! Scan the QR code below to go straight to the Amazon review page for this book and share your feedback.

`https://packt.link/r/1803249013`

Your review is important to us and the tech community and will help us make sure we're delivering excellent quality content.

Free Benefits with Your Book

This book comes with free benefits to support your learning. Activate them now for instant access (see the "*How to Unlock*" section for instructions).

Here's a quick overview of what you can instantly unlock with your purchase:

PDF and ePub Copies

Next-Gen Web-Based Reader

Access a DRM-free PDF copy of this book to read anywhere, on any device.

Use a DRM-free ePub version with your favorite e-reader.

Multi-device progress sync: Pick up where you left off, on any device.

Highlighting and notetaking: Capture ideas and turn reading into lasting knowledge.

Bookmarking: Save and revisit key sections whenever you need them.

Dark mode: Reduce eye strain by switching to dark or sepia themes

How to Unlock

Scan the QR code (or go to `packtpub.com/unlock`). Search for this book by name, confirm the edition, and then follow the steps on the page.

Note: Keep your invoice handly. Purchase made directly from packt don't require one.

Part 1: Foundations for System Design

Before writing a single line of code, we need to understand what we're building. This part focuses on dissecting product requirements, organizing them into actionable development tasks, and structuring domain models that will form the backbone of our system. By the end of this part, you'll have a clear path from abstract business needs to a concrete technical vision.

This part includes the following chapters:

- *Chapter 1, What are Product Requirements?*
- *Chapter 2, Sorting Complex Requirements into Features, Use Cases, and Stories*
- *Chapter 3, Defining Domains for Your Application*
- *Chapter 4, Defining Services for Your Domains*

What are the Product Requirements?

Welcome to a fascinating journey through the Spring Framework!

In this chapter, we will cover the world of the so-called "business" or "product" requirements that can be used across any kind of development work, regardless of the tech stack. These are the system's heart and soul, the first thing we need to know about our apps. Requirements are what make a product tick. After all, if we're creating software, we need to have a reason why. It's important to understand that best practices for software development are not just required in the middle or end of development, but instead, they begin right as we start conceptualizing the project.

That being said, in this chapter, we're first going to figure out the problems that we're solving and then we'll begin to clearly articulate the solutions to those problems.

Here's what we'll unpack:

- Unlocking your finances with the Spring Framework
- How is this book structured to help you succeed?
- Why do we need to understand business requirements?
- Crystal-clear needs – ensuring businesses get requirements right
- The pitfalls of product requirements

The world of business requirements is packed with insights waiting to be uncovered. As I dove deeper, I was very surprised by the treasures I could mine from past experiences. Missing out on these could mean wasted time, money, and effort. Imagine you're building your dream house without a blueprint. Sounds risky, right? That's exactly how vital our software's blueprint—the requirements—is.

> **Free Benefits with Your Book**
>
> Your purchase includes a free PDF copy of this book along with other exclusive benefits. Check the *Free Benefits with Your Book* section in the Preface to unlock them instantly and maximize your learning experience.

Unlocking your finances with the Spring Framework

Understanding the significance of the Spring Framework in today's backend development landscape is crucial. It stands as one of the most valuable tools out there. Period.

Much of its prestige is due to its foundation on the **Java Virtual Machine** (**JVM**), a cornerstone of technology that's over 30 years old and boasts extensive market maturity.

The JVM, along with the Java programming language, creates a formidable platform for software development, thanks to its standout features:

- The universal compatibility of its compiled packages across operating systems
- JVM bytecode's ability to run on nearly any hardware
- The Java JIT compiler's optimization of bytecode into native code at runtime, offering high performance close to that of C-language programs without the complexity of memory management
- A vast global developer community
- Ongoing support and yearly improvements
- Access to top-tier IDEs, enhancing the development experience for all programmers

These are just a few of the reasons Java and JVM together form such a powerful platform. And that's only one reason for the Spring Framework's acclaim.

Spring Framework experts are highly sought after, and will be into the future.

Moreover, the Spring ecosystem has secured its status as the most beneficial, quickest to implement, and simplest Java programming framework to understand. This distinction is due to the Spring Framework's adoption of superior design principles among all frameworks available on the market.

Created in 2003, the Spring Framework boasts over two decades of refinement. With each release, the Spring community has diligently preserved the best patterns and standards, discarding what no longer serves its purpose. Can you envision accessing such an extensive collection of tried-and-tested concepts and ideas for your benefit, free of charge?

By specializing in Spring, you gain expertise in the top framework built upon the best programming platform for the most demanding use case: enterprise applications. The Spring Framework is particularly crucial for developing backend microservice architectures, currently the foundation of the world's largest companies.

Backend microservices in enterprise companies constitute a multi-billion-dollar industry, with Java playing a leading role. Thus, by mastering the Spring Framework, you become an exceptionally valuable professional in the industry, globally. You elevate yourself to a world-class, highly esteemed professional status.

While many excellent frameworks and languages are used in enterprise backend systems, none other offers a framework for enterprise backend scenarios with such a large, active community, numerous job opportunities, and a combination of a well-structured language with an equally structured framework. The Spring ecosystem is unmatched in the market.

"But the Spring Framework is such a complex beast!" This is a common sentiment? The vast landscape of Spring projects can seem overwhelming at first glance.

Diving into the Spring ecosystem might feel like exploring a labyrinth of endless possibilities. For many, sifting through the Spring documentation can seem like a daunting endeavor.

Even the most seasoned developers, including tech leads and staff engineers, often admit to lacking a clear overview of the entire Spring project.

Whether you're a seasoned programmer in other languages or frameworks or just dipping your toes into Spring, you'll likely encounter essential questions:

- What are my options for building systems with the Spring Framework?
- What are the key components for system development in Spring?
- When should I prefer one component over another?
- How do Spring components and projects work together?
- What's the primary use of each Spring project?

By the end of this book, you'll find yourself able to confidently answer these questions, equipped with a solid understanding of how Spring's diverse components address real-world development challenges. While no system is without its flaws (yes, bugs are part of the journey), you're now on the path to learning the Spring ecosystem. Ready to embark on this adventure?

While others may feel uncertain of how to choose Spring components for their specific implementation and business needs, this book offers a clear roadmap. It guides you from understanding the initial business requirements to confidently programming software with the right approach, simplifying what can often seem like a daunting process.

How is this book structured to help you succeed?

By diving into this book, you'll learn how to decipher even the most challenging business needs. You'll learn how to transform these needs into clear, actionable use cases, akin to drawing a detailed map that guides how a system should come to life.

Starting with the map (use cases), you will move on to designing a vibrant city (domains, services, and sequence diagrams), and, finally, to constructing the buildings (coding) that stand tall in production. Along the way, we'll embrace automated tests like a trusted compass, ensuring our development process is not only swift but also efficient and fail-safe.

In this section, we're tackling the "software developer dilemma" head-on.

In the world of big enterprise companies, software engineers often find themselves at a crossroads—deciding whether to become visionary architects or coding wizards:

- Architects spend considerable time in discussions with product teams, working out how to decompose business needs into large work units: services, APIs, and interfaces. They are the professionals skilled in creating high-level designs and distributing well-defined tasks across teams and individual members. Many of them may not have written a line of code in some time, yet their expertise in design and planning remains critical.

- On the other hand, most programmers prefer working with the well-defined tasks that architects and technical leaders prepare. They enjoy coding independently, often seeking quiet away from business discussions, which they might find less engaging. Programmers typically focus more on the technical aspects of development, rather than directly extracting services from business-centric conversations.

This book is crafted to merge the two worlds of high-level design and detailed programming. It is structured as follows:

- Initially, you'll learn how to discern requirements and translate them into high-level service designs in the first three chapters.

- Subsequently, *Chapters 4* to *10* guide you through addressing technical and non-functional requirements to implement straightforward services with Spring. This includes writing APIs, managing data, ensuring security, and more sophisticated tasks like working with events-based architectures.

- Advancing further, *Chapters 11* and *12* elevate your understanding to construct a complete microservice cloud using Spring, featuring self-recovery, alongside with principles and tips to optimize your service performance.

This book encapsulates this entire journey. I'm excited for you to uncover the full potential of the Spring Framework for both the industry and your career.

I have just one request as you embark on this journey:

Always carry a big smile, especially through the challenges.

Persist in your learning journey; it's the essence of a fulfilling career in IT and software development. We navigate complex topics with countless variables. Remember, you're only human, and perfection in software is an evolving target. Your initial code might need refinement, and that's perfectly normal. Next week, you might spot opportunities for improvement—this cycle is almost inevitable.

Embrace the occasional mistake and address bugs promptly; this mindset will reward you immensely in your career.

Are you ready to adopt this approach and become a leading Spring expert in your organization? Do you aspire to be the top Spring Framework architect where you work?

Let's dive in without delay!

Why do we need to understand business requirements?

Let's dive into coding already...

Not so fast! A lack of understanding of business requirements will lead to a lot of misuse of the Spring Framework.

I recognize your eagerness to delve into creating Spring services using the best and most reliable design patterns available in our industry.

I could start by showcasing services built on Spring right at this moment. However, the challenge lies not in the absence of willingness but in the foundational knowledge of where to initiate. The Spring ecosystem is pretty broad, catering to a myriad of use cases, which begs the following questions: What are the pivotal elements? What defines the "beginning" and the "end"?

Indeed, there is no clear "beginning" or "end" within the Spring ecosystem; each component is designed to complement the others. Therefore, the key lies in understanding the specific needs that drive the selection of each component or Spring project. A common hurdle is that many lack insight on which Spring project to choose for their software solutions. More crucially, there's a widespread challenge in translating real-world demands into effective Spring Framework architecture and implementation strategies.

This gap in the industry stems from developers struggling to grasp customer perspectives, rooted in years of technology-focused discussions and coding, with minimal emphasis on customer engagement or adopting alternative viewpoints. Many software developers find themselves ensnared within their technological paradigms, unable to easily step beyond their confines. Grasping business requirements emerges as a fundamental skill for programmers aspiring to enhance their development capabilities and architectural acumen. It is precisely this skill that we aim to develop through this book.

Perfecting business requirements

This principle will help you avoid very big losses in your Spring implementation, because business requirements are the highest leverage point for steering you and your team toward success—or, conversely, toward failure.

The nuances and variables at play are numerous. A thoroughly crafted requirements document can instill a sense of clarity within the team, making the necessary steps forward appear intuitive. On the other hand, gaps in these requirements can lead to confusion, delays, and, often, unwelcome surprises in daily operations.

I have witnessed numerous adverse outcomes resulting from poorly outlined requirements:

- Teams might find themselves discarding months of development work

- Systems could be launched with missing functionalities, impacting user experience

- Integration issues may only come to light at advanced stages of the project

- Project timelines could be repeatedly pushed back, disrupting planned launch dates

- The quality assurance team might struggle with what and how to test, leading to potential oversights

- Poor architectural decisions are more likely to be made, impacting the project's long-term sustainability

- Short-sighted choices could incur significant future costs

- Additional hours may become necessary to meet deadlines, impacting team morale and project budgets

And so it goes. If you breeze past these initial chapters, heed this playful prophecy: thou shall not know peace in thy projects. Mornings will dawn with the suspense of what fresh chaos awaits in your Slack chats. But fear not! Be the guardian of ensuring all requirements align with these best practices. Do this, and thou art destined for a far more delightful existence as a Spring developer.

What are business requirements?

Business requirements, *product requirements*, and *functional requirements* are terms companies use to encapsulate the solutions their systems will provide to customer issues.

Understanding business requirements first requires a grasp of what constitutes a customer's problem.

So, what exactly is a problem?

Can you succinctly define a customer's issue? Many have an intuitive sense of problems but struggle to articulate them clearly. It's a common oversight but many are unaware of their own gaps in specifying or handling business requirements.

This gap in understanding can significantly impact the quality of architectural decisions.

I've seen numerous instances where teams went in circles, attempting to pinpoint a product's purpose. However, with the simple concepts, definitions, and tools I'm about to introduce, organizing and clarifying business needs becomes straightforward. Imagine converting weeks of circular discussions into a productive one-hour session. It's both powerful and straightforward.

Let's demystify business requirements with this simple yet profound definition of a "customer problem":

A customer problem arises from an undesirable situation.

This succinct phrase carries immense weight. It implies that software development should always aim to transition customers from undesirable states to solutions—desired states. Thus, your software should act as a gateway, guiding the customer away from their issue toward a resolution.

Now, getting back to what a business requirement is.

If we understand a problem as an undesirable situation, and the solution as the future, sought-after state, then the business requirement is essentially a compilation of precise statements detailing the actions your software must take to transition the customer from their current predicament to the desired resolution.

Let's delve deeper into this concept.

Crystal-clear needs – ensuring businesses get requirements right

The methodology that we'll discuss in this section helps to bring structure and clarity to the conversation about requirements. I have developed it using core concepts I learned in the neuro-linguistic programming field. While we don't need to get into the technicalities of NLP here, I think learning this way of structuring business requirements will be beneficial in helping you understand the very nature of business requirements.

Business people will usually freely write about the characteristics of the solutions they want to create. But, in fact, there are a few hidden variables at play in that usual, free-text form. When you really understand them, you will be able to spot gaps and missing pieces in any business requirements.

Visualizing timelines for problem-solving

Utilizing a visual timeline simplifies the definition of a business requirement by focusing on two critical junctures: the present and future *states*. The present state details the customer's current challenges, while the future state envisions their circumstances after implementing your solution.

Visuals are super important, as we have discovered from brain science. When we use pictures or diagrams, our brain just "lights up" in more places. By using more of our neurons, we understand things better. Our brain is really good at seeing and making sense of pictures. For example, think about how we understand time like it's a straight line in our heads. That's us using a picture to grasp a tricky concept. So, when we use visuals to explain systems, it taps into our brain's strong suit of working with images, making it easier for us to get the hang of things, including very complex business requirements. In short, using pictures isn't just helpful; it's a smart and necessary way to make the most of how our brains like to learn and solve things.

The following figure offers a clear framework for understanding the transformative journey your software facilitates for its users:

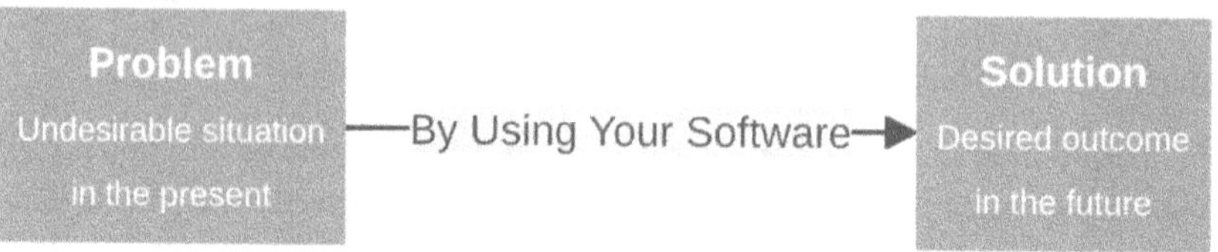

Figure 1.1 – From problem to solution by using software

For a comprehensive and effective business requirement document, it's essential to compile statements that vividly illustrate the contrast between the current and future states of the customer. Visualize this document as a two-column layout: the left side details the customer's present, undesirable situation, while the right side outlines the desirable future state after using your software. Importantly, the document must also specify how the software will facilitate the customer's transition from the undesirable present to the desirable future.

This structure not only clarifies the purpose and function of the software but also ensures that all stakeholders have a shared understanding of the objectives and the transformative potential of the project.

Taking the example of what problem social media platforms solve, we could put the elements in a basic timeline:

Figure 1.2 – What problem does social media solve?

In the chart, we observe two contrasting phases that delineate life before and after the advent of social media platforms.

On the left side, the scenario depicts a time when customers faced challenges in swiftly and effortlessly staying updated with their friends' lives on a daily basis. The right side, conversely, portrays the transformative impact of adopting social media, where customers enjoy the convenience of easily and instantly connecting with friends, marking a significant shift toward enhanced communication and social interaction.

This stark contrast highlights the role of social media platforms in bridging communication gaps and fostering connections among users. Of course, there are more problems solved by social media. This is just an example for illustration purposes.

Crafting business requirements

Now that we've delineated "problems" and "solutions" within our timeline model, the next crucial step is a comprehensive description of your product. Essentially, your product acts as the conduit transporting customers from their current predicaments to the envisioned solutions.

To ensure your product delivers on its promise, it's vital to define the attributes and qualities required for it to effectively transition customers from their "problem" state to the "solution" state. This is where the terms *business requirements*, *product requirements*, or simply *requirements* come into play, often used interchangeably across different organizations.

Crafting a complete set of business requirements typically involves a four-step process:

1. Identify all the *problems* faced by your customers that your product aims to solve.

2. Define the *solutions* to clearly articulate how your product should transform the user experience.

3. Outline the *high-level requirements* for each problem-solution pair, detailing what is necessary to achieve the desired outcome.

Turn the high-level requirements into *refined requirements* for specific use cases, business rules, and processes that will guide the development and implementation of solutions.

For a more visual representation of these steps, take a look at this figure:

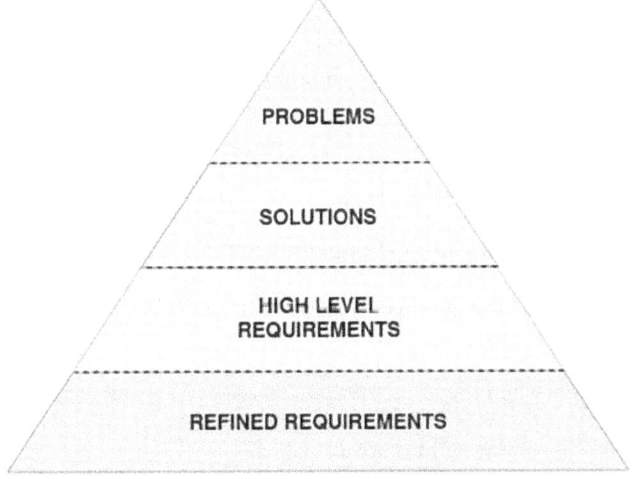

Figure 1.3 – From problems to refined requirements

In the upcoming sections, we'll dive deeper into each of these steps, providing a clear framework for translating customer needs into actionable product features and functionalities.

Identifying customer's key problems

Imagine you have recently joined a start-up called *HomeIt*—a company specializing in helping tenants find the perfect apartment that fits their lifestyle needs.

What could be the problems faced by tenants?

Here are some possible problems we can list. Remember, a "problem" is a description of a present issue, or an undesirable situation faced by your target users:

- Not all realtors are trustworthy

- Rental property ads sometimes hide existing problems

- Relationships with landlords and realtors can be difficult to manage

- There are a limited number of payment options available

- Contracts take a long time to be finalized

- There is a lack of good insurance options

What other problems can you imagine that tenants face during the experience of renting a home? Take some time to think about it before moving on to the next section.

Creating a matrix of problem-solution statements

Now that we have created a list of current problems tenants face, let's create a list of possible solutions to each problem. There could be more than one solution to each problem:

- Not all realtors are trustworthy:

  - Provide a list of trustworthy realtors

- Rental property ads sometimes hide existing problems:

  - Allow tenants to report issues not mentioned in the property ads that they might find when moving into a rental property

  - Compensate tenants when they find unreported issues in rental properties

- A limited number of payment options are available:

  - Offer different types of payment options

  - Make payments easy and fast for all parties—realtors, landlords, and tenants

  - Provide financial guarantees for landlords, in case tenants cannot pay their rent in a specific month

  - Provide a financial guarantee for tenants, in case they cannot pay their rent in a specific month

I'm not considering that some of these solutions might not be commercially viable. The examples offered here are for illustration purposes only.

Now that I have provided some solution samples, you can continue the exercise and provide new samples for the other problems mentioned in the earlier section. You can also use the problem samples you came up with to create new solutions.

Take some time to carry out this exercise before moving on to the next section.

Describing the high-level requirements for a solution

Now that we've pinpointed the issues our customers face and the solutions they need, let's outline the kind of software necessary to transition them from facing problems to embracing solutions.

Consider this scenario for HomeIt:

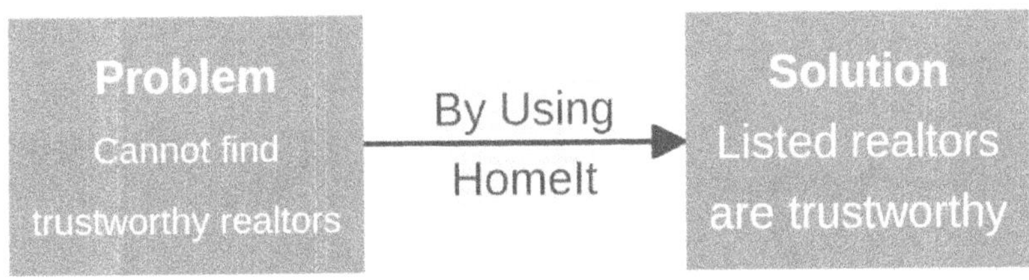

Figure 1.4 – HomeIt problem and solution sample

What are the required features that the HomeIt system should provide in this case?

Let's work with some simple paragraphs that illustrate the product's value, as an example:

Our system will equip every realtor with a business quality score, a 1- to 5-star rating derived from feedback given by tenants and landlords after successful dealings. This feature will act like a trust meter, helping users make informed decisions by choosing to partner with highly rated professionals.

Moreover, the HomeIt platform will include a mediation feature, enabling tenants, realtors, and landlords to address and resolve conflicts directly within our system. This ensures that any bumps along the road can be smoothed out efficiently, fostering a trusting and supportive community.

Additionally, HomeIt will offer insurance options for both tenants and landlords to safeguard against unexpected incidents potentially caused by other parties.

This trio of features—reliable realtor ratings, straightforward conflict resolution, and comprehensive insurance—lays the groundwork for a trusted environment where everyone can conduct business with peace of mind.

This sample provides a broad overview, focusing on the general actions a system should undertake to transition users from facing problems to enjoying solutions in the future.

At this stage, detailed specifics, business rules, or processes are less critical. Think of this high-level requirement as the initial brainstorming phase, which will be refined later. While we could delve into some rules and details, the main objective now is to lay out ideas openly, without too much concern for precision.

These overarching product requirements outline the vision of our solution.

Adopting this structured approach simplifies identifying customer problems, envisioning goals that resolve these issues, and defining requirements to guide customers toward our envisioned system.

Now it's your turn. Reflect on the problems and solutions we've discussed and outline some high-level requirements for the HomeIt start-up.

In upcoming chapters, we'll delve into the "Refine" phase, discussing use cases, sequence diagrams, domains, and so on.

In the next section of this chapter, we'll examine potential pitfalls in defining business requirements. Those principles will save you a ton of time.

The pitfalls of product requirements

The following guidelines were learned through personal experience throughout the years of working on different projects. Even multi-million-dollar monthly revenue products could bear such mistakes. Letting these things happen can cost the company a lot of extra time and money, and can lead to technical debt, bad architecture design, delivery delays, and so on. Learn from my experience; you don't want to let these mistakes happen to you as well.

Are mock designs business requirements?

Though visual mockups and Figma designs are integral to software development today, they are essentially interpretations of well-defined business requirements.

This is important to note, as sometimes you may question whether a mock user journey for a feature will actually and fully deliver the requirements. As a software engineer and analyst, it is also your responsibility to double-check whether the suggested visuals will lead to issues during development, in the user journey, or in performance—or even if the visuals identify business rules that were not made explicit in the business requirements and use cases (more about use cases in the next chapter).

In instances where visual representations are provided without explicit business requirements, development risks become pronounced. Clear, written statements defining the product team's expectations are indispensable for a smooth development process.

Requirements should not express technology choices

It's common in our field to encounter business requirements that prescribe technical methods for implementing a feature. However, it's crucial to understand that technical suggestions should not be confused with what defines a "business requirement."

Falling into the habit of treating technology directives within requirements as non-negotiable can trap you into limited choices, closing off the possibility of discovering better solutions. This practice can create significant blind spots for businesses.

Another downside of incorporating technology choices into business requirements is it can limit the product team to the capabilities of the chosen technologies. The development team, with its deep understanding of various technologies and their trade-offs, is better positioned to determine the most suitable technology for meeting the requirements.

Pointing out that business requirements should avoid containing technical instructions opens up opportunities for the product team to define features more broadly, with more freedom of thinking. This approach allows for more innovation, giving the development team the freedom to select the optimal implementation methods.

Does a customer know the problems they are experiencing?

It's quite fascinating that some problems are invisible to customers until solutions are presented. Often, innovative companies are the ones that shed light on these hidden issues, offering solutions to problems customers didn't even know they had. Indeed, customers might be in less-than-ideal situations without realizing there's an alternative.

Consider the invention of social media platforms. They introduced a new way for people to quickly share and receive updates from friends. Initially, this service was catered to tech-savvy individuals while others were hesitant or unaware of its benefits. I remember trying to get my friends on board, but they were largely indifferent.

Over time, however, social media has become a universal tool, with even tech-averse grandparents finding value in staying connected. Today, it's hard to find someone who doesn't use at least one social media platform. My grandmother, for instance, is now more active on Instagram than I am, and she thoroughly enjoys it.

This shift highlights how social media addressed a need that was once unrecognized. Initially seen as unnecessary by many, it has now become integral to our daily communication.

Are solutions the final step?

Of course, every situation can represent a problem. In such a way, moving the customer to a solution state might actually reveal new situations that could represent problems.

Take our social media scenario as an example. People flock to these platforms for the chance to stay connected with a wide circle of friends and influencers across various life stages. It's a modern marvel of connectivity.

Yet, here's the twist: becoming an avid social media user can lead to spending excessive hours scrolling, a potential drain on one's time, and a source of envy and psychological strain from constant comparison. Not to mention the encouragement to overshare, risking privacy for a moment of online validation. It's a paradox, right? This incredible solution to foster connections simultaneously breeds a host of new challenges.

This cycle is the heartbeat of innovation. Every solution we devise sheds light on new areas for improvement, signaling endless opportunities for refining and evolving our products. Developing software, much like navigating the waters of social media, is an ongoing cycle of release, feedback, and iteration.

Breaking the curse of technical debt

A *technical debt* is akin to a financial debt in the realm of software development. It represents coding choices that, while expedient, may lead to complications down the line:

- Code lacking automated tests is more susceptible to disruptions from changes

- Poorly designed software can compromise system stability in live environments

- An inefficient delivery pipeline might result in downtime during updates

In my experience across various companies, balancing technical debt repayment with feature development isn't always straightforward. Many teams prioritize new features over addressing underlying issues. Here's how we can shift that mindset.

Incorporating technical debt solutions into feature delivery

Make it a standard practice to include refactoring efforts with feature updates. This approach ensures that with most new deliveries, we're also enhancing the system's architecture and engineering quality.

Actively seek opportunities to integrate refactoring into your technical solutions for product implementations. It's part of our responsibility to preempt potential issues by improving the system proactively.

A very simple example here would be to mandate the creation of automated tests with every release. This should not only cover new features but also extend testing coverage to existing functionalities that might be under-tested. This strategy gradually increases our system's reliability, instilling greater confidence in its performance in live settings.

By treating technical debt with the seriousness it deserves, we can ensure a more stable, efficient, and future-proof software ecosystem.

Clarifying how technical debts are letting users down

By examining technical debt and tracing its effects on the user journey, we can identify and measure the problems it causes within the system. Here's how technical debt might be letting your users down:

- **Performance issues**: Similar to being stuck in a traffic jam, technical debt can slow down processes to the point of user abandonment

- **Data inconsistencies**: Users may lose or see their critical data messed up, leading to frustration and trust issues

- **Poor usability**: Complex, unintuitive, or flat-out non-working interfaces can confuse users, making them disappointed or irritated

- **Deployment delays**: Slower updates mean users wait longer for improvements and the company's time to market can be very badly affected

To truly understand the impact, take the time to quantify how many users are affected by specific instances of technical debt and the severity of these impacts.

When you can directly link poor design decisions to user dissatisfaction, quantifying the wasted time, money, and effort and convincing your product team to prioritize resolving technical debt become significantly easier. Making these connections clear is crucial to advocating for the necessary changes to improve your users' experience.

If you put a dollar sign to the issues created by technical debt and prove there is a lot of money waste going on, it is basically impossible for the high managers not to prioritize those changes.

Both strategies—making tech debt payment a part of the current release development tasks and measuring the direct user impact—are quite good for gradually allowing the system's improvements to come about more easily.

Dense documentation

In the realm of bad agile practices, it's not uncommon to stumble upon requirements documents that are so dense with information that they become indecipherable. This method harks back to the early 2000s when software was delivered on installation CDs, and development cycles could stretch from six months to several years to roll out a bundled update of features.

Fast forward to today, where applications often consist of a network of microservices, occasionally accompanied by legacy monolithic systems. This shift means updates are handled feature by feature, or even partial updates are released daily in production, until a whole feature is ready to be enabled with a feature flag. Realistically, a feature's description shouldn't sprawl across more than 1,000 lines, let alone span hundreds of pages.

If you find yourself navigating a sea of details for upcoming feature releases, expected to launch everything simultaneously... it's time to voice your concerns. Launching a product this way severely deviates from agile principles, which in general are great for implementing smooth transitions and improvements on user journeys. Being off-track from those good agile practices significantly increases the risk of things going awry. Let's not forget that in the digital age, agility and clarity aren't just nice to have; they're essential to success.

Vague documentation

On the flip side, encountering requirements documents that offer nothing more than high-level business goals raises a significant red flag. This lack of detail brings developers to a standstill, unable to initiate coding due to missing processes and business rules.

Developers, while adept at translating complex user needs into functional code, aren't typically versed in the intricacies of business operations. They're tech enthusiasts, focused on the latest and greatest in technology, not the minute details of a specific market or the legal nuances of a product. Their strength lies in building, not in divining the unspoken needs of the business or its customers.

In today's fast-evolving tech landscape, finding talented developers who also grasp user needs is increasingly feasible. These developers, akin to explorers in the vast universe of technology, are always on the lookout for the next ground-breaking tech. Their journey, however, often takes them far from the realms of market specifics and legal intricacies surrounding a product. Unlike product and support teams, who interact closely with customers, developers might not have the same depth of understanding of customer needs or the legal frameworks that shape product development.

If you're handed requirements that feel more like a teaser than a script, it's crucial to push back. Request the full story—complete flows and business rules—from the product team. Diving into project planning without this information forces a shift away from your technological expertise and into a realm where, despite your best efforts, the results may not align with the project's needs. Remember, your primary role is to bring technical solutions to life, not to guess the missing pieces of the business puzzle.

Looking beyond the happy path

In the world of product development, requirement documents often paint a picture where everything runs smoothly, a scenario we fondly refer to as the *happy path*. It's like envisioning a road trip with perfect weather and no traffic jams; however, reality begs for a plan B.

Effective requirement documents delve into the realm of "what ifs" to ensure robustness:

- What if users stray from the intended use of the product?

- What if there's a hiccup in the system's performance?

- What if our third-party services temporarily go down?

Good requirements anticipate and plan for any less-than-ideal situation. Ensuring that the requirements document is equipped to navigate the "bad days" is essential. By planning for exceptions and bad scenarios, we equip ourselves to face challenges head-on, and the system will be much more prepared from the start.

Disregarding other business areas and processes

Occasionally, a product manager will provide requirements that do not account for what should happen in other company areas. In product development, ensuring every department is ready to play their part is key to launching a successful service.

Let's say your company tasks you with developing a groundbreaking new service for the website. You and your team deliver this service to production at an astonishing pace, passing every quality and user acceptance test with flying colors. The launch is a success, customers are thrilled, and purchases are through the roof. But then, a curveball: the department responsible for delivering this service was out of the loop during development. Suddenly, there's a bottleneck—they're unprepared for the unique requirements of this new offering.

No matter the size of your organization, it's vital to ensure no department is left in the dark; to ensure that, you can do the following:

- Engage all relevant departments from the start.

- Ask probing questions to understand how this service integrates into the broader company ecosystem.

- Ensure the business requirements document reflects the roles and needs of every sector.

- Have documents signed off by all possible departments, even from the ones not impacted by the changes. It is always good to demonstrate which teams are not involved as well.

By adopting a holistic approach to project planning, you not only prevent last-minute hurdles but also foster a culture of collaboration and innovation.

Assuming too much about other areas

It's not rare to see product folks bring requirements that might not fully grasp how different parts of the company interact.

For instance, consider you're working on the product mentioned earlier, and you need to forward a request to the shipping department. It's crucial not to proceed, even during testing, without first syncing up with the development team in that area.

This advice ties back to a key point: has the requirements document been approved by all crucial stakeholders across the company? It's essential for this document to be vetted by those who understand the intricacies of our various systems and departments.

Imagine you're about to embark on a journey. You wouldn't start without a map that everyone agrees on, right? Jumping into coding based on an unchecked document is like navigating with a misleading map. You risk following the wrong path, built on assumptions that might not stand.

Summary

That's a wrap on this chapter. We've delved into the dos and don'ts of crafting business requirements that pave the way for successful software development.

Here's the key takeaway: impeccable, well-organized requirements don't just support good architecture—they're the foundation. A great system design stems from clearly articulated business needs. Remember, you're setting the stage for success right from the start.

It's your turn now: set aside some time to think about some existing problem that would be interesting to solve. Do not take this exercise too seriously. Just be playful and pretend you're able to solve any problem with software. You can work a bit more with the HomeIt scenario. From the start-up problems we laid out, consider the following:

- Expand to other existing problems in the rental properties sector.

- Create a vision that could represent the solutions to the problems you have imagined.

- Write some high-level requirements to deliver the solutions you defined. Remember, it is possible to imagine several different requirements and features to strengthen a desired solution.

In the next chapter, we will talk about how to organize requirements into use cases, stories, and everything related to adding details, cycles, flows, and business rules to your requirements. We will bring life and joy to the visions we created with the high-level requirements you learned in this chapter.

Get This Book's PDF Version and Exclusive Extras

Scan the QR code (or go to packtpub.com/unlock). Search for this book by name, confirm the edition, and then follow the steps on the page.

Note: Keep your invoice handly. Purchase made directly from packt don't require one.

2

Sorting Complex Requirements into Features, Use Cases, and Stories

In this chapter, we will continue our conversation about how to structure strong requirements. In the previous chapter, we created high-level requirements. Although useful for setting the direction of the products we are going to create, they are vague. In other words, they do not tell the whole story. They lack details that would allow us to start writing our software. If you have too many details at that phase, you have done it wrong.

In this chapter, we will look at the following topics:

- Naming the distinct features of your product
- Identifying actors, events, life cycles, stages, types, levels, and loops
- Creating user journeys, use cases, and stories
- Structuring the final business requirements document
- Which of these artifacts should come first?
- Scaling results with long-term business requirements

If high-level requirements are the "bones" of a system development process, this chapter revolves around the "muscles," "skin," and "organs."

We are going to ground the visions and dreams of high-level business requirements by distinguishing specific features, life cycles, use cases, and roles. These elements allow us to start projecting domains, which will eventually become well-designed Spring services. Let's now get started.

Naming the distinct features of your product

In this section, we will go back to our HomeIt startup example. But before that, it is important to clarify something.

The previous chapter was all about expanding our ideas. We were in brainstorming mode. During a brainstorming process, we don't care too much about structure or specifics. Brainstorming is meant to be an exercise in free thinking and creativity. We don't want to constrain ourselves too much with the *how* but are instead interested in the *what*.

This awareness is profoundly critical in software development. You don't want to limit your thinking by asking, "Is this solution even possible? How is this supposed to work? Who is going to build this? Which technology are we using to create this service?" Those reality-inquiring questions should come later in the process, and understanding this is key.

Now, after a blatant exercise in mind expansion in *Chapter 1*, we will add more structure to our product requirements. To do that, recap the high-level product requirements we imagined in *Chapter 1* for the HomeIt startup system.

To maintain clarity at this stage, we should identify and name the different solution requirements. By naming them, they will be easier to refer to. Here are the features of our HomeIt system:

- Realtor quality score

- Mediation

- Insurance

Now, let's proceed to the next step: identifying the structure of the system we want to create.

Identifying actors, events, life cycles, stages, types, levels, and loops

By understanding the conflicts and different features of our system, we know where our customers are and where we want to lead them. The next step is to ensure we understand the real structure of our system. In other words, what are the key elements that will enable the journey to the future solution we want to provide?

The following sections are crucial for understanding how to dissect your product requirements and uncovering many of the hidden features you could offer users.

Who will perform actions in your system?

Returning to our HomeIt startup idea, we have a variety of actors within our system. Each of these actors will be allowed to perform a well-defined set of actions. We can also refer to actors as *roles* in our system.

Let's take a quick look at some of the actors:

- **Tenants**: Users who will join the website to search for rental properties.

- **Landlords**: Users who will make their rental properties available to tenants.

- **Realtors**: Users who will facilitate the rental agreement. They are the people who connect tenants to landlords.

- **Admins**: Users who have extremely high administrative privileges in the system. These admin tasks include, for instance, blocking users who have attempted to commit fraud.

As illustrated with the admins, a system doesn't just comprise the end users on the website; it also includes several different flows and possibilities, incorporating internal users to whom we need to provide special permissions to assist in operating the system.

Here are other examples of internal users:

- **Legal**: Users who can edit contract models that landlords could use.

- **Finance operators**: Users responsible for ensuring the payment systems are functioning correctly, performing tasks such as authorizing refunds from insurance policies on the website.

- **Mediators**: Users responsible for conducting conflict resolution between two roles on the website. The goal of the mediator is to ensure different users can get along and reach an agreement in the case of disputes.

Imagine some other actors for our HomeIt system, but be aware of the challenges that might come with them.

Identifying key roles in a system

Just as with our HomeIt system, in every system analysis you conduct with your product team, you will have to go through the process of identifying the key roles/actors. Some product teams will have those roles very well defined. However, in some cases, some roles are not very well distinguished in the product requirements. If you can spot the missing roles, you will provide a lot of value to the company. This will also facilitate system development and architecture decisions.

Now that we understand the basics about who is going to take action in our system, the next step is to reveal the system flows. Let's take the first step to make that happen.

Defining critical events for each actor

Once we identify the key roles in your system, it's time to understand the power they will have. In this context, we will refer to these powers or actions as **critical events**. In other words, what are the possible behaviors we want to allow for each role?

In the case of the HomeIt system, we know we are providing tenants with a more trustworthy experience in choosing the right rental properties. You probably noticed that we are also allowing landlords to partner with realtors, which can bring benefits to both.

Let's go through some exercises for critical events, so you have a better understanding of how these can be identified. In this case, we will start from ground zero, but in the market, it is much more common to have many of these already defined by the product team. You will need to be aware that many critical events could be missing. Try to identify those missing events as early as possible. This is important to help you plan the right architecture and the best services.

Critical events for tenants

The critical events we see in this section are the actions our tenants will be able to perform in the system.

Let's start with an exercise. Think of all the functionalities a tenant will need. This can be anything from registering themselves as a tenant to searching for properties to making an offer. But one thing to bear in mind is that, when conducting this exercise, you may identify events that are not related to the key features we distinguished in the previous sections (such as mediation, insurance, and realtor quality score). These new events will then belong to new features that we must identify.

The way we organize it works as follows: after listing all possible events we want to implement in the system, we will *assign* each event to the features we want those critical events to be part of. These features could be anything from signing up to searching for a property.

The following list essentially attributes each event to one of the features:

- Sign up: Register a tenant account on the website
- Property search:
    - Search for rental properties
    - View rental property details
- People search:
    - Search for realtors
    - View a realtor profile page
- Property rental:
    - Schedule a visit to a property
    - Make a rental offer
    - Sign a rental contract
- Payment: Pay for a rental contract

- Messaging:

    - Send messages to a realtor

    - Send messages to a landlord

- Notification: View the latest updates – new messages, contract updates, etc.

- Cancellation: Cancel a rental contract

- People search: Search for a landlord

- Realtor quality score: Give a rating to a realtor

These actions, or critical events, represent what we might allow our users to perform in this system.

One key characteristic of critical events is that even though they might not have a clear and complete description of what it takes to perform each event, they do provide a much more comprehensive list of possible actions compared to the high-level requirements.

Let's now proceed to examine the next set of roles and their respective critical events.

Critical events for landlords

Of course, creating our HomeIt system involves more than just enabling tenants to act on the website or mobile app. We also need to allow realtors and landlords to interact, so that these three roles can bring value to the market.

In this step, we delve deeper into the world of landlords. What kind of critical events will we allow them to perform? Here are some examples, along with the features we expect to assign those events to:

- Sign up:

    - Register as a landlord

    - Fill in their personal details

- Rental property registration:

    - Register a new rental property

    - Set available dates for accepting visitors to their property

    - Enable/disable a property for renting

- Realtor partnership: Approve/reject a realtor in a property

- People search:

    - View a realtor's profile details

    - View a tenant's profile details

- Property rental: Approve a rental offer

- Account:

  - View the rental account balance

  - Withdraw funds from the rental account

Another interesting aspect of writing critical events is that you should be able to almost visualize the user taking the action. You might not be able to picture every visual detail of the system, but with critical events, you will always have a sense of an action taking place. This perspective helps in grounding abstract ideas into tangible functionalities that contribute significantly to the UX and the overall system design.

Critical events involve individuals taking steps to achieve their goals within the system. These steps should guide them toward the solution envisioned in the high-level requirements.

Some systems will always have standard features, such as the signup process and the ability to view another user's profile, among others. It's essential to always remember these core features; otherwise, you might leave open gaps and missing pieces, making it difficult to fully describe your system in a consistent and realistic manner.

Now, over to you: What other critical events would you assign to landlords in this system? Remember, we have some named features that have not been touched upon at this point. For example, we have not assigned any critical events that would represent the mediation or insurance features we discussed earlier.

Compile a list of critical events for the mediation or insurance features for landlords. After completing this exercise, you can move on to explore some examples of critical events for realtors.

Critical events for realtors

The same as the last two sections, we will create a sample of the critical events for realtors. Let's take a look at them here:

- Property search:

  - Search for rental properties

  - View a rental property's details page

- Realtor partnership:

  - Send a partnership proposal for a property

  - Cancel a partnership proposal

  - Set available dates for accepting visitors to a property

- Messaging: Read messages related to a rental property

- Account:

  - View the account balance

  - Withdraw the account balance

- Mediation: Open a dispute with a realtor/tenant

Now it's your turn: What else do you think realtors could be doing in the system? What other critical events could occur that would provide value for both tenants and landlords?

Before moving on to the next step, take some time to think about critical events for realtors. Also, consider the other roles in our system. What could mediators, finance operations, legal, and admins be doing to provide value and facilitate interactions among our three key external roles (tenants, realtors, and landlords)?

As you can see, planning the vision for a system from scratch is a considerable task. It all starts with understanding the key problems, brainstorming solutions, creating high-level requirements, and then expanding these requirements into a list of roles and critical events.

Now, let us lay down the key features of our system. This is a pre-condition for something even more important, which is organizing the events timeline.

Listing the main features of the system

So far, we have explored and identified some interesting new features in this exercise, and I hope you have also identified some new ones through your free-thinking exercises.

Here are the current features we have found:

- **Property search**: The ability for users to search for rental properties and view their details
- **Realtor partnership**: The ability for realtors to partner with landlords and present their properties to new tenants
- **Messaging**: The ability for users to exchange messages
- **Account**: The ability for users to manage their account balances in the system
- **Mediation**: The ability for users to have conflicts resolved within the platform
- **Rental property registration**: The ability for landlords to manage their properties in the system
- **Payment**: The ability for tenants to pay for their rent
- **People search**: The ability for users to search for other users in the system
- **Realtor quality score**: The reputation system for realtors
- **Cancellation**: The ability for tenants to cancel their rental contracts

What other features have you discovered during your system exploration? Now, let's move to the next step in our system analysis: creating a feature timeline.

Extracting a feature's events timeline

Now that we have brainstormed several events for each role and identified many new key features, we need to explore how to detail a single feature and place it on a timeline. This means describing each feature through an ordered sequence of critical events.

Additionally, we aim to create this feature timeline in such a way that we can also map the dependencies of a given feature. In other words, what is the proper order of events over time, and what conditions must be met by the user in order to utilize that feature?

In this section, we will not delve into every feature we've discovered so far. That would require a lot of pages and time, and this book is about creating systems with the Spring Framework. We will run through a few key examples, and it is up to you to apply your feature thinking by following the same process for other features we have discovered.

> **Should we fully replace UX/UI work with the techniques in this chapter?**
>
> You might look at the following pages and wonder: Is the author proposing that we replace the standard practices of UX/UI research with the tools laid out here? My answer is, "No!" We should never consider these pages as replacements for proper market research and specialized UX/UI methodologies. The pages here are meant to complement the work of great professionals in their UX research. This is simply a way to write event sequences in a very "dry," straight-to-the-point manner. This will aid engineers in making more sense of the systems they are building. However, occasionally, you might find that there are many gaps in how even UX work is being conducted in a specific project. In such instances, you might resort to crafting timelines to help refine product and business requirements.

Let's take a first shot at creating timelines for some of the most important features in the HomeIt system.

Organizing the sign-up feature on a timeline

There are no prerequisites for performing this task, since this is step 1 of using HomeIt. You can follow these steps to organize the sign-up feature:

1. The user lands on the initial website page.
2. The system validates the provided information.
3. If necessary, the user can correct any invalid or missing information.
4. The user submits the information.
5. The account is successfully created, and the user is now logged in.

Notice that we are ordering the events, but we are not assuming too much about the specific information needed at this point. We are drilling down enough to understand, at a high level, how the events should be organized in the feature.

Now, let's move on to the next feature.

Organizing the rental property registration on a timeline

To organize the rental property registration on a timeline, there must be a registered landlord who is in the main logged-in area. Then, the following steps are carried out:

1. The landlord chooses the option to add a new rental property.
2. The landlord provides the required information to register the rental property.
3. The system validates the information sent.
4. The landlord corrects the rental property information if needed.
5. The landlord finishes submitting all the information (description, address, price, etc.).
6. The landlord lands on the new property page, which now has an inactive status.
7. The system presents an option for the landlord to upload media files (pictures or videos).
8. The landlord chooses the option to upload the media files.
9. The landlord provides the required media files to register the rental property.
10. The rental property moves to the *processing media files* status.
11. The system starts to process the provided media materials (results to be defined).
12. When the media process is finished, the rental property moves to the *ready* status.
13. The landlord is presented with the option to *publish* the rental property and make it available to tenants and realtors.
14. The landlord selects the option to publish the rental property.
15. The rental property is now in the *published* status, available when using the property search feature.

As you can see, this specific feature outlines what we call an **object life cycle**. The rental property begins in an "inactive" state, then progresses through the statuses of "processing media files," "ready," and finally "published" as the landlord advances through the various steps of the feature.

We will delve deeper into life cycles in the subsequent sections and chapters of the book. However, it is evident that identifying life cycles is only possible when we carefully lay out a feature through critical events on a timeline.

Organizing the property search feature on a timeline

To organize the property search feature, it is required that there be a registered landlord who has registered a rental property. The rental property is in the "published" state. An optional requirement is a registered tenant. The following steps are carried out:

1. The user lands on the first page of the HomeIt website.
2. An unregistered/registered user types in the desired rental property location in the search bar of the first page (ZIP code, street name, state, city, etc.).
3. The user can provide a filter for ordering (by price, ascending or descending; by street name; by proximity; etc.).
4. The system provides a list of the listed properties found and their respective pictures.
5. The user can view the pictures for each property in the list.
6. The user can click to see the details page for the listed property and view all the information the landlord has provided.

As you can notice, this feature has many requirements or prerequisites. This means that other features should be present before we are able to use this one. This starts to give us some clues about which features should be developed first. But there is much more to consider, which we will explore by the end of this chapter. Now, let's move on to another interesting feature.

Organizing the realtor partnership on a timeline

The prerequisites for organizing the realtor partnership are a registered realtor, a registered landlord, a registered rental property, and the property search functionality implemented. It is also required that the realtor and landlord are logged in. The following steps are carried out:

1. The realtor is logged in and, after searching for a property, lands on a property details page.
2. The realtor selects the *Partner with the Landlord* option.
3. The realtor informs which days of the week they are available to receive tenants in the property.
4. The realtor specifies the time of day they are available on each day of the week to receive visitors.
5. The realtor indicates the percentage of the rent they want to receive as a partner.
6. The realtor finishes submitting the partnership proposal.
7. The partnership proposal is now in the pending partnership approval state.
8. The landlord views a list of their current partnership proposals.
9. The landlord visits one of the partnership proposals.
10. The landlord can view the realtor's information on the proposal page (user details, address, quality score, available days and hours to receive visitors, etc.).
11. The landlord chooses to accept the partnership proposal.

12. The partnership moves to approved status.

13. The realtor can see the approved partnership in the partnerships list.

14. The realtor's contact information is now shown on the rental property page.

In this feature, several important aspects need to be noted. The first is that this feature depends on a lot of prerequisites and involves interaction between two different users. Just like in the rental property object case, there is now a life cycle defined for the partnership object. These objects move from the pending partnership approval to approved status. We have also referred to a "list of partnerships" in the description, but we have not defined that feature anywhere so far. That is, we need to be aware that when writing a feature in a clear timeline, we will often reveal the need for other essential features. This new list feature should now be included in the prerequisites section as well.

This feature description only refers to the "happy path" – when a successful partnership is celebrated. Remember what we discussed in *Chapter 1*, when we talked about mapping possible errors and mistakes the users could make. We should also address questions such as what happens if the landlord rejects or never responds to the partnership proposal.

As you can see, things can become quite complicated over time when it comes to complex features. Now, let's move on to the last two features we want to outline here.

Organizing the property rental feature on a timeline

For this section, it is required that there is a registered landlord, a registered rental property, the property search functionality, and a registered tenant who is logged In. Along with that, we also need payment methods and HomeIt's finance details.

Here are the steps:

1. The tenant visits a property page.

2. The tenant selects the option to send a rental proposal to the landlord.

3. The tenant reviews a rental agreement contract and signs it in the system.

4. After the signing, a rental proposal is created in the pending approval status.

5. The landlord reviews the rental proposal and visualizes the relevant tenant information (to be defined).

6. The landlord chooses the option to accept the rental proposal.

7. A rental agreement document is produced with both electronic signatures.

8. The rental proposal moves to the accepted status.

9. The tenant is informed that the rental proposal was approved.

10. The tenant chooses the option to select a payment method.

11. The tenant sends the payment information.

12. The payment is carried out successfully.

13. HomeIt gets its share of the payment in the company account.

14. The realtor, if there is one, gets their share of the payment directly in their account.

15. The landlord gets the outstanding amount in their account

16. Every month, the payment happens again, and all parties receive their share of the amount

This is a very complex feature we have outlined, and the following observations need to be added here:

- There are possibly three users interacting in this flow: tenants, realtors, and landlords.

- The HomeIt finance workflow needs to be in place so that the company can receive its share of the payments.

- There is a recurring loop in this flow, which is the monthly payments that need to occur.

- This feature must also be expanded to accommodate exceptional use cases, such as the following:

  - What if the payment does not go through in a month due to a system failure?

  - What if the user (tenant) does not have the balance to pay for the rent in a given month?

  - When distributing the payment share to each party, what if one of the transfers fails?

  What other exceptional behavior can you find here?

- We have several possible payment methods available. In fact, depending on the countries where HomeIt will operate, there could be dozens of different payment methods available:

  - Different payment methods operate in different ways. Therefore, a critical question here is: How can we prepare this system to receive payments in the most flexible manner, making it easy to quickly integrate payments from different countries as soon as possible?

This type of analysis summarizes some of the critical steps we need to take in order to create the proper requirements for a system. It can become complicated over time. However, that is what software engineering is all about: ensuring that we can lay out the requirements as clearly as possible so that our architecture choices are made easier in the future.

Simplifying requirements

From all these exercises, you might think that implementing these requirements will take a lot of time, and you are right. Demanding that the development team implements every feature perfectly before publishing a website will make it very complicated and costly. That is not typically what we do in the world of software development. Perfect requirements are not always possible to implement. So, how do we proceed with a more practical approach in light of such complexity?

In cases where the requirements become too complex, costly, and time-consuming to develop, one critical approach is to reduce the scope of the work. To establish our online presence with minimal cost, we can reimagine the HomeIt system to achieve similar results with simpler features.

This is what we refer to as **scope reduction**. By omitting certain features, we can achieve a successful release within a shorter timeframe.

A simple example of simplifying complex requirements in the context of the HomeIt system study could be as follows:

- We can begin by developing a basic website that enables landlords to register their accounts and list their rental properties. We will exclude registration features for other user types.

- HomeIt will initially not process monthly rent payments.

By omitting many other features, we ensure the website launches with the essential components to establish an online presence. Additional features can then be incorporated over time. This approach is known as a **roadmap**.

Now, let's delve deeper into the stages and loops within our system.

Understanding stages, levels, types, life cycles, and loops

Every system will be built using a combination of stages, levels, types, life cycles, and loops. Let's define them now for our understanding.

Stages

This means a series of "phases" or "statuses" an entity will go through across time as the user progresses in their journey. In the HomeIt system, so far, we have stages for the following objects:

- **Rental property**: Inactive, processing media files, and published
- **Partnership proposal**: Pending partnership approval, accepted, and rejected
- **Rental proposal**: Pending approval, accepted, and rejected

Think of stages as the maturity steps an object could be represented within your system. It is common to have stages represented by a "status" attribute in the object, meaning we could monitor an object at different developmental steps over time.

Levels

A "level" is a set of distinctive features or qualities that you might want your entities to acquire in a system that makes it stand out from other objects on other levels. One key aspect of creating levels for an object is that any object could potentially navigate through the levels and be enriched in its life cycle. As the object evolves in your system, it achieves different levels and gathers more value and some privileges.

In other words, during the evolution of an object in the system, different levels could be attributed to it, each bringing special properties to the object. In our HomeIt startup, so far, we have not found any different levels in the requirements. However, we could design some, such as the following:

- **Realtors**: To provide incentives for our realtors, we could implement a tiered system based on reputation score. Newly registered realtors could be designated as Bronze Realtors, limited to partnering with no more than four rental properties. Upon achieving a reputation score of 3 stars, they would become Gold realtors, with the ability to partner with up to 10 rental properties. Realtors with a reputation score of five stars would be designated as Diamond Realtors, with no limit on the number of rental properties they can partner with.

- **Landlords**: Incentives for landlords could involve reducing fees based on the number of active rental agreements. For example, having five simultaneous agreements could result in a 10 percent fee discount.

- **Tenants**: To incentivize tenants and landlords, discounts on insurance prices could be offered based on the rental property's history. Properties rented without any incidents for a certain number of months would qualify for lower insurance prices. This creates a quality tier system, where higher-quality properties result in lower insurance prices, making them more appealing to tenants and encouraging landlords to maintain their properties well.

You can think of levels as "ascending layers" for objects in the system. They serve as a way to distinguish valuable behaviors in our systems and grant more rights, permissions, power, bonuses, or privileges to the best users.

Types

An object could have different types within a system. A clear example in our HomeIt startup is the various roles we have identified. While all actors are "users" on the website, they possess different characteristics because they aim to accomplish different tasks within the system.

We could design other types, such as the following:

- **Property types**: By distinguishing between houses and apartments in the HomeIt system, we can implement more effective filters to better serve our customers in the property search feature

- **Rental agreement types**: Offering a variety of agreements can be useful to represent different types of insurance with varying coverages and clauses

Think of types as a means to distinguish between completely different packages of attributes and behaviors that an object could possess in the system. We are not necessarily suggesting that one type is superior to another; rather, they are simply distinct and serve different purposes.

Life cycles and loops

You can think of a life cycle as the progression of an object across different levels or stages over time. It is crucial to distinguish and represent life cycles visually to better understand and communicate all the possibilities in the system.

By allowing life cycles to emerge, we can create state diagrams, which become key artifacts for developers. With these state diagrams, we can map test cases with a high degree of accuracy.

In our HomeIt startup case study, we can visualize life cycles for several objects. Let's go through some examples. The first one is the *rental property life cycle*:

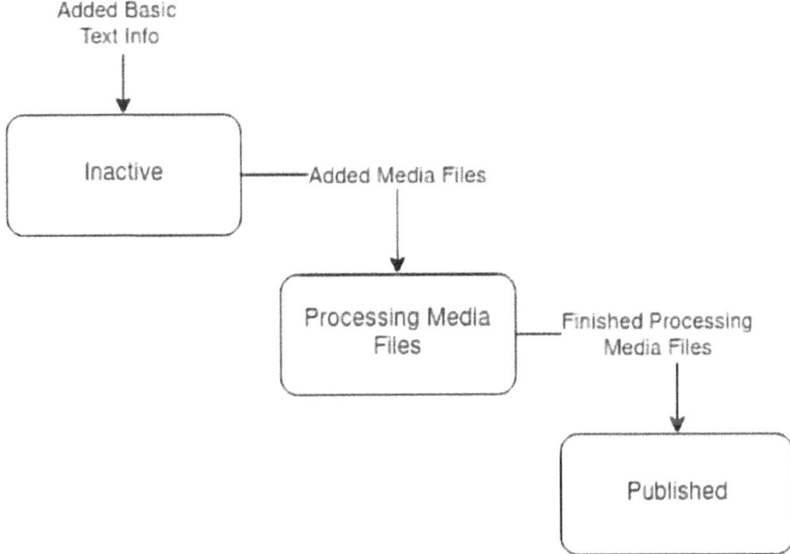

Figure 2.1: Rental property life cycle

As you can see in *Figure 2.1*, visually representing stages of the rental property life cycle – in this case, moving from inactive to processing media files to published – makes it easier to understand the entire history of an object in the system. Additionally, when transitioning to different stages, we can visually identify the triggers that cause the transition to occur.

Next, let's visualize the life cycle of *realtor levels*:

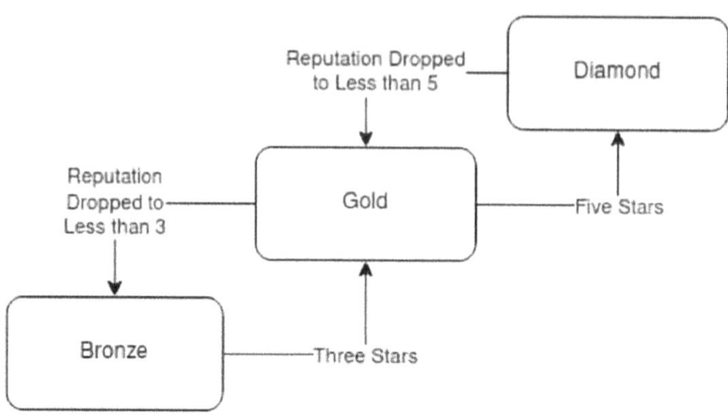

Figure 2.2: Realtor levels life cycle

As you can see in *Figure 2.2*, the reputation levels we created for the system allow a realtor to move from lower levels to upper levels, then to lower levels again. Sometimes an object's life cycle will become a loop. In fact, we can consider that our users will always go through a loop in our system, since they can start as newly registered users from the "outside world," become customers, then go inactive for a while, and eventually reactivate their account.

Understanding the user's life cycle as an overarching loop is important because we want to develop retention strategies in our systems. See the last diagram in this example:

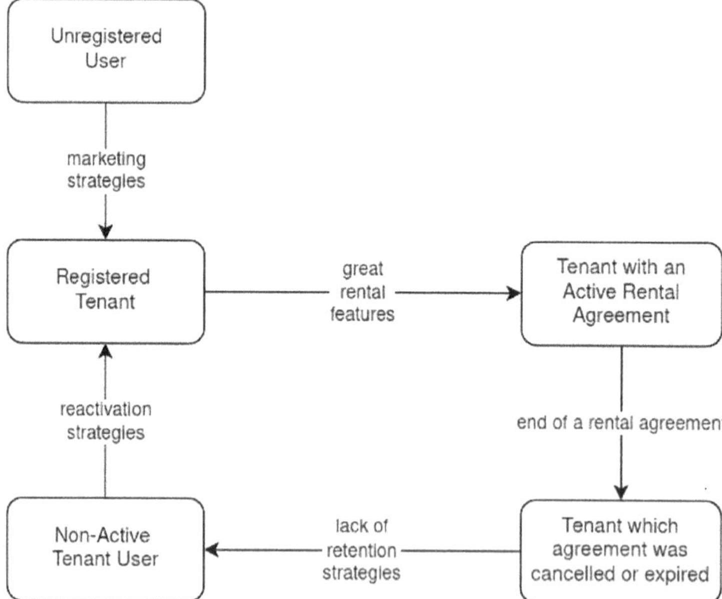

Figure 2.3 – Tenant's website loop

Finally, as in *Figure 2.3*, we have a more general description of the conditions that create a life cycle loop – in this case, a user moves from an unregistered to a registered tenant, then moves to a tenant with an active rental agreement, and so on. We don't necessarily need to have a specific "status" attribute in an object to design a systemic loop or a life cycle. It's essential to be aware of the existing, implicit loops in our systems. This awareness allows us to identify leverage points to ensure we can consistently provide more value as time passes.

It's very important to note here that failing to recognize loops and life cycles risks overlooking valuable insights and strategies. Creating visual representations of these structures is one of the most important tasks in requirements analysis.

> **Warning**
>
> I've encountered countless projects where the life cycles and loops in the systems were not documented at all. Statuses and levels would be defined in software, only to become loosely designed entities and features. Providing clear diagrams with all existing statuses and situations, along with the transition triggers, can offer a powerful and straightforward way to help your product team gain more insights that will enrich your UX.
>
> In many cases, while documenting and visually representing levels, stages, loops, and life cycles, you may discover that not all transition triggers are clear or even present in the software or the business requirements. There are often hidden opportunities in these seemingly simple visual diagrams. In fact, much of the best feedback I've received in my career was due to my habit of creating these visuals whenever possible. I recommend practicing creating these diagrams, even when working on a project with others.

The value of projecting requirements in this step-by-step manner is that we have a very good amount of freedom to imagine whatever we want for our system. It also helps that this is a very powerful brainstorming method. We don't start by trying to define a specific feature. Instead, we begin by expanding the possibilities we can envision for the system we're building.

If you are a developer, understanding these "dimensions" of software requirements (problem, solution, high-level requirements, roles, critical events, levels, stages, life cycles, and loops) will be really helpful, as you will be able to dissect the requirement documents that usually come with a lot of assumptions and vague information. These are tools for ensuring that the specific business requirements clearly express a consistent journey for the users in your system.

Creating user journeys, stories, and use cases

In this section, we will produce three key artifacts that will integrate all the business requirement elements we have seen until now in a way that makes sense from a business requirements perspective.

We will first explore how to assemble separate features into higher-level **user journeys** that better illustrate the strategy we want to accomplish with our software.

We will learn how to write **user stories** that summarize and articulate our features from a business perspective.

We will also write **use cases** that allow us to clearly communicate the value creation process that we aim to provide, expressing our business requirements with a high level of clarity and consistency.

> **Attention**
>
> The requirements building blocks we have seen up to this point function like LEGO blocks that can be used to explain things at different levels of detail. It's essential to recognize that different blocks are used to communicate with different levels in the company, enabling us to understand which people will be more interested in which kind of artifact. We will revisit this concept in a later section of this chapter.

Let's define and illustrate each of these artifacts and examine the relationship between all of them and other models we have seen so far.

User journeys

User journeys can provide a very high-level overview of how users will navigate through the experience of using your software, although they are not as vague as the high-level business requirements we saw in *Chapter 1*.

User journeys allow us to visualize user behavior over a long timeframe. In a sense, the user journey can be considered a specific way of making the entire user life cycle more explicit regarding the actions the user will take in your system.

A user journey can also be used to express the relationship between different users in the system over an extended period. While the critical events we have assembled in a feature will describe a finer level of detail, the user journey will illustrate larger chunks of the user actions in a few blocks.

Creating user journeys for one user at a time

Let's get back to our HomeIt startup. Look at this user journey:

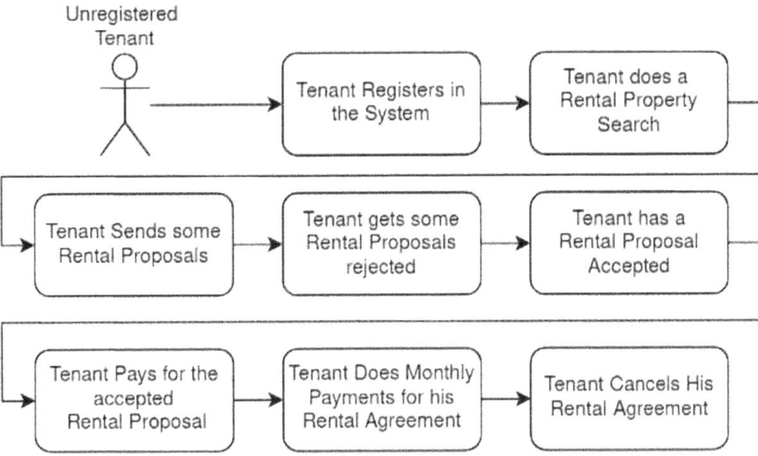

Figure 2.4: Tenant user journey

In this first example, as seen in *Figure 2.4*, we can communicate the entire tenant journey on the HomeIt website by summarizing their actions one block at a time. Each block represents a whole feature that can, in turn, be decomposed in different ways.

Let's take a look at the landlord user journey now:

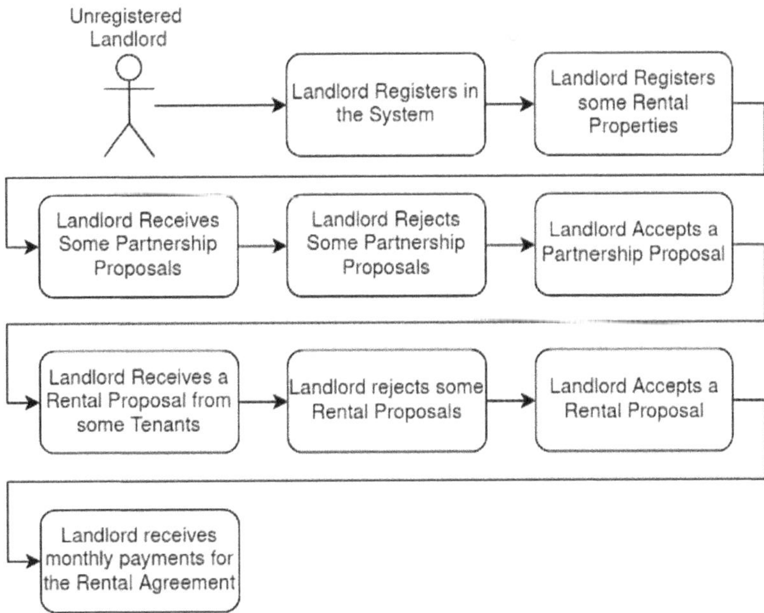

Figure 2.5: Landlord user journey

As you can see from the example in *Figure 2.5*, it is possible to concisely summarize the entire landlord journey on the website.

This method of using user journeys focuses on one user. In both examples, we are omitting some actual features, such as mediation and the insurance feature. Of course, if you have practiced creating requirements on your own, we are also leaving out the features you have discovered. However, you can get the idea. A user journey is capable of conveying a lot in just a small visual space.

Let's explore another way of creating user journeys.

User journeys with multiple users

In this case, we are involving multiple users in the same user journey. Take a look at *Figure 2.6*:

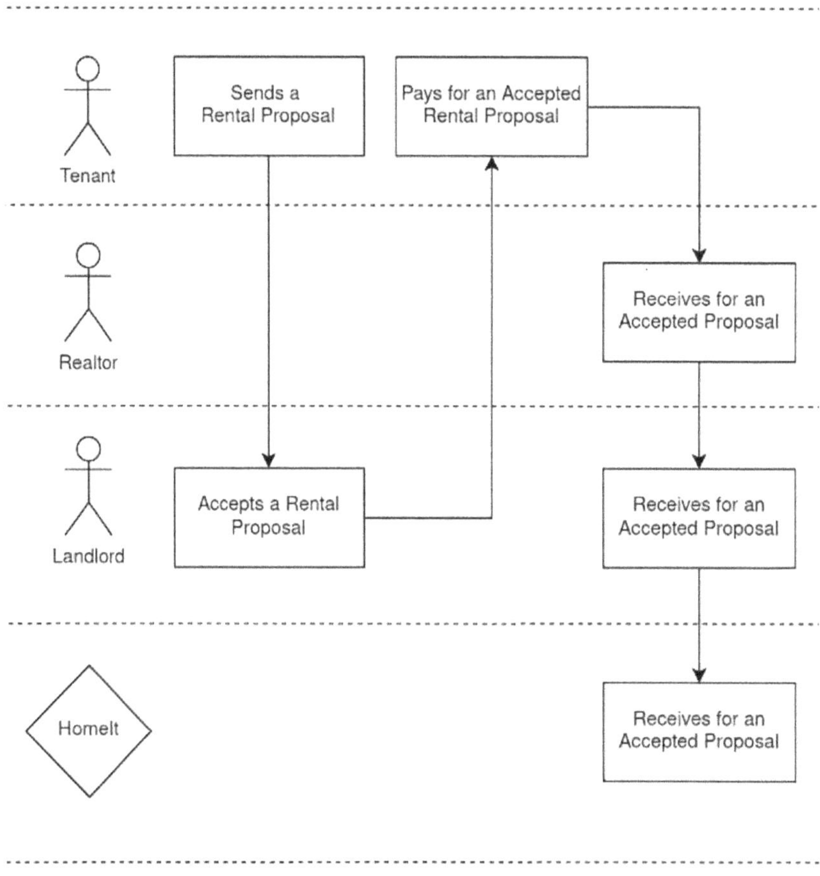

Figure 2.6: Multiple users in the same user journey

Due to space constraints, I have included just a section of the entire user journey that involves four actors: a tenant, a realtor, a landlord, and HomeIt. The user journey is divided into horizontal lanes, with each lane representing a user. The actions in a lane are displayed on the left side, and the boxes follow the order in which those actions occur over time.

It is quite easy to follow the actions of each user and the sequence in which they occur. In the real world, you can create extensive user journeys that span several departments and involve various types of users.

This type of user journey, involving several different users, can be created for very high-level processes or very specific detailed processes as well. It all depends on your needs.

As an exercise, create a user journey for the mediation flow. Take some time to think it through and create the lanes and all the different users involved, along with the actions that should take place over time for each user.

User stories

Because team members often get deeply engrossed in the technical details of a project, it can be challenging to encourage them to think from the end user's perspective. When we fail to adopt our users' viewpoint, we risk creating products or features that don't align with their needs. Unfortunately, this is a common occurrence in the market.

This is where user stories prove to be invaluable. These artifacts are designed to convey requirements from the user's perspective, making them particularly effective for helping team members empathize with users. User stories enable colleagues within a project to "wear the user's hat," so to speak. They aim to shift everyone's focus toward understanding and prioritizing the user's needs over the intricacies of the software.

The user story template

A user story is essentially a brief description that follows a specific template to convey a requirement from the user's perspective. The most common format for a user story is as follows:

Title: Realtor Sends a Partnership Proposal for a Rental Property

As a realtor, I want to send a partnership proposal for a rental property so that I can assist landlords in finding great tenants. This will not only help me increase my monthly income but also generate income for the landlord. Moreover, the partnership proposal will aid tenants in finding their desired home.

Acceptance Criteria:

The realtor can send a partnership proposal for a rental property.

The partnership proposal becomes available for the landlord to review.

As you can see, the user story is a focused part of the action. The ability to create a visual in the reader's mind is a very important goal to work toward. User stories should be all about describing events that are easy to visualize in a summarized manner.

It's clear that a user story can be combined with a list of critical events that should occur, allowing us to communicate the step-by-step value creation process we aim to implement in software effectively.

What questions does a user story answer?

User stories play a crucial role in the software development process by providing answers to key questions, such as the following:

- Who is attempting to accomplish what?
- What action is the user supposed to take in this story?
- Why is it important for the user to be allowed to perform that action?
- Which other users are affected?
- Why is the action in this story also important to these other users?

In many cases, the user story initially may not encompass numerous business rules. I prefer to view them as tools to illustrate actions, the relationships between users within the system, and the value created through those actions.

When writing user stories, it's generally advisable not to describe too many actions at once. If your story is too lengthy, it could indicate that it should be divided into multiple stories.

> **Learning to think outside the technology box**
>
> As mentioned earlier, an effective user story does not delve into the technical specifics of what is being developed. It is crafted specifically to help people focus on users, relationships, human actions, and the motivations of all involved parties. If you find yourself mentioning the latest JSON format or which HTTP method should be used, you're missing the mark. User stories are about understanding the "why" behind the feature, not the "how."

Crafting a great title for a user story

The best way to introduce a user story is with a title that is simply a brief description of the action the user needs to perform in the system. How would you describe the user action in a concise sentence without including any software-specific details? In other words, how would you explain what the user should do with the system without mentioning the system itself?

User stories are essentially an explanation of the process. Yes, you can include important business rules if necessary, but there's no need to focus too much on them. My preferred approach is for business rules to be more thoroughly addressed in use case documents, which I will explain later.

For many, avoiding discussions of software and technology is not an easy task! We must describe what the users should be able to do without referring to screens, buttons, data formats, network protocols, design patterns, and so on. We should remove all technical terminology from user stories, both in their titles and descriptions.

What are the acceptance criteria?

A crucial component of every user story is the acceptance criteria section. It ensures that we have completed the story's implementation in the software. An excellent acceptance criteria section provides a comprehensive list of business tests that can be conducted to determine whether the development is fully complete.

The acceptance criteria play a key role in creating our tests, marking the point where we begin to delve into software analysis. A well-crafted acceptance criteria section in user stories will guide the creation of a detailed, concise list of automated tests to be conducted in the software. With clear acceptance criteria, there will be no dispute about whether the software is ready for release. The acceptance criteria section acts as the gatekeeper for deploying our product in production.

Now is a great time to pause your reading and practice crafting some outstanding user stories for our HomeIt system. You can follow this template:

Title: <<User X performs an action described in a brief sentence.>>

Description:

As a <<add role here>>, I want to be able to <<add the action here>> so that I will be able to <<add the desired result here>>.

Doing that will allow me to <<consequence 1, consequence 2, consequence 3>>.

This will also allow me to avoid <<negative consequence 1, negative consequence 2>>.

This will also impact <<other users or roles>> in the following ways: <<add a list of consequences here>>.

Business Rules:

<<You might want to add business rules here, never talking about technical details, buttons, screens, etc.>>

Acceptance Criteria:

- <<The action we need to verify that is happening correctly in the system>>
- <<Other actions or consequences for which correctness can be verified after the software is done>>

If you search for user stories online, you'll encounter various templates. I prefer this custom-made one, allowing for a deeper exploration of relationships and benefits beyond what other common templates might permit.

After practicing writing some user journeys, move on to the next section.

Use cases descriptions

So far, we have explored various tools that assist in articulating our business requirements. If you were a painter, these requirement tools could be likened to the distinct colors that enable you to paint the portrait of your software.

The use case description is another crucial tool I prefer for ensuring developers understand what needs to be built. Its purpose is akin to that of user stories: with a use case description, we can depict a process that the user will undertake to interact with our system.

> **Beware**
>
> Before we delve into use case descriptions, I'd like to clarify a potential source of confusion. In the realm of software engineering, there exists a widely recognized tool known as the use case diagram. When I refer to use case descriptions, I am not talking about use case diagrams. Given their popularity, I won't be discussing use case diagrams in this context. Additionally, I prefer using user journey diagrams over use case diagrams for explaining user actions from a very high-level perspective.

Comparing user stories to use case descriptions

Returning to our main topic: if use case descriptions are similar to user stories, what differentiates the two? Here's my perspective: user stories are intentionally kept brief to avoid excessive detail about the process being described. The process is intended to be illustrated by another tool. In contrast, use case descriptions are where we aim to provide more detail – indeed, significantly more.

Here's how it works: while user stories are meant to avoid delving deeply into the system's specifics, use case descriptions allow for a combination of the user story with other artifacts we've discussed.

For instance, a use case description might begin with the text of a user story and then detail the sequence of critical events that make up the process we need to program. It might also include relevant diagrams within a use case description to give developers a clearer understanding of how the system operates.

The use case description acts as comprehensive documentation of a use case. Starting with the user story enables people to grasp the action, motivations, and relationships behind it. Progressing to a sequence of critical actions lays the groundwork for developing the process in software. Adding object stages or a life cycle diagram enhances the visualization of transformations over time.

In use case descriptions, the combination of visuals, the accompanying user story, and critical events forms a potent tool for conveying your software's objectives. Incorporating additional diagrams, such as one explaining various system levels, further enhances clarity.

A final thought on use case descriptions is that they should be viewed as the canvas on which you add the colors and sketches to express what the software is intended to do.

Triggers

Another crucial element to incorporate into use case descriptions is triggers, which I consider the context enabling the user to initiate the action proposed by the story. Indeed, there can be multiple avenues through which a user may begin to engage with a user story. For example, in our HomeIt system, when a tenant is searching for a rental property, we could consider the following triggers:

- **Direct property search**: The tenant initiates a search through the app's search feature to find available properties matching their criteria.

- **From a mobile phone**: The user is starting to search for a rental property from a mobile phone. In that case, starting from their mobile might change the process significantly. What could we have work differently in that case? Maybe we can use the mobile phone localization features to find properties that are geographically close to the user. In that case, it may be interesting to add a feature where the user chooses the distance from their location to find properties while searching.

- **From a personal computer**: If the user is starting their search from a computer, we can consider providing a very different layout that would take advantage of the larger screen space. Using a grid with high-resolution images might help captivate the user a bit more. Perhaps we could have a feature for comparing images from different homes on the same screen. Who knows?

- **Recommendation system**: The tenant receives personalized property recommendations based on their search history and preferences.

- **Notification alerts**: The tenant signs up for notifications and receives alerts when new properties that meet their criteria become available.

- **Agent contact**: The tenant contacts a realtor through the app for assistance in finding a property.

This simple example illustrates that although we have just one use case (in this example, the rental property search), the way that feature could work will be context-dependent. We use the term "trigger" to refer to each different context from which the user could start their user story.

> **Attention**
>
> It's very important to keep this clear in your mind: we could have a different set of critical events for different triggers within the same use case.

Now, let's see a useful template for creating our use case description. You are free to use it for any use case description:

Use Case Name: Follow the same rules as for user story titles.

User Story: Introduces the action that will take place, along with the motivations and relationships in the system. It includes the acceptance criteria used to assert that we have finished developing our story.

Trigger #1 – Title of the trigger: Identifies the unique context from which the user will perform their action:

- *Trigger Description*
- *Critical Events Timeline for the Trigger*
- *Stage, Levels, Types, Life Cycles, Loops* (or any other relevant diagrams that will aid in understanding the system)

Finally, let's take a look at a sample use case description, where a landlord publishes a new rental property.

Use case sample

Title: Landlord Publishes a New Rental Property

Description:

As a landlord, I want to be able to publish a new rental property in the system so that I can make my property available for rent. Doing so will allow me to attract prospective tenants, select the best tenant, create a new income stream when the property is rented, and attract a new realtor as a partner to reach even more tenants. This will also help me avoid having my property remain empty and without a new income stream. Additionally, this will impact realtors by providing them with an additional property to show their prospects and enabling them to gain a new income stream as they assist me in managing the property.

Business Rules:

Properties will be fully available for rental and partnership proposals only after all media is provided.

Landlords must always provide the full address of the property, the price of rent, and the conditions and features of the property, besides the media files.

Acceptance Criteria:

A landlord user is able to publish a new rental property in the system, with photos and videos attached to it.

Trigger #1: The rental property is published on the website.

Critical Events Timeline:

1. On the website, the landlord selects the option to add a new rental property.
2. The landlord provides the required information to register the rental property.
3. The system validates the information sent.
4. The landlord corrects the rental property information if needed.
5. The landlord completes the submission of all information (description, address, price, etc.).
6. The landlord is directed to the new property page, now in the inactive status.
7. The system offers an option for the landlord to upload media files (pictures or videos).

8. The landlord chooses to upload the media files.

9. The landlord uploads the necessary media files for the rental property registration.

10. The rental property status changes to processing media files.

11. The system begins processing the uploaded media materials (specific results to be defined).

12. Upon completion of media processing, the rental property status updates to ready.

13. The landlord is given the option to publish the rental property, making it available to tenants and realtors.

14. The landlord selects to publish the rental property.

15. The rental property is now in the published status and appears in the property search feature.

In short, this use case is about the landlord adding all the required info to register a rental property, so that it is available in the search feature.

Let's visualize the property life cycle again:

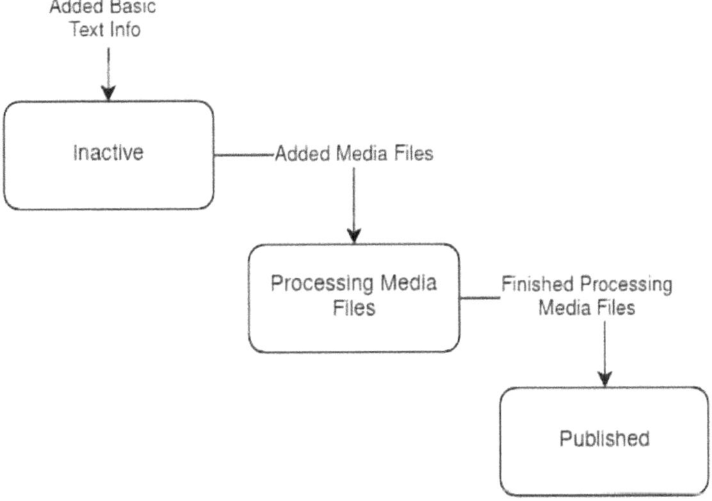

Figure 2.7 – Rental property registration life cycle

This is a very effective way of structuring a single use case within a complete business requirements document.

Let's now examine how a final business requirements document is created.

Structuring the final business requirements document

This section discusses the features of a great business requirements document. Remember to check whether these aspects are covered when creating or reviewing your own documents. This will put you in a good place for almost any project.

A single concept/feature with a well-defined scope

A business requirements document should focus on the delivery of just "one concept." What exactly does that mean? It means the document often includes a set of use cases, but they all contribute to a single "piece of value" that your software aims to provide. This piece of value is self-contained, not reliant on anything else to enhance user value. The flow is constructed in a *complete* way, from start to finish.

For instance, we discussed earlier the idea of launching a first simplified version of the HomeIt website that would only allow landlord registrations. Everyone else would be visitors who could obtain the landlords' phone numbers from the published properties. This means that a business requirements document created for the first release (let's refer to it as the *landlord flow release*) would contain essentially the following use cases:

1. A landlord registers on the website

2. The landlord publishes a new rental property

3. An unregistered visitor searches for a rental property

4. The unregistered visitor visits a rental property page

As you can notice, it is possible to create value in the market for all parties by providing only four use cases. This approach helps in going to market much faster than trying to implement all the use cases/features that we have uncovered so far.

But what do you do when there are other systems in place already?

You will often join companies that already have numerous systems in place. In such cases, the requirements documents typically focus on a new feature that adds value to existing flows. Suppose you join HomeIt as a programmer right after the initial landlords flow release. A logical next step might be to deliver the tenants flow, which could include these features:

1. A tenant registers on the website

2. The tenant sends a rental proposal for New York properties

3. A landlord accepts a rental proposal

4. The tenant sends the payment information

5. The payment is processed every month

In this case, for a second release, we are adding five new use cases to our system that will enable us to manage payments. Even so, we are limiting this feature to properties in New York only. This approach could be useful if, for instance, the finance team is still quite small and the HomeIt startup wishes to start in a reduced geographic area to focus its efforts more efficiently.

Clear inputs and outputs

We will delve much deeper into inputs and outputs in the upcoming chapters. But essentially, this means that the use cases should describe the processes' inputs and outputs as accurately as possible. For instance, here are some important questions to consider when dealing with inputs for rental property registration:

- What are the exact attributes we expect to register for a rental property in the HomeIt system?

- What kind of media files do we expect to support?

- What is the maximum acceptable length for rental property descriptions?

Here are some questions we expect to answer to clarify the outputs:

- What types of media files do we expect to produce after processing the media files?

- What is the acceptable resolution we expect the videos to have after we process them?

If we do not know what inputs and outputs are expected in our requirements, this could block programmers later down the road.

Exceptional use cases made explicit

When accepting and reviewing the business requirements documents from the product team or area, make sure to take these actions:

- **The user alternative behavior question**: First, after reading the descriptions and critical events, make sure to identify where in the system flow users could diverge from the expected path. For each of these junctures in the user journey, it's crucial to ask: "What if the user behaves differently from what is expected at point X? How should our system respond to that?"

  You'll often find that the product team has not thoroughly considered alternative behaviors. The issue is that, in systems experiencing high volumes of requests, users will engage in many new and creative actions. It's vital that programmers understand how to handle these alternative flows.

- **System errors and failures**: Second, when reviewing the documented features and requirements, you should also mark every step where a system failure could occur. While a business requirements document is not the precise place to start discussing technical issues, it may reveal important points for consideration.

  For instance, if you know that a requirement relies on a specific partner system that could go offline, you need to highlight this concern. How does the product team intend to handle a failure in that system? Do they aim for seamless recovery without the customer being aware of the failure? Or does the business plan to redirect customers to a customer support team? These questions are equally important.

Looking at how things could be misused or go wrong is a very important step in planning your development. Next, let's see how to guarantee that you can get the most eyes and fresh perspectives and ideas in the process you are documenting.

Complete signed-off flow with all impacted areas

In a product requirements document, you might want the product team to provide a process map of the end-to-end flow that spans across all different areas impacted by the release, detailing which users are taking actions throughout the process until the flow ends.

As stated in the previous chapter, having everyone in all areas aware of a new release is key to the success of new software. This is why you should, as a programmer, require these flows to be signed off by the different teams. If we get a well-detailed user journey that shows what should be done in different areas, and management in each area is signing off on that document, it is much safer to assume that the flow is correct.

Avoiding blocks when writing the documents

In some cases, when writing or reading requirements documents as well as other documents, there will be many open, undefined points. What do you do then? Should you start guessing what should happen? Should you wait for the next team meeting to report that you are blocked?

Such situations occur frequently. We, as programmers, are often faced with requirements that are not as detailed as they should be, and many details will be missing. As a general good practice for moving forward in these times, I would recommend creating an open questions section in the document. You can continue writing the document, adding everything you are confident about and then setting aside the questions you want to be answered by someone else.

Which of these artifacts should come first?

As we reach the end of *Chapter 2*, you've seen there are many effective tools to use when writing detailed business requirements. A key question then arises: with so many starting points available, which artifacts should you create first?

The answer is straightforward: it depends on the current state of the software development life cycle. Here are some excellent starting points:

- **If you're refining well-defined requirements**: Perhaps the processes are clearly laid out, and all that's missing are the input/output formats

- **If you're defining how a system flow should work**: The requirements might be vague, but if you have a general understanding of the entire user journey, it's likely time to focus on the critical events

- **If identifying the biggest knowledge gaps in the team**: The requirements might be too specific, and if it's unclear how they fit within a larger scope user journey, designing the entire user journey from a high-level standpoint may be necessary

To determine the best requirements documents to produce, start by addressing these questions. Also, be mindful of the following:

- **The size of the company**: In organizations with many different areas, a general user journey map for each user type can greatly facilitate cross-company communication.

- **The maturity of current systems**: If adding features to existing systems, review current documentation to identify gaps.

- **Practices in small companies**: Programmers might rush into implementation with minimal documentation, which is a critical mistake. Future team members will need to understand what was implemented, and relying solely on code or programmers for this information is unsustainable and non-scalable.

Documentation is crucial for scaling processes and communication. Avoid letting your project suffer from a lack of documentation, or you risk becoming the go-to person for basic questions, creating bottlenecks and consuming valuable time. With a robust set of clear documentation, you free up time for higher-value activities, which can lead to greater future compensation.

Scaling results with long-term business requirements

This section is designed to assist you in a critical mission: uncovering and addressing short-term constraints in business requirements. Doing so can lead to significant cost savings in your engineering efforts and facilitate the effective scaling of engineering results over the long term.

This pro tip is something many developers overlook due to a habit of succumbing to short-term thinking. If you yield to the pressure from business areas for faster releases to generate new revenue streams in the near future, you are likely to incur exponentially higher engineering costs in the following year.

Let's begin by understanding this: when we develop software with only the next week or month's release in mind, we often overlook the multitude of similar tasks we'll need to undertake in the future for the company's product.

That is not a position you will want to find yourself in.

For instance, in our HomeIt system, we could begin by implementing just one payment system for tenants – credit cards in the US, for example. If we task a team of engineers with deploying credit card payments by next month, what comes after? Well, tenants in the US might also wish to pay their rent via wire transfers. This would necessitate additional engineering work, correct? And it would be a task similar to the first. Suppose we then spend another month introducing wire transfers, and subsequently, the product team requests the ACH payment method for the following month.

This scenario could be satisfactory for US-based operations, presuming we aim to offer only three payment methods. Nevertheless, we might encounter variations in process flows across different US states – for instance, the need for distinct tax handling per state. If we decide to automate tax payments as well, this could imply the necessity to engage engineers for each unique scenario.

You're probably getting the picture. Many companies overlook long-term thinking, and as a result, their architectures will require engineers to step in and create code for more similar use cases. This is sometimes discovered only after the first year of development – perhaps after the fourth similar use case has been released into production.

Well, in the case of our HomeIt system, let's say the product team wants to scale the company to be present in 30+ countries. If they are asking for new payment systems on a monthly basis without explicitly stating their intention to introduce 200+ payment methods for all countries in the next 5 to 10 years, several constraints will emerge:

- Perhaps it will be impossible to have many teams working in parallel since the services might be designed in a way that makes it difficult to orchestrate multiple teams working simultaneously without creating conflicts

- Maybe we will have to spend hundreds of hours on each new payment system, which will start making developers feel like they are doing the same work repeatedly

- It's possible that scaling to over 30 countries in 5 to 10 years will be impossible because the architecture was not created to accelerate the development of every use case

You get the idea, right? When we only focus on short-term thinking, we cannot anticipate good design decisions that will allow for faster scaling.

> **The long-term business requirement corollary**
>
> Indeed, this approach appears to contradict the **You Aren't Gonna Need It (YAGNI)** principle. However, by understanding and aligning with the long-term goals of the product team, you can build your code to scale appropriately from the beginning, thus avoiding the need for extensive rework or redevelopment in the future. This proactive approach ultimately leads to a more efficient and profitable software development process.

Now, how can you spot areas in which you could write scalable code?

Here are some questions you could ask your product team in order to determine how your software should be prepared to accommodate long-term goals (5 to 10 years):

- What new types will we create in this system in the next 5 to 10 years?

- What new levels will we create in the next 5 to 10 years?

- What new products will we release in the next 5 to 10 years?

- How much do we want to increase our sales in the next 5 to 10 years?

- In which new geographies are we planning to release our software in the next 5 to 10 years?

- How many more use cases are we planning to develop in the next 5 to 10 years?

Once you have answers to these questions, consider the following:

- Does my architecture provide a general approach for facilitating the addition of new use cases, levels, and types?

- Will the engineering team spend a significant amount of development time adding each new milestone, level, or use case?

- Can we effectively coordinate additional engineers to develop more use cases if needed?

- Is our development cost increasing linearly or exponentially as we add more use cases?

- Will the current architecture create unmanageable complexity after a certain number of new use cases are released?

- What changes to the architecture are necessary to enable the rapid delivery of multiple use cases with the same engineering effort?

- How can we reduce the number of lines of code needed to deliver a use case and scale our software more efficiently?

Asking these questions will help you design software that delivers exponentially more value over time and unlocks significant potential for your company.

Exercises

Well, there are many more important aspects to discuss regarding how to craft great business requirements that truly make a difference and add significant value to companies. We will revisit those additional principles later.

For now, the tools I have introduced here will be the ones I use to drill down into the more specific details having understood the general, high-level business requirements in *Chapter 1*.

This section will help remind you of what we learned in this chapter. Feel free to go back to the respective sections for the fine-grained details:

- *Naming features* will help you set aside the right chunks of your application.

    Take a look at the previously discussed high-level business requirements in *Chapter 1* to find some new features that you would like to expand in our HomeIt startup. What features would you be interested in drilling into?

- *Critical events* will help brainstorm the most important events that we need to ensure are happening in the system.

    For the features you have come up with, which critical events can you come up with? What should you *not* forget to add to a feature in your product?

- *The events timeline* will help to thoroughly understand how a feature should work on a step-by-step basis.

  For each feature in this exercise, how would you arrange the events timeline?

- *Stages, levels, types, life cycles, and loops* will help understand the value streams over time in your system and how to distinguish users and objects in special ways.

  Which of these five elements would you like to use in the features you're ideating?

- *The user journey* will help you understand the life cycle of your users across the system, that is, where they start, where they finish interacting, and how you keep them active.

  As you consider the whole journey across the HomeIt systems, where do your use cases fit? What user journeys are affected (if more than one) and how would you draw the end-to-end experience?

- *User journeys with multiple users* will help you understand visually how users should interact with each other.

  When you think about a feature that affects more than one user, how would you build the multiple user journeys across different lanes?

- *User stories* help you understand the key actions performed by users, their motivations, the value involved, and the relationship and impact on other users. They also help to strip away technical details, in order to keep people thinking about users and the business, instead of thinking about code.

  How would you state the user stories of the features you want to exercise? What relationships would you foresee, and which acceptance criteria would you use to make sure the features are prepared?

- *Use case descriptions* help combine the previous tools to provide a clear perspective of how a feature should work. They provide triggers from which we can differentiate different contexts in which a use case could be started from, which may help identify differences in business rules and flows.

  As an exercise, I would recommend that you write at least one full use case description. You can reuse the template suggested to fully explain what should be accomplished there.

- *Exceptional use cases* help identify how users could behave in unplanned ways and what to do in case of failures across the system.

  As you think about your use case description, which exceptional use cases would you find there? At which moments could users do something unexpected, and at which moments would you consider taking extra care in order to prevent a system failure?

- *Clear inputs and outputs* help identify the specific data the business is expecting to work with. What are we expecting to collect at the beginning of the process, and what data are we expecting to produce at the end of the process?

  As you consider your use case and the different processes contained in it, which inputs and outputs would you need to make it work?

- *Long-term business requirements* help you understand the hidden costs of your current architecture and what to do to help deliver more features with less code and less engineering effort.

  As you think about this system five years from now, which new use cases do you think will be important to handle? What restrictions do these suggest you should deal with?

Summary

There were a lot of useful things covered in this chapter. I have not taken these points from other books but from my own day-to-day experience as a software developer, tech lead, and manager, as I have taken on all these positions in the past.

These business requirement practices and thinking have rewarded me with very good financial return, great feedback, and greater professional development opportunities. I have not started talking about code yet, but about the things that make writing code exponentially easier.

Of course, I would also encourage you to immediately apply all of these tools to the software you are working on right now.

In the next chapter, we will begin to consider a system that would fulfill your business requirements in a modular, scalable manner. We will discuss how to prioritize deliveries, identify domains and services, and sequence activities across these components. From there, we will be able to write our software using the great Spring Framework tools.

Get This Book's PDF Version and Exclusive Extras

Scan the QR code (or go to `packtpub.com/unlock`). Search for this book by name, confirm the edition, and then follow the steps on the page.

Note: Keep your invoice handly. Purchase made directly from packt don't require one.

3

Defining Domains for Your Application

In this chapter, we will begin by identifying the most valuable features of our system. Given that the product team often has an extensive list of requests to be implemented, our primary concern is to start by delivering the highest-value features. Next, we will move on to discover the domains we will need to work with, which will inform the APIs we need to develop. Finally, we will conclude by outlining the information flow across these domains over time, creating a clear map for implementing our use cases in your project.

We will cover the following topics:

- Determining which features to deliver first
- Defining domains and boundaries for your application
- Defining the right services for your domain
- Crafting your domain diagram
- Sequencing activities across services

This chapter serves as the critical link between robust requirements and your code. Here, we begin to model your system. We will teach you how to extract key system components from the requirements, which we will refer to as *domains*, and how to create diagrams that simplify discussions about system programming with non-programmers. The content covered will enable you to involve cross-disciplinary teams in discussions about the architecture you are designing to articulate the requirements.

Understanding the tools and skills presented here will provide significant leverage in your journey to becoming a respected architect—capable of translating business requirements into simple, comprehensive system designs. If you master this, you are well on your way to a successful leadership career.

Are you excited about it? I know I am. So, let's get started!

Technical requirements

In this chapter, you will need to use two simple tools to accomplish the proposed analysis laid out in the sections:

- `draw.io`, an online diagramming tool
- PlantUML, a tool that helps in drawing sequence diagrams, which we'll see in one of the last sections

You can access all of the chapter's code at this GitHub repository:

```
https://github.com/PacktPublishing/Spring-System-Design-in-Practice/
tree/main/chapter-03
```

Determining which features to deliver first

If you've worked with any company—be it start-ups or big tech—you'll find this situation familiar: backlogs are endless. There are no limits to the number of features a product team can dream up. If you haven't worked at a large company yet, a backlog is essentially a list of features and ideas waiting to be assessed, refined, and developed by the development team.

Why do backlogs always become so large? Firstly, being a creative human means that, given enough time, you will continuously be able to answer these three questions about your customers' different life situations:

- Is this situation a problem?
- What if we did X in this situation?
- What else could we do in this situation?

This ongoing creativity ensures that we can always identify new problems to solve, and new use cases and scenarios where it might be beneficial to add new features to support our customers. As backlogs grow larger, the critical question naturally becomes how to select the best features to deliver first.

A big warning about useless features

Many companies struggle with choosing the most valuable features to work on. As the number of potential features increases, the likelihood of selecting the most useful feature for customers is directly proportional to how skillfully a product team can assess and compare the value of different feature ideas.

With the widespread adoption of Agile methodologies, I've noticed a "new features syndrome" emerging in product areas. This syndrome arises because agile methodologies emphasize releasing new things quickly, which incentivizes teams to constantly create new features, sometimes "just because." In other words, because teams are embedded in a process that prioritizes frequent releases, they continue to produce new features—even when those features may not be particularly useful.

This often happens because many teams lack the skills to think critically about the value that different features will bring to the market. As a result, many irrelevant features are added to products across various markets on a daily basis.

Now that we have looked at some of the important questions, let's answer another important one: which business requirement should we prioritize?

Criteria for prioritizing a business requirement

As a developer working with product teams, I constantly discuss the relevance of the features I am asked to work on. I employ several critical criteria and questions to assess how valuable a release will be to the market. I have observed many instances where, simply by raising these questions during product meetings, the product team is prompted to revisit the viability and priority of the features they plan to release. These discussions are essential for ensuring that each feature adds real value and aligns with market needs.

Vision alignment

As a developer, you need to be able to understand what the company's vision is. What is the company trying to bring to the world? What difference does your company want to make in the market? With that in mind, does the feature you are being requested to work on deliver on that promise? Or is this new feature just irrelevant to our customers?

I have observed many companies doing one of the following:

- *Changing product strategies frequently*, often in the short term, due to key directors and managers leaving or joining the company with different ideas.

- *Delivering projects hastily* because there is a need to use up a budget. This scenario typically arises from the fear of facing negative consequences for a business unit if funds are left unspent.

- *Chasing market trends* without a clear strategy. It's common for companies to develop features or products simply because they're currently popular in the market. Industries such as crypto and artificial intelligence often see a surge of interest based on market buzz, leading companies to jump on the bandwagon without a well-considered plan.

These behaviors can divert resources from truly innovative or necessary projects and result in the development of features that may not provide genuine value to the company or its customers.

When developing a new feature for your customers, the most relevant factor to consider is the specific problem it will address, making it crucial to engage your product team with tough questions. If the proposed feature doesn't solve a clear problem or isn't aligned with the company's long-term vision, it's essential to escalate this concern. Make it known that the feature may be inappropriate for release—or at least that it requires refinement until it clearly aligns with the long-term goals of the company. This approach ensures that every development effort contributes meaningfully to the company's objectives and truly addresses customer needs.

Market size

When evaluating a potential feature, it's crucial to assess the size of the market that the feature will reach or attract. Even if the problem you're addressing is highly relevant and aligns with the company's vision, the impact on the customer base is a significant consideration.

Features that solve widespread problems will naturally appeal to a larger audience. Consider whether your product team is planning to develop a use case that may not be universally needed or wanted by your user base. How significant would its contribution be to the overall market?

If you recognize that the feature you're working on may not interest the larger user base, it's vital to voice this concern, given that software development is a costly endeavor.

Another key aspect to consider is whether the feature can be adjusted to appeal to a wider audience. If there's a way to modify the feature so that it becomes relevant to more people, pursuing such adaptations is highly advisable. This approach not only maximizes the feature's market potential but also enhances its value to the company.

There is an important exception to the criterion of targeting a large user base: if the company recognizes that addressing a smaller, more specialized segment can still generate substantial revenue, then the overall market size becomes less critical. This approach allows the company to carve out a niche in the market, which can be strategically advantageous. By focusing on niche markets, companies often find opportunities to establish strong positioning and potentially gain a loyal customer base, even if the number of users is relatively small. This targeted strategy can lead to significant returns and a unique product identity in the market.

Problem frequency

Here's another essential criterion for deciding whether to develop and release a new feature: consider the frequency with which your customer encounters the problem that the feature aims to solve. Analyze how often this issue arises—daily, weekly, monthly, or yearly—and determine whether your customer will have enough opportunities to use your product regularly, or whether it will merely serve as a one-time solution.

It's crucial that your product can be integrated into your users' daily activities more frequently. If you can influence some of your customers' frequent behaviors in a way that leads them to use your products more often, then the feature is a strong candidate for release.

Problem intensity

When assessing a new feature's potential, it's important to consider the intensity of the problem it aims to solve. Ask yourself the following questions: Is the problem significant enough that it motivates users to seek out your feature? Is the issue so pressing that the mere existence of your solution could drive users to your product?

The marketplace is saturated with features that do not address particularly intense problems; while this may be acceptable in some cases, it is crucial to discern which features are truly beneficial in solving significant issues for your customers. Remember, a problem that causes high levels of discomfort or acute pain is more likely to motivate users to take action. Features that effectively alleviate such problems can greatly enhance user reliance on your product, bolstering customer satisfaction and loyalty.

Market purchase power

Evaluating whether your target customer can afford your product is a crucial aspect of software development. Many companies, particularly start-ups, develop products for customer segments that are unlikely to spend substantial money with them. There is a common belief among start-ups that building a large user base will eventually translate into significant business returns. This target market is often addressed with a *freemium* model.

Willingness to pay for a solution

This point ties closely to the earlier discussion about ensuring your target customer is financially able and willing to purchase your product. In some instances, customers may recognize they have a problem but are not willing to pay for a solution. Think about when you wanted to buy something interesting, for instance, but then you did not find it worth the price. You had the money, but the price charged for it made you give up spending money on it.

In such scenarios, it is vital to ask yourself several key questions:

- Are our customers already spending money to address the problem that our feature aims to solve?

- Are they actively seeking solutions to this problem?

- Is there evidence that the customer is prepared to invest financially to resolve this issue?

These questions are essential for determining whether there is a viable market for your feature. They help in understanding whether your potential customers not only need but are also willing to pay for the solution you offer. This assessment can guide your development efforts and ensure they are directed towards features that are both needed and financially sustainable.

Estimated cost of delivery

The cost of developing a solution—whether in terms of time, money, or other resources—plays a crucial role in determining its viability. Reflecting on my experience since 2000 in the industry, where a concept akin to a social network seemed impossible due to resource constraints, highlights how feasibility can change over time. Today, social networks are ubiquitous, but at that time, the resource demands made such a project impractical.

When considering a new development, it is essential to assess the costs associated with delivering the solution your product team envisions. Questions to consider include the following:

- What are the costs of development?

- Are there ways to reduce these costs?

- Does your team possess the necessary time, skills, technology, and personnel to execute the project?

If the costs are prohibitive to the extent that they could jeopardize the company's stability, it may be prudent to reconsider or delay the development effort.

Estimated return on investment

When considering the development of a new feature, it is essential to evaluate whether the potential revenue justifies the effort and aligns with the company's scale. Revenue projections for new features must be significant enough to merit the resources dedicated to them, especially in larger companies.

For instance, if a company generates $40+ million annually, introducing a feature projected to bring in only $100,000 in the first years might not make financial sense. Such a discrepancy was highlighted by a CEO I worked with in my career, who rejected a product team's proposal due to its minimal impact on overall revenue, demanding a more substantial contribution to justify the use of development resources.

This scenario serves as a critical reminder for product teams to do the following:

- **Evaluate the financial impact**: Ensure that the projected revenue from a feature aligns with the company's financial goals and the cost of development.

- **Assess contribution to growth**: Consider whether the feature will significantly contribute to the business's growth. It should not only pay for itself but also bring additional value.

- **Justify development efforts**: The cost of development, including time and resources, must be balanced by the feature's potential revenue.

When planning new features, it's crucial for product teams to create well-founded revenue projections that reflect the feature's true value to the company. This ensures that development efforts are both economically viable and strategically beneficial.

Cost of acquisition

The scalability of a product often hinges not just on its quality but also on the cost-effectiveness of its marketing strategy. This is a critical point, especially in the context of the widespread layoffs across the tech industry in recent years, where hundreds of thousands of developers have seen firsthand the consequences of unsustainable business models.

Many companies have been forced to conduct layoffs primarily because they could not afford the high marketing costs needed to acquire customers and maintain net positive results. Even if the products were well-designed and functional, prohibitive customer acquisition costs can drain resources, leading to a situation where businesses burn through investor capital without generating sufficient revenue. This issue has led to the downsizing or shutdown of operations in many firms.

Considering the financial strain associated with customer acquisition, it is essential for product teams to evaluate several key questions when planning a new feature:

- What will be the cost of acquiring a customer for this feature? It is crucial to understand whether the marketing spend to attract each customer is justified by the revenue they will generate.

- Does this feature increase the likelihood that customers will want the product? Features that significantly enhance product appeal or meet a critical customer need can justify higher initial costs because they contribute to longer-term customer retention and satisfaction.

- Can this feature improve purchase conversions and help reduce acquisition costs? If a new feature can increase the conversion rate of prospects to paying customers, it may offset higher initial marketing expenses and prove financially beneficial in the long run.

Addressing these 0questions can help ensure that new developments are grounded in financial reality and align with broader business objectives. This approach encourages product teams to maintain a pragmatic perspective, balancing innovation with cost-effectiveness to support sustainable growth.

Impact of delivery

When developing a product, it's crucial to evaluate not just the frequency and intensity of the customer's problem but also the actual impact of your solution. Ask yourself the following questions: What significant difference will your feature make for the customer? Will the impact of your feature be substantial? Will it completely eliminate the problem or only alleviate it partially? And for how long will the solution be effective? While it is valuable to address frequent problems, ensuring that your product has a significant, positive impact is equally important—even if it means completely resolving the customer's issues for a long time to come.

Mapping dependencies

Assessing whether it is the right time to develop a feature involves considering whether your software currently possesses the necessary foundation for users to easily benefit from this new addition. Mapping dependencies is crucial to ensure that the introduction of a new feature is timely and impactful. Is it the right time to deliver this feature?

I have seen instances where products were not performing well or scalable, yet product teams were keen on rolling out the next *killer feature*. This approach often led to issues such as slow API responses, reliance on customer support teams for manual interventions, and challenges in onboarding new customers. Despite these hurdles, the focus remained on introducing another significant feature.

This tendency among product teams to chase the next appealing feature, even when the basic infrastructure is not robust enough to support it, is common. As a developer, it is important to challenge these assumptions. By examining the prerequisites for a feature's successful integration, you can help the product team realize that certain foundational improvements are required first. This groundwork ensures that when the next shiny feature is introduced, it will truly be effective and appreciated by users.

Invisible problems

This is a fascinating aspect of market dynamics that can be noticed in sectors such as mental health and professional development, where potential users may not readily acknowledge the problems they face. This lack of awareness can significantly impact the adoption and effectiveness of solutions designed to address these issues.

When tasked with developing a new feature, it is crucial to probe deeper with questions that assess market awareness and receptivity:

- How many of our prospects are aware that they have the problem our software aims to solve?
- How easily can we demonstrate the necessity of our solution to potential users?
- What strategies could we employ to help them recognize the problem that our solution addresses?

By answering these questions, you can better evaluate the potential impact and relevance of the proposed feature. This approach not only aids in developing features that are more likely to be accepted and used by your target audience but also enhances the overall value proposition of your product. Being proactive in understanding and addressing user awareness can significantly influence the success of your development efforts.

UX impact

In the world of top-selling products, the introduction of too many features can sometimes lead to a degraded customer experience. It is essential to ensure that new features are simple to understand and seamlessly integrated into the existing product to maintain and enhance the value offered to customers. Moreover, it is crucial to ensure that these features do not confuse users or detract from the overall user experience.

To determine the validity of a new feature request, consider asking the following questions:

- Will the overall customer experience/user journey be improved by adding this feature?

- Will customers be aware that the new feature exists? Is it well integrated with the other features and the user journey?

- Could this new feature potentially confuse the customer in any way?

- Will this feature conflict with any existing features?

These questions are vital in understanding whether the new feature will be usable and beneficial to the customer.

Additionally, it is important to gather good metrics. Ideally, your product should have mechanisms in place to collect usage data. This data can help ensure that the user experience is not compromised over time as more features are added.

Uniqueness

The approach of looking at competitors' features and attempting to mimic their successes is indeed a common strategy in product development. It often starts with analyzing what already exists in the industry to try to improve upon it or gain an edge. However, this can lead to a cycle where competitors increasingly resemble each other as they continually adopt similar features, stifling true innovation and uniqueness in your product. This also leads to the market becoming saturated with similar offerings, eventually diminishing the distinct value of each product.

Additionally, it is important to ensure that your features are not easily replicable or replaceable by free tools available in the market. This can involve offering superior functionality, a better user experience, or unique services that free tools do not provide.

Sorting priorities

What we discussed in the previous section are the most effective criteria I have used in the past to help teams prioritize product requirements. It is wonderful for me to see them all laid out in an easy-to-remember format so that you can take advantage of it. It took me years of experience to know these are really important questions to address when choosing which feature to develop.

But how should you apply these criteria? There is not a one-size-fits-all approach to this. Each project may present different challenges, and certain criteria might be more relevant than others, depending on the situation. However, a general method to help you identify the best features to develop is to ensure that the product scores as highly as possible on each of the criteria.

If you're faced with a long list of potential features to implement, try rating each one against every criterion on our list. Then, organize the list from the highest-rated feature to the lowest. This will give you a rough estimate of what is most important to your customers.

Comparing and prioritizing HomeIt features

Now, we will go over some of the main features of our HomeIt start-up to understand how to better score the features against each other. You might be confused here as to what the "score" is, but do not worry; you will understand as we go ahead. We will be using the criteria laid out in the previous sections. Bear in mind that these explanations are subjective and open to debate. This is just a sample of the type of reasoning behind scoring features:

- **Property search**:

    - For property search, my scores are Vision: 10, Market Size: 10, Problem Frequency: 10, Market Purchase Power: 10, Willingness: 10, Estimated Cost: 10, Estimated ROI: 10, Cost of Acquisition: 10, Impact of Delivery: 10, Mapping Dependencies: 10, Invisible Problems: 10, UX Impact: 10, Uniqueness: 1, and the total score is 121.

    - Notice that the property search is central to our system because every tenant will have to use it. They are "searching" for a new property anyway. The only criterion this feature is scoring low is "uniqueness." Even so, we could imagine ways in which the property search works in unique ways, so as to outpace our competition.

- **Realtor partnership**:

    - For realtor partnership, my scores are Vision: 10, Market Size: 10, Problem Frequency: 3, Market Purchase Power: 10, Willingness: 5, Estimated Cost: 5, Estimated ROI: 8, Cost of Acquisition: 10, Impact of Delivery: 6, Mapping Dependencies: 4, Invisible Problems: 4, UX Impact: 6, Uniqueness: 10. The total score is 91.

    - For realtor partnerships, we get a lower general score. Many tenants and landlords actually do not care about having a realtor, in case they can easily talk to each other (makes "problem frequency" score low). Also, there are many people who do not want to deal with realtors, bringing "willingness" down. We expect that the introduction of realtors can help the system to be more scalable (sometimes, landlords are not available for visits as realtors can), bringing "ROI" up to 8. Many people do not see how a realtor can help, bringing the "invisible problems" score down to 4. I am considering the "dependencies" criterion down to 4 since many things need to be in place already for us to be able to introduce realtors to the system.

- **Messaging**:

  - For messaging, my scores are Vision: 10, Market Size: 10, Problem Frequency: 10, Market Purchase Power: 10, Willingness: 10, Estimated Cost: 10, Estimated ROI: 10, Cost of Acquisition: 10, Impact of Delivery: 10, Mapping Dependencies: 7, Invisible Problems: 10, UX Impact: 10, Uniqueness: 1. The total score is 118.

  - Of course, everybody needs to communicate, so messaging gets higher scores in almost everything, except for "uniqueness" and "dependencies." Even so, we could think in what ways messaging could happen in unique ways in our HomeIt system.

By looking at these sample scores, we have the following roadmap, sorted by the highest-rated features:

1. **Property search**: 121
2. **Messaging**: 118
3. **Realtor partnership**: 91

It is clear that we need the search feature before everything else, as all features depend on it. Taking this approach ensures that we can even let features out of scope. Seeing the scores, answer this question for yourself: Does HomeIt even really need a mediation feature?

By using these feature lists, sorted by their ratings, the team can now make projections for the coming months or even years. A good practice is selecting features to develop quarterly. Planning quarterly milestones makes it easier to communicate the product's direction to all stakeholders.

With the features prioritized and a milestones roadmap in place, we can now focus on modeling our software. At this point, we are officially done with handling, composing, massaging, exercising, exploring, and expanding business requirements. You now have the best tools I like to use to assist product teams in deciding which features should be developed and how to describe those features in a way that simplifies the job for software developers.

Let's now move on to the world of software modeling. I hope you are excited about what comes next!

Defining domains and boundaries for your application

Once you have decided which feature to develop next, it is time to identify the building blocks that will make up your actual system. This is where we begin to uncover the crucial components of the software modeling process.

In this section, I will demonstrate how to identify the key objects you need to code and how to determine the various services you will implement.

What are product domains and why are they important?

A domain can be considered the specialized business knowledge that you need to express in your software. In other words, whatever you build using Spring or any other tools or tech stack you choose, you should do it to best represent the expertise of the top specialists you can access. These are people who truly excel in your product-specific area within the market.

In your software, a well-expressed domain should include two indispensable features:

- **Well-designed entities**: These are a carefully refined set of objects that accurately reflect the concepts or things that exist in the business and the real world

- **Well-designed services**: These entail a thorough process through which the entities can be processed—created, moved through different lifecycle stages, and everything else that fulfills the business requirements you aim to deliver

> **Note**
>
> The foundation for delivering good software begins with excellently modeled entities and services. The prerequisite for achieving this is having well-written business requirements. This highlights the critical need for all the tools and techniques discussed in the first two chapters. Remember, even the best companies in the market may have significant gaps in the requirements they expect you to implement. You need the right tools to thoroughly analyze these requirements, ensuring they can be articulated in the best way possible, thereby simplifying the extraction of your entities and services.

This section summarizes the most important steps for engaging with domain modeling. However, as you might expect, there are comprehensive books dedicated to this subject. A foundational text I recommend is *Domain-Driven Design – Tackling Complexity in The Heart of Software* by Eric Evans.

Now, let's move on to the steps you need to follow to identify and implement the necessary entities and services.

Detecting common concepts and eliminating redundancy across use cases

During your domain modeling process, the first step is to identify the nouns or substantive terms that frequently appear across various use cases. These key terms will form the core vocabulary used to build your software.

For example, in our HomeIt system, some of the critical concepts we need to express through domain modeling include the following:

- Users, tenants, landlords, and realtors

- Rental properties, rental proposal, rental agreements, and partnership proposal

- Payments

- Reputation

An effective method to gauge the significance of a concept in your software is to observe how often that specific term is mentioned across different feature requests. This frequency indicates its importance and centrality to the functionality of your system.

During the domain modeling process, you may encounter instances where different terms are used interchangeably to describe the same concept in the requirements document. For example, in our HomeIt system, terms such as *landowners, real estate owners*, and *proprietors* might all be used to refer to what we simply mean by *landlords*.

As a developer, your role includes identifying these synonymous terms and working with the product team to standardize the terminology. For instance, you might agree to use *landlords* consistently across all documents. Consequently, whenever terms such as *proprietors* appear, they would be corrected to *landlords* to maintain consistency in terminology.

Conversely, there may be cases where a single noun is used to refer to two or more different concepts within the requirements documents. In our HomeIt example, the term *user* might be used across various use cases and feature requests but refer to different roles such as landlords, realtors, or tenants.

When you encounter an ambiguity such as the latter you would need to review your documentation to determine the specific context in which *users* are mentioned and then specify more precise terms for each case. This approach helps eliminate confusion and ensures that each term accurately reflects its intended meaning within the system.

For example, in a recent project I was involved with, one term was used to represent three vastly different things. It referred to a CMS platform, an important virtual server, and a third item I cannot quite remember. When I joined the project, discussions about that term were confusing to me because it was applied inconsistently. My confusion initially made me feel out of place, but upon further questioning, I realized that different people were using the same name for completely different elements. The issue was not with my understanding; it was with how the term was being misapplied. As someone new to the team, or even as an existing member, you will greatly benefit the project by clarifying and unifying the terminology used. This will help everyone communicate more effectively and avoid misunderstandings.

Setting up and defining domains for your product

If you effectively eliminate ambiguity and redundancy from the requirements documentation, identifying the actual domains needed for your software becomes a straightforward process. Essentially, you just need to list the most frequently mentioned nouns in your product requirements.

At this point, I want you to think about domains in an incredibly simple manner. Consider each noun, or concept, as a separate domain. For HomeIt, each of the keywords we mentioned earlier will represent a different domain. Therefore, we will have domains such as the *Tenants* domain, the *Landlords* domain, and the *Rental Proposal* domain. This approach simplifies the initial steps of domain modeling and sets a clear foundation for further development.

Setting up domain composition, boundaries, and limits

Now that we have identified the various domains, it is crucial to consider the boundaries and composition of each domain. This phase is more philosophical than technical and can lead to extensive discussions, as different team members may have diverse perspectives on how these models should be structured.

Using your critical thinking skills, you will need to define the actual responsibilities of each domain. These responsibilities should be based on the language used by the product team and how they describe their use cases.

In the previous chapter, we utilized tools to drill down into the requirements, designing inputs and outputs for processes. These inputs and outputs, along with the relationships described between concepts, will inform us about the composition of each domain. This step is essential for establishing clear domain boundaries and ensuring that each domain fulfills its role effectively within the system.

For instance, in HomeIt, we have discovered that a rental property contains essential information such as media (pictures, videos), address, number of rooms, and size in square meters. Additionally, tenants may have one or more *Payment Information* objects, assuming someone could use various ways to pay for the rental services.

Understanding how the domains are composed will lead us to the exact place we need to be. Here are four key sets of questions for you to answer when drilling down on domain boundaries:

- What domain/concept am I defining? What is this domain, and what purpose does it serve?

- What is this domain comprised of? What set of information makes up this domain?

- What does this domain not account for? What should be excluded from this domain, either because it belongs to another domain or because we want to establish certain limits to its definition?

- What other domains is this domain related to? Which other domains interact with this one, and how can these relationships be expressed or explained?

To effectively answer these questions for the *Realtors* domain in the HomeIt system, we can walk through each question systematically:

- What domain/concept am I defining? What is that domain? What is it used for?

  The domain being defined is *Realtors*. Realtors are users who facilitate the rental of properties in exchange for a commission. This domain is used to manage interactions related to property rentals and to bridge communications between tenants and landlords.

- What is a realtor comprised of?

  A realtor should have personal contact information to facilitate communication and a list of current rental proposals they are managing. A realtor should also have separate communication channels with each user (tenant, landlord) to maintain clarity and privacy in communications.

- What is this domain not accounting for? What should we leave out of this domain, either because it belongs to another domain or because we want to just establish some limits to the domain definition?

  A realtor will not directly own an availability calendar since that calendar is specifically tied to each rental agreement. However, because the realtor manages their rental agreements, they can access all related calendars by reviewing each agreement. We can also extract a consolidated calendar by looping through the agreements. This delineation prevents clutter in the *Realtors* domain and keeps the focus on their primary responsibilities.

- What other domains is this domain related to? What other domains will show up as a relationship to this one, and how can that relationship be expressed or explained?

  Realtors are essentially related to the domains of tenants, landlords, partnership agreements, and rental properties:

  - They have a communication channel with tenants for discussing rental opportunities and resolving issues

  - They enter into partnership agreements with landlords, which authorize them to manage properties and interact on the landlord's behalf

  - The relationship with rental properties is through the management of rental proposals and agreements pertaining to those properties

This discussion provides a glimpse into how we can propose and refine domains, which often form a significant part of conversations with your colleagues. As these discussions progress, clarity is enhanced, allowing the team to confidently document the domains and their interrelationships.

As a result of your domain modeling, some domains might be expressed as their own microservices, while others may be grouped together in the same microservice. Additionally, some domains may simply act as properties of other domains. This structuring brings us closer to actually starting the coding process.

Before moving on to the next section, I invite you to think about the domains we have in our HomeIt system. Besides the ones I listed, what other three domains would you add? How would you answer the key questions about these new domains? Consider these questions, and after you have formulated your thoughts, you can proceed to the next section where we will refine the services that belong to each domain. This exercise will help deepen your understanding of the domain-driven design fundamentals and prepare you for the practical steps ahead.

Defining the right services for your domains

Great! We have now mastered how to identify key domains within our system. The basic approach involves scrutinizing the nouns in requirement descriptions and understanding the relationships between these identified nouns.

It is advisable to do real-world system analysis by playing Sherlock Holmes with a team. The goal is to comb through the requirement documents to distill them down to the essential set of words that represent the entire system effectively.

Once you have identified the different domains, the next step is to understand how these domains behave. This involves identifying the verbs or actions that the domains perform. This is a crucial phase where we start to discover the operations or functionalities—essentially, the key services—associated with each domain. Understanding these services is the focus of this section, as they are integral to how the system will function and interact.

What are services and why should we think about them?

In this chapter, we define a service as any operation or action that can be performed within a specific domain. For example, in the HomeIt system, *Partnership Proposal* is considered a domain. Within this domain, various operations can occur, such as creating, sending, rejecting, or accepting a proposal. Each of these operations is viewed as a service within the *Partnership Proposal* domain.

Understanding these services is crucial. Neglecting to account for these specific domain operations can lead to significant blind spots and gaps for developers. A wise colleague and friend of mine often said, *"Everything is possible through the miracles of programming."* However, I argue that these programming miracles become less miraculous if we are unclear about the operations our domains should support.

Since the introduction of the RESTful API standard, many developers have aimed to design *the perfect API*. The specifics of crafting well-structured APIs will be discussed in later sections. However, it's important to recognize that many developers fall into the trap of merely representing basic objects and resources in their APIs. Here, "basic" refers to the most tangible objects, such as products, customers, shopping carts, and so on. They often focus on mapping key domain resources in their URLs because they are fixated on this approach. By not adequately representing operations and actions in the APIs, they inadvertently create a lot of confusing code, as those operations will have to be supported by extra logic added to the basic resources. It becomes a mess over time.

Such APIs that lack expressiveness often fail to adequately represent the actions of the system over time, which can lead to muddled code, parameter overload, bulky classes, and too few endpoints handling too many responsibilities.

Neglecting the design of services frequently results in what is known as *spaghetti code*. Consider trying to eat spaghetti: even with a fork, it is difficult to control and manipulate your food. Similarly, spaghetti code is challenging to manage due to its tangled lines, where numerous responsibilities are crammed into a few endpoints and methods. This complexity makes it nearly impossible to clearly understand and maintain your own code over time.

On the other hand, by carefully identifying and listing the key operations and actions your domain should express, you can more easily segregate these actions into distinct parts of your code. This separation allows for better isolation, making your code easier to manage. The advantages of modeling key actions for each domain will become evident as we begin writing our services in subsequent chapters. For now, in this chapter, our focus will be on understanding how to effectively document different services.

How to model and document domain services correctly

When it comes to doing excellent service modeling work on your domains within your software, the following four steps are essential:

- **Basic actions**: Define the fundamental actions that your domain will support. These are commonly known as **CRUD** (which stands for **Create**, **Read**, **Update**, and **Delete**) operations. These operations form the backbone of interaction within the domain.

- **Special actions**: Identify and document any special actions that your domain should support beyond the basic CRUD operations. These could include actions that are specific to the business logic or unique functionalities of the domain.

- **Actions to new domains**: Assess whether any of the actions currently within your domain could be better served as new, separate domains. This step involves evaluating the potential to modularize your architecture further, enhancing scalability and maintainability.

- **Inputs, processes, business rules, and output descriptions**: For each service, provide detailed descriptions of the inputs required, the processes involved, the business rules that apply, and the outputs expected. This documentation is crucial for ensuring clarity and consistency in service implementation and integration.

In the next section, we will go over the exercise of exploring and modeling a feature of the HomeIt system: the *Partnership Proposal* service.

Partnership Proposal service modeling

To effectively model the services within the **Partnership Proposal** domain of the HomeIt system, here's how you would apply each of the steps we previously outlined:

- **Basic actions:**

  - **Create**: To create a partnership proposal, inputs include the rental property ID, the realtor ID, and an introductory letter written by the realtor. Since a rental property has an owner (landlord), the owner can be identified using the rental property ID. The output of this action is the identification of the newly created *Partnership Proposal* domain object.

  - **Delete**: Instead of supporting hard deletion, which permanently removes records, the system will implement soft deletion. This action marks the proposal as *deleted* in the database, making it invisible on customer-facing interfaces but retaining the data for consistency purposes. Input required is the partnership proposal ID.

  - **Read**: This action retrieves a partnership proposal object using its ID, returning all relevant details associated with that ID.

  - **Update**: The update service allows changes to the partnership proposal's status only, such as updating from *open* to *accepted* or *rejected*. The input for this action is the new status and the partnership ID.

- **Special actions:**

  - **Sending a partnership proposal**: It is assumed that a partnership proposal is automatically *sent* when it is created in the system, making this one of the basic operations integrated during the creation process.

  - **Messaging service**: If there is a requirement for a chat feature that allows realtors and landlords to communicate directly within the context of a partnership proposal, a messaging service needs to be implemented. This service would handle the exchange of messages specifically tied to a partnership proposal.

- **From actions to new domains:**

  - **Messaging as a new domain**: Implementing the messaging service might necessitate treating messages as a new domain object within the partnership proposal. This implies that each message is part of a list of messages associated with a particular proposal. By defining messages as a new domain object, basic operations (CRUD) can be applied directly to each message, reflecting the dynamic interaction between the parties involved. Messages would be stored as child objects within the partnership proposal domain.

This approach ensures that the *Partnership Proposal* domain is robust, with clear responsibilities for each service and consideration for potential expansions such as messaging. This methodical breakdown not only simplifies system maintenance but also enhances functionality and user experience.

This section is an example of how to find key services for your domains and how to model them properly. This structured approach to defining actions and considering new domains helps ensure that the system's architecture remains robust, scalable, and easy to manage, providing clear pathways for future enhancements and maintenance. It follows the basic premise of domain-driven design, which prioritizes reflecting real-world business objects in your model.

Now, let's start to lay out the system domain components and the interaction of the different domains over time.

Crafting your domain diagram

So, here is the thing: if you are working with several domains and find that you have many of them and tracking starts to become difficult, you will probably find it much easier to map them visually. For the same reasons we discussed in the first chapter, a visual representation will accelerate everyone's understanding of your domain.

The process for crafting a domain diagram is quite simple. You will draw simple boxes where one domain points to another domain with which it has some relationship. There are several ways to craft this visual, so I will just provide an example of many of the HomeIt domains we have discussed so far. The diagram in *Figure 3.1* was created using the same free `draw.io` app I have recommended before.

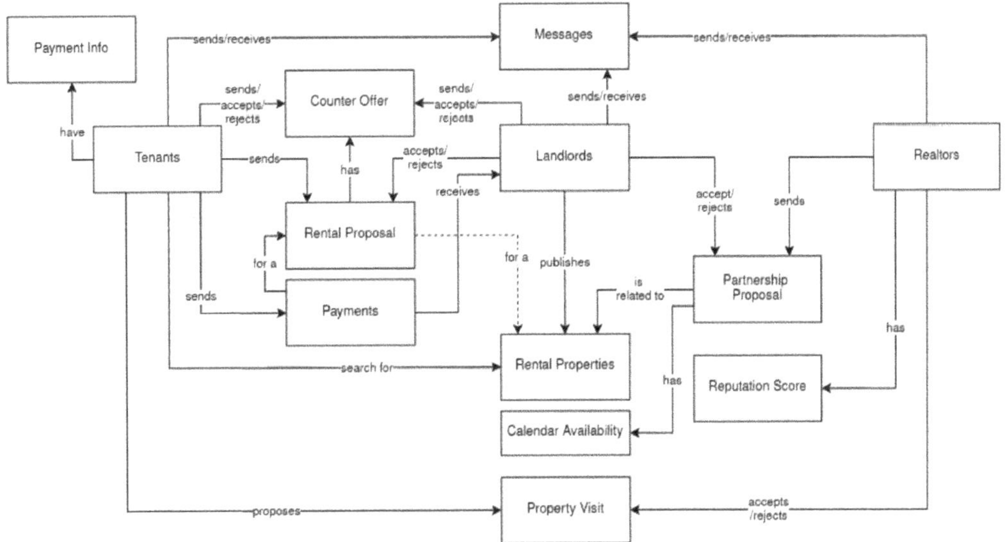

Figure 3.1: HomeIt domain diagram sample

As you can see, I have added verbs to the arrows, indicating that every domain acts in relation to another domain. This domain diagram helps us identify key flows in the system we are building and provides a more global view of what we want to build. And, as you can clearly notice, we are making it much easier to conceptualize the entire system on just a single page.

From this domain design, we can extract microservices, API contracts, classes, attributes, flows, and many other components that our Spring Framework will help deliver.

Note: the dotted arrow I drew in this diagram is to make it easier to follow the relationship between a rental proposal and a rental property.

I want you to notice another thing here: the *Counteroffer* domain was extracted from exploring the possibilities of allowing tenants and landlords to negotiate the price of a rental property during the *Rental Proposal* flow. This domain literally represents an important service we can provide to facilitate price negotiation, which is a key part of conducting business in the real world. Additionally, this price negotiation feature helps track the amount we will see in the payments after the contract is finalized.

In this sample of the HomeIt domain diagram, I have omitted several domains and use cases that we discussed in previous chapters—for instance, the *Mediation* feature. I did this to simplify the diagram so that we have a simpler sample to look at and leave some space for you to practice your own skills, in order to improve your understanding.

Before moving to the next chapter, I want to challenge you to represent other domains that I have intentionally left out. How would you design the domain diagram for these additional features?

After you have considered your own domain diagram for HomeIt or any other system you are interested in, we will proceed to learn how to sequence activities across domains and services over time, using sequence diagrams.

Sequencing the activity across services

Having drilled down into the requirements, we now understand how our system looks. The domain diagram we just constructed can serve as the basis for modeling our microservices. However, a crucial, timely question remains.

How do the domains interact with each other over time? Moreover, how can we express these interactions over time in the simplest possible manner, so that all teams understand what to build?

The Rental Proposal sequence diagram

To address these questions, we turn to the sequence diagram. During my experiences across various programming roles, I have found that this type of diagram is exceptionally effective in explaining how system flows work—specifically, how information is passed from one service to another—and in getting teams to collaborate effectively.

To explain it, see *Figure 3.2*:

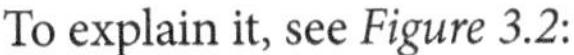

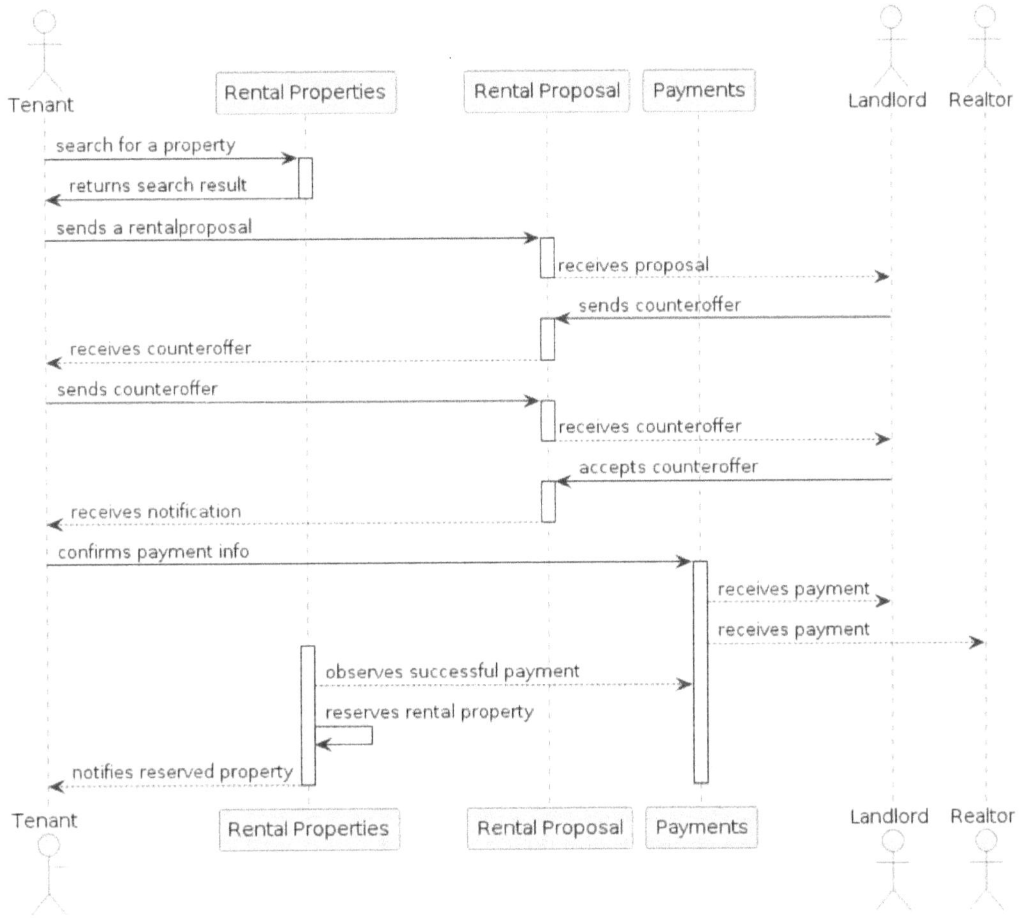

Figure 3.2: Complete rental flow sequence diagram

This sequence diagram illustrates how the core system of HomeIt operates. Importantly, we have different actors represented on both sides of the diagram: a tenant on the left, and both a landlord and a realtor on the right side.

Notice that the interactions between these actors do not involve direct communication from one person to another. Instead, the arrows point only to the domains, demonstrating that interactions occur through the system's structured domains. This design ensures that the domains facilitate and reflect real-world scenarios. For example, it is a natural process for a tenant to search for a property, negotiate an offer with the landlord, and handle payments using their bank accounts. This system setup enables clear and structured interactions that mirror the practical steps involved in real estate transactions.

In this diagram, I have highlighted three key domains: *Rental Properties*, *Rental Proposal*, and *Payments*. These domains effectively illustrate the search, negotiation, and payment flow within the system.

Every sequence diagram is structured to clearly show the order in which actions take place, with time progressing from top to bottom, following the arrows. This setup makes it very easy to understand how services exchange messages. Arrows in the diagram always point from the system sending the request to the system receiving the request, clarifying the direction of communication.

While we could discuss the creation of these domains and the specific order of components within the diagram, it is important to note that different developers might choose to create the diagram with layouts that best suit their own visualization of the flow. This flexibility is fine and expected, as it allows developers to adapt the diagram to their individual needs and understanding.

In this example, I have implicitly indicated that notifications are exchanged back and forth within the system, reaching all users. Observing the structure of this sequence diagram reveals that a notification service is crucial and utilized across different systems. In light of this, it would be reasonable to consider adding *Notification* as a new domain. Introducing this domain would necessitate some revisions to the domain and sequence diagrams. However, for the sake of time, and since the sequence diagram would be too confusing for a book page, I will invite you to make that change. Could you redesign these diagrams to include the notification service?

In this sample diagram, numerous details have been omitted. For example, the payment system's rationale for determining the amount, or how the payment system interfaces with the banks to execute the transactions is omitted. This raises an important question: how much detail should be included in a sequence diagram? The answer is as much as necessary to effectively communicate with stakeholders who will look at that specific sequence diagram. The level of detail will depend on the specific feature you are working on and to who you will address that diagram.

Now that we understand what a sequence diagram is, let's learn how to actually create one of them very easily, in the next section.

Introduction to PlantUML as a tool for building sequence diagrams

Using PlantUML to create sequence diagrams is a powerful way to visualize interactions within your system. PlantUML has been a significant tool in the market for many years, appreciated for its simplicity and effectiveness in diagramming complex systems.

To build similar diagrams, you can use the free online application available at `plantuml.com`. This tool allows you to quickly generate sequence diagrams (and other types of diagrams) by writing simple scripts. To get started, you can take as an example the script I used to render the sequence diagram we have discussed. You can find the script here: `https://github.com/PacktPublishing/Spring-System-Design-in-Practice/blob/main/chapter-03/sequence-diagram-sample.txt`.

To recreate the sequence diagram we discussed earlier, you can simply copy and paste the provided code into the text area on `plantuml.com`. This online tool will render the sequence diagram based on the script you input.

PlantUML is also capable of drawing other kinds of diagrams. But I just use it today for drawing sequence diagrams. There are plenty of tutorials on the internet that will teach you how to explore more features of this amazing and free tool.

Summary

In this chapter, we have covered how to prioritize features effectively to craft a roadmap, and how to identify and articulate the domains necessary for expressing the essence of our software. Understanding and defining these domains is crucial, acting as a bridge between robust requirements and the successful development of great software. An insightful engineer once emphasized to me the importance of taking considerable time to discuss naming conventions within software development, as these names fundamentally shape the outcome of our features and systems. The right names can significantly facilitate successful software construction.

Additionally, we have tackled a critical step in sequencing activities across domains to establish a complete flow for our use cases. This sequencing reveals more clearly which systems and services need implementation, enhancing our understanding and planning processes.

Before progressing to the next chapter, I encourage you to practice the concepts discussed. You might choose to apply these strategies to some use cases from our HomeIt system example, or perhaps explore feature prioritization, domain identification, and sequence diagramming for the systems you are currently working on.

Having thoroughly addressed business requirements, I hope you are excited to move on to the next chapter where I will introduce a holistic approach to selecting technologies and Spring projects for building our software, tailored to meet our specified requirements. This will involve diving into the world of **Non-Functional Requirements** (**NFRs**) and exploring how they influence the choice of technology and the architecture of our systems.

Get This Book's PDF Version and Exclusive Extras

Scan the QR code (or go to `packtpub.com/unlock`). Search for this book by name, confirm the edition, and then follow the steps on the page.

Note: Keep your invoice handly. Purchase made directly from packt don't require one.

4
Defining Services for Your Domains

I am very excited about this chapter. Here, you will be introduced to the world of technical requirements, or, to be more precise, non-functional requirements. We will go through a deep analysis of the system's technical qualities that you want to implement. This is crucial for ensuring your application will survive and stay online.

This chapter is an introduction to the world of thinking through the tech aspects of your system. We will explore this subject in more in future chapters, as we write the code for different services. Here is what we will cover in this chapter:

- What are non-functional requirements?
- Why do we need non-functional requirements?
- User handling
- Basic I/O and data maintenance questions
- Processing
- Testing
- AI, data engineering, and analytics
- Disaster recovery
- Protocols

Non-functional requirements, as we will see, are the best friends of business requirements. They are the backbone of the functions and processes we need to implement for the systems we are developing. Without non-functional requirements, the outcome and performance of a system are mostly unpredictable.

Understanding non-functional requirements

So far, everything we have discussed in the world of business requirements is considered functional requirements – that is, a business function represented in code. Such business functions are specific day-to-day processes your company needs to perform. In the HomeIt example, functional requirements are related to property searches, collecting payment information, and allowing proposals to be sent between parties. That is all just everyday business stuff.

Conversely, there are **non-functional requirements**. That is, the features you need to incorporate in your software such that the functional or business requirements are sustained over time and all users can benefit from your software.

Think about it this way: one requirement is the choice to support Visa credit cards on your payments. Another requirement is making sure your software can support up to one thousand credit card payments per minute. Those are requirements from different levels.

Supporting credit card payments is a functional piece of your software. Making sure you can process a lot of payments at the same time is a non-functional or supporting aspect of your software.

Now, you might ask yourself this: Why do we need non-functional requirements? Many big businesses do not actually think too much, or too thoroughly, about non-functional requirements. That is, they are too focused on the business process but not on ensuring the systems can support a wide range of challenging situations. Things such as a big spike in the number of users on a website can make it stop working completely. You want to make sure your systems can work under heavy loads. Your software cannot fail. Or, if it fails, you will want to ensure it can recover without making data inconsistent.

In the next sections, we will talk about the various aspects of non-functional requirements. I will equip you with loads of great questions to ask when designing software. This is my personal treasure chest of great questions I have collected through years of software development. I go back to it from time to time to ensure the systems I am working on have the right support for the situations we need to go through.

Bear in mind that many of those questions are half explained in this chapter. These are questions we will get back to exploring throughout the rest of the book. This chapter will become your go-to place for finding a very rich set of questions at once. However, the practical details will be explored in all future chapters. There is a lot to talk about, so let's start.

Handling user requirements

When we start building a system or a feature in a system, it is important to think about how to handle our users. Many of these questions, such as the type of users that will exist in the system, were already tackled in the previous chapters. Here are some other questions for user handling:

- What is the perfect user journey like?

- Are there user "levels," "types," or both?

- Do we have human users in our system?

- Do we have other systems as clients/users?

- How will each user onboarding be done?

- How will other systems be authorized to access the different system functions?

- How will authentication and authorization be handled by human users?

- What kind of devices will the users have, and how will they restrict/enable the user experience?

- What are the data formats each user can handle properly? What are the data formats we need to show to these users?

- Which important user actions need to be fed into BI systems (such as conversion data), and why? How will you anonymize user data so you can achieve data compliance standards such as GDPR, which requires user personal information to be fully protected? If your system requires personal information, how will users consent to use such data? How will you avoid the misuse of personal user information by any agent in your organization (from development to operations, marketing, etc.)?

- How will the frontend be best served to users? Through browsers, clients, or mobile apps?

- Is there any need to keep real-time, live connections among users or users and systems?

Let's explore and try to answer these questions using the HomeIt project. After reading these questions, we can sense that it could be a good opportunity to think about a mobile experience in which the user could search for nearby properties by using GPS. Maybe it is a clever idea to serve search results in CVS format if the user is in a desktop environment and prefers using Excel and other similar software for triaging properties. It is probably a good idea to use the OAuth 2.0 protocol to give access/permission for different users. Maybe we want to enable API access for other developers to be able to fetch data from our website. We probably want to track and log payment actions in such a way that it is easier to find out whether or not there are fraud attempts.

There are countless other things we could think of by thinking through those questions. What are other non-functional aspects you could think of?

Now, let's talk about how to handle data.

I/O and data maintenance requirements

This is where we think about how to handle data in our system. So, depending on the feature you are building, you will want to go through each of these questions in order to better think about which technology problems we're facing and how to solve them in our software. Here are the key questions you should address:

- What are the inputs and outputs expected? For instance, in HomeIt, what images do we need as input for a rental property registration, and what is the output format when we finish processing the media files?

- Which data types will be used? Are we expecting to receive PNG, JPG, or videos? What kind of data do we expect to receive in each important process in our system?

- Does data need to be geo-referenced?

- How many different entities or business objects do you have?

- What is the data structure used? For example, in our rental property search feature, what data should we return from the backend to the frontend? A list, a map? What is the best data structure given the requirements for the search feature?

- Are we generating combinations or permutations in an automated way? For instance, if we generate IDs for rental properties in an automated way, are we generating that data properly? Or does our algorithm fail at creating unique IDs for each property registered by landlords?

- What is the universe size of data, or how much space will it occupy? Are we able to generate as many combinations as we need for our use case? Is our data space too restricted or too big? For example, for identifying rental properties, how are we creating IDs for each one of them? Does our ID system allow us to generate as many IDs as our system needs in the long term? Or, are we constrained by the size of the data type chosen?

- What level of precision do we need to have in our data?

- Do we have an acceptable error tolerance margin?

- Is it transactional data that is important to keep?

- Does the data need to be 100% consistent right away? Or, are we OK with creating inconsistent data that can be sorted later by other processes, and consistency might be resolved later downstream in the process?

- What kinds of I/O channels should be used? Will your function require network access? Do you need to load or store data in a database or a hard drive? Do you have a memory-intense application or use case?

- Will we persist data? Which kind of persistence storage will be used?

- What is the required **input-output per second** (**IOPS**), storage volume, durability, and latency (how much time can we afford to wait for the system's response)?

- Will the persisted data use filesystems or databases? In the case of filesystems, which kind of persistent storage should we choose?

  - Should we pick an instance store? This is the hard drive of the server you will host your application on; this option is usually limited to a maximum size (it's considered a temporary storage type, but it's fast).

  - Should it be block storage? That is a persistent hard drive in the network, which is fast but dedicated to just one computer, some network filesystem (which you do not need to care that much about maximum size, it is not as fast but it can be attached on multiple computers)

  - Or, should it be object storage, such as Amazon S3 and other similar offerings from cloud vendors, which is extremely scalable?

- Will there be concurrent access or writes to the files?

- Which kind of protocols will be used to transmit/receive data? Will you need **Transmission Control Protocol (TCP)**, **User Datagram Protocol (UDP)**, FTP, HTTP, or GraphQL?

- Is a full text search needed?

- Which kind of sorting/querying patterns exist in the system? For example, in HomeIt, optimizing for queries around ZIP code or street names is expected. Sorting the system rental properties geographically (by ZIP code) might be interesting, depending on the expected user behavior.

- Which data representations will be used? Will it be XML, JSON, Avro, **Protocol Buffers (Protobuf)**, binary, tables, or files?

- Which protocols can support the data size and communication requirements?

- Is any optimization needed to store or transfer information? Do we need to work with different file resolutions, file types, and so on?

- Is there a pruning, **time-to-live (TTL)**, or data cleaning needed?

- Does data need to be encrypted in transit or at rest?

- Is data sharding needed? For your reference, see the following:

  - Vertical sharding is different tables on different servers.

  - Horizontal sharding is the same table spread across different servers, separated by attribute values

- Is the data accessed too frequently or infrequently, or is it archived data that is mostly not accessed? How fast should we be able to access the data if it is archived?

- How long does the data need to be kept? Are there different data categories with different time persistence requirements?

- Does data need to be masked? Do we have **personally identifiable information (PII)** that needs to be hidden from some users?

- Can async processing help speed things up?

- Is data pagination required for this service?

- Can some packages be lost in traffic (by using UDP, which is more appropriate when you are doing live streams, and you could have some packages lost without meaningful quality reduction in video, audio, etc.) or is there the need for high consistency (that is the case for TCP/HTTP, in which you cannot lose any bytes while transmitting information)?

- Are there any compliance restrictions regarding how, where, when, and for how long data should be stored? Which regulations are at play and need to be observed?

- What are the costs associated with data storage?

Again, there are a lot of questions here. Let us answer a few of the questions that pertain to our Homelt example's context. Let's consider that we are doing an analysis of the property search feature. In that case, we will certainly need pagination capabilities, and yes, we do have PII information that identifies the landlord. Perhaps we want to hide the landlord information from random, unregistered users? That is a possibility. The search feature needs to return exact data, so we will use TCP as the data transfer protocol. We also need to provide sorting capabilities for our searches. If we find out that our database has a lot of data, we need to work on the search feature in such a way that the time for the answer is short. We want a fast search implementation.

In the property registration, we are sending both text data and images. We must think about how to pay for image storage. We could assume we will resort to an S3 bucket to store all images since this cloud resource is great for dealing with such data. However, we would have to do a thorough study of how much data we will be storing and how much that will cost over time.

Considering that each rental property will take a fair amount of data storage space, due to the media resources we're allowing the users to upload, what could be the best way to pay for that? Should we assume that every user will be able to upload as many images as they want, and we can cover that cost from our service fees when we are helping landlords rent their properties? If yes, then the media storage space is an important part of our infrastructure cost.

As you go through the data storage questions, there are a lot of great insights you can study with the product team to make your service better suited for your current use case. What are other non-functional aspects you can think of when considering data handling needs?

After talking about data, let's have a quick look at other aspects of storing the data.

Exploring sizing requirements

Given the data structures and types you will be using, what is the size in bytes of the data created? How many bytes does a single object occupy in memory? How many bytes would a big list of those objects require? Those are important things to assess.

- How many objects will exist over time, and what is the growth plan of that object number?

- How much disk space is needed over time to account for storing those objects?

- How much RAM is needed to manage queries and the different data handling capabilities you will need to implement?

Depending on your use case, different algorithms will be recommended due to the size in bytes of your information. For instance, if you implement a feature that requires a query for a set of rental properties, you need to assess how many objects you will be able to load in memory at the same time. Ideally, if you need to load thousands or even hundreds of thousands of objects from a database, you will want to manage these objects using streams instead of whole collections, given collections load all objects simultaneously in memory, while streams are just like cycling through objects, loading and discarding one by one, as you operate through them.

Storage types

Here are some aspects of dealing with different kinds of data that you will want to consider:

- **SQL Databases (Live Transaction Data)**: First, if you are dealing with important live transaction data in such a way that you need it to be fully consistent, you will want to use SQL databases (Oracle, SQL Server, Postgres, MySQL etc.). For example, you should use SQL databases if you are programming a feature that deals with money, such as payment systems and money exchanges of any sort, or if you need to keep a record of some product inventory. Perhaps you just want to get a safe and consistent place to store user data. All these are great use cases for SQL databases because they enforce data and transaction consistency when done right.

- **NoSQL Databases**: If you are dealing with unstructured data (a classic example of this is the product information in an e-commerce catalog), or if you are dealing with just text data that forms entities that do not have a totally enforced format, then **NoSQL** databases, such as MongoDB, will be great. NoSQL databases will usually have fewer restrictions to data access, which basically means that they can be faster than SQL databases (that is not true in all cases, though). Other NoSQL examples are Couchbase, Cassandra, DynamoDB, and so on.

- **Binary Files**: When dealing with files themselves, it would be good to use Amazon-S3-like services, which allow you to store and retrieve individual files using HTTP requests. For blob data, static files, and media (images, video), you might also think about using **Secure File Transfer Protocol (SFTP)** or **Network File System (NFS)**; when files are extremely large, you do not need to expose them directly in websites but you need access to them as if you were accessing a regular filesystem. Do you need to make heavy files available for a partner? Maybe an SFTP is good enough, which allows encrypted access to a directory that can be mapped remotely and behaves like a local hard drive directory. Do you just need your services to have access to some heavy files and do you want a specific filesystem in place to manage the large objects as if they were local directories to your services? Then, maybe you need a shared filesystem using NFS.

- **Content Delivery Network (CDN)**: When dealing with static files, if you need to deliver them to your users in a very low-latency mode – in other words, if you need a blazing fast retrieval time for your users, especially when they are using a browser or a mobile app – you should consider using a CDN. It will keep a cached version of your system's static files geographically closer to your user. CDNs are typically used for accelerating the retrieval of website resources, such as images, videos, fonts, static HTML pages, and so on.

- **Text Search**: If you need to provide specific search capabilities to your website, then you cannot go wrong with Elasticsearch. Bear in mind that Postgres also has great search capabilities (actually, Postgres has a lot of use cases for data storage and management, in a brilliant way).

- **Fast and Highly Available Data**: If you need a large set of data that should be very fast to consume and you have simple tables with simple queries to access, maybe you will want to use Cassandra as your database. It also has incredibly special capabilities for making data highly available. I have seen Cassandra used very effectively to store user cookies and credential hashes, in such a way that retrieving that data for validating user actions was an extremely fast operation. Another option for bringing the same fast-retrieval qualities for simpler data structures is using DynamoDB, a cloud-native service from AWS.

- **Events Hub**: If you need to choose a storage system for your events, there are great alternatives: either you will choose Apache Kafka (the obvious choice for the market) or a cloud-native service, such as Kinesis, from AWS. Although they have different properties and serve different purposes, they are both used to provide real-time processing capabilities for your systems.

- **Mobile data storage**: If you need data storage for mobile devices, you can consider choosing SQLite or Realm as great solutions. They have excellent features that work on devices with restricted hardware.

- **Analytics**: When you think about analytics data storage, you will need to think a bit about your use case. If you have very large sets of data that you want to batch process in parallel ways, you can choose Hadoop. If what you truly want is a very fast processing time of data streams, you will need Apache Spark. If you just want a data warehouse that can store very large sets of data for your reports, you will want to use something like Snowflake. As you can tell, there are other very good options in this area, but they are mostly fine-tuned to specific usage scenarios.

- **Geospatial Databases**: If what you want is to store geographic data in your application, that means your database needs to support special geographic data types. Most big SQL vendors already support them. Oracle, MS SQL Server, and even Postgres bring support to those special data types.

- **Graph databases**: Suppose you want to represent your data as a network, or a graph. A classic example of this would be a social network, in which people follow other people. To represent that kind of data in storage, you can use special graph databases. Two examples are Neptune and Neo4J. Graph databases make it much faster to operate searches and navigate through relationships since the relationships themselves are represented in storage. In comparison, SQL databases will usually be slower, since the relationships are represented with foreign keys, and they need to be calculated during the query. Graph databases maintain the relationship representation in primitive database structures.

- **Caching**: If you need to store and access simple data structures with extremely fast retrieval time and you don't care too much about the actual persistence of that data, you can go with in-memory databases, such as Redis and Memcache. Although having different features (Redis offers data persistence and supports more complex data structures), they serve the same purpose. Usually, both databases are used in front of persistent storage to speed up data retrieval by creating temporary data caching.

- **Time Series Data**: When your information is time-sensitive – in other words, if optimized time-ordered data will make a difference in your use case – you can choose what we call a *time series database*. InfluxDB is an example of this use case. It makes it much faster to retrieve data ordered by time, and it makes it faster to also slice your data in a time-sensitive manner. Time series databases are also optimized for writing and their data ingestion is much faster. It does not seem too much, but think about use cases for reporting, for example. If you want to plot charts in real time and you are showing events on a chart, time series databases will be the best choice for that. Another great technology for handling time series data is Prometheus. The twist in this case is that this database can pull data from sources over time and helps create alerts for metrics. This makes Prometheus a great choice for monitoring systems.

- **Aggregated Logging**: A special case for search-capable databases is log aggregators. In the past, when monolithic applications were the norm, it was a common situation to just have a single, huge log file for our applications and triaging issues was nothing but a matter of logging in a server and filtering files for exceptions. Those were the days of monolithic architecture. Today, microservices are very common; we have dozens of containers with lots of smaller applications. What do you in that case? How can we troubleshoot our apps? Enter log aggregators. Technologies such as Sumo Logic, Datadog, and Splunk are special databases used for, among other things, aggregating and indexing logs from diverse services and their respective pods/containers. They make it quite easy to query logs across dozens of microservice instances.

Now that we have talked a lot about data storage, let's study how we process our data.

Requirements for data processing

Besides users and data handling, we also need to think about how we are processing the data we are storing and representing. These are the questions I have used repeatedly to think through data processing matters when dealing with systems design and programming:

- What algorithms can be used to solve the problem quickly?

- What latency or time response is needed by your remote client systems?

- Is geographic proximity relevant?

- What are the data states?

- What is its life cycle? How is an object created? How does it live through time? How does it die?

- Is lagging in information allowed?

- Is high availability necessary?

- What kind of scalability do you need? Which of the following should it be?

    - **Horizontal**: Should multiple servers handle your requests?

    - **Vertical**: Should you upgrade your server hardware to deal with heavier workloads?

- How about resiliency? Do you need your services to be able to keep serving requests when a failure happens at some point in your architecture? Do you need to implement fault tolerance, such as making your application capable of recovering from failure without losing meaningful data?

- What is your expected **throughput** (**TP**)? How many requests per second do you expect to handle? How many read and write attempts will you need to deal with? How much input or output in bytes per second? Do these TPs change during the day/weeks/months/years, meaning do you have more operations happening at a specific time?

- Is there any single point of failure?

- How many concurrent users are there at a time?

- What are the possible bottlenecks, and how do you solve them?

- Is there any delayed operation allowed or needed?

- Is any recurring operation needed on your system? Do you need batch jobs to consolidate data once a day? Do you need to regularly export data to other systems on a regular schedule? Do you need to transform data and send it to other systems, such as data warehouses?

- Is there any bulk data operation necessary? Do you need any system that will process a lot of data at once? For instance, suppose that in HomeIt, you add all media for different properties to a queue, then at an hourly basis, a single process moves through the entire queue and works the entire media batch at once, producing optimized images of different sizes for different parts of your website.

- Is streaming data needed?

- Will data need to be treated with buffering?

- Can the processing be done in parallel?

- For the data amount projected, is there any need for high-performance computing?

- Do you have concurrency happening on your system, with different requests trying to access the same resources? Do you face race conditions, in which two requests try to change the same resource simultaneously?

- Is there any need for adjusting algorithms or data formats at runtime, depending on devices?

- Does the system support offline usage?

- Is caching needed for processing stuff or consulting external systems?

- Is clustering needed?

- How much will the data amount handled vary at runtime?

- What is the maximum time tolerated for spinning up a service?

- Is real-time computation a critical feature?

- Which events need to be published, regular states or errors, and why?

- Which other systems need to be notified by this system?

- Which kinds of failures are possible?

- What kind of errors will the system return in case of failure?

- How will the system try to recover from errors?

- What error alarms will be available?

By using these processing questions to think about our HomeIt system, we can think of a few interesting points. For instance, when we are considering the rental property media, it seems likely that we will need to provide fast computation time to create thumbnails from the original user images. We also need to make sure that we can recover from image processing failures. When considering the times at which the system has a heavier load, we could think that between 9 a.m. to 5 p.m. are the busiest hours. In that case, we should probably have some infrastructure in place that is capable of scaling up and down to deal with heavier or lighter loads, depending on the time of the day. We want a cluster capable of doing image processing for multiple users at the same time. But how many users do we want to simultaneously serve? We certainly do not want the image processing service to become a bottleneck. Otherwise, we will face a lot of delays and errors when multiple landlords are trying to register their rental properties concurrently.

Which other aspects of the HomeIt system call your attention when you go over the different questions in this section?

In the next section, we will look at a few important testing questions.

Testing requirements

We will look at testing across the book. However, for starters, let's consider the following questions, which will help us understand how we will design a test approach for our applications. Here are the questions:

- How will your features be tested?

- Are there different kinds of testing required for different parts of your system?

- How much unit testing do we want to do?

- How much integrated testing do we want to have?

- Will we have behavior or UI testing?

- What are the collateral effects of this design choice? Are there unintended consequences for choosing the program structure in the way we did? If there are collateral effects, are they desirable or completely undesirable?

Just to explore it a bit with a good scenario, we could assume that the HomeIt systems will have both unit tests and integration tests. UI tests are not a subject for this book, since we are mainly talking about backend software development using Spring 6.

AI, data engineering, and analytics requirements

I have a few critical questions for data analysis. They help guide the main concerns regarding data. This book will have some chapters devoted to data analysis techniques using Spring 6, but you should look for more references if you genuinely want to get a deeper understanding of how to work with data. Here are the main questions:

- Which kinds of reports and analyses will be needed in these systems?

- What are the key business performance indicators we need to track?

- Are we able to extract those **key performance indicators** (**KPIs**) from the current data?

- Are we able to project those KPIs from the current data design?

- Will any ETL be needed? How would we build the extraction, transformations, and data loading?

- Is machine learning needed in this product? Do we need any data tagging/categorization systems?

- Do we need to use any regression techniques?

- Do we need to use generative AI somewhere?

Data analytics is a very crucial topic for businesses for multiple reasons. If we think about the HomeIt startup, we could project dashboards to show revenue on a daily basis. We could also report the number of proposals that were closed/rejected. We could show the number of counteroffers that were created in a proposal, on average. Additionally, we could report the number of users registering on the website (even by separating the users of different types in the analytics dashboard).

On another note, we could automatically create easy-to-use tags for filtering properties, depending on the content of the property descriptions. We could also help landlords improve their descriptions using generative AI to correct texts, create more enticing descriptions, and things like that. Of course, to build dashboards, we will need to think about the kind of technologies we need to have in place to allow superior performance on ETL systems. We could also have a real-time fraud detection system by using machine learning to react to important user attempts.

The possibilities are endless regarding reporting and data analytics.

Disaster recovery capabilities

Another key system aspect to think about – and this is a very important one that many companies will overlook – is thinking about disaster recovery capabilities. Suppose your company building is set on fire by accident. Will you be able to keep all key systems operational? If a hacker manages to invade your servers, how will you be able to shut down their access and get the systems to operate normally again? How fast will you be able to do such things? Here are some more questions to help your assessment:

- What is the frequency of the needed backup?
- How much time can be tolerated from data loss to the last backup point?
- How many backup events will be kept?
- How is the backup data stored?
- Will there be any redundancy of backups?
- Who will have access to the backups?
- What is the target recovery time from disasters?
- How much downtime is tolerated?
- How will the restoration process be done? What will trigger it?
- What geographic regions will be used to prevent disasters?
- Which strategy will be used? Would it be backup/restore, pilot light, or hotsite/multisite?

In our home IT system, there are simple things that can be done, such as choosing policies for a daily backup of the database. In fact, there are cloud providers that have those capabilities out of the box. The retention window is also another important thing to consider. For example, we could define that a database snapshot can be done every day. Also, the retention window could be a whole week. In that way, we always have the last seven snapshots.

Depending on the size of the damage and recovery capabilities you want to account for, we could set different policies for allowing faster or slower recovery. For instance, if you want to have a fully operational database replica ready for your application to connect to, in case of a failure of the primary database instance, then you will need to pay for that additional instance and set up your system in a way that you get all write operations immediately applied to the disaster recovery database, as they are happening in real time. That is, there are a lot of different and possible configurations and designs you can use to make sure the system will be able to come back online if some outage happens.

In the next section, we will discuss the different protocols used to implement communication on your applications.

Choosing protocols

In the last few sections, we talked about storage, processing, data formats, how users are onboarded, kinds of users, and so on. Now, we need to be mindful about how to transfer objects. Which protocols will we choose in order to exchange data between services?

- **RESTful APIs**: We choose simple **Representational State Transfer** (**REST**) designs when we want to allow our service to be accessible in a straightforward, standard way, using the basic HTTP protocol methods. As the most used data transfer pattern today, you can safely make your services available using this standard. There are a few drawbacks to REST services, though. The biggest one is that the JSON object representation is considered to consume too much bandwidth, compared to newer protocols, such as **Google's Remote Procedure Calls** (**gRPC**). Rest services make it very simple for users to read and understand the data being exchanged and represented. All in all, it is pretty easy to go with this option when implementing services since there are a lot of people who know how RESTful services work.

- **gRPC**: If you're seeking a less verbose protocol with higher TP than REST, gRPC is a strong alternative. It uses HTTP/2 for transport and Protobuf for efficient data serialization, offering low latency and bidirectional streaming. gRPC is suitable for resilient, high-performance applications, especially in event-driven architectures.

- **WebSockets / WebRTC**: WebSockets provide a full-duplex communication channel over a single TCP connection, allowing real-time data transfer between clients and servers. They enable efficient, persistent connections, which are ideal for chat applications, live data feeds, and collaborative tools.

- **Web Real-Time Communication (WebRTC):** This is a protocol suite enabling peer-to-peer audio, video, and data sharing directly between web browsers or apps. It powers application features such as video conferencing and file sharing, offering low-latency communication without intermediaries.

- **GraphQL:** GraphQL is a query language and runtime for APIs developed by Facebook that provides a flexible, efficient approach to data retrieval. GraphQL allows clients to request exactly the data they need, reducing over-fetching and under-fetching. It organizes data in a schema-based, strongly typed structure, enabling clients to query multiple resources in a single request. It also supports real-time data with subscriptions and allows developers to shape their API responses precisely to match frontend requirements.

As you can see, there are very different approaches to enabling data exchange between your different services.

Summary

In this chapter, we had an overview of the different technical aspects you need to think about when designing your application. This chapter is not supposed to be the only resource you will use to dive into the technical requirements. It usually takes a whole team with different specialists to make such decisions.

When you are in a big company, many of those decisions will already be made for you. However, it is important to know how to raise the discussions and understand what assumptions are currently made, and how they affect the overall application performance. With this guide, you will probably be much more effective at raising good questions and exposing risks and weak spots in the systems you are working with.

There are other aspects of software development you will need to think through to deliver great systems. For now, this is a great starting point. The following is a checklist I often go back to, and it helped me to assess many applications and find opportunities for improvement.

When thinking about your systems, you should consider these questions:

- How will you handle your users?

- How will you represent the application data?

- How will you process the application data?

- How will you store your data?

- How will you transfer your data?

With these aspects and analysis in mind, we can finally start to understand how Spring can help you in building such systems. In the next chapter, we will dive into Spring Framework coding. Let's talk about service design and programming.

Get This Book's PDF Version and Exclusive Extras

Scan the QR code (or go to `packtpub.com/unlock`). Search for this book by name, confirm the edition, and then follow the steps on the page.

Note: Keep your invoice handly. Purchase made directly from packt don't require one.

Part 2: Designing Great Spring Services

With a solid foundation in place, it's time to start coding. This part covers the process of translating requirements into well-structured APIs and services using the Spring Framework. We'll define REST APIs, implement service layers, manage dependencies, and ensure that our services communicate effectively with databases and external systems.

This part has the following chapters:

- *Chapter 5, Writing Your Services – Introducing REST APIs with the Spring Framework*
- *Chapter 6, Translating Business Requirements into Well-Designed Spring APIs*
- *Chapter 7, Handling Data and Evolving Your Microservice*

Writing Your Services – Introducing REST APIs with the Spring Framework

We are finally ready to start coding! This chapter provides the link between all the product and system analyses we have done in previous chapters and what it takes to get those ideas to solid Spring services.

These are the topics we are going to cover in this chapter:

- Moving from domain design to programming
- Introducing the HTTP protocol
- Writing your first Spring app
- Designing your API services
- How Spring apps run internally
- Creating RESTful APIs in Spring

Some sections will feel a bit like a review for more experienced developers. If you prefer, you can skip the sections in which we go back to some HTTP fundamentals.

After reviewing the important HTTP knowledge needed to understand how the protocol works, we will introduce you to the inner world of Spring beans and how the framework handles key objects for you. Then, we will move on to how to write good controllers using the Spring Web project, which enables your API to properly handle HTTP requests. Also, we will have plenty of examples of how to add validation to our input data.

Alright, enough of introductions. Let's start our journey!

Technical requirements

You will need the following tools installed:

- **Java 21 SDK**: The standard Java Software Development Kit, version 21

- **Gradle**: An industry-standard built tool

- **IntelliJ Community edition**: The free version of one of the lead **integrated development environments (IDEs)** for the Java language

- **SDKMAN**: A package manager software we use to install Java and Gradle

Moving from domain design to programming

Let's recap what you have learned so far. By going through our HomeIt example across the first chapters, if you followed all the proposed exercises, we did a series of business requirements analyses for your product. We delved into the details of how a feature should work. We studied lifecycles, inputs, outputs, users, and so on. We ended up with user stories and use case descriptions for different features. We then defined domains and services for our application and created great domain and sequence diagrams. After all this, we studied how to think about non-functional requirements – that is, how to think about our system constraints so that we can choose the right technologies to implement our services.

This chapter is the first one in which we will write our first services using the Spring Framework. Are you excited? By learning the first lessons in this book, we have been equipped with great tools that turn us into true system analysts. Next time you get a ticket to implement something, you can now go back to the foundations of those tickets and user stories and dive deep into a series of critical reasoning processes that will help you lead a boatload of great conversations with your team.

For instance, how do we go from our domain and sequence diagrams to effectively writing our software?

The first thing we will want to discover is how many actual "programs" we will need in our system. Back in the old days of the internet, we used to have just one backend service for a whole website. The code we had written would basically implement all domains and services in a single code base and would be compiled in just one binary – or in the case of PHP, the pages would be "packaged" into one directory that would be served by a single HTTP server (Apache, for the vast majority). Then there were server replicas: the same program was run across multiple computers so that we could serve more users. That was it.

The old days were simpler, and these were called **monoliths**. But that design carried many issues. The main one was that monolithic programs would grow into an enormous amount of code that would become unmaintainable. Another huge problem was that big monolithic services would require an enormous amount of system resources – CPU, memory, and so on. Developers started to realize that, to avoid those big constraints (and many others), services could be broken down into different smaller and simpler programs. Today, there are companies with dozens or even hundreds of those different programs. These are called the **microservice architectures**.

The idea in the microservice architectures was that your domains and services would be split across a certain number of programs so that they could talk to each other. The promise in the land of microservices was that programming would become simpler, by allowing us to maintain smaller services separated from each other. Each service would use fewer resources, the code base would be smaller, and a team could be specialized into just a few domains, instead of carrying the responsibility of maintaining a whole monolith with many business areas implemented in the same code base.

However, the microservice hype did not live up to its promise. Microservice architectures can become very complex. For example, when we have a transaction going, how do we guarantee that different programs maintain 100% consistency across the sequence diagram flow? If one of the systems fails during an update, how can we guarantee that other services do not keep the wrong object states if they are using different databases? That is just for starting the conversation. There are many other drawbacks to choosing to write microservices.

Well, today, monoliths and microservices will co-exist. It is up to you to understand when you should write one or more programs to reflect your domain diagram. This figure illustrates what usually happens between both extremes of monolith and microservices architectures:

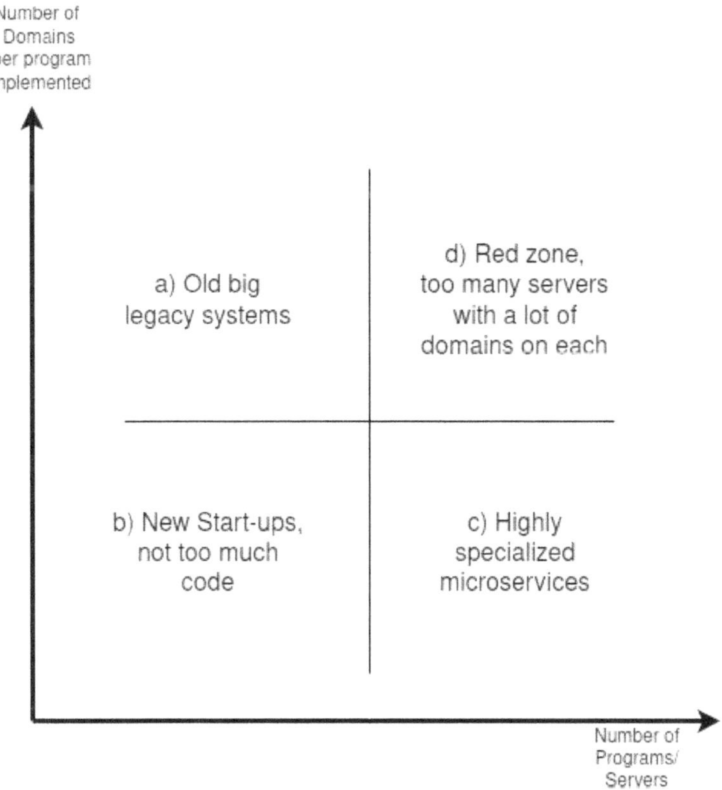

Figure 5.1: Company size versus number of server applications

By looking at the different quadrants in the figure, you can see the relationship between the number of servers and the number of domains in each server.

What should drive your decision when implementing a new feature? Should you just add that feature to an existing code base or should you just start a new service from scratch on a brand-new Spring project? Here is a good set of steps to help you decide:

1. If you are dealing with legacy code, you will face a few servers with a lot of code in each one, reflecting an enormous number of domains in each (*quadrant a*). If that is the case and your product team decides to release something new, avoid changing the legacy server. Otherwise, you will deal with things such as not being able to even run the server on your machine (that is a common problem with legacy servers). To help you implement microservices on top of legacy services, go for what we call the "strangler pattern" – that is, implement a new program that will override and replace the services implemented inside the old legacy service. There is a whole book to learn about all kinds of strategies for implementing the strangler pattern and its variations called *Monolith to Microservices: Evolutionary Patterns to Transform Your Monolith*, by Sam Newman.

2. If you are working for a start-up (*quadrant b*), you might do well by starting with a monolith, as start-ups usually choose speed over optimization. Writing a monolith will help you release things faster in the beginning. Also, since start-up services will not have too much request volume at first, you should be able to move things to production and iterate faster by just having one system to take care of, even if it is not fully optimized. When the user volume starts to scale up and the most successful services start to show up, you can think about moving them to their own microservices, optimizing them for performance, scalability, and maintainability. This monolith-to-microservice bootstrap process will help you avoid spending too much money and time on configuring a microservice cloud in the beginning, which can be detrimental to the speed a start-up needs to be successful.

3. If you work for a company that has some maturity, a lot of microservices, and a strong budget for software development, you will probably work with dev teams for different systems and areas (*quadrant c*). In that situation, you can evaluate the need for creating new microservices when adding features to your software. Unless there is already a service to take care of a specific domain you were asked to develop, you will be fine by creating a brand-new program/microservice for tackling some new requirements.

4. If you work for a company with too many systems that have a lot of code and domains inside, feeling like a multi-monolith architecture (*quadrant d*), that will mean you got the worst of both worlds: bloated code that is difficult to understand, manage, and develop and a lot of servers requiring heavy resources. This is what I call the *red zone*; you should avoid that scenario at all costs. If you find yourself in that environment, you should evaluate the possibility of refactoring your services, moving them to more general approaches that can reduce the lines of code required to release something new. The key is to find similar domains, use cases, and objects that could be collapsed into a single service. That service should implement different use cases by using configuration objects and files, instead of relying on new code for new releases. Moving the differences between similar objects to configuration files will be key to allowing for more manageability, speed of implementation, and time to market.

Preparing the right way for the upcoming features

The scenarios under each quadrant are pretty easy to understand, but I would like to expand a bit on *quadrant d* by circling back to something we talked about in *Chapter 2*, which is thinking in the long term. Suppose the HomeIt company wants to operate in 10 countries and already has a different code base for 4 payment methods in the country they operate in today. That amounts to lots of different implementations of the same thing (a payment method) for the new countries they will enter in the next years. You will want to provide a faster way of implementing the different payment methods in the future. In that case, you can look at what is common across the different payment method services and create just one service to support all future payments. The idea is that you should be able to configure new payment methods, instead of having to write them in code.

So, let us wrap this up by doing some more HomeIt examples. Let's start by considering these different microservices to be programmed:

- User service, which allows registering, storing, and retrieving user data for tenants, landlords, and realtors

- Rental property service, which helps register new properties and retrieve data through high-performance search capabilities

- Partnership proposal service, which helps register and manage rental proposals

- Payment service, which allows both storing user payment data and processing the user payment

These are some examples of the actual programs and microservices that could help us develop the HomeIt startup sample project. What other services or programs do you think would be interesting to have on this list?

Microservice communication

Okay, so we have given some thought to whether or not we should add new microservices to our architectures. Now, since this book is mostly about microservices, we need to understand how they actually communicate with each other. In order to learn that, I would like you to look at this next diagram:

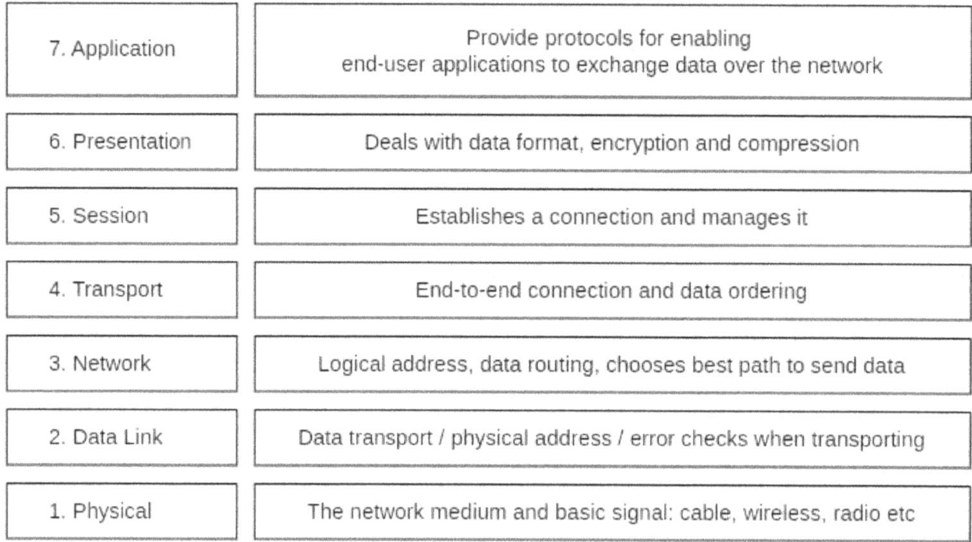

Figure 5.2: The OSI model

This model is what we call the **Open System Interconnection (OSI)** model. This is a conceptual model designed by the **International Organization for Standardization (ISO)**. It makes it easy to understand our regular network stack and identify exactly how internet applications are developed, from wiring technology up to your application.

There are many great articles about the OSI model on the internet, and since it is not the main topic of the book, we will not explore it further. I just wanted to call your attention to it so you have a clearer perspective on what your application is sitting on top of. From the base physical layer up to the data link, network, transport, session, and presentation layers, our application will generally use the protocols in layer 7, the application layer.

In the next section, we will dissect the different pieces of the HTTP protocol – the main one we will be using to create our services.

Introducing the HTTP protocol

Sitting on layer 7 of the OSI model, the **Hyper-Text Transfer Protocol (HTTP)** is the railroad through which our applications will send and receive data over the network. It was created originally by Tim Berners-Lee to transfer HTML pages between browsers.

> **Your browser works on top of HTTP**
>
> This section introduces the exact way in which your browser connects to websites. There might be some differences, which we will highlight in the next chapters. But the essence of browsing the internet is the explanation we will go over here.

The beauty of HTTP is that the protocol is readable by humans. By using simple commands, it is possible to actually understand what data the client and servers are exchanging.

We can get a glimpse of the exact power of the HTTP protocol by using the `curl` command. This terminal command is available in all major operating systems, including Windows 10+.

For example, this is the output of a `curl -vvvvv httpbin.org/ip` command in my machine on Ubuntu Linux. It is querying for a service that will inform my own computer IP (`http://bin.org/ip`). The `-vvvvv` parameter will take the `curl` execution to its maximum verbosity level. In other words, it will throw in the console output all the actual exchanges between client and server:

```
curl -vvvvv httpbin.org/ip
*   Trying 3.233.6.75:80...
* Connected to httpbin.org (3.233.6.75) port 80 (#0)
> GET /ip HTTP/1.1
> Host: httpbin.org
> User-Agent: curl/7.84.0
> Accept: */*
>
* Mark bundle as not supporting multiuse
< HTTP/1.1 200 OK
< Date: Tue, 14 May 2024 12:00:22 GMT
< Content-Type: application/json
< Content-Length: 32
< Connection: keep-alive
< Server: gunicorn/19.9.0
< Access-Control-Allow-Origin: *
< Access-Control-Allow-Credentials: true
<
{
   "origin": "45.228.146.86"
}
* Connection #0 to host httpbin.org left intact
```

Figure 5.3: The raw request and response to/from an HTTP server using curl

You can test this same command on your machine. After you do this, we can dissect this output:

- The first and second lines show the IP (3.233.6.75) and port (80) of the target server. The IP was found under the hood by using the DNS protocol, which maps readable addresses to structured numbers that identify where to find the servers on the internet. The IP is a part of layer 3 in the OSI model. The port is a part of layer 4. The string saying we are connected to the server is a part of layer 5, the session layer. The second line also shows the connection number (#0). A complex HTTP exchange with multiple requests can lead to multiple connections to the same server/port.

- The third line onward starts with two characters: > or <. The right arrow represents the data we are sending to the server. The left arrow represents the data we received from the server.

- In the data we send to the server, we can see the following:

  - GET /ip HTTP/1.1: GET is the command we are executing in the target server. In this case, we are asking the service to retrieve a resource, which is the /ip directory. In this case, we are using the HTTP 1.1 version. The GET command is also referred to as an HTTP verb. We will dive into the main verbs available shortly.

  - Host, User-Agent, and Accept: These are called the headers in the HTTP request. They help structure the request in all kinds of ways. The headers in this example are used to identify the target domain and the curl version used to execute the request and to set the type of data our command accepts back (in this case, we accept any format). We will dive deeper into the role of important headers in the future.

- This execution does not support multi-use. This means a new connection must be established if we need to execute other HTTP commands.

- In the data we receive from the server, we can see the following:

  - HTTP/1.1 200 OK: The 200 number tells our curl client that the request was successful (OK). It is also called the return code. There are a lot of important return codes for HTTP requests, and we will learn about the main ones in the next sections.

  - We then have a series of headers: Date, Content-Type, Content-Length, and so on. They tell us the date of the execution, the return content type (JSON, which we will look further into), the length of the data in bytes, and the actual server and version that is being run (in this case, gunicorn, which is a Python-based HTTP server).

- Finally, we can see the actual IP result, which is called the **payload**. In this case, it contains the IP address of my own computer (the origin of the request). The JSON content type is key to developing microservices, as it is 100% readable by humans.

I love using `curl` when troubleshooting systems. For general development efforts, there are great alternatives such as Postman, Insomnia, and Bruno. They all allow creating request collections so that we can easily test various aspects of our services.

Of course, your browser can be used as a tool to access websites using HTTP as well. In the real world, the browser acts as the client (`curl`), and the website is served by a web server. Your browser will generally either fetch HTML pages issuing `GET` commands or fire HTTP requests to the backend services, which allows using other HTTP commands, which you will learn about shortly.

Most backend services that are exposed on the internet today will be built on top of the HTTP protocol. That means, when building a new service, we will always have a request to a service and a response back to the original client that fired the request. All requests will have key parts, such as the HTTP verb that defines the action, the response code that summarizes the result, the HTTP headers, and the payloads.

Let's see some of these aspects of HTTP closely.

What are the main HTTP verbs?

In our previous example, we saw the `GET` HTTP verb in action. Let us look at all the main verbs now:

- `GET` allows fetching a resource. It can be used for retrieving web pages or some domain representations (we will look at that shortly). It could be used to fetch a list of the rental properties found during a search on the HomeIt website, for instance.

- `DELETE` allows issuing a command for the service to remove some object from their domain. It could be used to delete some pictures of a rental property in the HomeIt system.

- `POST` allows sending a new resource to a backend service so that it can be persisted and accessed later using `GET` requests. It could be used when landlords are submitting new rental properties that would later be found during searches.

- `PUT` is used when we need to fully update an existing resource. It could be used for uploading a profile picture, for instance, or a simple object such as the user details.

- `PATCH` allows updating some fields of a resource, without touching other fields. It could be used to update just some fields of a rental property, such as the description, for example.

There are other important HTTP verbs, but these are the main ones we need to study. Let's stick with them for now. By implementing these five verbs for a domain, we have fully implemented the CRUD operations – create (`POST`), read (`GET`), update (`POST`, `PUT`), and delete (`DELETE`). These are the main operations in basically every software.

Let's now go over the main return codes.

What are the main HTTP response codes?

As you saw in our `curl` example, when you send an HTTP request to a server, it will always respond with some code. These are the main response codes we will use in most systems:

- `200 OK`: The request has succeeded. For instance, when you issue a `GET` request, receiving back a `200` code means the resource has been fetched and is transmitted in the message body.

- `201 Created`: The request has been fulfilled and resulted in a new resource being created. It is usually a response to a `POST` request.

- `202 Accepted`: The request has been accepted for processing, but the processing has not been completed.

- `204 No Content`: The server successfully processed the request but is not returning any content.

- `301 Moved Permanently`: The address of the requested resource has been changed permanently. The new address is usually provided in the response.

- `400 Bad Request`: The server cannot or will not process the request due to some client error, usually a malformed message.

- `401 Unauthorized`: Although the HTTP standard specifies `Unauthorized`, semantically, this response means *unauthenticated*. That is, the client must authenticate themselves to get the requested response.

- `403 Forbidden`: Although the client is authenticated, its credentials are not enough to access the specified resource.

- `404 Not Found`: The server cannot find the requested resource.

- `500 Internal Server Error`: A server error, meaning some unrecoverable error happened.

- `502 Bad Gateway`: The server, while acting as a gateway or proxy, received an invalid response from the upstream server.

- `504 Gateway Timeout`: The server, while acting as a gateway or proxy, did not get a response in time from the upstream server.

Again, there are other possible HTTP codes that you might want to use in your implementation. These are some ideas of the ones people use the most. You can find other HTTP return codes in a lot of places online, such as `http://http.cat` – a funny website that mixes HTTP return codes with cat pictures.

Writing your first Spring app

How about we rewrite this IP service using Spring Boot (which is the main Spring Framework project we will talk about in a bit), just so that we can have our very first app running and you can get a feel of how Spring works? We can start with this very quick practice, and then we can get back to explaining the Spring Framework.

Using SDKMAN to manage your tool versions

To install all the needed programs, we can use a smart tool called **SDKMAN**. It is software capable of maintaining different versions of your Java SDKs in the same computer environment. With SDKMAN, you will be able to work with different versions on demand. Let's say you need Java 8 today, you can just install it and instruct SDKMan to let Java 8 be your default tooling in your terminal. If you want to change your current SDK version to Java 17, you can do this as well. You can even set a directory with a default Java version of your choice so that when you are running Java commands inside that directory, your preferred Java version will be used. This is useful when you are working with different projects that require different Java versions.

SDKMAN works with both Linux (including macOS and Windows WSL) and Windows. You can install it on your machine by following the instructions here: `https://sdkman.io/install`.

Beware that SDKMAN is capable of also managing other tools, including Maven and Gradle. In our case, we will work with Gradle in this book.

The SDKMAN website contains a very easy-to-follow manual page so that you can learn about the main commands and how to use them: `https://sdkman.io/usage`.

For this book, it is enough to run just a few commands to have the right tooling installed. First, you can list the available versions of Java with this command:

```
> sdk list java
```

The result will show you several Java versions that you can install:

```
================================================================================
Available Java Versions for Linux 64bit
================================================================================
 Vendor        | Use | Version   | Dist  | Status      | Identifier
--------------------------------------------------------------------------------
 Corretto      |     | 22        | amzn  |             | 22-amzn
               |     | 22.0.1    | amzn  |             | 22.0.1-amzn
               |     | 21.0.3    | amzn  |             | 21.0.3-amzn
               |     | 21.0.2    | amzn  |             | 21.0.2-amzn
               |     | 17.0.11   | amzn  |             | 17.0.11-amzn
               |     | 17.0.10   | amzn  |             | 17.0.10-amzn
               |     | 11.0.23   | amzn  |             | 11.0.23-amzn
               |     | 11.0.22   | amzn  |             | 11.0.22-amzn
               |     | 8.0.412   | amzn  |             | 8.0.412-amzn
               |     | 8.0.402   | amzn  |             | 8.0.402-amzn
```

Figure 5.4: SDKMAN listing Java versions

When installing the Java 21 SDK, you will need to choose whatever version you prefer. For this book, I will generally use the Java 21 version. Just as an example, this is the command you need to run if you are working with the Amazon Corretto package:

```
> sdk install java 21.0.3-amzn
```

As you can see, the last part of the command is the same as in the Identifier column in *Figure 5.4*. Choosing the right Java SDK package is a matter of little concern, but for our code samples, we will use the Temurin SDK, which we see in the next section.

Installing the Java SDK

There are several Java SDK distributions available for you to choose from. For example, the following figure shows you the output of the command for installing a different version from the amzn one, called **Temurin**. This is the SDK I am using throughout the book:

```
~ (34.307s)
sdk install java 21.0.3-tem

Downloading: java 21.0.3-tem

In progress...

####################################################################################################

Repackaging Java 21.0.3-tem...

Done repackaging...

Installing: java 21.0.3-tem
Done installing!

Do you want java 21.0.3-tem to be set as default? (Y/n): Y

Setting java 21.0.3-tem as default.
```

Figure 5.5: SDKMAN installing a new Java version

As you can see, I have actually chosen to set the Temurin version as my default one, by answering Y to the question. In regards to why I am using Temurin, there is not really a strong case for it. Different Java SDK providers will generally build their tools following Java specifications, so there is no strong advocacy about which one to choose. But as a general rule, if you are using **Amazon Web Services** (**AWS**), you might prefer to use Corretto as your preferred Java SDK. Since Amazon built it, it has supposedly been battle-tested to use in conjunction with AWS.

Installing Gradle

Now, we are going to install Gradle 8.7, which is the latest stable version:

```
sdk install gradle 8.7

Downloading: gradle 8.7

In progress...

#############################################
#############################################

Installing: gradle 8.7
Done installing!


Setting gradle 8.7 as default.
```

Figure 5.6: SDKMAN installing Gradle

Since I do not have any Gradle version installed yet, SDKMAN decided to make 8.7 my default version.

Alright, we have now installed Java and Gradle, which is enough to run future Java projects. You can make sure they are correctly installed by running these two commands:

```
> java --version
> gradle -version
```

This is what I get when I run both commands. You should get a similar output:

```
java --version
openjdk 21.0.3 2024-04-16 LTS
OpenJDK Runtime Environment Temurin-21.0.3+9 (build 21.0.3+9-LTS)
OpenJDK 64-Bit Server VM Temurin-21.0.3+9 (build 21.0.3+9-LTS, mixed mode, sharing)


~ (0.57s)
gradle -version


Welcome to Gradle 8.7!

Here are the highlights of this release:
 - Compiling and testing with Java 22
 - Cacheable Groovy script compilation
 - New methods in lazy collection properties

For more details see https://docs.gradle.org/8.7/release-notes.html



------------------------------------------------------------
Gradle 8.7
------------------------------------------------------------

Build time:   2024-03-22 15:52:46 UTC
Revision:     650af14d7653aa949fce5e886e685efc9cf97c10

Kotlin:       1.9.22
Groovy:       3.0.17
Ant:          Apache Ant(TM) version 1.10.13 compiled on January 4 2023
JVM:          21.0.3 (Eclipse Adoptium 21.0.3+9-LTS)
OS:           Linux 6.5.0-28-generic amd64
```

Figure 5.7: Checking the newly installed software versions

Easy-peasy, isn't it?

SDKMAN is my go-to package installer for all things related to the Java ecosystem.

Now, let's actually write some Spring code. I will be occasionally adding screenshots from my code, but I'll add a link to the complete source code in the sections.

Using Spring Initializr

There is a very important tool for kickstarting Spring projects. It is called Spring Initializr, and it can be accessed at this address: `https://start.spring.io/`.

When you visit the website, you will see two panels side by side. The left one requires a general setup for the versions used and the names of the applications, packages, and so on. I have set these values, and you can do the same to follow along this process:

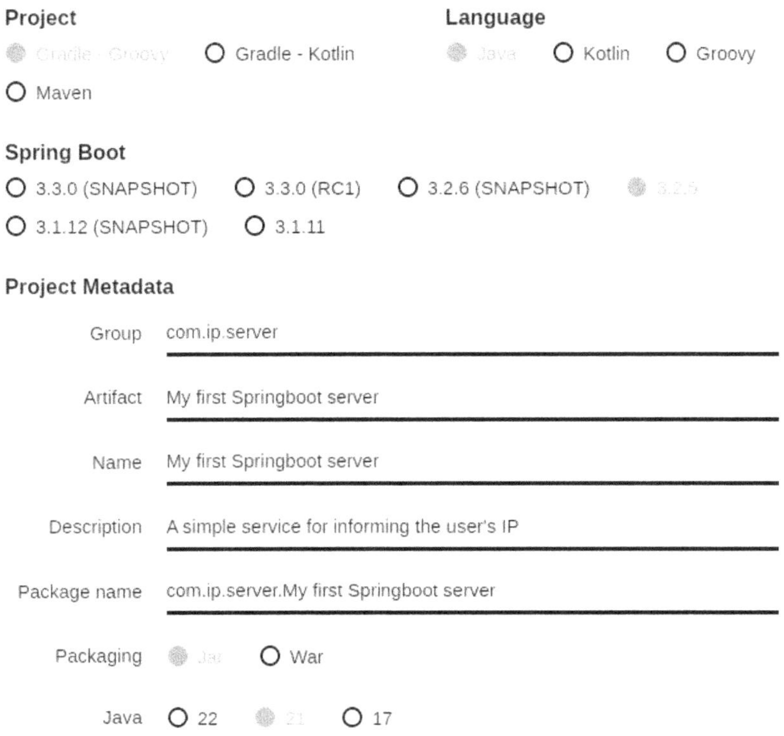

Project

◉ Gradle - Groovy   ○ Gradle - Kotlin

○ Maven

Language

◉ Java   ○ Kotlin   ○ Groovy

Spring Boot

○ 3.3.0 (SNAPSHOT)   ○ 3.3.0 (RC1)   ○ 3.2.6 (SNAPSHOT)   ◉ 3.2.5

○ 3.1.12 (SNAPSHOT)   ○ 3.1.11

Project Metadata

Group   com.ip.server

Artifact   My first Springboot server

Name   My first Springboot server

Description   A simple service for informing the user's IP

Package name   com.ip.server.My first Springboot server

Packaging   ◉ Jar   ○ War

Java   ○ 22   ◉ 21   ○ 17

Figure 5.8: Creating an app with Spring Initializr

The right panel is where you choose which Spring projects will be used in your service; these are actually the Java dependencies you will need. In this very first sample project, we will need nothing besides the Spring Web project. This is how you should parameterize your Spring starter:

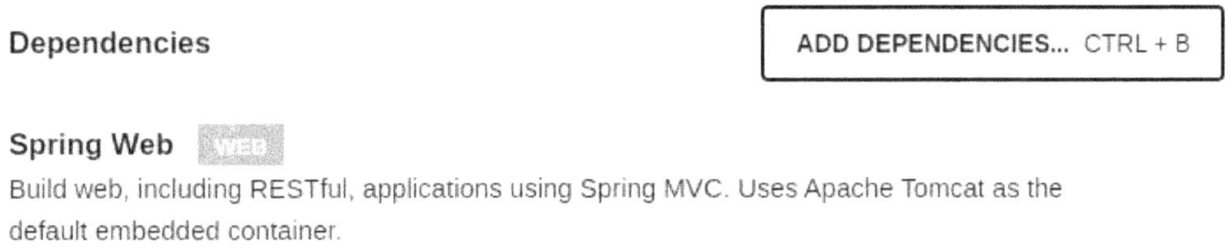

Dependencies

ADD DEPENDENCIES... CTRL + B

Spring Web WEB

Build web, including RESTful, applications using Spring MVC. Uses Apache Tomcat as the default embedded container.

Figure 5.9: Choosing dependencies in Spring Initializr

To select the Spring Web dependency, just make sure to click on **ADD DEPENDENCIES** and you will be presented with an intimidating list of components. Just forget about the substantial number of options; I will show you all these components one by one throughout the chapters.

With the Spring Web project enabled as a dependency, we can click on **Generate** in the page footer. The website will create a package containing a ready-to-implement basic Spring project. Download it and open it in your favorite IDE. If you still do not have a preference, I recommend downloading the IntelliJ Community edition, which is free. If you are a student, you can even have access to the paid version. It is by far the best IDE for Java-related projects.

Opening your Spring project

After you unpack your first server, you will be presented with the following directory structure:

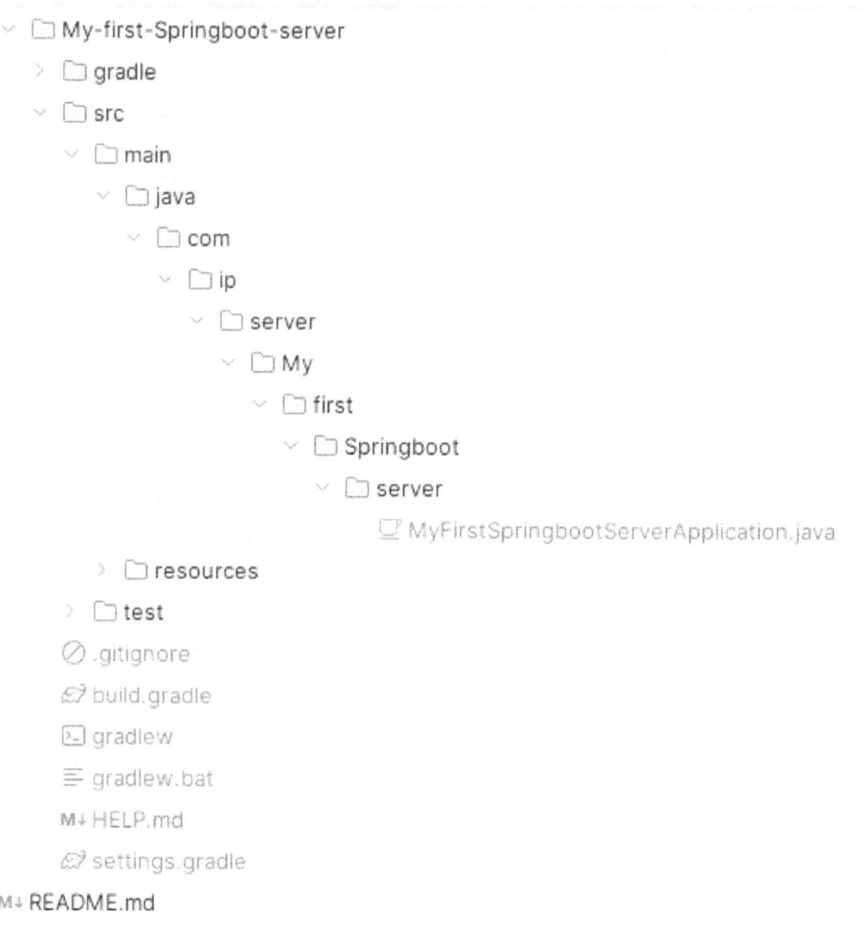

Figure 5.10: Spring Initializr basic app structure

This is a basic structure for a Spring project. I will dive into more background explanations in a bit. For now, let's understand the different parts:

- The `/gradle` directory actually contains a whole version of the Gradle software, our package builder. It is there in case you don't have Gradle installed on your machine.

- The file called `MyFirstSpringbootServerApplication.java` is the main application class of your server. This is the class that can run an entire set of Spring services.

- The `/test` directory contains an initial test class, which we are going to be using to speed up our application development.

- There are other Gradle `config` files that we are going to deal with in the next sections. For now, it is important to state that `gradlew` and `gradlew.bat` are actually executable files from which you can run a Gradle build in this project, even if you do not have Gradle installed on your machine.

- The file named `build.gradle` is where we declare the Java library dependencies (the `.jar` files containing the Spring classes you will use in your project).

Next, we will learn how to compile and build our package.

Building your application using Gradle

In order to build your Spring application, you need to switch to your directory and run either one of these commands on a terminal window:

```
> gradle jar
> ./gradlew jar
```

The first command will execute a build using the default Gradle version that you installed on your machine using SDKMAN. The second command will use the built-in Gradle version that comes with the Spring project you generated using Spring Initializr.

Let us check the output of the build command:

```
gradle jar

BUILD SUCCESSFUL in 1s
3 actionable tasks: 3 up-to-date
```

Figure 5.11: Gradle build command output

When you run your application, Gradle will compile it and build it automatically and the following things will happen:

- Your Java dependencies will be downloaded to a local cache directory directly from the Maven Central website by default, but it is fully customizable. In some companies, severe network restrictions might have been applied, meaning that you will not be able to download your dependencies from Maven Central. In that case, it is possible to configure your build to get dependencies from the company's own repositories.

- The Java compiler will compile all your classes and package your Spring application.

- The project's test suite will be run, making sure all the tests you wrote pass.

- Your Spring application `.jar` file will be created.

After you run the `gradle jar` command, this is where you will find your created `.jar` file:

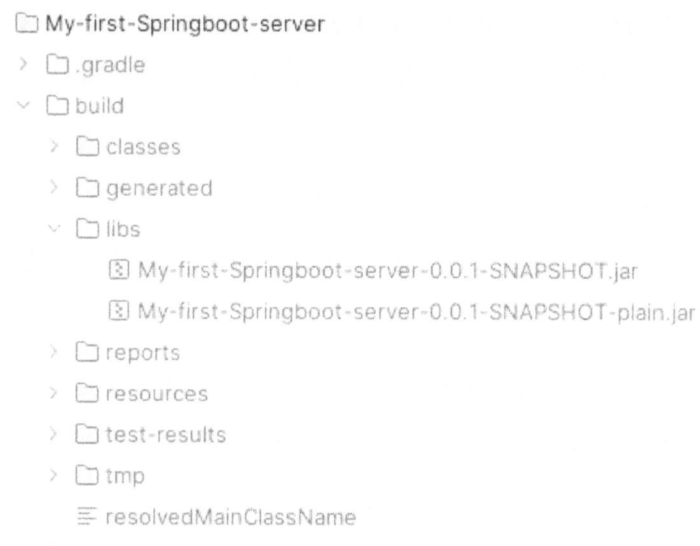

Figure 5.12: The application .jar file created by the build process

The `build` directory is where all compiled classes and resources generated during the build process will go. Now, let's implement the actual IP extractor.

Implementing your first Spring Controller class

A **Controller** class is a Spring class capable of handling HTTP requests. In order to implement your IP extractor class, you will need to add a new `IpController` class in this directory:

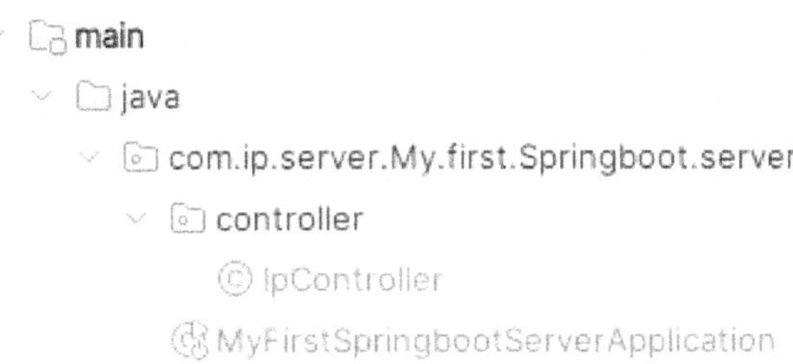

Figure 5.13: Creating a new Controller class

Generally speaking, every new Spring component needs to be included in a child directory from your main application class (in our case, `MyFirstSpringbootServerApplication`). That will help Spring automatically find your classes and make them available at runtime.

The body of your class should look like the following:

```
@RestController
public class IpController {
    public IpController() {}

    @GetMapping("/get-ip")
    public String getIP() {
        ServletRequestAttributes requestAttributes =
            (ServletRequestAttributes) RequestContextHolder
                .getRequestAttributes();

        if (requestAttributes != null) {
            return "Your IP Address is: " +
                requestAttributes
                    .getRequest()
                    .getRemoteAddr();
        }
        return "Error while trying to get your IP.";
    }
}
```

As you can see, the implementation is pretty simple, but let me break down the different parts for you to understand:

- The `package` and `import` statements inform where this class belongs in the project, and which Spring classes will we use to implement our service

- The `@RestController` annotation tells Spring that this class will implement API endpoints that will handle HTTP requests from remote servers

- The `@GetMapping` annotation tells Spring that the `getIp()` annotated method will handle HTTP GET requests in the `/get-ip` **Unique Resource Identifier** (**URI**) – we will explain this in a bit

- The method implementation basically uses the `getRequestAttributes()` static method from the `RequestContextHolder` class, which makes the current request available to our method

- Finally, we recover the IP address that is stored in the `HTTPServletRequest` object and return to the remote client that issued the HTTP request

Now, let's learn how to run our Spring application.

Running your Spring Application

In order to see your application at work, just run the following command from the root of your Spring project:

```
> gradle bootRun
```

You will see your application going online. The actual screenshot will be unreadable, but you can look at the details in your own console:

```
gradle bootRun

> Task :bootRun

  .   ____          _            __ _ _
 /\\ / ___'_ __ _ _(_)_ __  __ _ \ \ \ \
( ( )\___ | '_ | '_| | '_ \/ _` | \ \ \ \
 \\/  ___)| |_)| | | | | || (_| |  ) ) ) )
  '  |____| .__|_| |_|_| |_\__, | / / / /
 =========|_|==============|___/=/_/_/_/
 :: Spring Boot ::                (v3.2.5)

2024-07-15T22:48:57.803-03:00  INFO 130951 --- [My-first-Springboot-server] [           main] f.S.s.MyFirstSpringbootServerApplicati
on : Starting MyFirstSpringbootServerApplication using Java 21.0.3 with PID 130951 (/home/rodrigo/IdeaProjects/pro-spring/profession
al-spring-system-design-patterns/chapter-05/My-first-Springboot-server/build/classes/java/main started by rodrigo in /home/rodrigo/I
deaProjects/pro-spring/professional-spring-system-design-patterns/chapter-05/My-first-Springboot-server)
2024-07-15T22:48:57.805-03:00  INFO 130951 --- [My-first-Springboot-server] [           main] f.S.s.MyFirstSpringbootServerApplicati
on : No active profile set, falling back to 1 default profile: "default"
2024-07-15T22:48:58.509-03:00  INFO 130951 --- [My-first-Springboot-server] [           main] o.s.b.w.embedded.tomcat.TomcatWebServe
r  : Tomcat initialized with port 8080 (http)
2024-07-15T22:48:58.519-03:00  INFO 130951 --- [My-first-Springboot-server] [           main] o.apache.catalina.core.StandardService
   : Starting service [Tomcat]
2024-07-15T22:48:58.520-03:00  INFO 130951 --- [My-first-Springboot-server] [           main] o.apache.catalina.core.StandardEngine
   : Starting Servlet engine: [Apache Tomcat/10.1.20]
2024-07-15T22:48:58.557-03:00  INFO 130951 --- [My-first-Springboot-server] [           main] o.a.c.c.C.[Tomcat].[localhost].[/]
   : Initializing Spring embedded WebApplicationContext
2024-07-15T22:48:58.558-03:00  INFO 130951 --- [My-first-Springboot-server] [           main] w.s.c.ServletWebServerApplicationConte
xt : Root WebApplicationContext: initialization completed in 718 ms
```

Figure 5.14: Spring application console logs

There are two lines at the end that will help you to know whether your application is online:

```
Tomcat started on port 8080 (http) with context path ''
Started MyFirstSpringbootServerApplication in 1.615 seconds (process
running for 1.924)
```

This means you are exposing your server in port 8080 of your computer, which is the default Tomcat web server port. It is important to notice this because Spring uses Tomcat behind the scenes. You can also change Tomcat to Jetty, Undertow, and other containers, depending on your needs.

Finally, you can test your own application with the `curl` command on a different terminal. Just use the following command:

```
> curl -vvvvv localhost:8080/get-ip
```

Just for the record, `localhost` means you are calling a service that is on your own machine. This is the execution result:

```
curl -vvvvv localhost:8080/get-ip

*   Trying 127.0.0.1:8080...
* Connected to localhost (127.0.0.1) port 8080 (#0)
> GET /get-ip HTTP/1.1
> Host: localhost:8080
> User-Agent: curl/7.81.0
> Accept: */*
>
* Mark bundle as not supporting multiuse
< HTTP/1.1 200
< Content-Type: text/plain;charset=UTF-8
< Content-Length: 29
< Date: Thu, 16 May 2024 13:48:56 GMT
<
* Connection #0 to host localhost left intact
Your IP Address is: 127.0.0.1
```

Figure 5.15: Calling our new IP service

And that's it! You have your first Spring service up and running. The IP address 127.0.0.1 means your Spring application knows that you are calling from the device that is running the application itself. In this case, we have implemented the application in a way that returns a basic text string. We will improve on that later; this was just for getting you a first experience with running Spring services.

After this lab, we have some interesting questions to discuss, such as the following:

- How does the Spring Framework know which classes to run?

- What are the most important annotations?

- What are the best actual conventions for organizing Spring services?

Let's discuss those in the next sections.

Designing your API services

Now that you have seen a bit of how Spring applications work, it is important to know how they are actually organized. There are some key terms for you to learn here.

In general, professional teams will look to create *APIs* with *RESTful* standards, documented with the *OpenAPI* specification.

What are all these buzzwords, and why they are important? That is a long story that we will uncover in the next sections and the next chapter.

What are APIs?

When you write a service that other people can use by means of other programs, we say you are creating an **API**, which stands for **application programming interface**. It means you can give other developers special documentation and credentials so that they can call your program in different ways. In this book, we are working with the Spring API in order to create our own APIs for other systems to use. In other words, we are using the Spring Framework API so that we can provide our own API to other developers. One API is leveraging another.

Think about that for a second. In the software world, it is APIs all the way down. The Spring Framework leverages the Java programming language API as well, and Java leverages the operating system's APIs. It is one API on top of the next one, in layers.

APIs facilitate the work of other developers. Let's look at this diagram, which illustrates that organization:

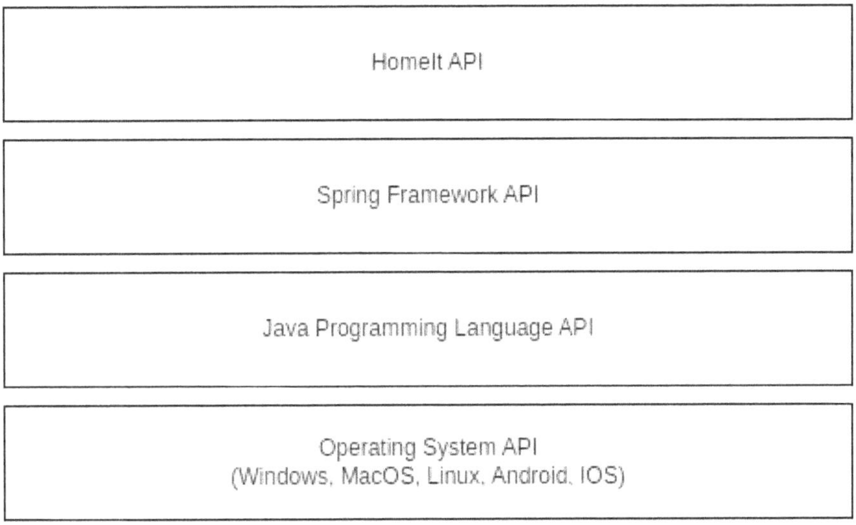

HomeIt API

Spring Framework API

Java Programming Language API

Operating System API
(Windows, MacOS, Linux, Android, IOS)

Figure 5.16: The OS-Spring application stack

As you can see, developers are building APIs on top of other developers' APIs.

In our example, as we want to provide a nice backend interface for our HomeIt systems, we will need to build our API on top of the HTTP protocol, and that is exactly one of Spring Framework's specialties. Great APIs will always accelerate the next level of development.

To provide great APIs on top of the HTTP protocol, we need to understand the RESTful standard.

Why do we need RESTful standards?

As we saw before, the HTTP protocol allows for several different actions, which are represented by the verbs we saw beforehand. The most important ones are GET, POST, PUT, PATCH, and DELETE. If those are the actions available, what are we acting on? And how should we organize those actions?

Enter the **RESTful** standard. It was created in 2000 by Roy Fielding. The name stands for **Representational State Transfer**. It proposes that an application should be exposed over HTTP as a set of URIs, which are actually a part of the browser URL. The URIs would represent the application objects' directories and instances (our domain objects, basically). Each URI was subject to actions fired by users by basically sending HTTP requests to those URIs.

For example, in our HomeIt exercise, RESTful applications would make URIs available for the main domain directories:

```
/users
/rental-properties
/rental-proposals
/partnership-proposals
```

And so on, and so forth. These URIs will allow sending HTTP requests using different verbs. These are some examples:

- A GET request to `/users/{id}` would return the details of a single user

- A GET request to `/users` would return a list of users registered on the website

- A POST request to `/rental-properties` would allow registering a new property in the system

- A GET request on `/rental-proposals/{id}` would retrieve the information for the rental proposal ID provided in the request

You get the point, right? A RESTful API will allow you to act on all available domain objects by basically sending HTTP requests with the right verbs.

Circling back to *Chapter 3*, when we were extracting our services from the actual business requirements, the RESTful APIs are powerful ways to design those services.

Another critical point is that RESTful APIs will always be **stateless** services. That means the program should not keep any user session state between requests. Every request is treated as an entirely new interaction. The only persisted state is applied to the resources we are acting on. For example, when we create a rental property through a POST request, the data is saved in a database and made available for future requests. But there is no other user data kept between requests (such as a login context, for example). That design guarantees that we can fire requests to any server replica that might exist. This facilitates scalability, making sure that whenever we need to serve more users, we just need to spin up more servers and distribute requests across the server instances equally.

Dissecting a RESTful resource address

Just to restate an important concept: a **resource**, in a RESTful service, is an address that refers to an object from a particular domain. All resources are represented as URIs, and URIs are contained within URLs, which are basically the browser addresses. This schema will help you understand the structure of a RESTful address:

```
{protocol}://{base-addr}:{port}/{api-name}/{version}/{URI}
```

For example, these are URLs that contain a URI:

```
http://homeit.com/api/v1/rental-properties
http://homeit.com/api/v1/rental-properties/123
http://homeit.com/api/v1/rental-proposal/345
```

Let's break down the different parts of a URL:

- `protocol`: The network protocol used to access the resource. It will usually be HTTP or HTTPS (which we will talk about later).

- `base-addr`: The base address, or the root domain of your URL.

- `api-name`: A directory that you can use to segregate a series of resources as suffixes.

- `version`: A way for you to be able to update your APIs without losing backward compatibility. That means you can upgrade an API and still leave the old version online so that other developers can still do their requests and have their own client systems working before they can update the APIs to the new version.

- **URI**: The general identification of a resource. You can use a resource address to access both a set of resources or individual resources.

And here is the kicker: a resource URI is commonly referred to as an **endpoint**. Endpoints are represented as the resource locations in RESTful APIs.

Adding parameters to your API endpoints

Besides exposing resource locators, the RESTful API endpoints will also provide ways in which you can filter your request. For example, let's say you have 10,000 users in the HomeIt system. If you fire a `GET` request to the `/users` endpoint, you do not want your server loading every user in memory, as that might break the system, especially if many users are requesting data like that. So, we need a way to tell our system that we need to get just a limited list of users. We usually do that with pagination parameters that are made available in the URL for other programmers to use.

There are two common ways to add parameters to a RESTful endpoint: path parameters and query parameters.

Path parameters are part of the URI directory path and are used to uniquely identify a specific resource or to affect the resource's representation returned by the API. Here is an example of how that could work for our HomeIt system:

```
http://homeit.com/api/v1/rental-properties/123/EUR
```

In this case, `123` is a path parameter that identifies the specific object instance you want to retrieve from the database. You could add the `/EUR` path parameter if you want the rental price of the `123` ID property to be retrieved in Euros instead of US dollars.

Then there are **query parameters**, which you can add after the URI directories. These are generally written by appending a question mark after the URI, and then appending pairs of parameter names and values we want to expose, as in this example:

```
http://homeit.com/api/v1/rental-properties/123/EUR?page=3&size=10
```

As you can see, there are two parameters after the question mark, `page` and `size`, which represent the page number you want to access and the size of each page, respectively. You can add several query parameters to your request.

We can design query parameters for whatever we need our service to perform. Path parameters and query parameters will be useful when we do not want to design really straightforward parameters that can be added to the URL itself.

Then, there are payloads, which represent a block of content we can send in our request. Let's look at these in the next section.

Using payloads in RESTful services

In RESTful services, a **payload** is a block of data that might be present in HTTP exchanges. When firing a request to a REST endpoint, you can either send a payload with whatever data the servers require or you can receive a payload as a response from the server after your request is handled.

Requests and response payloads could contain any type of data: PDF, XML, CVS, and image formats. But in our case, when dealing with REST endpoints, we are mostly interested in JSON payloads. JSON is a standard for data representation that makes it very easy for humans to read.

Here is an example of a JSON response using `curl`. Simply type this command in your terminal:

```
> curl ip-api.com
```

Here is the output I got by executing this command in my terminal. This time, I got my API and a lot more information. This data is represented in JSON format. Bear in mind that I am not using the -vvvvv flag this time, as I have already presented you with what happens "behind the scenes" during a request. Here, we are basically seeing a very simple request from our `curl` client and a JSON response from the server. You can apply the -vvvvv flag to your own execution if you want so that you get a full scoop of what happened in this HTTP exchange. Here's the command execution:

```
curl ip-api.com
{
  "status"          : "success",
  "continent"       : "South America",
  "continentCode"   : "SA",
  "country"         : "Brazil",
  "countryCode"     : "BR",
  "region"          : "PB",
  "regionName"      : "Paraíba",
  "city"            : "João Pessoa",
  "district"        : "",
  "zip"             : "",
  "lat"             : -7.114,
  "lon"             : -34.8605,
  "timezone"        : "America/Fortaleza",
  "offset"          : -10800,
  "currency"        : "BRL",
  "isp"             : "Proxxima Telecomunicacoes Ltda",
  "org"             : "Proxxima Telecomunicacoes SA",
  "as"              : "AS262773 PROXXIMA TELECOMUNICACOES SA",
  "asname"          : "PROXXIMA TELECOMUNICACOES SA",
  "mobile"          : false,
  "proxy"           : false,
  "hosting"         : false,
  "query"           : "45.228.146.111"
}
```

Figure 5.17: Calling ip-api.com using the curl command

As you can see, a JSON payload is pretty easy to read. Without the verbose flags on `curl`, we will not see the HTTP method (`GET`), the headers, and the whole conversation that happens underneath.

If you want to send a JSON payload on your `curl` requests, just use the following command:

```
> curl -X POST \
  -H "Content-Type: application/json" \
  -d '{"key": "value", "id": 123}' \
  http://example.com/api/resource
```

Let`s break down each line:

- In the first line, we are specifying that the `curl` command should use the POST HTTP method in a request to a remote server.

- In the second line, we are specifying in the HTTP header the kind of payload we are sending. In this case, `application/json` is the right string for specifying the JSON format.

- In the third line, we are specifying the actual payload in JSON format.

- In the last line, we type the URL of the endpoint that will receive the request with our payload.

- The backslash is basically a way for complex commands to be issued using more than one line in a Linux terminal. If you are using Windows, the character will be different.

As stated at the beginning of this section, sending or receiving payloads will be key to be able to offer inputs and receive well-structured responses from our services. In RESTful services, a well-designed JSON request or response will typically represent an entire domain object or its partial representation (this is especially important for PATCH requests, which will update just a portion of your domain object).

As an example, when sending a POST request to our `rental-properties` endpoint, we could make it so that a `curl` request would look like this:

```
curl -X POST \
  -H "Content-Type: application/json" \
  -d '{"address": "the address st, 32", "rooms": 3}' \
  http://homeit.com/api/v1/rental-properties
```

Since the POST request is used conventionally to create an object, our API service could send back a JSON payload as a response to our client, with the actual full JSON representation of the new rental property. That would include an ID among other fields. The ID would be used to uniquely represent and refer to the rental property across all HomeIt services. Speaking of IDs, let's talk about them next.

Using UUIDs to uniquely identify objects

When creating objects in our systems, we need to make sure that we can identify them by a strong ID system. Many systems in the past would create IDs for objects by starting to assign 0 (zero) as the first object's ID, and incrementing the IDs one by one as more objects are created. That, unfortunately, leads to a very insecure system, in which an attacker can derive valid IDs very easily. If they know an endpoint and have a valid credential, retrieving valid and sensitive data is just a matter of testing natural numbers as IDs. This brute force could easily lead to personal data leakage.

In contrast, modern systems will use the UUID system.

A **Universally Unique Identifier** (**UUID**) is a 128-bit number that is generated randomly, bit by bit. There are 2^{128} possible UUIDs to be created. That amount is so big that a single software system can generate UUIDs randomly for thousands of years, and the likelihood that the same UUID will be generated twice is ridiculously small. Most programming languages have the proper implementation of a UUID generator, as designed by the **Internet Engineering Task Force** (**IETF**), in RFC 4122. The IETF is an open society of IT professionals that provides open standards for different subjects related to computer sciences.

Here is an example of a UUID. It was generated using the `uuidgen` command on Linux:

```
uuidgen
966c807f-5131-49ca-bdfa-b8b889392935
```

This string sequence is the randomly generated 128-bit number, represented with alpha-numeric characters. This is the standard I would recommend you use when creating IDs for your domain objects. The main goal of the UUID standard is to make it possible to generate IDs without having to use central authorities, which makes it the perfect case for distributed microservice applications. With UUIDs, you don't need counters, iterators, or any repository to ensure you are not generating duplicates of the same UUID. Whatever UUID you generate means you have a unique number in your hand if the algorithm is properly implemented.

We will see an implementation of UUID generation shortly in another Spring service. Before that, we still need to learn about the last piece of REST requests: headers.

Using HTTP request headers

If payloads are the actual content of a request or response between HTTP server and client exchanges, **headers** offer a place to add additional content about that request.

Payloads will always refer to your application domain. In the HomeIt system, payloads will always contain specialized knowledge from the business itself (landlords, rental properties, rental proposals, partnership proposals, etc.). Headers, on the other hand, always contain data that is used to facilitate handling the requests themselves. You will add the data about your data to headers. Hence, we say that an HTTP header contains metadata (data about other data).

Let's learn about some common headers used in HTTP requests today:

- `Host`: Indicates the host and port number of the server to which the request is being sent. Essential in determining the destination of the request, especially on servers hosting multiple domains.

- `User-Agent`: Provides information about the software used to make the request (browser or otherwise), allowing the server to tailor responses suitable for the client's software capabilities.

- `Accept`: Specifies which media types, expressed as MIME types, the client understands, and their preferences. This allows the server to select appropriate content or encoding methods. We have been talking about the JSON format, but it can really be any format.

- `Authorization`: Contains credentials for authenticating the client to the server, which is essential for areas requiring user verification (we will dive into authorization methods in future chapters).

- `Cookie`: Sends stored cookies from the client to the server, allowing the server to recreate the state of a client's session, thus maintaining stateful interaction. This will not be used in stateless REST services.

These are commonly used HTTP response headers:

- `Set-Cookie`: Instructs the client to store a cookie and send it in subsequent requests to the server, essential for session management and maintaining user state. Not used in stateless REST services.

- `Content-Type`: Indicates the media type of the resource, telling the client what the content is and how it should be processed (e.g., `text/html` or `application/json`).

- `Content-Length`: Specifies the size of the response body in bytes, which is critical for the client to know how much data it is expected to receive.

- `Cache-Control`: Specifies directives for caching mechanisms in both requests and responses. It controls resources' cache behavior to reduce bandwidth and improve performance (e.g., `no-cache` or `max-age`).

- `Location`: Used in redirections (3xx response codes) and when a new resource has been created. This header informs the client of the exact URL to redirect to or the new resource's location.

Now we have seen the basic elements of an HTTP request, let's see in practice how to create HTTP request handlers in Spring.

How Spring apps run internally

In the first Spring app, which we created a few sections ago, something might have caught your attention. Let's take a look at the `MyFirstSpringbootServerApplication.java` class:

```java
@SpringBootApplication
public class MyFirstSpringbootServerApplication {
    public static void main(String[] args) {
        SpringApplication.run(
            MyFirstSpringbootServerApplication.class,
            args);
    }
}
```

As a Java developer, you know that the `main()` method is the one that Java uses to start any application. Isn't it intriguing that we were able to download a sample project and write a new class from scratch without referencing it in this `MyFirstSpringbootServerApplication` class?

Since the `getIp()` method in the `IpController` class is not a static method but an instance method, the only way for the Spring framework to use it in Java was to have an instance of the `IpController` class *somewhere*. How did the Spring Framework know how to instantiate that class and bring our first HTTP handler online, making the `getIp()` method available for our `curl HTTP GET` requests?

We know that it is impossible for a Java application to instantiate a class without having it configured somewhere. In the Spring Framework, there are several ways to configure a class to be instantiated, such as the `IPController` class we wrote:

- XML configuration

- Annotation-based configuration

- Java-based configuration

- Groovy-based configuration

- Property files

- YAML files

- Environment variables

- Command-line arguments

- Profiles

We will explore some of those different configuration types throughout the book. For now, we just want to answer our question: with so many possible ways for configuring our classes, how did the Spring Framework know how to instantiate the `IpController` class? And another important aspect: why, as Java developers, did we not have to write the methods for instantiating the `IpController` class?

This is a major source of confusion in the minds of Spring Framework beginners. If classes can be instantiated by the Spring Framework alone and developers do not need to write that code for providing the class instances, it feels like magic that an object is "just there," completely ready for use, after the application starts.

I know, right?! That was the way I felt when I first saw this. And the piece of the puzzle responsible for answering this mind-boggling question is the Spring Framework component lifecycle.

Introducing the Spring Framework component lifecycle

The short answer to this mystery is that once the key classes in a system are configured by the developers, the Spring Framework is capable of detecting those classes and instantiating them automatically for the users during startup time. Unless stated otherwise, the Spring Framework will provide just one instance of each configured class, which will be made available during execution time. When shutting down the whole application, the Spring Framework will destroy those instances. We call this the **Singleton** pattern: guaranteeing just one instance for each important class during execution time.

Alright, let's unpack this a bit more: what do we mean by a *key class*, and why can (and should) the `IpController` class have just one instance available during the execution time?

If you remember, when writing the `IpController` class, we added the `@RestController` annotation to the `IpController` class and the `@GetMapping` annotation to the `getIp()` method. When our Spring application starts, what these annotations do in the background (among many other things) is to create a network listener on port `8080` by default, using our operating system's native API. And that listener will know how to call the `getIp()` method once it receives an HTTP GET request that targets the `/get-ip` URI. In other words, the Spring Framework somehow knows how to orchestrate all the OSI model layers for you, so that you focus solely on your Java methods (more on that later). When you do a `curl localhost:8080/get-ip` on a terminal, the Spring Framework is there to take that request and deliver it right to your `IpController.getIp()` method.

Also, because a single network listener can handle multiple HTTP requests separately from each other, it makes sense to have just one Java class instance to handle as many GET requests as possible for the same URI (`/get-ip`). Each remote HTTP client request will be delivered to a single call to the `getIp()` method. Hence, `IpController` is a key class that we can declare as a singleton (we just need one instance of that class).

Finally, since the Spring Framework is using Tomcat, Jetty, or Undertow behind the scenes, they are able to handle different HTTP requests in separate threads, making it reasonable that your `getIp()` method from a single `IpController` class instance will even be called in parallel by different processors on your machine if you have a multi-core CPU. In other words, you can use just one class instance to serve as many parallel requests as needed. This parallel processing and thread management is automatically handled by the **Java virtual machine** (**JVM**), and Spring does not even need to be aware of it.

Here is a visual that illustrates that concept:

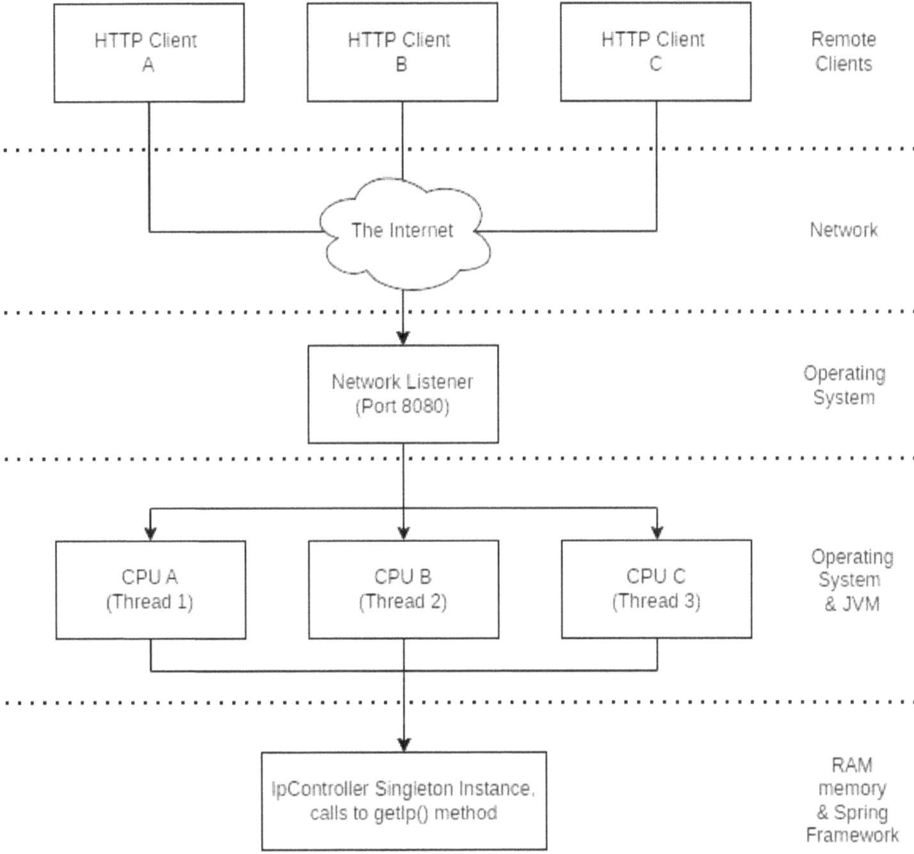

Figure 5.18: How Spring deals with a network request

Okay, so now you know how the Spring Framework works conceptually and architecturally. This prepares the background story for understanding an important keyword in the Spring Framework world: Spring beans.

What are Spring beans and why are they important?

The idea that the Spring Framework application will have some core services implemented in singleton classes is not new: the J2EE architecture also works from that assumption. These reusable singleton Java classes implementing core services of your software are what people refer to as **Java Beans**. Conversely, in the world of the Spring Framework, we just call these core singleton classes the **Spring beans**.

I think it is very important to fully explain this term here. I was personally very confused about this mysterious word *beans* for a long time. Many books will use this term without proper explanation, which makes things very confusing for many beginners.

The word *bean* was chosen for those reusable classes as a metaphor that matches the Java programming language name. *Java* refers to a type of coffee that was originally grown on the island of Java in Indonesia. The coffee metaphor was used because, back in the early days of Java, the programmers felt excited and energized by the possibilities of the language. Many programmers love coffee for the energy it brings to their day-to-day work, so this is where they took the inspiration from: that programming language was as good as their beloved coffee.

The word *bean* is an allusion to *coffee beans*. The Spring application will need several beans to execute its logic. A bean is a singleton class that can be used in conjunction with other beans to make your app work properly and serve a business function.

Alright, that should be enough to dismiss any confusion about the use of the word *bean* that you will find in many places. And that makes our `IpController` class a Spring bean in our first sample application. You now understand a lot about the architecture background, but we are still following the breadcrumbs to completely and unquestionably answer these questions: How did our Spring app know how to instantiate our `IpController` bean? And even before that, how does the JVM even know that our application is built with the Spring Framework and will follow its processes?

Introducing the Spring Boot project

If you take a closer look at our main application class, you are going to notice that the `MyFirstSpringbootServerApplication` class is tagged with the `@SpringBootApplication` annotation. That is one of the key components of the Spring Boot project. That annotation alone will configure an entire Spring app with default options that make the app run basically out of the box. The `main` method has nothing but a call to `SpringApplication.run()`, which takes the main project class itself as a parameter.

That is the power of the Spring Boot project: it provides key components to make your application configuration very easy. With the `@SpringBootApplication` annotation alone, your app becomes a full Spring app, and it will know how to look for the classes that should be instantiated as Spring beans. You do not need to write anything else in your main class. It just knows! This feels like pure magic for beginners.

We will explore a lot of other interesting things in the Spring Boot project in the next sections and chapters. But first, we still need to follow the track we are on: now that we know how the Spring app came into existence, how exactly does it know which classes are to be treated as Spring beans or singletons?

Understanding the Spring Framework component scan

When starting an application, the Spring Framework will scan for all classes that are tagged with some special annotations. Those annotations tell Spring that the tagged classes should be managed as Spring beans. In other words, the Spring Framework will automatically create a single instance for those annotated classes.

The main annotation that marks a class as a Spring bean is the `@Component` annotation. Other annotations are themselves tagged with the `@Component` annotation. Guess what? The `@RestController` annotation, used in our `IpController` class, indirectly inherits the `@Component` annotation as well. Here is the annotation chain:

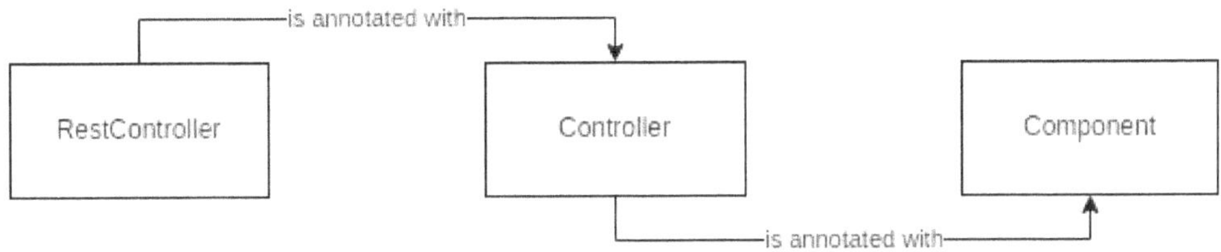

Figure 5.19: The RestController annotation class hierarchy

And voilá! There are a series of annotations that inherit from `@Component` and there are other ways to create Spring beans. We will have plenty of pages devoted to teaching you how they work.

Where are Spring beans stored at runtime?

The memory area reserved for storing and managing Spring beans is called the **application context**. In fact, that is itself a Spring bean, whose class is called `ApplicationContext`. This bean allows you to have access to all the Spring beans instantiated in your application.

We will generally not access this bean, but it is nice to know about it so that we have a clear picture of how Spring applications will organize things in memory. Knowing these details basically reveals the mystery behind the Spring Framework magic.

How to easily access a Spring bean

As you know, in our first application, the `IpController.getIp()` method will be called automatically by Spring whenever a new HTTP request is fired to the `/get-ip` URI. In that example, we do not need to directly access the `IpController` class from any other classes, since the Spring Framework will do all the work for you out of the box.

But what if you have two Spring beans with important services in your application, and they need to access each other? That is actually a very common scenario, in which we have one bean depending on another. So, in the Spring Framework, instead of you having to manually instantiate the beans with factories and setting the reference in another bean programmatically, you can instruct the Spring Framework to "inject" a bean reference into another. That is called **dependency injection**, and it is also one of the core Spring Framework features.

The best way for you to inject a Spring bean into another bean you are writing is by doing something like this:

```
@Component
public class DependencyInjectionSample {
    private final ApplicationContext applicationContext;

    public DependencyInjectionSample(
        ApplicationContext applicationContext) {
        this.applicationContext = applicationContext;
    }


    @PostConstruct
    public void init() {
        System.out.println("Initializing MyComponent");
        for (String beanDefinitionName :
            applicationContext
                .getBeanDefinitionNames()) {

            System.out.println("Bean Name: "
                    + beanDefinitionName);
        }
    }
}
```

As you can see, we have declared the `DependencyInjectionSample` class with the `@Component` annotation. That tells Spring to create a single instance of this class at runtime, after the component scan phase. Also, we have a constructor that takes the `ApplicationContext` bean as a parameter and sets it in a private class attribute. During startup time, the Spring Framework will check for the bean dependencies and create the beans in the right order, so that a bean will only be built when its dependencies are already finished building. This ensures that all beans can receive their dependencies as arguments when the application is starting. Plus, if you have a circular dependency (bean A depends on bean B and bean B depends on bean A), Spring will throw an explicit exception, since circular dependencies are not possible to solve during build time (and frankly, it is just bad design).

You may have noticed the init() method in *line 18*, which is tagged with the @PostConstruct annotation. That tells the Spring Framework that this method should be executed right after the bean's instantiation. This is a part of the Spring Framework component lifecycle, and it makes it easy to take initial actions in each bean when your application is starting. This init() method will basically access and print all existing bean names in the console output, whenever your application is starting. There are dozens of Spring beans created automatically by the Spring Framework itself, but your own beans will be present in that output as well. Here is just a slice of the output I get when executing this app in my console:

```
gradle bootRun
```

```
Bean Name: myFirstSpringbootServerApplication
Bean Name: org.springframework.boot.autoconfigure.internalCachingMetadataReaderFactory
Bean Name: ipController
Bean Name: dependencyInjectionSample
Bean Name: org.springframework.boot.autoconfigure.AutoConfigurationPackages
```

Figure 5.20: Listing the available Spring beans at application start

As you can see, all our classes in this first project are considered beans by the Spring Framework: the ipController, dependencyInjectionSample, and myFirstSpringbootServerApplication classes.

Now, let's understand what inversion of control is and how it facilitates Spring application and services management.

Spring container and inversion of control

This all gives you a great deal of understanding of what the Spring Framework is and how it operates its magic behind the scenes. If you understand these concepts, you are off to a great start, because most developers have a hard time grasping what happens automatically in Spring.

This way of letting the framework control the creation of your beans is called **inversion of control (IoC)**. Instead of you, the developer, having to program the factories for instantiating the main services, you can leave it for the core Spring Framework to do. The Spring ApplicationContext class is also referred to as the **Spring IoC container** – in other words, the class that contains the Spring beans. You just need to declare where you want them passed as constructor arguments. The framework takes care of the rest.

There are other aspects of the Spring Framework and the Spring Boot project that we will learn about throughout the book. For now, you just need to have a good grasp of the following:

- The Spring Framework contains a set of core features such as the Spring IoC container and several projects – Spring Boot being one of the projects
- You need to understand the purpose of each project in order to know when to use them

- The Spring Boot project helps you quickly pull out an application by using a set of easy-to-use annotations

- All Spring Framework projects provide really helpful annotations and great patterns to speed up your work as a developer

With that, let us now implement our first REST API for our HomeIt service.

Creating RESTful APIs in Spring

So far, we have used just two annotations for declaring REST services in Spring – `@RestController` and `@GetMapping`. These represent only a tiny fraction of the possibilities we have using this framework for writing web services. There are two main ways to write REST applications in Spring:

- The *Spring Web* project, which these annotations came from. This implements a thread-blocking model.

- The *Spring WebFlux* project, which brings a non-blocking, reactive model.

We will check a sample implementation of both models in the next pages of this book. We will first get you to understand how to implement the REST interfaces. This section will not have too much business code or persistence layer implementation. We want to keep things simple so that you understand exactly what these two projects – Spring Web and Spring WebFlux – are used for.

Writing a rental property REST API with Spring Web

The Spring Web project used to be the right choice whenever you had APIs that you wanted to quickly pull out and you did not have thousands of concurring requests to handle. But nowadays, with a few tweaks from Java 17+ and the virtual threads implementation, you can make Spring Web very close to Web Flow's performance for high-volume, concurrent request processing.

That is, if you need a servlet-based framework for writing REST APIs, you can go the very safe route with Spring Web. It can be very fast and has low latency, but if you do not use virtual threads, it will block one thread per request, which could be an issue, especially when doing I/O operations, such as database access, requests for other remote services, and so on.

If you need to handle thousands of concurring requests, if you have too many I/O operations on your endpoints, or if your app needs to wait for long I/O operations that take a lot of time to complete, and you want to have an edge, you could consider using WebFlux. WebFlux does not block your threads while waiting for these operations to complete (more on that later). But again, with the virtual threads tweak I will show you here, Spring Web is probably best for all use cases, due to its easier-to-understand programming patterns.

We have a full Spring Web REST API implementation example for you here: `https://github.com/PacktPublishing/Spring-System-Design-in-Practice/blob/main/chapter-05/My-first-Springboot-server/src/main/java/com/ip/server/My/first/Springboot/server/controller/RentalPropertyController.java`. All the explanations in the next pages come from the code at the provided link.

Let us break down this code example for you.

In this exercise, we are going to implement an API example for the rental property microservice for our HomeIt startup. In general, a Spring Web API will look like this:

- A REST API should be able to deal with HTTP requests, generally handling JSON payloads.

- Each domain in a REST API will be implemented as a single `Controller` class. The domain class implements the *Controller* layer in the traditional **Model-View-Controller (MVC)** design. So, in the HomeIt startup example, we should have at least one class for each domain (Rental Properties, Users, Partnership Proposals, etc.).

- The *Model* and *View* layers will not be covered in this book, since we are all about microservices and the other layers are more used for rendering HTML pages. If you want to know more about Spring MVC, there are plenty of resources available on the internet.

Alright, let's start our REST API example.

Declaring the dependencies

First, let's look at our Gradle dependencies. The full Gradle build file we are using can be accessed at `https://github.com/PacktPublishing/Spring-System-Design-in-Practice/blob/main/chapter-05/My-first-Springboot-server/build.gradle`.

Here is where we start the `build.gradle` file, which instructs Gradle on how to build the application:

```
plugins {
    id 'java'
    id 'org.springframework.boot' version '3.2.5'
    id 'io.spring.dependency-management' version '1.1.4'
}

group = 'com.ip.server'
version = '0.0.1-SNAPSHOT'

java {
    sourceCompatibility = '21'
}
repositories {
    mavenCentral()
}
```

All these lines come by default from the Spring Initializr website we used to create the sample application. Here are some important explanations:

- We see the block with the list of plugins used to build and run this application. We have added Java and Spring Boot to the `plugins` section, which allows us to easily configure our Spring apps, and the *Spring Dependency Management* plugin, which manages Spring Boot dependencies for us so that we do not need to keep track of every dependency version.

- Since we will need virtual threads, it is important to set the Java `sourceCompatibility` at a minimum of `17`, which is the minimum recommended Java version for Spring 6. In our case, I am setting it to `21`, just to get the virtual threads feature, which we will explore in future chapters to make our API more performant.

- Maven Central comes configured automatically as well from the Spring Initializr website.

Now, let's look at the rest of this file. Here is an important section that declares the Spring Web dependency:

```
dependencies {
    implementation 'org.springframework.boot:spring-boot-starter-web'
    testImplementation 'org.springframework.boot:spring-boot-starter-test'
    implementation 'org.springframework.boot:spring-boot-starter-validation'
    testRuntimeOnly 'org.junit.platform:junit-platform-launcher'
}

tasks.named('test') {
    useJUnitPlatform()
}
```

As you can see, we have included other important dependencies here:

- Spring Web dependency is declared, which allows writing a REST API

- The Spring Test dependency is declared, which allows us to write automated tests for our API

- We will also need the Spring Validation dependency to ensure our REST requests will only be processed if they are correct

- Finally, we define that we want to run the test classes with JUnit

In the next section, we will jump to the code lines for the `RentalPropertyController` class itself. It will clearly illustrate how to write a `Controller` class using Spring Web.

Writing the RentalPropertyController class

Look at this class definition:

```
@RestController
@RequestMapping("/api/v1/rental-properties")
@Validated
public class RentalPropertyController {

    private final RentalPropertyService
        rentalPropertyService;

    public RentalPropertyController(
            RentalPropertyService rentalPropertyService) {
        this.rentalPropertyService = rentalPropertyService;
    }
    // ... the rest goes here
}
```

These are the important points for this beginning:

- We are declaring that this class will be a `RestController` class. Since this annotation inherits from the `@Controller` annotation, which inherits from `@Component`, Spring will treat this class as a Spring bean and will instantiate it for you during the application start.

- The `@RequestMapping` annotation is used to define the actual API root directory. Since updating endpoints can break clients, the best pattern for maintenance is to add a version to the root API directory. When you need to release new versions of the same API, it is advisable to create the other versions on separate classes, with an updated version number.

- We declare that this class will have method parameters validated by Spring at execution time. We will see how that is done in a few sections.

- Another interesting thing we can see is that this Spring bean depends on `RentalPropertyService`. We will talk about service classes in the future, but in essence, these are the classes that should segregate our business rules. For now, it is enough to say that this is the same syntax used previously for dependency injection. These lines declare for the Spring Framework that it needs to provide an instance of the service class whenever it is instantiating the `Controller` class during the API boot time. Spring will find and instantiate the service class.

Let's now jump to the actual endpoint declarations, starting from the GET request to retrieve a rental property from a property ID:

```
@GetMapping(
    value = "/{id}",
    produces = "application/json")
public ResponseEntity<RentalPropertyDTO> getPropertyById(
    @PathVariable UUID id) {
    return rentalPropertyService.get(id)
        .map(ResponseEntity::ok)
        .orElse(ResponseEntity.status(HttpStatus.NOT_FOUND)
            .body(null));
}
```

This shows how to implement the GET HTTP endpoint using Spring Web:

- We see how to use the @GetMapping annotation. This is the one that makes Spring forward the GET requests it receives from the network straight to your annotated method. The full endpoint address will then include the value we added to the @RequestMapping annotation at the top of the RentalPropertyController class. The whole address for this GET endpoint will be /api/v1/rental-properties/{your rental property id}.

- We define what format the application will produce. In this case, whatever object we return inside ResponseEntity will actually be automatically turned into a JSON string by the Spring Framework.

- We define that the method should return ResponseEntity, and this is a standard return type for HTTP requests in Spring. The return is actually typed with the RentalPropertyDTO class, which is our **data transfer object (DTO)** class. In other words, the RentalPropertyDTO class is the Java POJO that carries the properties of a rental property over the network. We will look at it in just a second.

- We declare a variable in the endpoint address – the {id} part, which we call a **path parameter**. We also declare that part of the request address will be extracted to a variable. To extract a path parameter from the request URI, we need to use the @PathVariable annotation, and the name of the method parameter should match the path parameter declared in the value attribute of the @GetMapping annotation.

- We have declared the code with a functional pipeline, from which we retrieve the rental property from the service class, and then we map it to a ResponseEntity object if the rental property object is found. The ok method in this line will set the rental property DTO as the response payload and the HTTP response code as 200. We also implement a fallback so that we return a 404 status code (NOT FOUND) in case the GET request is fired with an invalid rental property ID. This pipeline was built using the Java Optional object, which helps avoid if sentences and null pointer exceptions in Java. The code feels more fluid and readable, but it can be a challenge to read if you are dealing with functional code for the first time. I felt confused the first time I read code like this, but eventually, I got used to it.

Now, let's jump to the POST request implementation:

```java
@PostMapping(
    consumes = "application/json",
    produces = "application/json")
public ResponseEntity<RentalPropertyDTO> createProperty(
    @Valid @RequestBody RentalPropertyDTO property) {

    RentalPropertyDTO createdRentalProperty
            = rentalPropertyService.create(property);

    return ResponseEntity.status(HttpStatus.CREATED)
        .body(createdRentalProperty);
}
```

These are the highlights from this code. I will not repeat the explanations that I gave for the GET endpoint:

- As with the `@GetMapping` annotation we just saw, we are using `@PostMapping` now to declare an HTTP POST endpoint implementation.

- We declared that this endpoint would accept JSON payloads from the clients. This means that the only way to send new information for creating a rental property is by sending a JSON payload in our request to the API (we will look at a request execution sample in a minute).

- We are declaring the `property` parameter in the method, of the `RentalPropertyDTO` type since this is the class we use to transfer rental property information over the network. We tagged this parameter with two annotations: `@Valid`, so that Spring needs to check for some rules before accepting the request and executing our method, and `@RequestBody`, which means Spring will parse your POST request payload into a `RentalPropertyDTO` object. This is basically how we can parse payloads to method parameters using Spring Web.

- We ask our service class to create the property and return it to a variable.

- Finally, we illustrate how to create the default `ResponseEntity` object used as a standard return type for the Spring Web implementations. The HTTP status of CREATED is the one numbered 201. The payload of the return, of course, is the newly created rental property, set as the `body`.

Let's now jump to the PUT mapping to see what we've got:

```java
@PutMapping(
    value = "/{id}",
    consumes = "application/json",
```

```
    produces = "application/json")
public ResponseEntity<RentalPropertyDTO> updateProperty(
    @PathVariable UUID id,
    @Valid @RequestBody RentalPropertyDTO updatedProperty) {

    return rentalPropertyService
        .update(id, updatedProperty)
        .map(ResponseEntity::ok)
        .orElse(ResponseEntity.status(HttpStatus.NOT_FOUND)
            .body(null));
}
```

Here:

- We have used the `@PutMapping` annotation, which tells Spring to create a `PUT` endpoint from our method. This is the same as the other annotations but for a different HTTP method.

- The `PUT` request needs both a payload and a path parameter since we are sending updated information to an existing rental property object. The payload is, of course, declared with the `@RequestBody` annotation, and the path parameter is declared with the `@PathVariable` annotation, just like in previous examples.

- We show a similar functional pipeline as we had in the `GET` implementation. However, this time, we are first calling the `update` method of our service class.

The `PATCH` implementation looks just like the `PUT` implementation:

```
@PatchMapping(
    value = "/{id}",
    consumes = "application/json",
    produces = "application/json")
public ResponseEntity<RentalPropertyDTO> patchProperty(
    @PathVariable UUID id,
    @RequestBody RentalPropertyDTO partialUpdate) {

    return rentalPropertyService
        .updateSomeFields(id, partialUpdate)
        .map(ResponseEntity::ok)
        .orElse(ResponseEntity.status(HttpStatus.NOT_FOUND)
            .body(null));
}
```

- We have a proper `@PatchMapping` annotation, of course

- We also need a request body for handling partial updates

- We have the functional pipeline in the method implementation

The DELETE implementation changes things a bit:

```
@DeleteMapping("/{id}")
public ResponseEntity<Void> deleteProperty(@PathVariable UUID id) {
    return rentalPropertyService
        .delete(id)
        .map(opt ->
            ResponseEntity.noContent()
                .<Void>build())
        .orElse(ResponseEntity
            .status(HttpStatus.NOT_FOUND).build());
}
```

- Of course, we have the @DeleteMapping annotation, which will tell Spring that the method is implementing the DELETE HTTP method endpoint.

- When deleting an object successfully, the standard return code we should use is 204 (success, no content). However, some developers will also use 200.

- Since we are not returning a payload in our request, we need to make it explicit, with the <Void> declaration.

Now, let's go to the /search endpoint:

```
@GetMapping(
    value = "/search",
    produces = "application/json")
public ResponseEntity<List<RentalPropertyDTO>> searchProperties(
    @RequestParam(required = false) String name,
    @RequestParam(required = false) String address,
    @RequestParam(required = false) String city,
    @RequestParam(required = false) String country,
    @RequestParam(required = false) String zipCode) {

    return ResponseEntity.ok(rentalPropertyService.search(
        name, address, city,country,zipCode));
}
```

- This is just another use case of the @GetMapping annotation, which declares a GET HTTP endpoint. This time, our full endpoint address will be /api/vi/rental-properties/search.

- Instead of a path parameter, this time, we are using a series of request parameters through the use of the @RequestParam annotation. None of the request parameters are required since we will usually look for properties using just a few criteria.

- Since the return of the service class is a list of properties found, we do not have to add the optional implementation. If we do not have a property, we can return an empty list.

Okay, this covers a lot of cases and almost all of the essential Spring Web annotations for declaring REST endpoints, which is amazing, but what if we need to extract a header from our HTTP request? Let's take a look at the next code sample:

```java
@GetMapping(
    value = "/headers",
    produces = "application/json")
public ResponseEntity<String> getHeaderInfo(
        @RequestHeader("User-Agent") String userAgent) {
    return ResponseEntity.ok("User-Agent: " + userAgent);
}
```

In this implementation, these are the important things to consider: this implementation is not quite related to our rental property. I added it to our sample code just to show you how to extract the User-Agent header from the request. This is done by declaring the @RequestHeader annotation, in which you add the name of the header you would like to extract.

Let's now take a quick look at RentalPropertyDTO, which is the basic Java object that we used to implement the payload:

```java
public record RentalPropertyDTO(
        UUID id,

        @NotNull(message = "Landlord id is required")
        UUID landlordID,

        @NotEmpty(message = "Name is required")
        String name,

        @NotEmpty(message = "Address is required")
        String address,

        @NotEmpty(message = "City is required")
        String city,

        @NotEmpty(message = "Country is required")
        String country,

        @NotEmpty(message = "Zip code is required")
        String zipCode,

        @NotNull(message = "Rent is required")
        Double rent
) { }
```

As you can tell, the @NotEmpty and @NotNull directives come from the Spring validation project. It makes it easy to define what is acceptable in our HTTP requests.

And that's it for the essential Spring Web implementation. There are a lot of interesting advanced parameters you can explore in the Spring Web documentation, but with these foundational annotations, you are fully equipped to write a very comprehensive set of endpoints for your API.

Let's see our API in action, and then I will leave you with a nice cheat sheet of the essential annotations of the Spring Web project.

Using the Rental Properties API

Let's execute a request to all these endpoints using curl so that you know exactly how they behave.

Remember, we can run your Spring application with this command in the terminal:

```
> gradle bootRun
```

Let's see the result. This is the start of the execution. Since the logs are massive, I'm only adding some slices of the output here:

```
gradle bootRun


> Task :bootRun


  .   ____          _            __ _ _
 /\\ / ___'_ __ _ _(_)_ __  __ _ \ \ \ \
( ( )\___ | '_ | '_| | '_ \/ _` | \ \ \ \
 \\/  ___)| |_)| | | | | || (_| |  ) ) ) )
  '  |____| .__|_| |_|_| |_\__, | / / / /
 =========|_|==============|___/=/_/_/_/
 :: Spring Boot ::                (v3.2.5)


2024-05-21T23:53:49.347-03:00  INFO 14825 --- [My-first-Spr
ingboot-server] [           main] f.S.s.MyFirstSpringbootSe
rverApplication : Starting MyFirstSpringbootServerApplicati
on using Java 21.0.3 with PID 14825 (/home/rodrigo/IdeaProj
ects/professional-spring-system-design-patterns/chapter-05/
My-first-Springboot-server/build/classes/java/main started
by rodrigo in /home/rodrigo/IdeaProjects/professional-sprin
g-system-design-patterns/chapter-05/My-first-Springboot-ser
ver)
2024-05-21T23:53:49.349-03:00  INFO 14825 --- [My-first-Spr
ingboot-server] [           main] f.S.s.MyFirstSpringbootSe
rverApplication : No active profile set, falling back to 1
default profile: "default"
```

Figure 5.21: Spring application console output

This is the very beginning of the execution. As you can see, the Spring Boot ASCII header is the first thing that is logged in the terminal.

Now, let's guarantee that our beans for this chapter are all online:

```
Bean Name: org.springframework.context.event.internalEventListenerFactory
Bean Name: myFirstSpringbootServerApplication
Bean Name: org.springframework.boot.autoconfigure.internalCachingMetadataF
Bean Name: ipController
Bean Name: rentalPropertyController
Bean Name: dependencyInjectionSample
Bean Name: rentalPropertyServiceImpl
Bean Name: org.springframework.boot.autoconfigure.AutoConfigurationPackage
```

Figure 5.22: Listing the available Spring beans

As you can see, because we created `dependencyInjectionSample` in our project, we can now see the `rentalPropertyController` bean instantiated:

```
2024-05-21T23:53:50.426-03:00  INFO 14825 --- [My-first-Springbo
ot-server] [            main] o.s.b.w.embedded.tomcat.TomcatWebSe
rver   : Tomcat started on port 8080 (http) with context path ''
2024-05-21T23:53:50.434-03:00  INFO 14825 --- [My-first-Springbo
ot-server] [            main] f.S.s.MyFirstSpringbootServerApplic
ation : Started MyFirstSpringbootServerApplication in 1.391 seco
nds (process running for 1.628)
<=<==========---> 80% EXECUTING [24m 21s]
> :bootRun
```

Figure 5.23: Checking how long the application is alive

And by the end of the boot log, we can see the success message. In this case, the app is running for 24 minutes.

You can also run this app by finding the `.jar` file in the `build/libs/My-first-Springboot-server-0.0.1-SNAPSHOT.jar` location:

```
java -jar build/libs/My-first-Springboot-server-0.0.1-SNAPSHOT.jar
```

```
  /\\ / ___'_ __ _ _(_)_ __  __ _ \ \ \ \
 ( ( )\___ | '_ | '_| | '_ \/ _` | \ \ \ \
  \\/  ___)| |_)| | | | | || (_| |  ) ) ) )
   '  |____| .__|_| |_|_| |_\__, | / / / /
 =========|_|==============|___/=/_/_/_/
 :: Spring Boot ::                (v3.2.5)

2024-05-22T00:23:33.786-03:00  INFO 18320 --- [My-first-Springboot-server] [
OT using Java 21.0.3 with PID 18320 (/home/rodrigo/IdeaProjects/professional-sp
SHOT.jar started by rodrigo in /home/rodrigo/IdeaProjects/professional-spring-s
2024-05-22T00:23:33.789-03:00  INFO 18320 --- [My-first-Springboot-server] [
 "default"
2024-05-22T00:23:34.997-03:00  INFO 18320 --- [My-first-Springboot-server] [
2024-05-22T00:23:35.022-03:00  INFO 18320 --- [My-first-Springboot-server] [
2024-05-22T00:23:35.023-03:00  INFO 18320 --- [My-first-Springboot-server] [
2024-05-22T00:23:35.054-03:00  INFO 18320 --- [My-first-Springboot-server] [
2024-05-22T00:23:35.055-03:00  INFO 18320 --- [My-first-Springboot-server] [
177 ms
Initializing MyComponent
Bean Name: org.springframework.context.annotation.internalConfigurationAnnotat
Bean Name: org.springframework.context.annotation.internalAutowiredAnnotationPr
Bean Name: org.springframework.context.annotation.internalCommonAnnotationProce
```

Figure 5.24: Running a Spring application .jar file

As you can see, the command for you to run your application is this one:

```
> java -jar <path of your spring app jar>
```

This is the command through which you want your application to run in production. It is as simple as that. The fact that your application .jar file is named with the SNAPSHOT suffix will be explained in future chapters. This is due to deployment and versioning strategies. Let's forget about this for now.

Creating a rental property

Now that we have confirmed that our application is running correctly, let's create a rental property. Use the following curl command for that:

```
> curl -X POST "http://localhost:8080/api/v1/rental-properties" \
    -H "Content-Type: application/json" \
    -d '{
        "address": "456 New St",
        "landlordID": "80b0da3f-0568-4eff-b665-26372b853242",
        "city": "New City",
```

```
      "country": "New Country",
      "zipCode": "67890",
      "rent": 1500.0,
      "name": "rental property sample"
  }' -vvvvv
```

I created the `landlordID` value using the `uuidgen` command in Ubuntu, just as I explained earlier.

The execution goes as follows in my terminal:

```
curl -X POST "http://localhost:8080/api/v1/rental-properties" -H "Co
ntent-Type: application/json" -d '{
  "address": "456 New St",
  "landlordID": "80b0da3f-0568-4eff-b665-26372b853242",
  "city": "New City",
  "country": "New Country",
  "zipCode": "67890",
  "rent": 1500.0,
  "name": "rental property sample"
}' -vvvvv
Note: Unnecessary use of -X or --request, POST is already inferred.
*   Trying 127.0.0.1:8080...
* Connected to localhost (127.0.0.1) port 8080 (#0)
> POST /api/v1/rental-properties HTTP/1.1
> Host: localhost:8080
> User-Agent: curl/7.81.0
> Accept: */*
> Content-Type: application/json
> Content-Length: 211
>
* Mark bundle as not supporting multiuse
< HTTP/1.1 201
< Content-Type: application/json
< Transfer-Encoding: chunked
< Date: Wed, 22 May 2024 03:34:21 GMT
<
* Connection #0 to host localhost left intact
{"id":"93f2ec4a-e774-4eca-81d7-f7e66457f0bf","landlordID":"80b0da3f-
0568-4eff-b665-26372b853242","name":"rental property sample","addres
s":"456 New St","city":"New City","country":"New Country","zipCode":
"67890","rent":1500.0}
```

Figure 5.25: Getting a response from the server

As you can see, we are correctly receiving the JSON with the result of the API request.

Retrieving the created rental property

Let's fire a request for retrieving this property. It is as easy as appending the declared API URI to our base URL (`localhost`, port `8080`) and adding the resource (`rental-properties`), and the ID generated in the previous POST request goes as the path parameter. We are also sending the `accept` header in order to notify our API that we can receive JSON as a response:

```
curl -X GET "http://localhost:8080/api/v1/rental-properties/93f2ec4a
-e774-4eca-81d7-f7e66457f0bf" -H "accept: application/json" -vvvvv
Note: Unnecessary use of -X or --request, GET is already inferred.
*   Trying 127.0.0.1:8080...
* Connected to localhost (127.0.0.1) port 8080 (#0)
> GET /api/v1/rental-properties/93f2ec4a-e774-4eca-81d7-f7e66457f0bf
 HTTP/1.1
> Host: localhost:8080
> User-Agent: curl/7.81.0
> accept: application/json
>
* Mark bundle as not supporting multiuse
< HTTP/1.1 200
< Content-Type: application/json
< Transfer-Encoding: chunked
< Date: Wed, 22 May 2024 03:39:46 GMT
<
* Connection #0 to host localhost left intact
{"id":"93f2ec4a-e774-4eca-81d7-f7e66457f0bf","landlordID":"80b0da3f-
0568-4eff-b665-26372b853242","name":"rental property sample","addres
s":"456 New St","city":"New City","country":"New Country","zipCode":
"67890","rent":1500.0}
```

Figure 5.26: Retrieving an existing rental property

Next, we will update our new property.

Updating the rental property

With the following command, we are updating the entire object. Note that we are appending both the path parameter in the URL and the payload with the updated fields:

```
curl -X PUT "http://localhost:8080/api/v1/rental-properties/93f2ec4a
-e774-4eca-81d7-f7e66457f0bf" -H "Content-Type: application/json" -d
 '{
   "address": "updated address",
   "landlordID": "80b0da3f-0568-4eff-b665-26372b853aaa",
   "city": "updated City",
   "country": "updated Country",
   "zipCode": "11111",
   "rent": 11111.0,
   "name": "updated rental property sample"
}' -vvvvv
*   Trying 127.0.0.1:8080...
* Connected to localhost (127.0.0.1) port 8080 (#0)
> PUT /api/v1/rental-properties/93f2ec4a-e774-4eca-81d7-f7e66457f0bf
 HTTP/1.1
> Host: localhost:8080
> User-Agent: curl/7.81.0
> Accept: */*
> Content-Type: application/json
> Content-Length: 233
>
* Mark bundle as not supporting multiuse
< HTTP/1.1 200
< Content-Type: application/json
< Transfer-Encoding: chunked
< Date: Wed, 22 May 2024 03:45:25 GMT
<
* Connection #0 to host localhost left intact
{"id":"93f2ec4a-e774-4eca-81d7-f7e66457f0bf","landlordID":"80b0da3f-
0568-4eff-b665-26372b853aaa","name":"updated rental property sample"
,"address":"updated address","city":"updated City","country":"update
d Country","zipCode":"11111","rent":11111.0}
```

Figure 5.27: Updating the rental property

As expected, this request returns 200 as the update was successful, and the new fields are also returned by the API.

Sending missing data when a field is required

Note that if we skip sending some fields, the Spring validation feature will act on it and we will be able to see some interesting feedback. This is the request that should fail. I am skipping sending the `landlordID` attribute, which is declared as `@NotNull` in `RentalPropertyDTO`:

```
curl -X PUT "http://localhost:8080/api/v1/rental-properties/93f2ec4a
-e774-4eca-81d7-f7e66457f0bf" -H "Content-Type: application/json" -d
 '{
  "address": "updated address",
  "city": "updated City",
  "country": "updated Country",
  "zipCode": "11111",
  "rent": 11111.0,
  "name": "updated rental property sample"
}' -vvvvv
*   Trying 127.0.0.1:8080...
* Connected to localhost (127.0.0.1) port 8080 (#0)
> PUT /api/v1/rental-properties/93f2ec4a-e774-4eca-81d7-f7e66457f0bf
 HTTP/1.1
> Host: localhost:8080
> User-Agent: curl/7.81.0
> Accept: */*
> Content-Type: application/json
> Content-Length: 177
>
* Mark bundle as not supporting multiuse
< HTTP/1.1 400
< Content-Type: application/json
< Transfer-Encoding: chunked
< Date: Wed, 22 May 2024 03:48:45 GMT
< Connection: close
<
* Closing connection 0
{"timestamp":"2024-05-22T03:48:45.071+00:00","status":400,"error":"B
ad Request","path":"/api/v1/rental-properties/93f2ec4a-e774-4eca-81d
7-f7e66457f0bf"}
```

Figure 5.28: Sending missing data on purpose in a request

As you can see, the return code is now 400, meaning that the request was malformed. The payload returned reflects this. In this case, the client will not receive too much information about what is missing, but we can still see it in the server console logs:

```
2024-05-22T00:48:45.070-03:00  WARN 18320 --- [My-first-Springboot-s
erver] [nio-8080-exec-9] .w.s.m.s.DefaultHandlerExceptionResolver :
Resolved [org.springframework.web.bind.MethodArgumentNotValidExcepti
on: Validation failed for argument [1] in public org.springframework
.http.ResponseEntity<com.ip.server.My.first.Springboot.server.dto.Re
ntalPropertyDTO> com.ip.server.My.first.Springboot.server.controller
.RentalPropertyController.updateProperty(java.util.UUID,com.ip.serve
r.My.first.Springboot.server.dto.RentalPropertyDTO): [Field error in
 object 'rentalPropertyDTO' on field 'landlordID': rejected value [n
ull]; codes [NotNull.rentalPropertyDTO.landlordID,NotNull.landlordID
,NotNull.java.util.UUID,NotNull]; arguments [org.springframework.con
text.support.DefaultMessageSourceResolvable: codes [rentalPropertyDT
O.landlordID,landlordID]; arguments []; default message [landlordID]
]; default message [Landlord id is required]] ]
```

Figure 5.29: Getting a specific error from the Spring validation dependency

As you can see, the very last line of this log refers to the fact that the landlord ID is required, which was exactly what we wrote in the `RentalPropertyDTO` validation rules.

There are ways to improve the message for the customer. If you look closely, you will find that this 400 request didn't even call our Java method – the one that is marked with the `@PostMapping` annotation. That is because Spring validation works prior to the request reaching `RentalPropertyController`. Spring takes care of notifying our clients that the request is malformed, and we do not need to worry at all about it in our code.

Partially updating the rental property

This is the `curl` test for demonstrating how to update only one of the fields of our rental property object. The rental property ID is from an already existing property:

```
curl -X PATCH "http://localhost:8080/api/v1/rental-properties/ad4459
d1-79a3-4f4c-9382-c9c584105ea6" -H "Content-Type: application/json"
-d '{
  "name": "Partially Updated Property"
}' -vvvvv
*   Trying 127.0.0.1:8080...
* Connected to localhost (127.0.0.1) port 8080 (#0)
> PATCH /api/v1/rental-properties/ad4459d1-79a3-4f4c-9382-c9c584105e
a6 HTTP/1.1
> Host: localhost:8080
> User-Agent: curl/7.81.0
> Accept: */*
> Content-Type: application/json
> Content-Length: 42
>
* Mark bundle as not supporting multiuse
< HTTP/1.1 200
< Content-Type: application/json
< Transfer-Encoding: chunked
< Date: Wed, 22 May 2024 23:50:12 GMT
<
* Connection #0 to host localhost left intact
{"id":"ad4459d1-79a3-4f4c-9382-c9c584105ea6","landlordID":"80b0da3f-
0568-4eff-b665-26372b853242","name":"Partially Updated Property","ad
dress":"456 New St","city":"New City","country":"New Country","zipCo
de":"67890","rent":1500.0}
```

Figure 5.30: Updating just a portion of a property

As you can see, this request only sends a partial JSON representation of the rental property object. We are sending only the name of the object. The returned JSON contains the updated name of the rental property.

Deleting the rental property

Here is an example of how you can send a DELETE request to an existing rental property:

```
curl -X DELETE "http://localhost:8080/api/v1/rental-properties/7db53
d95-bd51-4c54-b57b-35851a900ed3" -H "accept: application/json" -vvvv
v

*   Trying 127.0.0.1:8080...
* Connected to localhost (127.0.0.1) port 8080 (#0)
> DELETE /api/v1/rental-properties/7db53d95-bd51-4c54-b57b-35851a900
ed3 HTTP/1.1
> Host: localhost:8080
> User-Agent: curl/7.81.0
> accept: application/json
>
* Mark bundle as not supporting multiuse
< HTTP/1.1 204
< Date: Wed, 22 May 2024 23:53:28 GMT
<
* Connection #0 to host localhost left intact
```

Figure 5.31: Deleting a property

As you can see, the HTTP return code is 204, as we have programmed it in the former pages. 204 stands for *no content*; saying that, after an HTTP DELETE request, we should not find the entity anymore.

Making sure the rental property was deleted

If we try to fetch the deleted property, we get a 404 code, which means *not found* in the HTTP protocol:

```
curl -X GET "http://localhost:8080/api/v1/rental-properties/7db53d95
-bd51-4c54-b57b-35851a900ed3" -H "accept: application/json" -vvvvv

Note: Unnecessary use of -X or --request, GET is already inferred.
*   Trying 127.0.0.1:8080...
* Connected to localhost (127.0.0.1) port 8080 (#0)
> GET /api/v1/rental-properties/7db53d95-bd51-4c54-b57b-35851a900ed3
 HTTP/1.1
> Host: localhost:8080
> User-Agent: curl/7.81.0
> accept: application/json
>
* Mark bundle as not supporting multiuse
< HTTP/1.1 404
< Content-Length: 0
< Date: Wed, 22 May 2024 23:58:33 GMT
<
* Connection #0 to host localhost left intact
```

Figure 5.32: Trying to fetch a deleted property

Let's now search for a rental property.

Searching for a rental property

This is probably the key functionality we were expecting to see. In this case, we are arguing that the endpoint for searching for a rental property can support different query parameters. This is not supposed to be "the final right answer" since there are a lot of ways to implement a /search endpoint. But since this is an exercise to show how a Spring Web REST API should work, I am showing you one of the many possible ways to do this:

```
curl -X GET "http://localhost:8080/api/v1/rental-properties/search?n
ame=rental%20property%20sample" -H "accept: application/json" -vvvvv
Note: Unnecessary use of -X or --request, GET is already inferred.
*   Trying 127.0.0.1:8080...
* Connected to localhost (127.0.0.1) port 8080 (#0)
> GET /api/v1/rental-properties/search?name=rental%20property%20samp
le HTTP/1.1
> Host: localhost:8080
> User-Agent: curl/7.81.0
> accept: application/json
>
* Mark bundle as not supporting multiuse
< HTTP/1.1 200
< Content-Type: application/json
< Transfer-Encoding: chunked
< Date: Thu, 23 May 2024 00:35:43 GMT
<
* Connection #0 to host localhost left intact
[{"id":"e0e421e6-c2bb-4b09-a443-ecf6d1a583ef","landlordID":"80b0da3f
-0568-4eff-b665-26372b853242","name":"rental property sample","addre
ss":"456 New St","city":"New City","country":"New Country","zipCode"
:"67890","rent":1500.0}]
```

Figure 5.33: Searching for a rental property

Also, I think you noticed that the -H flag is used to specify a new header to be sent on your request. We have used it in every request to specify that we can accept JSON payloads in the response.

> **Warning**
>
> Bear in mind that you need to program your endpoints to return whatever you want them to return. Those return codes are nothing but a convention for the HTTP protocol that you need to be keen on. The Spring Web project will not force you to use the right codes – you, as a developer, need to choose them wisely. Otherwise, you will risk programming your API to do weird things.
>
> I used quite a few APIs that would return `200` for whatever requests I would make, even if the request found an error. Those APIs will return a JSON with some `error` attribute in it, or `success=false` in the JSON. This is just wrong from an API standpoint. Your return code should inform the API user whether the API request was successful or not. You can even include some special response payload to explain the error, but the HTTP error code should be chosen according to the conventions. When you are in doubt, just use the HTTP Cats website (`https://http.cat/`), which is both informative and fun!

Spring Web cheat sheet

Here is a useful list for you to quickly refer to whenever you need to remind yourself of which Spring Web annotations should be used and where:

- `@RestController`: This should be added to the class definition. It tells Spring that your class will handle HTTP requests.

- `@RequestMapping("api/v1/your-resources")`: This should be added to the class level as well. It tells Spring the resource address of your REST API. A resource address is a directory in the API in which you can find the domain and domain objects. It is a good convention to use the resource name in the plural (`rental-properties`, `landlords`, `payments`, and so on).

- `@GetMapping`, `@PatchMapping`, `@PostMapping`, `@PutMapping`, and `@DeleteMapping`: These should be used at the method level. They define which HTTP verb will be handled by your class method. You should define the path parameters in them if you are to take the domain object ID as a part of the URL. You also need to define here what you accept and produce in the request and response payloads.

- `@PathVariable`: This should be added before a method parameter. It helps extract a path parameter out of the URL directly to your method parameter. It only works if the method parameter name is the same as the path parameter defined in the URL mapping annotations (please refer to the examples we have shown in previous sections).

- `@RequestParam`: This should be added to a method parameter. It helps extract query parameters from the URL.

- Validation-specific annotations at the class level are as follows:

  - `@Validated`: This should be added at the class level. It helps inform that the Spring validation feature will be used in some method parameters.

  - `@Valid`: This should be added to a parameter in a method. It helps automatically validate input rules from the parameter class types.

- Validation-specific annotations at the field level are as follows:

  - `@NotNull`: This ensures that the annotated field is not null. Use this for mandatory fields.

  - `@NotEmpty`: This ensures that the annotated collection, map, or string is not null and not empty. Use this for non-null, non-empty strings or collections.

  - `@NotBlank`: This ensures that the annotated string is not null and not empty after trimming. It is suitable for mandatory, non-whitespace strings.

  - `@Size`: This validates the size of collections, maps, arrays, or the length of strings. It specifies the min and/or max attributes to set boundaries.

  - `@Min`: This ensures that the annotated numeric value is not less than the specified minimum. Use this for setting lower bounds on numbers.

  - `@Max`: This ensures that the annotated numeric value is not greater than the specified maximum. Use this for setting upper bounds on numbers.

  - `@DecimalMin`: This ensures that the annotated decimal value is not less than the specified minimum. It supports strings for large numbers or floating-point precision.

  - `@DecimalMax`: This ensures that the annotated decimal value is not greater than the specified maximum. It supports strings for large numbers or floating-point precision.

  - `@Positive`: This ensures that the annotated numeric value is greater than 0. Use this for validating positive numbers.

  - `@PositiveOrZero`: This ensures that the annotated numeric value is 0 or greater. Use this for validating non-negative numbers.

  - `@Negative`: This ensures that the annotated numeric value is less than 0. Use this for validating negative numbers.

  - `@NegativeOrZero`: This ensures that the annotated numeric value is 0 or less. Use this for validating non-positive numbers.

  - `@Digits`: This ensures that the annotated numeric value has an exact number of integer and fractional digits and specifies integer and fraction attributes.

  - `@Pattern`: This validates that the annotated string matches the specified regular expression. Use this for custom string formats.

  - `@Email`: This validates that the annotated string is a valid email address and ensures the proper format of email addresses.

- `@Past`: This ensures that the annotated date or time is in the past. Use this for historical dates.

- `@PastOrPresent`: This ensures that the annotated date or time is in the past or present. It is suitable for historical or current dates.

- `@Future`: This ensures that the annotated date or time is in the future. Use this for dates that must occur later.

- `@FutureOrPresent`: This ensures that the annotated date or time is in the future or present. It is suitable for future or current dates.

- `@AssertTrue`: This ensures that the annotated Boolean field is `true`. Use this for Boolean conditions that must be `true`.

- `@AssertFalse`: This ensures that the annotated Boolean field is `false`. Use this for Boolean conditions that must be `false`.

- `@CreditCardNumber`: This ensures that the annotated string is a valid credit card number (Luhn algorithm) and validates credit card numbers.

- `@URL`: This ensures that the annotated string is a valid URL and validates the proper format of URLs.

Summary

We covered a lot of ground in this chapter. We went through a full revision of how network requests happen and the HTTP protocol and its main parts, and learned how the Spring Framework works internally and manages Spring beans for you. Then, we wrote our first Spring Web REST API.

In the next chapter, we will cover great topics and patterns that complement this one, such as learning how to test our APIs; how to use localization patterns so that we can have our API working with multiple currencies, measurements, and languages; how to write WebFlux apps; and learning about saga patterns, logging patterns, and other important additions that you will find important in many projects you will face.

Get This Book's PDF Version and Exclusive Extras

Scan the QR code (or go to `packtpub.com/unlock`). Search for this book by name, confirm the edition, and then follow the steps on the page.

Note: Keep your invoice handly. Purchase made directly from packt don't require one.

6

Translating Business Requirements into Well-Designed Spring APIs

Welcome to *Chapter 6*! In this chapter, we will talk about how to develop your core business logic using Spring Framework conventions. Also, we will talk about many things related to improving our API design's clarity. Another important aspect we will dive into in this chapter is how to create the tests we need to ensure our APIs are working as expected.

We will turn our requirements into test cases and guarantee that our APIs are working according to what the product team wants. These are the topics we are going to cover:

- Mastering the blueprint for any Spring microservice

- Error handling in REST APIs

- Implementing business services in Spring

- Writing automated tests for your Spring applications

- Tuning Spring Web for peak performance

- Making your API design a lot better

This will be an exciting journey that focuses on translating the product desire into actual models that provide the right logic for delivering business value. You will start by learning about the only template you will ever need to write a Spring microservice. How about that? Let's get into it!

Technical requirements

All the code in this chapter is in this GitHub repository URL: `https://github.com/PacktPublishing/Spring-System-Design-in-Practice/tree/main/chapter-06/rental-property-microservice`.

Mastering the blueprint for any Spring microservice

Now that we know exactly how to produce a good HTTP interface for our remote clients with Spring Web, let's look at the critical pieces of a server. Most Spring-based servers that can serve remote client requests will follow the pattern shown in *Figure 6.1*:

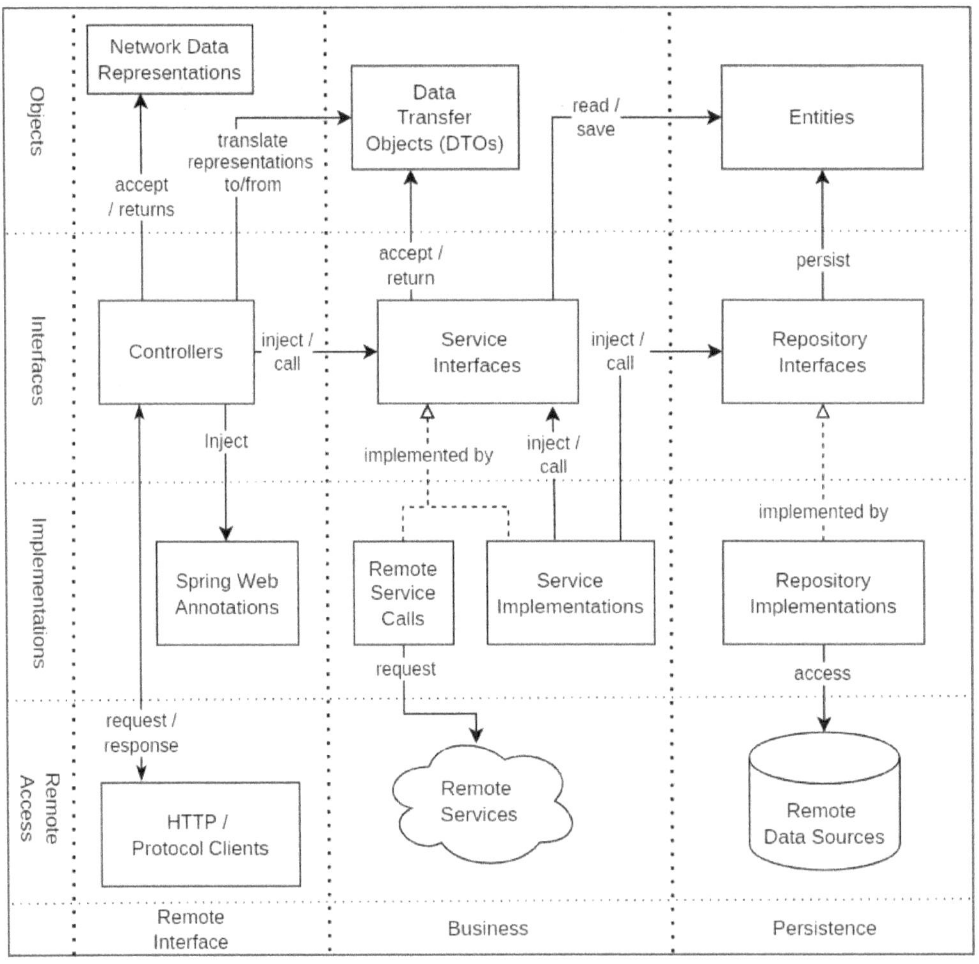

Figure 6.1: Spring services master blueprint

As you can see, there are three vertical layers and four horizontal layers in this diagram. We will conceptually explain the vertical and horizontal layers, and we will go over each of these aspects in future sections and chapters.

Exploring the vertical layers

The three vertical layers you can see in *Figure 6.1* will help you to organize your source code in such a way that you can isolate three special categories, client interface code, internal services, and the data persistence layer, so that your app can maintain a long-term state if you need it. They are not strictly required every time, but they are truly useful for organizing your mind. In the sub-sections that follow is a more thorough explanation of each layer.

Remote interface

This left vertical layer contains the set of classes that will be concerned solely with interfaces for serving remote clients. This is the client's entry point. In the example in the previous chapter, using Spring Web, we learned how to implement HTTP and REST APIs. But this remote interface layer can be implemented in diverse ways, depending on our use cases (we will see this throughout the book). You should avoid at all costs adding business rules to this set of classes since, in this remote interface layer, your code is required to only capture the client requests and delegate them to business services in the central vertical layer. This approach is similar to the one we wrote in our past chapter example, when we injected the `RentalPropertyService` Spring Bean into our `RentalPropertyController` class. This layer is also responsible for formatting data to be transmitted over the network. In REST APIs, that means we can accept JSON objects, for instance.

Business

This central vertical layer represents the set of classes where you should code your domain business rules. Whatever specialized knowledge you have about the product should be represented and implemented in this layer, and nowhere else. The typical class that performs a business action and enforces its specific rules is called a **service**, and it will accept and return **Data-Transfer Objects (DTOs)**, which are basic Java classes representing structured business objects. These service classes also interact with remote services (other microservices that we need to call from within the service we are writing) and repositories (the data sources we need to use in order to store long-term data) to save data and delegate calls to other servers in the network.

Persistence

This is the right vertical layer and is responsible for making sure we can store and retrieve structured data from a data store. It usually implements connections to databases of distinct types, or some sort of blob storage mechanism, or whatever interfaces we need to store and retrieve data to (it could be a remote filesystem, such as FTP, NFS, or even a Google Sheet in the cloud).

These three vertical layers will be made clearer as we proceed.

Understanding the horizontal layers

The horizontal layers will separate each vertical layer into some common areas. They will give you four distinctions: the top one consists of the objects that you will use to handle data in your system (hence, each vertical layer has its own data object format). The middle layer consists of interfaces (literally Java interfaces that you will use to define system functions – what input they need and what output they return). The third layer is the Java code that will drive the implementation of the service interface you have defined. And the fourth layer describes a remote system that you are relating with (it could be a customer, another microservice, or a database, for instance). Let's have a more thorough description of our horizontal layers.

Objects

The top horizontal layer contains the actual data structures we will work with. There is a special need to separate implementations for the network objects, the service objects, and the storage objects because these data structures, although representing the same business concepts, will have different needs. The network data representations could be JSON objects in REST APIs. The DTOs are plain Java objects with raw attributes and very simple methods for handling whatever business rules we need to enforce. They are usually the input and output parameters of our service classes. Entities, on the other hand, are classes representing whatever requirements for data persistence we need to enforce. We will often see service classes translating DTOs to entities and vice versa, with a 1-1 mapping, especially when they are too similar. Spring Web is capable of automatically turning JSON objects into DTOs. On several occasions, a single call to a service class with quite a simple DTO could result in many entity objects being created and persisted in a repository. Because of those different factors, we will usually have these three core types of data:

- Network data representations
- DTOs
- Entities

Interfaces

This middle horizontal layer represents the methods that are available throughout the whole application, stripped of their implementations. For Java programmers, that means we should only add interface classes in this layer, or very thin implementations (for instance, our `RentalPropertyController` contains very few lines of code in each method). This layer will help you to keep your abstractions as clean and organized as possible so that you can think in business terms without concerning yourself too much about how to implement those methods, or which technologies you are interfacing with. This is great for expressing the concepts and philosophies of your servers in an isolated manner. On the left side of the interfaces layer, we will have all interfaces that handle remote communication. In the center, we will have business interfaces. On the right side, we will have persistence interfaces.

Implementations

This third horizontal layer, from top to bottom, is where you create classes to implement the interfaces from the interfaces layer (the second layer, from top to bottom). As a rule of thumb, on the *left* side, the implementations for REST controllers are provided by the Spring Web dependency and the annotations we have learned about. You can use other Spring Web annotations to enrich your HTTP protocol handling, such as `@RestControllerAdvice`, to map how Java exceptions will lead to proper HTTP responses (we will look at that in this chapter).

Throughout the entire layer, you will be using whatever annotations are available in Spring Projects to implement specific behaviors for your application (you will also use Spring AOP for this, which will be presented later in the book).

In the *central* part of the implementations layer, a service implementation can be of two types: either you are implementing a call to another remote service (remote service calls), and that implementation will encapsulate whatever boilerplate code is required, or you are implementing business rules (service implementations), which means you can handle DTOs and entity objects, and injecting other services interfaces in that implementation. You should never let an implementation class inject another implementation class directly because when a service needs to call another service, if you inject the implementation classes directly, that will expose your specific implementation detail to the rest of your code, and this will risk making your code harder to maintain in the long term. Instead, you should just inject the service interface into whatever class needs it to keep your abstractions clean and the implementations isolated from each other. Spring Framework knows how to provide the proper implementation classes for your services; we will see some examples of that.

On the *right* side of this layer, we can find the implementation for storing and retrieving objects from different databases and other kinds of persistence mechanisms. These are usually given by annotations that you will take from the right Spring dependency. There are different Spring Projects that you can include in your server that will allow you to connect to whatever databases you want, for example.

Remote access

Finally, the lower horizontal layer is there to make you aware of the external connections your Spring server is maintaining. On the *left* side, for REST APIs, we are talking about your remote clients' HTTP connections. In the *center*, it lets you know that your service could execute requests to other remote servers. On the *right* side, the remote access is, of course, your database of choice. With this single diagram, you can understand the entire philosophy of how to create any microservices with Spring Framework. This is truly all you need to see how a Spring server should be implemented. It might take a bit to really understand this, but once you re-read these sections a couple of times and go through our upcoming examples, you should have a better understanding.

Remember that, in general, each Spring microservice will serve just one or a few very closely related domains or concepts in your application.

Here is an example, based on our HomeIt start-up.

Rental proposal service design

We can think of a rental proposal service that will use Spring Web as the left vertical layer (remote interface – a REST API), will implement a few services in the middle vertical layer (business) to translate a DTO to a rental proposal entity, and will save the rental proposals as documents in a MongoDB database in the right vertical layer (persistence). Turn the book to the right so that you can see the whole image properly.

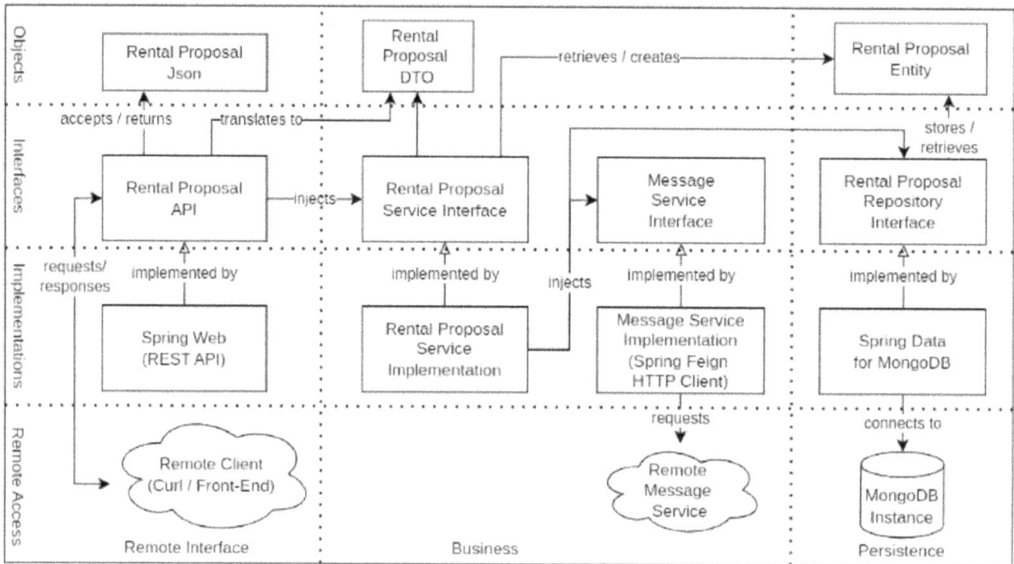

Figure 6.2: Rental properties service Spring layout

To implement this service, we should do the following:

1. Create the `RentalProposalController` remote interface, defining the API and the HTTP methods using Spring Web.

2. Create the `RentalProposalDTO` class, which contains the rental proposal fields. The JSON structure should come out of the box, as Spring Web automatically translates DTOs to JSON and vice versa.

3. Create a `RentalProposalService` Java interface with all the operations we need for creating/storing rental proposals.

4. Create a `RentalProposalServiceImpl`, which will implement the methods in the interface.

5. Create a `MessageService` interface, which encapsulates the messages we are sending to users when a rental proposal is created or changed.

6. Create a `MessageService` implementation, using the Spring Feign client to fire HTTP requests to our message service (we will look at how the Feign client works in a future chapter).

7. Create a `RentalProposalEntity` class that will be used to store and retrieve our rental proposal objects from MongoDB.

8. Create a `RentalProposalRepository` interface that will declare all possible operations over our repository.

9. The implementation for accessing MongoDB will be provided by the Spring Data MongoDB instance (we will look at that during *Chapter 10*, when we will show you how to work with NoSQL databases).

10. We will need to implement automated tests to make sure all these classes are working properly.

We will see that implementation in upcoming sections. For now, this step-by-step plan is basically to show you a different service in our HomeIt startup.

In the next section, we will discuss and practice an important but often overlooked aspect of Spring software development: how to deal with exceptions and errors in a very structured, clear way.

Error handling in REST APIs

Since we were talking about REST services in the prior chapter's examples, let's extend this a bit to solve a critical problem in Spring REST APIs.

Suppose there is a specific exception that is issued by various endpoints in your application. How could you implement the proper error handling and return meaningful responses to your remote clients without replicating code with the same `try/catch` statements all over the place?

A useful example would be the `500` error code in HTTP. How many times you have seen unexpected server errors that are fully unformatted and irrelevant, or just empty? It is basically impossible to anticipate every situation in which your code can break in production. So, it is at least advisable to have something in place that can catch all the unexpected exceptions thrown in your code and just handle it in such a way that your remote clients will receive a standard, well-formatted message in every case.

In these annoying situations, we can standardize our responses using the `@ControllerAdvice` and `@ExceptionHandler` Spring Web annotations, and the `ProblemDetail` class as a standardized return object.

Let's see how it works. First, we will create this sample *defective* endpoint in our current `RentalPropertyController` class that will purposefully throw a `RuntimeException`:

```
@GetMapping(value = "/error")
public ResponseEntity<List<RentalPropertyDTO>>
runtimeExceptionSample() {
    throw new RuntimeException
        ("This was a sample unhandled runtime exception");
}
```

This exception is just to symbolize a runtime error that could happen anywhere in your application.

Next, let's use `curl` to fire a request to this endpoint:

```
curl -X GET "http://localhost:8080/api/v1/rental-properties/error" -
H "accept: application/json"

{"timestamp":"2024-05-29T02:47:45.840+00:00","status":500,"error":"I
nternal Server Error","path":"/api/v1/rental-properties/error"}
```

Figure 6.3: A sample request to an endpoint that always triggers an exception

As you can notice, we get an internal server error that does not give any useful data from the exception we originally fired.

Now, let's create this simple class to handle all uncaught runtime exceptions that happen throughout our code:

```java
@RestControllerAdvice
public class SampleExceptionHandler {

    @ExceptionHandler(RuntimeException.class)
    public ResponseEntity<ProblemDetail>
        handleGenericException(RuntimeException ex) {
            ProblemDetail problemDetail =
                ProblemDetail.forStatus(
                    HttpStatus.INTERNAL_SERVER_ERROR);

            problemDetail.setTitle(
                "Customized Internal Server Error");
            problemDetail.setDetail(
                "An unexpected error occurred: "
                    + ex.getMessage());
            problemDetail.setInstance(
                URI.create(
                    "/api/v1/rental-properties/error"));
            problemDetail.setProperty("timestamp",
                LocalDateTime.now().toString());

            return new ResponseEntity<>(problemDetail,
                HttpStatus.INTERNAL_SERVER_ERROR);
    }
}
```

Here are some highlights:

- I am annotating the class with the `@RestControllerAdvice` Spring Web annotation, which lets Spring know this is a bean that's used to handle whatever exceptions are declared in the methods. We can have as many `@RestControllerAdvice` classes as we want in our code, but many projects will only maintain one of them. Unless you have very complicated exception handling and need to isolate them in other classes for clarity, having just one `@RestControllerAdvice` tagged class will be OK.

- We are tagging a single method with the `@ExceptionHandler` annotation, which lets us specify which exception should be handled in this method. In our case, we just want a method that can capture all runtime exceptions so that we can better format `500` error messages to our HTTP clients.

- We are creating an instance of the `ProblemDetail` class, which has very useful fields for informing remote clients about our errors.

- If you have several different exceptions that you want to handle in your code using the `RestControllerAdvice` mechanism, you can create different methods for handling each one of the exceptions you want to address.

Now, let's see it in action. Once you have written a `RestControllerAdvice` class, Spring *just knows* how to forward errors to an instance of this class by using the Spring Beans management mechanism we talked about in the previous chapter.

The `@RestControllerAdvice` annotation will signal Spring Framework to create a Spring Bean out of it, and to keep that instance throughout the whole application lifecycle.

Here is an attempt to fire the same GET request, but this time the response is customized by our `@RestControllerAdvice` bean:

```
curl -X GET "http://localhost:8080/api/v1/rental-properties/error" -
H "accept: application/json"
```

```
{"type":"about:blank","title":"Customized Internal Server Error","st
atus":500,"detail":"An unexpected error occurred: This was a sample
unhandled runtime exception","instance":"/api/v1/rental-properties/e
rror","timestamp":"2024-05-29T00:07:27.656941842"}
```

Figure 6.4: A customized response returned by the RestControllerAdvice class

As you can see, our original exception message is now being carried over the remote client. Notice that this can help with troubleshooting important error messages, but it can also lead to security breaches if you don't handle the error messages properly. Letting error messages flow to your remote HTTP clients can leak important security details about your architecture. You need to be very careful about these error messages.

Implementing business services in Spring

Now, let's answer another very important question about the Spring Frameworks' magic and how it fits in the generic design diagram we showed you at the beginning of this chapter.

When implementing a Spring Server application and writing the business vertical layer, how should we declare our service interfaces and implementations?

Declaring service interfaces in Spring

The answer is rather simple, and we can illustrate it with our `RentalPropertyController` service classes in a few minutes. First, Spring will basically require you to follow these four steps:

1. For every special domain in your server, you can have one or more service interface classes that represent the special operations you can perform over your domain objects.

2. For each service interface you have declared, you need to have an equivalent service implementation class that will extend your service interfaces and add code to its methods. We usually name these classes `YourServiceNameImpl` as a convention.

3. You should always tag those service implementation classes with the `@Service` annotation. That is all Spring needs to know in order to transform your service interface into a Spring Bean during runtime.

4. You can inject your services into other Beans by using the interface name only. Spring knows how to search for the right implementation class for that interface at startup time.

Let's see how it happens in our `RentalPropertyService` class. This is our service interface:

```
public interface RentalPropertyService {
    List<RentalPropertyDTO> getAllProperties();

    Optional<RentalPropertyDTO> get(UUID id);

    RentalPropertyDTO create(RentalPropertyDTO property);

    Optional<RentalPropertyDTO>
        update(UUID id, RentalPropertyDTO updatedProperty);

    Optional<RentalPropertyDTO>
        updateSomeFields(UUID id,
            RentalPropertyDTO partialUpdate);

    Optional<RentalPropertyDTO> delete(UUID id);
```

```
    List<RentalPropertyDTO> search(String name,
        String address, String city, String country,
        String zipCode);
}
```

As you can see, the `RentalPropertyService` interface maintains all possible operations pertaining to a rental property object. We can either get a rental property by its UUID, create a new rental property, update the whole object, update some fields, delete, or search for a rental property.

Writing the implementation class for your service

Now, for this interface object, we need to add an equivalent implementation class. Let's go over some important parts:

```
@Service
public class RentalPropertyServiceImpl
        implements RentalPropertyService {

    private final Map<UUID, RentalPropertyDTO>
            rentalProperties = new HashMap<>();

    @Override
    public List<RentalPropertyDTO> getAllProperties() {
        return List.copyOf(rentalProperties.values());
    }

    @Override
    public Optional<RentalPropertyDTO> get(UUID id) {
        return Optional.ofNullable(
            rentalProperties.get(id));
    }

    // ... the other methods go here
}
```

The following points are important here:

- We can see the `@Service` annotation, signaling to Spring Framework that this is a Spring Bean. So, by default, any time we try to inject the `RentalPropertyService` interface, Spring will take this class as the Bean that implements it. Magic!

- You can see that this class implements the `RentalPropertyService` interface, which is the domain we decided to represent in this microservice.

- You can see that I have used the naming convention. This is the `RentalPropertyServiceImpl` class. In other words, an implementation of the `RentalPropertyService` class.

- We can see that I have used a simple `HashMap` instance to store our `rentalProperties`. We are currently not persisting our domain objects in a database yet; this will be a topic for the next chapter.

- You can see two of the several method implementations of the `RentalPropertyService` interface.

Now, this illustrates basically every Spring Service implementation you will find in any company. This is the standard way to organize your code, and every time I see code written with different conventions, it carries quite a bit of technical debt and it is hard to maintain.

There are some advantages to this approach:

- By setting aside service interfaces and implementation classes, it becomes extremely easy to create functional prototypes by providing very basic implementation classes and prove that your interfaces are working properly in the general context.

- You can switch implementations as you need to. Once we get to implementing the database interfaces, we can add a new implementation class that injects the database interface and uses it, instead of the in-memory HashMaps.

Now, let's revisit how our `RentalPropertyController` is injecting the `RentalPropertyService` and using the implementation class. This is how we declared the controller class:

```java
@RestController
@RequestMapping("/api/v1/rental-properties")
@Validated
public class RentalPropertyController {

    private final RentalPropertyService rentalPropertyService;

    public RentalPropertyController(
            RentalPropertyService rentalPropertyService) {
        this.rentalPropertyService = rentalPropertyService;
    }

    // ... the rest of the controller class goes here
}
```

Again, to use a service class in one of your Beans, you just need to declare a private reference to your desired service interface and add that interface as a property to your constructor. Spring will know how to instantiate the required implementation service class if you tag it with the `@Service` annotation.

Now, let's look at how this Rental Property API is structured in our general template:

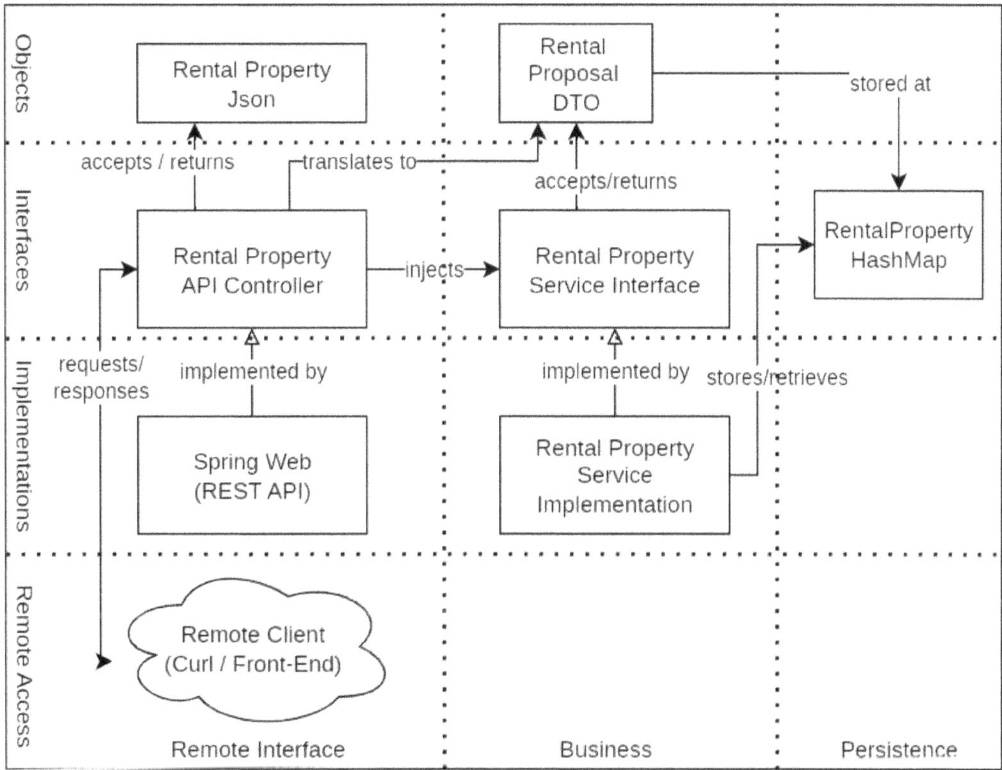

Figure 6.5: Rental property service class layout

In this sample, we have worked with an extremely poor persistence layer, just because we wanted to focus on how to declare Spring Web REST APIs.

I hope this visual representation helps you make sense of how people in general structure their Spring applications. The next chapter will be dedicated to talking about the data and persistence layers in Spring applications.

Organizing your Spring classes

This screenshot illustrates how to organize your different classes in a Spring application:

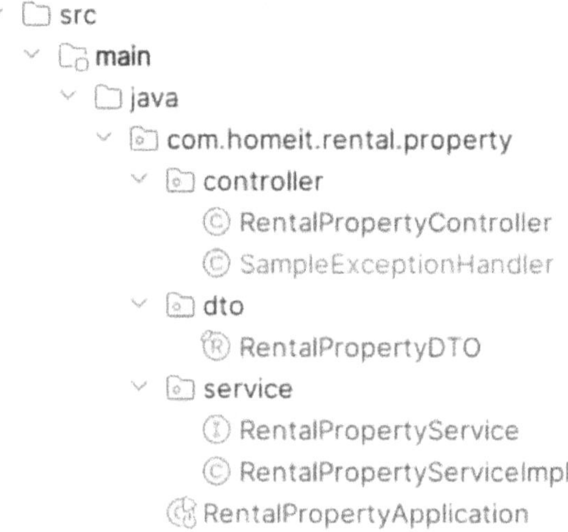

Figure 6.6: Rental property packages organization

As you can see, there are three main packages so far: `service`, `dto`, and `controller`. The service interface and respective implementation class reside in the same service folder. Similarly, the controllers and exception handlers reside in the same folder as well. There are some variations of this structure, but this is enough of a convention for you to start.

In this example, we created a series of methods in the same service interface. That was just a convention we followed because the methods implemented were pretty thin. If your service implementations are huge and take a lot of code, you can break your service interfaces into more files.

An alternative route that you can take in your project is segregating each individual service method into a separate interface, then creating an implementation class for each interface with just one method in each. That is a decision you and your team will have to make.

When you and your team are deciding about how to organize interfaces and implementations (and even the controllers, for that matter), ask these important questions:

- Is the number of files in your project manageable? Is it possible to easily look at the project structure and navigate the different interface/class files?

- Is the number of packages and the directory structure also manageable and easy to navigate? Does the name of the packages make sense in the context of your product? Can the developers find the interfaces and implementation classes they want by intuitively navigating the package folder structure?

- Are the interfaces and implementation classes easy to read? Is it possible to read, learn, and maintain the service implementation methods?

If you find yourself having a tough time understanding a service implementation class, it is most probably time to do some refactoring. You can break interfaces into smaller interfaces and make them more specialized. You can refactor big service classes by extracting new classes and utility methods to other files and packages. You can do all sorts of re-organization in your code.

Now, over to you. Before going to the next section, take some time to plan and maybe even implement a Spring Web REST application. Maybe you want to take one of our microservices in the HomeIt system? Or would you like to create a RESTful microservice for another enterprise? It is up to you. Just do not let that change of practicing escape from your hands. It is pretty easy to create nice APIs using Spring, since most complicated implementations are provided by the Spring project dependencies, such as Spring Web. You might have noticed that your only work when using Spring Framework is twofold:

- Knowing what Spring Project you will use to provide implementations for your technology choices for storage and remote connections

- Knowing a lot about your product domain so that you can create the best interfaces for your key services

Are you up to the challenge of learning by doing? I will wait for you in the next section.

Writing automated tests for your Spring apps

Now that we have gone through how Spring applications are structured, let's take a look at how to write automated tests for your apps. When writing software, you should never leave tests outside of your plans because you do not want to spend your time manually testing everything important every time you release a new feature. Or even worse, you do not want to release new versions without testing everything you can. That will lead to a very bad result in production, with a lot of bugs and incidents.

An automated test suite will guarantee your software is always compliant with the requirements. A good set of automated tests is actually a guarantee that the business will be working fine. Also, automated tests make your development much faster and easier, as we will see. Once you have a great test automation suite, you will feel very confident whenever you release new software.

Understanding the basic test pattern

So, let's learn how to write automated tests. First, you need to understand the basic automated test pattern, also called a **test case**. Every automated test case – even the manual ones – is created from the same pattern, as shown in *Figure 6.6*:

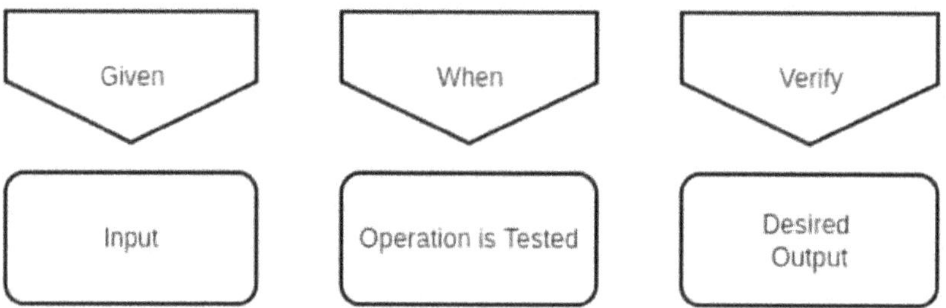

Figure 6.7: The test pattern

This three-step process, which you follow from left to right to create a test case, means this:

1. **Given – Input**: This is a set of background objects from which you want to start your test. It means the test setup. This is also called the **test scenario**. In this phase, you are simulating, replicating the scene from which you want to start your test.

2. **When – Operation Is Tested**: This is where you use the prepared setup (the input, or test scenario) to fire the actions you want to test. It means simulating the behavior that your user will have when the app is running in production.

3. **Verify – Desired Output**: This phase means that your operation will generate an output, which you can now compare with the desired output. If the tested operation output equals the output you expect, your test was successful. If not, some error happened in the app, and you need to fix your code.

This test case pattern is pretty easy to understand. When designing a test, you should always know which output you are expecting to receive from the test scenario. Otherwise, why bother testing something?

Creating integrated tests with Spring Test

OK, enough of theory. In our code base, we have provided an example implementation of a test suite for the `RentalPropertyController` class. It is located in the chapter's repository. We are going to look at this first sample, then step back to explore different test approaches using Spring.

First, let's start by looking at the test class location. This is the same place you will find test classes in typical Spring projects everywhere:

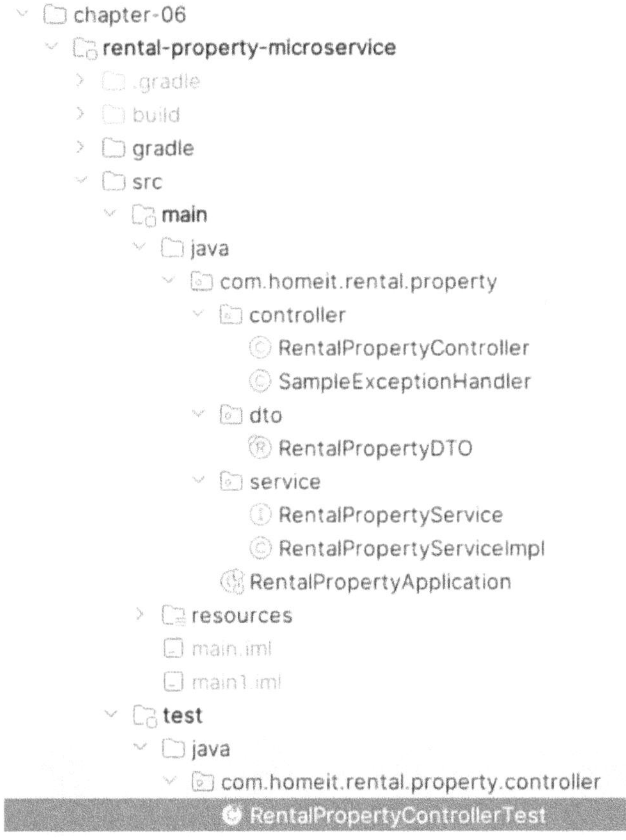

Figure 6.8: The test class location

The test file is usually named after the original class you are targeting. In our case, we are going to test `RentalPropertyController`, which is the origin of the `RentalPropertyControllerTest` class. All test classes are stored in the `test` directory and should reflect the tested class' package structure.

This test class contains different test cases, which we call a **test suite**. A test suite contains a set of test cases that follow the same pattern we talked about earlier.

Another important thing to understand is that tests in Spring are driven by a specific project, Spring Tests, which we need to include in our project build file:

```
dependencies {
    implementation 'org.springframework.boot:spring-boot-starter-web'
    testImplementation 'org.springframework.boot:spring-boot-starter-
test'
    implementation 'org.springframework.boot:spring-boot-starter-
validation'
```

```
        testRuntimeOnly 'org.junit.platform:junit-platform-launcher'
}
```

Since Spring Test is integrated with JUnit out of the box, these are the two directives we need to include in our `build.gradle` file. These dependencies are automatically included in the Spring Initializr website generated project.

Now, let's head to our `RentalPropertyControllerTest` class declaration:

```
@SpringBootTest
public class RentalPropertyControllerTest {

    private final WebApplicationContext context;
    private final ObjectMapper objectMapper;

    @Autowired
    RentalPropertyControllerTest(
            WebApplicationContext context,
            ObjectMapper objectMapper){
        this.context = context;
        this.objectMapper = objectMapper;
    }

    // ... the rest of the test goes here
}
```

These are the important highlights from this code:

- We are including the `@SpringBootTest` annotation. That means that once Spring starts to run your tests, it will actually create an entire Spring ApplicationContext for you. In other words, your entire Spring application will run while the test is running. And yes, that includes your database connections if you do not mock some services (we will see later how this works).

- We are declaring a reference to the web application context. We will need it in order to be able to target our application with our test cases.

- We are declaring a JSON parser. The `ObjectMapper` class will help extract the DTOs from our API responses.

- We are declaring the test class constructor. We are asking Spring Boot to inject the `ObjectMapper` and `WebApplicationContext` Beans. Remember that Spring Framework will automatically create and manage a singleton of each class for us.

- We are required to add the `@Autowire` annotation to the constructor so that Spring can inject the Beans in the test environment. This annotation is only strictly required when running test classes, but you can also use it in your application code as well. There are several ways to use the `@Autowire` annotation in Spring, but since the constructor injection is a better way to get references for other Beans, we will not cover `@Autowire` in this book.

This summarizes how to declare your test class. Now, let's see the following parts:

```
private RentalPropertyDTO createdProperty;
private MockMvc mockMvc;

@BeforeEach
void setUp() throws Exception {
    mockMvc = MockMvcBuilders
        .webAppContextSetup(context).build();
    createdProperty = createProperty();
}


private RentalPropertyDTO createdProperty;
private MockMvc mockMvc;

@BeforeEach
void setUp() throws Exception {
    mockMvc = MockMvcBuilders
        .webAppContextSetup(context).build();
    createdProperty = createProperty();
}
```

The following observations are important:

- We are declaring the `MockMvc` class reference, which is the class we use to fire HTTP requests to your endpoints.

- We are declaring a `setUp` method that needs to be run before every test method is called. The `@BeforeEach` annotation means exactly that. Use it to tag a method that you need Spring to run in order to prepare a clean context for a test case. This preparation method is a part of the *Given – Input* step in our test case pattern.

- We are defining that Spring will create a new instance of `MockMvc`, a class used to fire the HTTP requests, as we stated earlier.

- We are declaring an instance attribute of type `RentalPropertyDTO` called `createdProperty`. That object will be re-created every time a test case is run, providing a clean setup for every test case to run.

- We can see the call to the `createProperty()` method, which is firing a real HTTP request to our API and inserting a fresh instance of the rental property in the API repository.

Alright, now that we have learned how to prepare your test case context, let's see how a new rental property is created before every test case:

```java
private RentalPropertyDTO createProperty() throws Exception {
    RentalPropertyDTO property = new RentalPropertyDTO(
    null, UUID.randomUUID(),"Test Property",
    "123 Test St","Test City",
    "Test Country", "12345",1200.0);

    // Simulate creating a property
    String responseBody = mockMvc.perform(
            post("/api/v1/rental-properties")
            .contentType("application/json")
            .content(objectMapper.writeValueAsString(property)))
        .andExpect(status().isCreated())
        .andReturn().getResponse().getContentAsString();

    return objectMapper
        .readValue(responseBody, RentalPropertyDTO.class);
}
```

In this code, we have the following:

- We create a sample of the new rental property object to be sent in our API request as a JSON payload
- We perform a POST request to our API to create the rental property
- We specify the POST address
- We specify the content type of the request
- We parse the `RentalPropertyDTO` to a JSON string, included as the content (payload) of the request
- We verify that the HTTP return is `201` (created), which is what we expect from our API when a new property is successfully created
- We extract the response content to a string called `responseBody`
- We use the `objectMapper` object to parse our JSON string to a new `RentalPropertyDTO` instance, then return it

This is nice, isn't it? We are actually verifying the results as we are setting up the other tests. That means if something goes wrong while creating the new properties for the test cases, Spring Test will notify us that something went wrong.

Let's see now an example of an actual test case implementation:

```
@Test
void testGetPropertyById() throws Exception {
    mockMvc.perform(
            get("/api/v1/rental-properties/{id}",
                createdProperty.id())
            .contentType("application/json"))
        .andExpect(status().isOk())
        .andExpect(jsonPath("$.name")
            .value("Test Property"));
}
```

The following considerations apply:

- We are naming a method with the test case we want (`testGetPropertyById`). In this case, the method should test whether the GET property request will work in our application. Every test method should clearly be named as the test case we want to execute.

- We are indicating with the `@Test` annotation that Spring should automatically run this method when automated tests are run so that every time we run our automated test suite, this method will be executed by Spring Test and the designed test case will be executed and verified.

- Remember that this method will be called only after Spring Test calls the `setUp()` method because we declared it with the `@BeforeEach` annotation. That means a brand-new rental property instance will be available for this test case to use.

- We are using `mockMvc` to perform an action.

- The performed action is the GET call to the `/api/v1/rental-properties/{id}` endpoint. The `{id}` path parameter will be replaced by the new rental property ID. This is the *When – Operation Is tested* step in our basic test case pattern.

- The GET request is also added with the `contentType` header.

- The final piece is the `Verify - Desired Output` step in our test case pattern:

  - We make sure that the HTTP return code is `200` (OK)

  - We use a JSON path query to make sure our response payload attribute name in the root of the object contains the string `Test Property`, which is the name of the property we created before this test was run.

This summarizes how Spring Tests are created, concisely. You can look at other test cases by reading the whole example test class in this chapter's repository.

Testing Beans in isolation

Although remarkably effective, this model I just showed you, in fact, will test the entire Spring application, with all original Spring Beans created for you. That means your entire application will behave in the way it was originally intended to.

This should be enough for you to do an integrated test, which is great. But sometimes, you will want to test nothing but a single Spring Bean, or an extremely specific scenario, which might be difficult to set up using this automated test model. The complex test scenarios here are examples in which you want to have more control over the application context:

- If your test case will cause your application to fire requests to other remote apps or try to connect to external services, such as databases, you might find it difficult to run integrated tests in your local machine because your environment may not have access to an instance of the external app.

- If a determined test case requires your external apps to return specific results to your tested app, even if your Spring app can connect to other apps, it might be impossible to make them return what you want.

- If you have an overly complicated service class implementation that has a lot of complex business rules and references to other injected Spring Beans, it might be impossible to make other Beans behave exactly how you want in an integrated test model.

For all these complicated scenarios, wouldn't it be useful for Spring Test to inject fake Beans for you as you see fit? Imagine you can provide a new implementation of any Spring Bean method during test time and get that Bean to respond in the exact way you want during a test case.

That is possible using the `@MockBean` annotation.

Let's see a test class that illustrates this. Do you remember when we briefly talked about how to set up a default exception handler for your Spring app? Let's force the services to throw exceptions using the `@MockBean` annotation, then we can make sure that the `RestControllerAdvice` class is working properly. How about that?

The complete code for the exception handler test class can be found in this chapter's repository:

```
@SpringBootTest
public class SampleExceptionHandlerTest {

    private final WebApplicationContext context;

    @MockBean
```

```
    private RentalPropertyService rentalPropertyServiceMock;

    private final ObjectMapper objectMapper;

    @Autowired
    SampleExceptionHandlerTest(
            WebApplicationContext context,
            ObjectMapper objectMapper){
        this.context = context;
        this.objectMapper = objectMapper;
    }


    private MockMvc mockMvc;
    // ... the rest goes here
}
```

Most of this code is familiar to you, except the part in which we declare that we want to take control of the `RentalPropertyService` Spring Bean. The `@MockBean` annotation will create a wrapper around the original `RentalPropertyService` bean, and we will be able to override any behavior of that bean during our test cases.

This is how it works:

```
@Test
void testGetPropertyById() throws Exception {
    Mockito.when(rentalPropertyServiceMock.get(any()))
        .thenThrow(new RuntimeException(
            "an unexpected 500 error"));
    mockMvc.perform(
            get("/api/v1/rental-properties/{id}",
                UUID.randomUUID())
            .contentType("application/json"))
        .andExpect(status().is5xxServerError())
        .andExpect(jsonPath("$.title")
            .value("Customized Internal Server Error"));
    Mockito.verify(rentalPropertyServiceMock,
            times(1)).get(any());
}
```

This is a test case in which we are forcing our `RentalPropertyService` Spring Bean to throw a runtime exception when its `get()` method is called with any value by any class in our Spring app.

You could even customize the parameter to suit your needs in case you are expecting an exact match in your test case. You can see that we are using the `Mockito.when()` method for that. Any time our conditions are met, the mocked response will be activated with the `thenThrow()` method. We are basically passing a new instance of a runtime exception there so that it can be thrown by Mockito when it is the right time.

By the way, you may have noticed that Mockito is a transient dependency of the Spring Test project. This means you do not need to manually include this library in your app dependencies because Spring Test already imports it.

Here are some useful Mockito methods for you to use during your test cases:

- `thenReturn(T value)`: Specifies the value to be returned when the method is called

- `thenThrow(Throwable... throwables)`: Specifies the exception(s) to be thrown when the method is called

- `thenReturn(T value, T... values)`: Specifies multiple values to be returned sequentially each time the method is called

- `thenDoNothing()`: Specifies that nothing should be done when the method is called, typically used for void methods

How amazing is it? Now we test any aspect of our Spring app during test time. We can manipulate responses as we see fit. During the test verification step (the third step of our test case pattern), we can also verify that a specific method was called and how.

Other testing options

On some occasions, you will not want to run an entire Spring ApplicationContext during your tests, since it could take a lot of time on your build pipeline. In that case, you can resort to regular unit tests. Here is an example:

```java
public class SampleExceptionHandlerUnitTest {
    private final SampleExceptionHandler handler
        = new SampleExceptionHandler();

    @Test
    public void testHandler() {
        ResponseEntity<ProblemDetail> mySampleException
            = handler.handleGenericException(
                new RuntimeException(
                    "my sample exception"));
        ProblemDetail problemDetail =
            mySampleException.getBody();
```

```
    assert problemDetail != null;
    String detail = problemDetail.getDetail();
    Assertions.assertEquals(
    "An unexpected error occurred: my sample exception"
    , detail);
    }
  }
```

In this case, we are testing the `SampleExceptionHandler` class, which is called by our Spring app whenever it finds an unhandled runtime exception. In the `testHandler` method, we are just testing that the `ProblemDetail` class comes as the content of the `ResponseEntity` object returned by the `handleGenericException()` method. It is as simple as that if do not want to add this test case to your entire integrated Spring application test environment.

You can find the full code for this unit test in our chapter repository.

We will not extend ourselves too much with regular unit tests, since this is beyond the scope of Spring Framework. But we will go back to writing other test cases in the future. I hope this was enough to give you some clarity about how to start writing your Spring application tests using the Spring Test dependency.

Coming up with a test case list

Just as a last reminder, since writing an app will always combine thousands of variables, it is imperative that you write tests that tap into the key combinations and hottest spots of your application. You need to come up with a strong list of test cases that combines positive and negative scenarios:

- **Positive test cases** are the ones that assert your application is working properly if the right information is passed during the test scenario. For instance, in our API, a positive test case would be the one in which the API is creating objects when we pass the right parameters.

- **Negative test cases** are the ones in which the application reacts correctly to incorrect data. In other words, you want to make sure that your application is emitting the right errors when the wrong data is passed in the operation tests.

We have seen plenty of positive test cases for `RentalPropertyController` and a negative test case for the runtime exception. Now, let's see another negative test case. We will send the wrong data in our request when creating a rental property. We expect the Spring Validation dependency to do its job:

```
@Test
void testCreatePropertyErrorNullAddress() throws Exception {
    RentalPropertyDTO newProperty = new RentalPropertyDTO(
            UUID.randomUUID(), UUID.randomUUID(),
        "New Property", null,
```

```
                    "New City", "New Country",
                    "67890",1500.0);

        mockMvc.perform(
            post("/api/v1/rental-properties")
            .contentType("application/json")
            .content(objectMapper.writeValueAsString(
                newProperty)))
            .andExpect(status().isBadRequest());
    }
```

As you can see, this test case method's name states the exact scenario we want to test: a client sends a null address, and an error is expected. The null address is inserted on purpose. We verify that our app has returned 400, the bad request HTTP code, in the very last line. A bad request will be returned by default any time the Spring Validation dependency finds a data violation in the data sent by the customer. Of course, we could implement a new `RestControllerAdvice` bean so that we can return a clearer answer to our users as to which fields are invalid in the request.

The code for this test case can be found in this chapter's repository.

Perfecting the application tests over time

OK, now you can write your own test suite. When creating your test cases, you must be thorough to ensure the tests guarantee the application's robustness. But remember, you can never be perfect.

It does not matter how much you try to create test cases for every combination of variables, you will always miss some interesting combinations in your test suite. This is what defines a bug. More important than trying to be the perfect software developer is being a developer who can react quickly and find great solutions when problems and missed test cases are found. And oh, boy, you will find a lot of problems, because that is the nature of software.

As soon as someone on your team reports a bug, make sure to fix the code and do your best to include new test cases in your suite to cover that scenario. If you do that over the years, your application will achieve a remarkably elevated level of maturity.

Running your tests in the console

In order to run your tests, we need to instruct Gradle to make its results very clear in the console. You will have to add the `testLogging{}` directive to your `build.gradle` file, inside the `tests` section:

```
tasks.named('test') {
    useJUnitPlatform()

    testLogging {
        events "passed", "skipped", "failed"
```

```
    }
}
```

Then, you will be able to run the following command in your console, in your project's root folder:

```
> gradle clean test
```

The `clean` directive gets Gradle to empty its build cache and re-run all its build tasks. If you do not add it, Gradle might store the build and test results in its cache and will not run the tests again unless you change some code. You can remove the `clean` directive once you are used to how it works and just run this command:

```
> gradle test
```

This is the output I get when doing it on my computer:

```
gradle clean test
OpenJDK 64-Bit Server VM warning: Sharing is only supported for boot
  loader classes because bootstrap classpath has been appended

> Task :test

RentalPropertyControllerTest > testPatchProperty() PASSED

RentalPropertyControllerTest > testUpdateProperty() PASSED

RentalPropertyControllerTest > testCreateProperty() PASSED

RentalPropertyControllerTest > testGetHeaderInfo() PASSED

RentalPropertyControllerTest > testCreatePropertyErrorNullAddress()
PASSED

RentalPropertyControllerTest > testDeleteProperty() PASSED

RentalPropertyControllerTest > testSearchProperties() PASSED

RentalPropertyControllerTest > testGetPropertyById() PASSED

RentalPropertyControllerTest > testGetAllProperties() PASSED

SampleExceptionHandlerTest > testUpdateProperty() PASSED

SampleExceptionHandlerTest > testExceptionEndpoint() PASSED

SampleExceptionHandlerTest > testGetPropertyById() PASSED

SampleExceptionHandlerUnitTest > testHandler() PASSED

BUILD SUCCESSFUL in 5s
5 actionable tasks: 5 executed
```

Figure 6.9: The Gradle output with the test results

As you can see, each test class and test method is transparently run, and you can see which ones passed and which ones did not pass. Every IDE has a special feature for running tests as well so that you can see the logs for everything you are doing.

We will talk about logs and transparency a lot more in *Chapter 11*, when we will show you how to prepare your service for production. That's it for testing in this chapter. Now, it is time to enhance your Spring Web app's performance.

Tuning Spring Web for peak performance

As we mentioned when we introduced the Spring Web project, in the past, Spring Web was not highly recommended for handling a large number of parallel client requests (in the order of thousands of simultaneous calls) or for addressing many I/O operations in the same call, such as connections to databases, transactions, and requests to other microservices.

I/O operations can add significant latency to APIs because accessing networks and even local hard drives is much slower than processing in-memory data. Before Spring 6 and Java 19, Spring Web relied solely on thread pools to handle these parallel requests. These thread pools were managed by the OS, and once your API initiated an I/O operation, the entire OS thread would be stalled, waiting for the operation's result. Managing a large number of threads was impractical because each thread consumed substantial CPU and memory resources, making it less feasible to run APIs under heavy server load.

With the introduction of Java 19, we saw the arrival of the Loom project, which introduced **virtual threads**—a feature that reduces the cost of suspending thread execution by using internal JVM mechanisms. Virtual threads are much lighter than traditional OS threads, enabling the handling of many more concurrent tasks with less resource overhead. Spring 6 now offers a way to enable virtual threads in your API.

The effect of enabling virtual threads is significant, making it very efficient to process parallel requests and I/O-bound operations. This enhancement brings Spring Web performance much closer to that of Spring WebFlux, which is a hyper-performant architecture for microservices that we will learn about in the future. Generally, Spring Web is more readable and easier to understand and debug than WebFlux, so enabling virtual threads is a genuinely beneficial feature that substantially reduces development costs.

Let's see how to enable virtual threads for your Spring Web API. We will look at how to configure your application in the future by using property files, environment variables, and so on. This will be important when we are discussing deployment strategies and configurability with Spring. For now, let's keep things as plain and simple as possible by just changing our `RentalPropertiesApplication` class. It will be rewritten like this:

```
@SpringBootApplication
public class RentalPropertyApplication {
    public static void main(String[] args) {
        SpringApplication app =
```

```java
        new SpringApplication(RentalPropertyApplication.class);

    app.setDefaultProperties(
        Map.of("spring.threads.virtual.enabled", "true"));

    app.run(args);
    }
}
```

As you can see, we are setting a default property value for the `spring.threads.virtual.enabled` key. This is pretty much all you need if you are using Java 21 and Spring 6. You can make sure you are using Java 21 by looking at your `build.gradle` file. If you have instructed Spring Initializr to create your app with the latest Java version, this is what you will see there:

```java
java {
    sourceCompatibility = '21'
}
```

To make sure we are really using virtual threads, I have added a utility endpoint in our `RentalPropertyController` class:

```java
@GetMapping("/thread-model")
public String getThreadName() {
    return Thread.currentThread().toString();
}
```

All this code does is access the current thread and call its `toString()` method. You will be able to see the name of the class used to create the thread. This is what we get when firing a `curl` request to this endpoint:

```
curl -X GET "http://localhost:8080/api/v1/rental-properties/thread-model"
 -H "accept: application/json"

VirtualThread[#57,tomcat-handler-1]/runnable@ForkJoinPool-1-worker-8
```

Figure 6.10 : Firing a curl request

As you can see, the class used to create the thread for responding to your request is the `VirtualThread` class. If we set the `spring.threads.virtual.enabled` property to `false` instead, this is what we get:

```
curl -X GET "http://localhost:8080/api/v1/rental-properties/thread-model"
 -H "accept: application/json"

Thread[#42,http-nio-8080-exec-1,5,main]
```

Figure 6.11: Knowing if your system is using virtual threads or threads

As you can see, by setting the virtual threads property to `false`, you will get your `curl` calls running over a common `Thread` class.

The performance assessment and comparison is beyond the scope of this book, but there are numerous studies on the internet that compare threads, virtual threads, and async processing with Webflux performance. In general, there will be a lot of improvement of thread vs virtual thread use, and virtual threads are a lot closer to Webflux performance. Still Webflux should be your option of choice when dealing when very high throughput is needed on your application.

Next, we will see how to write API endpoints with a great structure.

Making your API design a lot better for clients

Now, let's jump to another important subject. Suppose we have published our Rental Property API to the HomeIt website. Take this endpoint URL as an example:

```
https://homeit.com/api/v1/rental-properties/c2d538fa
```

Let's review the anatomy of this address:

- `https`: This is the protocol of the request. In this case, we are dealing with a secure HTTP connection, which we will discuss when addressing API security.

- `homeit.com`: This is what we call the **base URL**. It represents the domain in which your API is published.

- `/api`: This is the root API directory where all APIs from HomeIt are published.

- `v1`: This is the version of your API.

- `rental-properties`: This is the name of your API, which corresponds to the name of your domain or resource.

- `/c2d538fa`: This is the ID of your domain object.

- `rental-properties/c2d538fa`: This is what we call a **Unique Resource Identifier (URI)**. It tells you the exact HTTP address where you can find this specific rental property object.

It is important to review these elements because now, we are going to talk about API maturity levels. In other words, we want to answer the following question: How do we know our REST API is well structured and properly documented? The best answer for that lies in a special model we will learn about now.

Richardson Maturity Model for creating/documenting REST APIs

Leonard Richardson is an influential writer who noticed that some REST APIs are better than others in providing an intuitive design and, more importantly, adherence to the original REST standards proposed by Roy Fielding. The REST standard is like an ideal implementation of a service, and Leonard's design provides information about how far a real implementation is from the state of the art.

In the next few subsections, we are going to review the four levels of maturity, which are: Remote Procedures (level 0), Resources (level 1), HTTP Verbs (level 2), and Hypermedia Controls (level 3).

Exploring remote procedures at level 0

Many HTTP API designers will follow the strategy of creating arbitrary URLs that reflect the name of the operation they are with to provide to remote clients. If our Rental Property API was done that way, at level 0 of maturity, we would have something like the following examples:

- POST `https://homeit.com/api/createRentalProperty`

- POST `https://homeit.com/api/deleteRentalProperty`

- POST `https://homeit.com/api/updateRentalProperty`

- POST `https://homeit.com/api/sendRentalProposal`

- POST `https://homeit.com/api/acceptRentalProposal`

As you can see, the URLs all make the operation to be done explicit, which means clients need to understand and memorize a series of specific addresses for each possible operation. This leads to a very unstructured set of URLs that could lead to totally unexpected designs in the future as the API grows to support more functions and features. This is confusing for users, who have no idea how many domains and entities they need to deal with, let alone what is possible to do with the API.

This is what we consider the level 0 API maturity level. The URLs and the HTTP protocol are used without any commitment to the original design standards and intentions. Verbs are chosen from the developers' gut feelings. The URLs are truly a horror show and resemble the names of the functions in code.

If you have spent at least a couple of years in the industry, you certainly will have stumbled on such APIs. If you have designed something like that (I know I have), you need to step up to the next level.

Creating directories at level 1

At the second level, the API is considered to have entered the realm of REST. Here, the APIs will consistently use URL patterns for creating directories for the objects you are going to manipulate. Those directories will also allow you to address the objects directly by just appending the object IDs as the path parameters. Here are some examples:

- POST `https://homeit.com/api/rental-properties`

- GET `https://homeit.com/api/rental-properties/123`

- POST `https://homeit.com/api/rental-properties/123/delete`

- GET `https://homeit.com/api/rental-proposals/456`

- GET `https://homeit.com/api/rental-proposals`

As you can see, in the first, second, and third examples, we are able to address a single object, the ID of which is `123`, to fire different operations over it. But this time, we can use different verbs in the same URL, which will lead to different results. As we saw before, this unique address that refers to the same object instance is called a URI. That means your objects now have their own unique addresses in an API, and you can fire different operations to manipulate that object from that URL.

The root directory of an object is a resource. In these examples, we have two represented resource types: rental properties and rental proposals. Every resource type address should be named in plural.

OK, we have now got some consistency in creating specific URL addresses for our resource instances. But in our examples, we can see that there is no consistency in using the right HTTP verbs. We can see that there is a POST request pointing to a `/delete` URL, which is nonsense, since the POST verb in HTTP was originally designed to create a new resource. Level 2 fixes that.

Using HTTP verbs in level 2

At level 2, we now are consistently using HTTP verbs and the right response codes when handling client requests. That will guarantee that the original intent of the HTTP protocol is satisfied in your API. Achieving this level of maturity means that you are providing a highly structured and intuitive API for your clients. See the following examples:

- POST `https://homeit.com/api/v1/rental-properties`

- GET `https://homeit.com/api/v1/rental-properties/123`

- DELETE `https://homeit.com/api/v1/rental-properties/123`

- POST `https://homeit.com/api/v2/rental-properties`

- GET `https://homeit.com/api/v2/rental-properties/123`

- DELETE `https://homeit.com/api/v2/rental-properties/123`

By versioning your API, you will also guarantee that any changes can be published with new versions using new URLs. That will make you confident that you are not breaking the code of the clients that use old versions. The API users can then start to use more recent versions of the same URIs as they see fit.

At level 2, as I said before, you are also required to respond to requests with the right HTTP response codes. That means answering with 201 when a POST request to create a rental property is successful, answering with 400 when required data is not present in the request, or answering with 409 when the input data format is correct but there is some other conflict (such as trying to create a rental property with an ID for a landlord that does not exist).

The key point of Level 2 is evening out differences, making all resources behave basically in the same standard way. As we said a couple of chapters earlier, by understanding the basic operations an object should have, we are able to design the API and discover new resources that should exist in the API.

Level 3 – Hypermedia Controls

At this level, your API will not only provide standard operations and responses using the right HTTP verbs, but will also provide responses that inform the clients about the available operations for a given object. This means that once a client performs a GET request over a specific resource instance, they will not only receive the object representation but will also receive a structure that lists the next possible URIs that clients can use with new HTTP requests to perform other operations on that object.

Since this is our ideal level of maturity, let's see how it works.

Spring Web will allow you to create whatever URLs and URIs you want, so it is up to you to follow good practices, such as the ones I have just shared with you. But there is a tool called Spring HATEOAS that will help you to create level 3 APIs.

HATEOAS stands for **Hypermedia as the Engine of Application State**. That is a term coined by Roy Fielding, one of the key designers of the open HTTP protocol, which proposes that HTTP client applications should be able to guide themselves based on options returned by the HTTP-based applications. In other words, the idea is that every mature application that uses HTTP should return not only the result of the operation requested by the client but also a list of control options that could enable the application to expose those actions to the user automatically.

The ultimate result of HATEOAS – client applications that just know how to guide themselves based on hypermedia controls – is pretty hard to achieve since developers will need documentation to fire HTTP requests to a service. But it might be very useful for our clients if you make the extra actions available in the responses.

Differentiating DTOs from descriptors

So, we know that in order to have level 3 APIs, we need to offer new URIs in our HTTP responses so that the remote clients can discover further actions linked to the objects they are retrieving from our endpoints.

The way we will do this here is through DTO descriptors. A **descriptor** is basically an object wrapped around a DTO. This approach provides a container for your DTOs, and that container can also include the links that represent actions about the business object we're retrieving. See the following diagram:

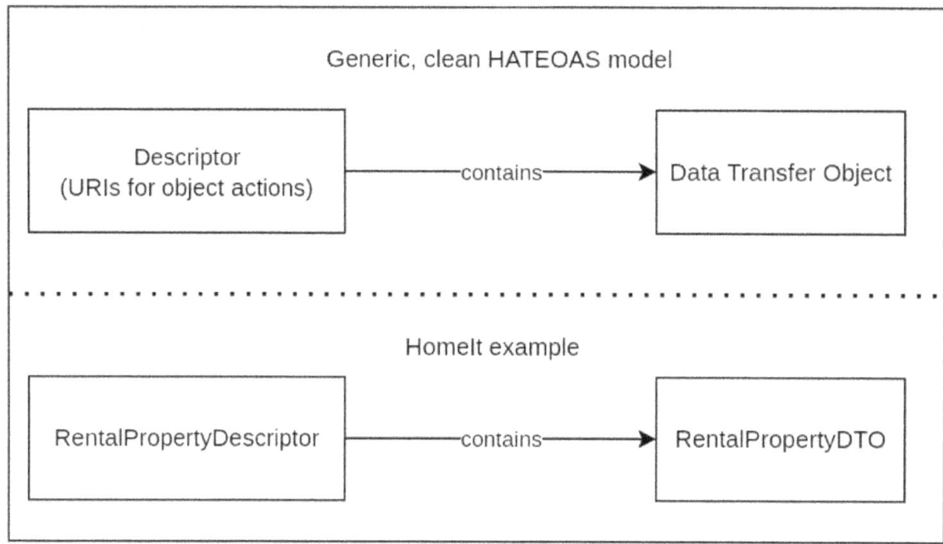

Figure 6.12: Home IT HATEOAS implementation example

Now, before looking at the code, let's see what our clients will get when retrieving the objects with their URIs.

First, when we run the API, we can create an example `RentalProperty` using our old `v1` POST method:

```
curl --request POST \
  --url http://localhost:8080/api/v1/rental-properties \
  --header 'Accept: application/json' \
  --header 'Content-Type: application/json' \
  --data '{
"id" : null,
"landlordID" : "6a1f992b-06f6-4583-b4a4-afc4ab21a3bd",
"name" : "rodrigo santiago",
"address" : "Example St 123",
"city" : "Strange City",
"country" : "US",
"zipCode" : "1111",
"rent" : 133.33
}' --silent | jq --monochrome-output

{
  "id": "ede78e6a-b25e-4446-b370-342e02baed74",
  "landlordID": "6a1f992b-06f6-4583-b4a4-afc4ab21a3bd",
  "name": "rodrigo santiago",
  "address": "Example St 123",
  "city": "Strange City",
  "country": "US",
  "zipCode": "1111",
  "rent": 133.33
}
```

Figure 6.13: A POST request for creating a rental property using curl

This time, we have used the `--silent` flag in the `curl` command, which will simplify the request and response. We are also using the `jq` command to better format the API response. The `jq` command can be installed on Windows, Mac, and Linux. It is open source and can be found here: `https://jqlang.github.io/jq/`.

OK, now we have created our new rental property. This is what we will get when retrieving a single `RentalPropertyDTO` class with hypermedia controls using Spring HATEOAS:

```
curl --request GET \
  --url http://localhost:8080/api/v2/rental-properties/ede
78e6a-b25e-4446-b370-342e02baed74 \
  --header 'Accept: application/json' \
  --header 'Content-Type: application/json' --silent | jq
--monochrome-output

{
  "rentalProperty": {
    "id": "ede78e6a-b25e-4446-b370-342e02baed74",
    "landlordID": "6a1f992b-06f6-4583-b4a4-afc4ab21a3bd",
    "name": "rodrigo santiago",
    "address": "Example St 123",
    "city": "Strange City",
    "country": "US",
    "zipCode": "1111",
    "rent": 133.33
  },
  "_links": {
    "self": {
      "href": "http://localhost:8080/api/v2/rental-propert
ies/ede78e6a-b25e-4446-b370-342e02baed74"
    }
  }
}
```

Figure 6.14: A GET request to retrieve a Rental Property

As you can see at the top of the screenshot, we are now using the v2 API URL. And the return contains an encapsulated `rentalProperty` class, as well as the URI for that rental property.

Let's see how we can retrieve a collection of rental properties using Spring HATEOAS:

```
curl --request GET \
  --url http://localhost:8080/api/v2/rental-properties \
  --header 'Accept: application/json' --silent | jq --monochrome
{
  "describedRentalProperties": [
    {
      "rentalProperty": {
        "id": "f09cdf3f-b9c5-421f-907d-89875490ece3",
        "landlordID": "6a1f992b-06f6-4583-b4a4-afc4ab21a3bd",
        "name": "property two",
        "address": "Example St 123",
        "city": "Strange City",
        "country": "US",
        "zipCode": "1111",
        "rent": 133.33
      },
      "_links": {
        "self": {
          "href": "http://localhost:8080/api/v2/rental-propertie
        }
      }
    },
    {
      "rentalProperty": {
        "id": "ea0da9c7-c6b0-4691-9519-50a83ba0a919",
        "landlordID": "6a1f992b-06f6-4583-b4a4-afc4ab21a3bd",
        "name": "property one",
        "address": "Example St 123",
        "city": "Strange City",
        "country": "US",
        "zipCode": "1111",
        "rent": 133.33
      },
      "_links": {
        "self": {
          "href": "http://localhost:8080/api/v2/rental-propertie
        }
      }
    }
  ],
  "_links": {
    "allProperties": {
      "href": "http://localhost:8080/api/v2/rental-properties"
    }
  }
}
```

Figure 6.15: A GET request to retrieve a list of properties

As you can see, each rental property comes with its own URI, and the whole collection comes with the URI for getting all the rental properties.

This is the kind of result we will learn to implement now, with Spring HATEOAS.

Let's now, with the following diagram, quickly look at the classes we used in our solution, which you can check out in our GitHub repository:

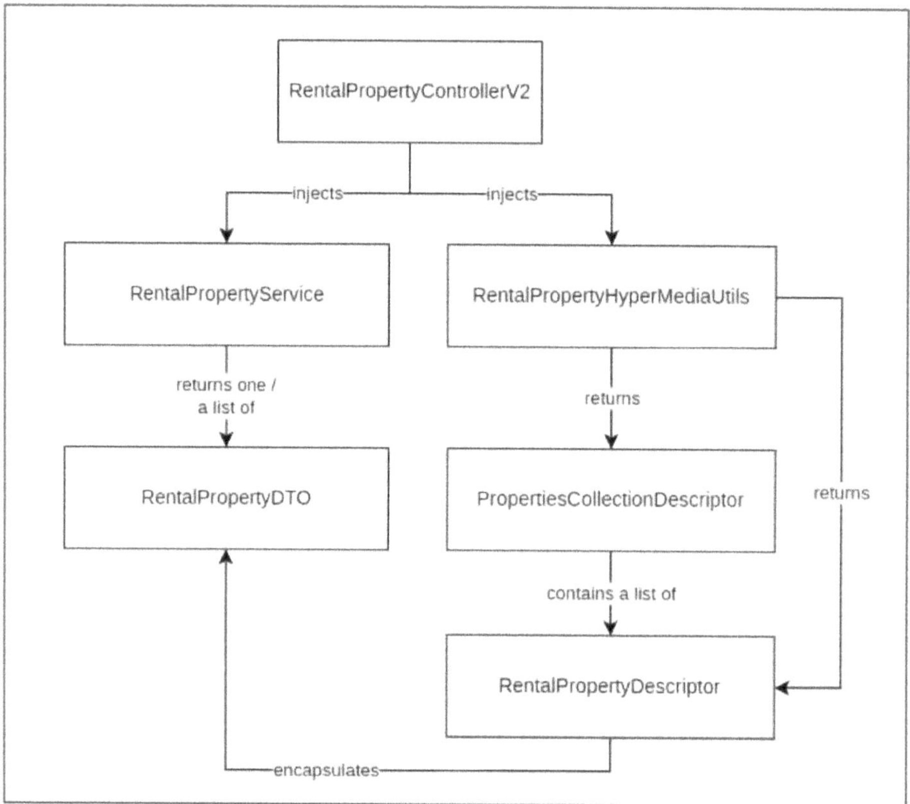

Figure 6.16: HATEOAS class structure

These are the classes used in this example:

- `RentalPropertyControllerV2`: Adds two new endpoints for retrieving one or a collection of rental properties, with the hypermedia controls (URIs) included

- `RentalProperty` and `RentalPropertyDTO`: The two classes that have existed in our system since our V1 controller

- `RentalPropertyHyperMediaUtils`: A helper bean that will create the hypermedia descriptors for us

- `RentalPropertyDescriptor`: Encapsulates a rental property and includes the URI for that rental property

- `PropertiesCollectionDescriptor`: Encapsulates a collection of `RentalPropertyDescriptor` objects and includes a URI for getting all properties at once

Alright, with that introduction out of the way, let's go to our implementation details.

Adding HATEOAS as a dependency

The first thing we should do here is to use HATEOAS as a Spring dependency. These are the changes we will make to our `build.gradle` file:

```
dependencies {
    implementation 'org.springframework.boot:spring-boot-starter-web'
    implementation 'org.springframework.boot:spring-boot-starter-
validation'
    implementation 'org.springframework.boot:spring-boot-starter-
hateoas'

    compileOnly 'org.projectlombok:lombok:1.18.32'
    annotationProcessor 'org.projectlombok:lombok:1.18.32'

    testCompileOnly 'org.projectlombok:lombok:1.18.32'
    testAnnotationProcessor 'org.projectlombok:lombok:1.18.32'

    testImplementation 'org.springframework.boot:spring-boot-starter-
test'
    testRuntimeOnly 'org.junit.platform:junit-platform-launcher'
}
```

The following observations are important:

- Spring HATEOAS is included as a dependency in the `build.gradle` file. It contains all the tools we need to create a level 3 hypermedia-based API.

- We will also include Lombok as a dependency of the `build.gradle` file so it is easier to write our descriptors. Lombok provides a series of annotations that simplify a lot of the usual Java verbosity. This dependency must be included in the compile and test phases of the build process.

With these new directives in the `build.gradle` file, we can move on to implementing the actual classes.

Writing RentalPropertyControllerV2 class

The next thing we will see is the new Spring controller class. We will write it as a new version of the API. This way, the old clients that still work with v1 will not be affected, since we are not editing old endpoints.

This is how we declare the new controller class (the entire controller code can be found in this chapter's repository):

```
@RestController
@RequestMapping("/api/v2/rental-properties")
@Validated
public class RentalPropertyControllerV2 {

    private final RentalPropertyService rentalPropertyService;
    private final RentalPropertyHyperMediaUtils
rentalPropertyHyperMediaUtils;

    public RentalPropertyControllerV2(
            RentalPropertyService rentalPropertyService,
            RentalPropertyHyperMediaUtils
                rentalPropertyHyperMediaUtils) {

        this.rentalPropertyService = rentalPropertyService;
        this.rentalPropertyHyperMediaUtils =
            rentalPropertyHyperMediaUtils;
    }
    // ... the rest goes here
}
```

You will recognize most patterns in this class, except for the following:

- We are now declaring that this URI will be nested inside the V2 version, so that we keep the old API with no changes

- We now have injected a `rentalPropertyHyperMediaUtils` Bean, that will help us render the URLs for our level 3 API.

Let's now look at how we will be retrieving a single rental property that will come with hypermedia controls (in other words, useful endpoint links that clients can use to perform actions related to the object we are retrieving):

```
@GetMapping(
    value = "/{id}",
    produces = "application/json")
public ResponseEntity<RentalPropertyDescriptor>
```

```
getPropertyById(@PathVariable UUID id) {
return rentalPropertyService.get(id)
    .map(rentalPropertyHyperMediaUtils::
        describeRentalProperty)
    .map(ResponseEntity::ok)
    .orElse(ResponseEntity.status(
        HttpStatus.NOT_FOUND)
            .body(null));
}
```

Let's analyze the current code:

- We declare that the method will return `RentalPropertyDescriptor` instead of the old DTO class

- We retrieve the usual `RentalPropertyDTO` from the `RentalPropertyService`

- We use the `rentalPropertyHyperMediaUtils` component to encapsulate our `RentalPropertyDTO` with a `RentalPropertyDescriber` (we will see how that works in a few minutes)

- Then, we proceed with the current algorithm that will return the found response, or `404 - NOT_FOUND` if there is no object for the ID we are looking for

Now, let's look at the method for retrieving all available rental properties, but now the entire collection will be encapsulated in a `CollectionDescriptor`:

```
@GetMapping(produces = "application/json")
public ResponseEntity<PropertiesCollectionDescriptor>
getAllProperties() {
    return Optional.ofNullable(
        rentalPropertyHyperMediaUtils
            .describeRentalPropertyCollection(
                rentalPropertyService
                    .getAllProperties()))
        .map( describedCollection ->
            ResponseEntity.ok().body(describedCollection))
        .orElse(ResponseEntity.noContent().build());
}
```

You can see the following:

- We are using the `rentalPropertyService.getAllProperties()` method to bring all the DTOs we have; then, we are using the `rentalPropertyHyperMediaUtils` component to encapsulate the DTO collection in a hypermedia descriptor for the entire collection. We will see how that is implemented in a few minutes.

- We state that the return of the collection descriptor can be `null` (in case no DTOs exist), which means the clients will receive no content in the payload. When a request has been successful but there is no payload to be received in the response, it is good practice to set the HTTP return code `204`.

As you can see, both methods are simple enough in the controller, which keeps things isolated and easy to read and understand. Let's now look at our descriptors, so that you know what we are returning when a client fires an HTTP request to any of the endpoints.

Writing the rental property hypermedia descriptors

This is how we implement the `RentalPropertyDescriptor` class, which is a container for the `RentalPropertyDTO` class:

```
@EqualsAndHashCode(callSuper = true)
@Data
public class RentalPropertyDescriptor
        extends RepresentationModel<RentalPropertyDescriptor> {
    private RentalPropertyDTO rentalProperty;
}
```

Easy enough, right? Let's break down this code (the entire class can be found in the chapter's repository):

- The class is tagged with Lombok annotations that reduce our boilerplate (`@EqualsAndHashCode` and `@Data`).

- `@Data` defines that this class should have getters and setters for all attributes, and Lombok will generate the bytecode automatically during compilation time.

- `@EqualsAndHashCode` annotation gives Lombok the directive to auto-generate both methods – `equals()` and `hashcode()`.

- We define that the descriptor should encapsulate the `RentalPropertyDTO` class, which keeps the DTO isolated from the relative links.

- We define that the descriptor class extends the `RepresentationModel`, which is a Spring HATEOAS class that adds support for the hypermedia links. This means our descriptor has a series of attributes and helper methods to add those links to our responses.

OK, that was simple and full of info. Let's now see how to create a descriptor for `RentalPropertyDTO` collection (this class can be seen in the chapter's repository):

```
@EqualsAndHashCode(callSuper = true)
@Data
public class PropertiesCollectionDescriptor
    extends RepresentationModel<PropertiesCollectionDescriptor> {
    private Collection<RentalPropertyDescriptor>
```

```
describedRentalProperties;
}
```

This class is very simple as well, with the following highlights:

- It is built as an extension of the `RepresentationModel` class, which adds attributes to store the hypermedia links

- This class maintains a collection of `RentalPropertyDescriptors` because we want to return descriptors for the individual DTOs and a descriptor for the entire collection

That's it for our descriptors. Let's go to the last piece in this solution.

Writing the RentalPropertyHyperMediaUtils Spring Bean

We can look now at the main piece of code in our chapter repository, which we decided to call `RentalPropertyHyperMediaUtils`. This creates the responses with the links. Let's first look at how we declare this class:

```
@Component
public class RentalPropertyHyperMediaUtils {
    // ... class body
}
```

The `@Component` annotation comes from the core of Spring Framework. That tells Spring that this class should be treated as a Spring Bean – the framework will create a singleton of this class and make it available for other Beans to inject. This is an annotation that you can use for services that are not business related but still provide some important functionality. In fact, the `@Component` annotation is the root annotation for creating Spring Beans. The `@Controller` and `@Service` annotations are two annotations that extend `@Component`. This is why Spring Framework knows to create Beans out of controllers and services as well.

Now, let's look at how we create `RentalPropertyDescriptor`:

```
public RentalPropertyDescriptor describeRentalProperty(
        RentalPropertyDTO rentalPropertyDTO) {

    return Stream.of(new RentalPropertyDescriptor())
        .peek( desc ->
            desc.setRentalProperty(rentalPropertyDTO))
        .peek( desc -> desc.add(
            WebMvcLinkBuilder.linkTo(
                RentalPropertyControllerV2.class)
        .slash(rentalPropertyDTO.id()).withSelfRel())

        // add as many links as you want for this entity
```

```
        // WebMvcLinkBuilder.linkTo(WebMvcLinkBuilder
        // .methodOn(RentalPropertyControllerV2.class)
        //     .getPropertyById(rentalPropertyDTO.id()))
        //     .withRel("anotherFunction");
        // WebMvcLinkBuilder.linkTo(
        //     RentalPropertyControllerV2.class)
        //.slash(rentalPropertyDTO.id())
        //     .withRel("anotherFunction"))

        .findFirst().get();
    }
```

Let's look at some important notes here:

- This class receives `rentalPropertyDTO` as input and returns its equivalent descriptor, which basically encapsulates the original DTO.

- We are creating a stream so that we can use the functional style, which is more concise and compact. The `peek()` method means we take the previous object, do some operations with it, and then move to the next functional operation, passing on the same object reference. It is different from `map()`, which will deliver the output object of the current operation to the next function. `peek()` preserves the original object in the functional pipeline, while `map()` uses functions to transform the input object into a different output object.

- Once we have created a `RentalPropertyDescriptor`, we add the `rentalPropertyDTO` to it, and then we add the links to the descriptor.

- The `add()` method comes from the Spring HATEOAS `RepresentationModel` class. We inherited it automatically.

- `WebMvcLinkBuilder` is the key utility class for building the URIs. I have added some examples here in some comments. It is possible to add as many URIs as you want to an object. It is up to you how many controls you add to your class.

- You can see that the link builder works by finding the address for the controller class of your choice and then adding the ID of the rental property to create a URI for the rental property we are retrieving.

Alright! You can go back a few pages to review the output and look at the URIs mapped in the API's JSON response if you want. Let's keep looking at our hypermedia `util` class. The next method returns the descriptor for a set of property descriptors:

```
public PropertiesCollectionDescriptor
    describeRentalPropertyCollection(
        List<RentalPropertyDTO> allProperties) {
```

```
    if(allProperties.isEmpty())
        return null;

    List<RentalPropertyDescriptor> parsedProperties =
        parseProperties(allProperties);

    return Stream.of(new PropertiesCollectionDescriptor())
        .peek( cDes ->
            cDes.setDescribedRentalProperties(
                parsedProperties))
        .peek(this::addAllPropertiesLink)
        .findFirst().get();
}
```

This method is quite interesting. Let's review it:

- We receive a regular list of rental properties to be encapsulated in descriptors.

- We define that this method should return `null` if the list is empty.

- We have a utility method for parsing our list of `RentalPropertyDTOs` to `RentalPropertyDescriptors`, and now we have a full list of descriptors, each one with URIs and hypermedia controls.

- Now, we create a root descriptor that will encapsulate our list of `RentalPropertyDescriptors`. We insert the list of `RentalPropertyDescriptors` to it and we add the `GET /properties` hypermedia link.

- Then we return the first result we find, which is actually the root collection descriptor we created before.

The `describeRentalPropertyCollection()` method is the most complex one, as it delegates some calls to other util functions. Let's look at these lasting utility functions now:

```
private List<RentalPropertyDescriptor>
    parseProperties(
    List<RentalPropertyDTO> allProperties) {

    return allProperties.stream()
        .map(this::describeRentalProperty).toList();
}


public void addAllPropertiesLink(
        PropertiesCollectionDescriptor collectionDescriptorDTO) {
    collectionDescriptorDTO.add(
        WebMvcLinkBuilder.linkTo(
```

```
                    RentalPropertyControllerV2.class)
                .withRel("allProperties")
        );
    }
```

We can see the method to parse `rentalPropertyDTOs` to their respective descriptors. This actually uses the function we have just seen, `describeRentalProperty()`. We create a `stream()` from the input list, and for each object, we use `map()` to transform the `rentalPropertyDTO` element into the `RentalPropertyDescription` object. That line contains special syntax for Java functional programming, which is beyond the scope of this book.

We have a simple utility method to add the `GET /properties` URI to the `RentalPropertyCollectionDescriptor`. You can use this method as a reference to add any link to any of your own descriptors in the future.

Now, let's finally check how the class and package structure was laid out.

This is what we got as a result of the Spring HATEOAS implementation of a level 3 REST API with hypermedia controls:

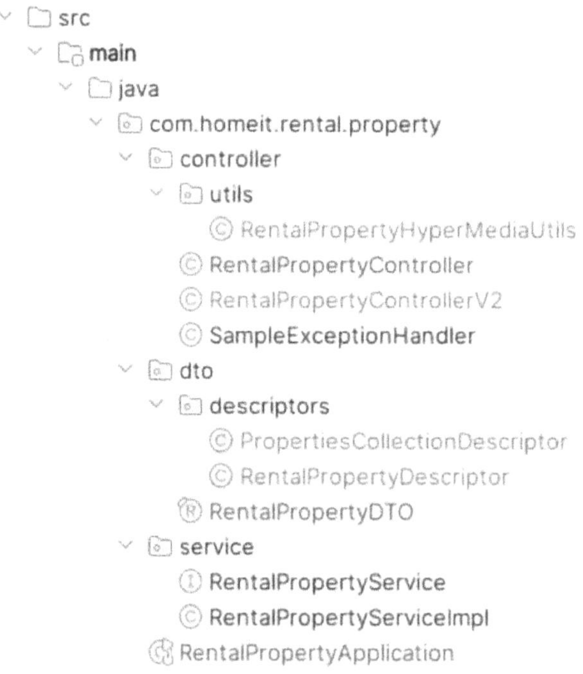

Figure 6.17: Class and package structure for a level 3 REST API

As you can see, a lot of work and thought has happened here, just to have the hypermedia links in your response objects.

Are level 3 REST APIs worth the effort?

Although HATEOAS is a useful tool, and the promised land of level 3 REST APIs creates the vision of objects that will help HTTP clients to discover functionality by themselves, the reality is that our API users will still need thorough documentation to know how to consume our APIs. As such, HATEOAS is not a bullet-proof strategy for creating great APIs. It can help our clients in some ways, but maybe it is not as good as people promise.

I have seen a great implementation of hypermedia controls, though. Maybe there is a special operation that you want your user to know about when they are getting the response of an HTTP call. An example is as follows: when a user is creating a security token that has an expiration time, you might want to consider adding the hypermedia URI to the response so that your user can see the token refresh the URL right there in the response. Critical operations such as that may be important to implement in your APIs. But do not bother to spend all your time adding all possible URIs to your responses. If you do that, your response object will become very confusing to developers.

The best way to make your API usable is to have the best possible documentation. We will see how to do that in a future chapter, when we are focusing on getting our services to talk to each other.

Summary

In this chapter, we covered a lot of ground to make your APIs well designed, well tested, and well structured internally, and we also talked about the Spring conventions to make sure your code is cleaner and more flexible. These were critical subjects to help you speed up your development process and lead you to think like a Spring Framework seasoned developer.

We have also learned how to create business interfaces that isolate implementation details from the definition of business processes. In the final sections, we dealt with improving your Spring Web API's performance, as well as how to make sure your API adheres to the HTTP standards. The Richardson Maturity Model is a great template that you can follow to make the lives of your API users much easier, and we have also seen how to create level 3 APIs by using Spring HATEOAS.

The last two chapters represent a critical step into microservice thinking from a business perspective. The next chapters will cover a lot of ground in the technical details that come from this core software development. We will now deal with non-functional requirements such as persistence, communication, security, deployment, and everything "techy" using Spring Framework. See you in the next chapter!

Get This Book's PDF Version and Exclusive Extras

Scan the QR code (or go to `packtpub.com/unlock`). Search for this book by name, confirm the edition, and then follow the steps on the page.

Note: Keep your invoice handly. Purchase made directly from packt don't require one.

7

Handling Data and Evolving Your Microservice

Welcome to *Chapter 7*! In this chapter, we will explore several topics regarding how to create the data persistence layer of your services. The topics here will be implemented using a SQL database, but we will dive into the architecture, which will help you understand how you should approach data modeling and persistence for any database type.

We will cover the following topics in this chapter:

- Data persistence in applications with Spring

- Reactive versus non-reactive data handling

- SQL versus NoSQL data storage

- Microservice versus monolithic applications data design

- Implementing a non-reactive, SQL database persistence layer

- JpaRepository: your go-to SQL interface in Spring Data

- Working with transactions in Spring Data

- Using `NamedParameterJdbcTemplate` to run raw SQL queries

The chapter starts with a general explanation of how to take architecture decisions on data modeling and the cost of each kind of approach. Then, we will move to the implementation, where we will show you the different levels of database interactions using Spring Data.

This chapter will also give you an understanding of how to evolve your service over time as we discuss each topic. You will often work with microservices that need some kind of reengineering. We will show you how to do that in Spring with the use of multiple implementations for the same service interfaces. In the end, we want to have a clear separation of concerns between the business interfaces we need and how we actually implement those interfaces. This is going to be a wild ride; let's go!

Technical requirements

Here is the full code for the classes and services we have created in this chapter: `https://github.com/PacktPublishing/Spring-System-Design-in-Practice/tree/main/chapter-07/rental-property-microservice`

Data persistence in applications with Spring

So far, we have focused on how to enable Spring Web APIs without caring too much about data persistence. In our RentalProperty API, the service layer implementation is currently just using a simple map to collect the rental property objects in run time. Of course, that is not enough to bring about a whole REST API. Obviously, objects need to be persisted correctly.

The fact is that adding support to a real database can be a really tiresome task if you are an application developer. When writing a Spring application, most developers just want to jump in and start coding, without caring too much about database infrastructure details. In fact, even choosing the database technology and how to connect to it will vary from company to company, and from cloud to cloud.

Here are some circumstances that might affect the choice of database technology:

- Your company might already have a favorite database instance for your app to connect to

- Big companies might use on-premises appliances, such as Oracle's Exadata server

- You could have a managed database in the cloud to connect to, such as Amazon Aurora

- The company might have a database pod deployed in a Kubernetes cluster using something like Postgres, for example

The options for database connections can vary a lot, so we will start by giving you a very flexible way to start coding your service. To understand what we are going to do, let's recap our universal Spring app anatomy diagram:

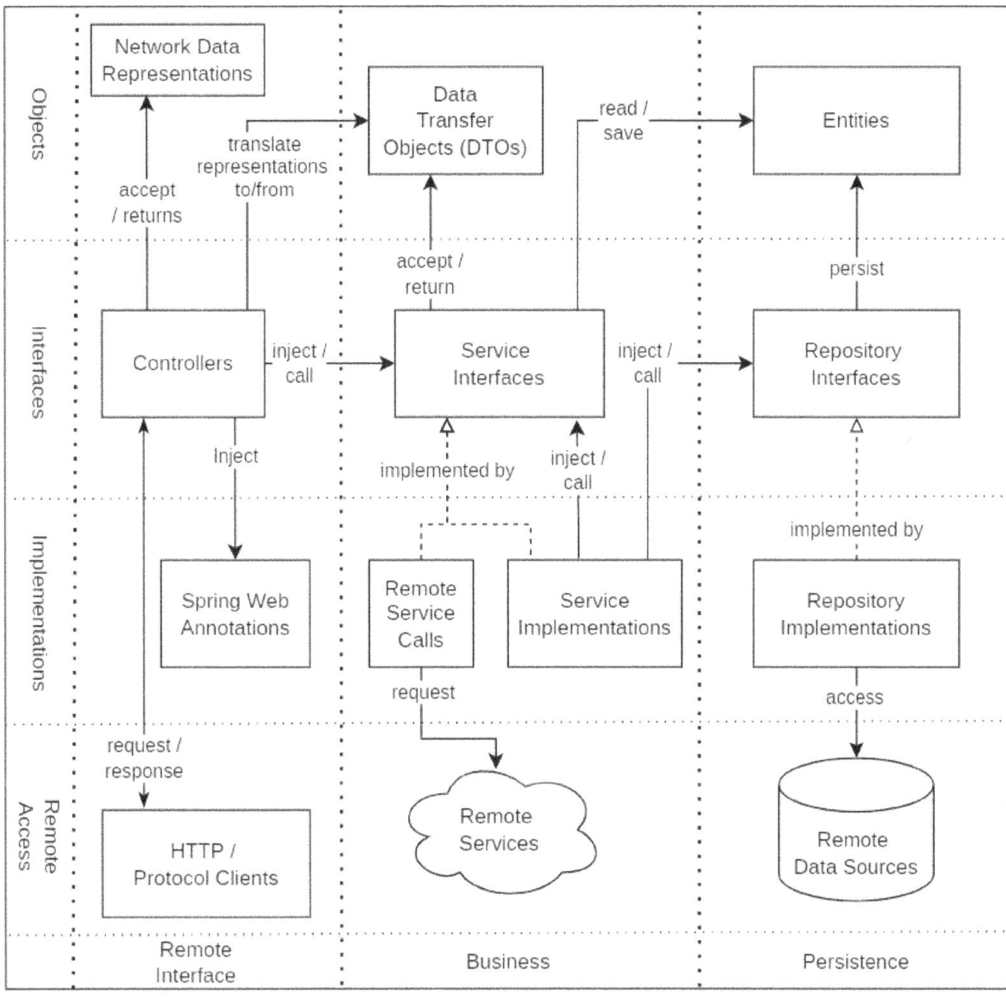

Figure 7.1: Spring application anatomy

When we look at this chart, we can see that the *Interfaces* and *Implementations* horizontal layers are built apart from each other. If you look at how they impact the *Persistence* vertical layer, this means that Spring was designed in such a way that you are geared toward writing persistence repository interfaces that are fully separate from the code that specifies the actual databases you will use.

In other words, the same code you will write to manage your data can be used without any changes with any database instance you like, given that the database is of the same type (we will work with SQL databases in this chapter). You can get a recap of the database types we have by reviewing *Chapter 4*. To change your database instance, just give Spring a few configuration options and some dependencies, and voilà: you can connect to a different database instance and even different database vendors. Spring will provide the infrastructure you need to connect to a different database.

Being able to point to different database types at any time by just changing your configuration files and dependencies is extremely helpful in the following circumstances:

- You are at the very beginning of writing your application, and the dev team still does not know exactly what database instance to connect to, so you can start with an in-memory database and be unblocked for doing the rest of the development.

- Your company is migrating to another database architecture, and you need to reconfigure your connection without impacting your implementation, for example, moving from on-premises to a cloud-managed database.

- You are deploying the same application in different environments, each one with a different database instance to connect to (dev, stg, prod, and so on). This is useful for running quality assurance processes before going to production (we will see how that is done in the next chapters).

- You are running integration tests and need to provide a test database without changing your code.

- Your company is moving to another database (such as moving from Oracle to Postgres) and you need to change your configuration and make very minor changes to your code.

There are other scenarios in which decoupling the data repository implementation from the database connection comes in handy. In this chapter, we will connect to in-memory databases so that we can free you from thinking about infrastructure for now and focus on understanding how data is stored, changed, and retrieved in a typical Spring application.

In the next section, let's talk about how to make your app faster by understanding reactive and non-reactive programming.

Reactive versus non-reactive data handling

Another key factor when thinking about data handling is that we have two basic options: reactive and non-reactive data handling.

Non-reactive data handling means this: every time your code tries to run a database query, the current thread will be stalled as it waits for the database result. A reactive query, on the other hand, will free your current thread as long as there are no results from the database. Also, if you are streaming data from the database, you will be able to return objects as they are returned from the database operation.

Let's talk briefly about both options in this section.

Non-reactive data handling

In **non-reactive data handling**, we write data persistence code that will block a single thread when doing database I/O operations. As you saw in the earlier chapters, thread-blocking operations can make your applications a lot slower when you have too many concurrent client requests. You can still enable virtual threads on your Spring app so that the application becomes a lot faster.

Non-reactive data handling is suitable for Spring Web apps, or for any apps that you can think of that do not have strict requirements for dealing with an exceedingly high volume of concurrent requests (in the order of thousands per second).

Reactive data handling

On the other hand, **reactive data handling** code will work without blocking a thread. Any time your app starts an I/O operation, that code will be put in waiting mode. When the requested data is available, Spring will run the rest of the code again in such a way that threads can be shared around thousands of requests.

In this chapter, we will concentrate on implementing non-reactive data handling. In the future, we will come back to reactive servers; then, we will be able to look at how different it is to write very high-performance servers.

Now, let's talk briefly about the two paradigms for organizing data.

SQL versus NoSQL data storage

Today, every developer with some experience knows that applications can have a wide variety of databases. We have plenty of ways that we can store our data. But all types can be separated into two major categories: SQL or NoSQL. Let's have see why using either of them would be a good choice.

SQL databases

Structured Query Language (**SQL**) databases are data storage mechanisms that help you keep the integrity of your data. They have several features:

- **Fixed table column format**: Your tables will enforce a regular format for your data, meaning all rows will have the same number of attributes (columns) and all attributes will have the same type. This means you have a very strong guarantee that all your data will be highly standardized.

- **Constraints**: You can set restrictions on how your data is created in relation to other data in different tables. In our HomeIt example, we could say that a rental property cannot be created unless it has a landlord. Those restrictions can add a lot of safety to your application.

- **ACID guarantees**: When using a SQL database, you can make it so that your transactions can handle a lot of data in different tables, and the transaction will be successful only if every single operation inside a transaction is successful. That means that if one of the operations fails, every other operation is rolled back to its previous state and the database is left with full data integrity. Also, concurrent transactions do not affect each other. **ACID** stands for **Atomic** (all operations in a single request should work as if they were just one), **Consistent** (constraints are used to guarantee data integrity), **Isolated** (one transaction cannot be interfered with by another concurrent transaction), and **Durable** (data will keep its state unless a transaction that changes it is successful).

Using SQL databases has two remarkably interesting implications. First, you will not be able to have as much flexibility on how your objects are created. Second, every object should have the same attributes and types.

Constraints are processed in the database, which means a data model with many constraints will be slower than data models with few constraints.

You will most probably want to use SQL databases when dealing with data that requires a lot of integrity. The most common application is, of course, registering financial transactions. Also, medical records, compliance requirements, and everything that smells like high-risk data should be a candidate for SQL databases.

NoSQL databases

When data integrity among different tables is not a particularly high-priority requirement, you can resort to other kinds of databases. All of them fall in the category of **Non-Structured Query Language (NoSQL)** databases. These databases will help in various kinds of use cases, depending on how they are structured. The most famous one is MongoDB, which is a document database.

MongoDB can be used to store unstructured data. This means that if your data is in some way unpredictable and you have high variability in its format, then MongoDB can be used to store that data successfully. For HomeIt, we could store rental property data as a NoSQL document and allow landlords to add as many description sections as they want to their registered rental property. Thousands of different documents representing different properties would be stored in a single MongoDB collection. Each section would be a different field of the document so that landlords can get more creative in their descriptions.

There are other great NoSQL databases that you can use in your Spring application:

- **Cassandra**: Implemented as a wide-column store, optimized for high availability and scalability, suitable for **Internet of Things (IoT)** data, time-series data, and real-time analytics

- **Redis**: Key-value store offering fast, in-memory data access, perfect for caching, session management, real-time analytics, and message brokering

- **Neo4j**: Graph database designed for handling highly connected data, useful for social networks, recommendation engines, and network analysis

- **Couchbase**: Document store with integrated caching and full-text search capabilities, suitable for interactive web and mobile applications

- **Elasticsearch**: Search engine optimized for full-text search, analytics, and complex search queries, useful for log and event data analysis

As you can see, there are a lot of use cases for NoSQL databases. Spring contains drivers and dependencies for using all of them.

Other important characteristics of NoSQL databases are the following:

- Because devs usually won't put a lot of constraints on NoSQL data design, that usually means faster processing times. But you can have almost the same effect by getting rid of constraints in SQL databases.

- If you have a lot of constraints that need to be applied to NoSQL data, that means you will have to implement them in your application. That means you can face a lot of complications if you have concurrent transactions accessing the same documents.

- Moving constraints outside the database means a lot more read/write performance for less money, but you are generally giving up the ACID guarantees. There is always a cost associated with architectural decisions.

As you can see, using a NoSQL database should be done with caution. You need to make sure that you do not need features such as ACID transactions.

> **Note**
>
> Since this chapter is mostly about how to manage your data in Spring applications, I need to acknowledge and warn you that there are entire books about how to properly deal with data. If you want to dive really deep into this subject, I recommend the book *Designing Data-Intensive Applications: The Big Ideas Behind Reliable, Scalable, and Maintainable Systems* by Martin Kleppmann as a great starting point. It will perfectly complement this chapter, making you a much better data architect.

Now, we need to discuss what level of complexity is required for you to implement data structures and persistence in your application.

Microservices versus monolith application data design

In the early days of the internet, data design was heavily focused on ensuring data integrity. Since most applications were monolithic, the database schemas would host all entities and objects from an application in one place.

This centralized approach was beneficial because it allowed the use of constraints to enforce various business rules effectively. Additionally, databases offered PL/SQL (Procedural Language extensions), which are essentially programs within the database for various purposes.

However, in modern times, extensive use of PL/SQL and large database schemas are often considered anti-patterns, as different domains are mixed in the same code base and database, making them harder to maintain.

With the advent of microservice architectures, the general rule is that each service should contain its own database. But as all dreams come to an end, microservice architectures also have their drawbacks. Over time, the limitations of the original microservice recommendations have become apparent. The primary issue with having a separate database for each microservice is the complexity that arises when trying to perform transactions that impact multiple services. For example, in our start-up, HomeIt, when a tenant pays for an approved rental proposal, the transaction must ensure consistency between the payment service and the rental proposal service. You do not want to accept the tenant's payment unless the rental proposal has been finalized, allowing the tenant to move in.

To ensure a distributed transaction such as this works properly, you need to design your services so that if one service fails, the state of the other services must also be updated accordingly. This example involves only two services, and the complexity can increase exponentially as you add more services to the transaction requirements. For instance, if you add a rule stating that a property should not appear in search results if it is currently rented, you must coordinate three services in the same transaction.

As you can see, microservice architecture is not without its challenges. Moving away from large, centralized schemas comes with significant costs. Running the same transaction on a single database is much simpler because you can ensure that updates to multiple tables occur within a single transaction. The database takes care of the ACID guarantees.

Overall, microservice architectures are here to stay, so you must design your services with a conscious trade-off. There are some key decisions that you will have to make. Let's see them in this section.

Data complexity and granularity level

When you are designing a service entity, such as our RentalProperty object, you will need to assess how much of a complex object you want. Do you want `RentalProperty` to just be a flat Java object with as few attributes as possible, or do you want to inflate it, with a lot of nested objects?

If you go for a more complete and more complex object with a lot of nested objects inside, your API will return a lot of data in a single call, which makes the object heavier to move around the network. Also, update operations might take longer because you might be changing a lot of nested data, which will potentially trigger a lot of foreign key constraints. The memory footprint of your microservices will also need to be bigger, especially if your application should be able to deal with a big list of objects.

It is not rare to find APIs that will allow a developer to retrieve a list of hundreds of very inflated objects, with lots of nested objects in each one of them (think about fetching a list of landlords with all their rental properties as attributes of the landlord). These operations are very expensive for your service's RAM, the network, and the database. You should use them with caution.

On the other hand, having thin objects on your endpoints could mean you need to fetch data multiple times from different services, putting a burden on the network with multiple requests. Imagine you need to fetch a list of landlords from one service, then fetch a list of their rental properties from another microservice. That could become intolerable, depending on how it is used on your application.

Let's look at another key driver of your decision.

Organizing databases

Another important decision is on how to organize your databases. Of course, if you have a lot of different database types, you can only store information in different instances. Suppose you have a NoSQL database for storing property attributes and maybe a SQL database for storing user info, and maybe a graph database for storing the connections between users and contracts... that means you can only host data in different places.

But if you are using just a single database type – let's say Postgres – you may be able to store schemas for different services in the same database instance. It would be possible to isolate each microservice in a different schema, which can become an advantage since you just have one instance to do backups and maintenance, but it can become a burden as well since all microservice instances would put a pressure in the same database instance. It is up to you and the architecture team to decide how to organize databases. The decision should take into account both functional and non-functional requirements. That means going back to the first chapters to understand things such as the following:

- Which users should be able to access this data, and when they are doing it?

- How many times will an operation be used every day?

- Can the user take a long time to wait for the result, or should the application return the result in a very low latency time?

- How many users will be accessing the same service at the same time?

Investigating how the application is being used, both from a product perspective and also from a frequency and situational perspective, is key to doing your best design.

This is a key question I like to ask the teams I am working with, whenever we have trade-offs such as these: *what problems do we want to have?*

Because problems will happen. As soon as you make an architectural decision, you will eventually face the burden of that choice. This means that if a system can fail, it will surely fail, eventually.

We will talk a bit more about performance, resilience, and resource constraints in future chapters. For now, without further ado, let's jump to coding our rental service with various kinds of data handling strategies that Spring makes available to us developers.

Implementing non-reactive SQL database persistence

SQL databases are, still to this day, the most important storage type for any kind of API. Since non-reactive implementations are so commonly used across the industry, let's start with this option to help you understand the various ways to implement persistence layers in Spring.

The Spring project that provides excellent features for whatever data architecture you would like to implement is Spring Data. Let's see how it works for non-reactive, SQL database persistence.

Adding support to a dev database

This chapter code will also be done on top of the RentalProperty Spring application. The full code can be found at `https://github.com/PacktPublishing/Spring-System-Design-in-Practice/tree/main/chapter-07`.

Because we are interested in enabling our application as fast as we can for coding our data persistence repositories, we will enable in-memory databases as a starting point for our development. The first step is to add the right dependencies. You can add this code to the `build.gradle` file, in the `dependencies` section:

```
implementation 'org.springframework.boot:spring-boot-starter-data-jpa'
// in memory database, for testing only
implementation 'com.h2database:h2'
```

With these lines, you will have all the dependencies you will need.

Now that we have the right dependencies, let's configure our in-memory database. You will have to set some properties on your rental property application. This is a handy method through which you can set up all the properties you need to run your persistence layer:

```
private static void databaseProperties
    (SpringApplication app) {
    // # H2 Database configuration in PostgreSQL mode
    app.setDefaultProperties(
        Map.of(
```

```
        "spring.datasource.url",
    "jdbc:h2:mem:testdb;DB_CLOSE_DELAY=-1;MODE=PostgreSQL",
        "spring.datasource.driverClassName",
            "org.h2.Driver",
        "spring.datasource.username",
            "sampleuser",
        "spring.datasource.password",
            "samplepass",
        "spring.jpa.database-platform",
            "org.hibernate.dialect.H2Dialect",
        "spring.h2.console.enabled",
            "true",
        "spring.h2.console.path",
            "/h2-console",
        "spring.jpa.hibernate.ddl-auto",
            "create",
        "spring.jpa.show-sql",
            "true"));
}
```

Spring allows you to set up all kinds of database connections with similar properties. In our case, we are signaling that this should be an in-memory database with support for Postgres syntax. This method should be called in your `main` class like this:

```
public static void main(String[] args) {
    SpringApplication app =
        new SpringApplication(
            RentalPropertyApplication.class);

    virtualThreads(app);
    databaseProperties(app);

    app.run(args);
}
```

Notice that I also extracted the `virtualThreads` method in order to add support for virtual threads.

After you add these directives to your application, your app will not only have access to an in-memory database, but you will also have access to a full SQL terminal when running your app. That is what the `spring.h2.console.enabled` property is about. In that way, you will be able to connect to the in-memory H2 database and run whatever SQL queries you want. That makes it easier to check the state of your persistence layer. H2 is a very lightweight, open source database written in Java. It is very useful for quickly adding SQL capabilities to your app, especially during prototyping.

When starting your Spring app, you should see this line in the console log:

```
o.s.b.a.h2.H2ConsoleAutoConfiguration     : H2 console available at '/
h2-console'. Database available at 'jdbc:h2:mem:testdb'
```

That means you will be able to connect to your in-memory SQL dev database instance by visiting this URL in your browser: `http://localhost:8080/h2-console`.

When visiting this URL, you will see the following page:

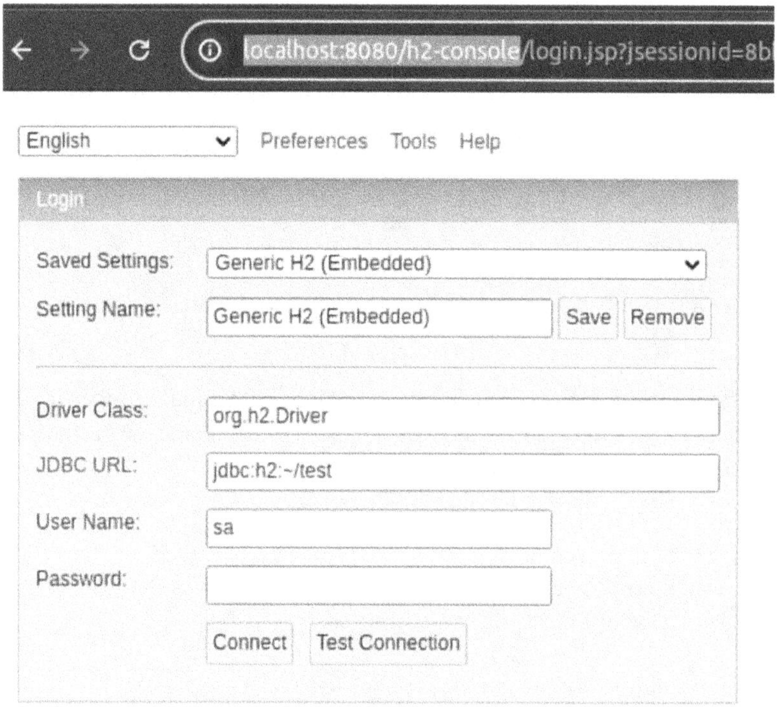

Figure 7.2: H2 database SQL login screen

As you can see from the log message, you will be able to connect to this database when you change **JDBC URL** to `jdbc:h2:mem:testdb`. Then, add `sampleuser` to the **User Name** field and `samplepass` to the **Password** field. Once you have set those fields and clicked on **Connect**, this is what you will see:

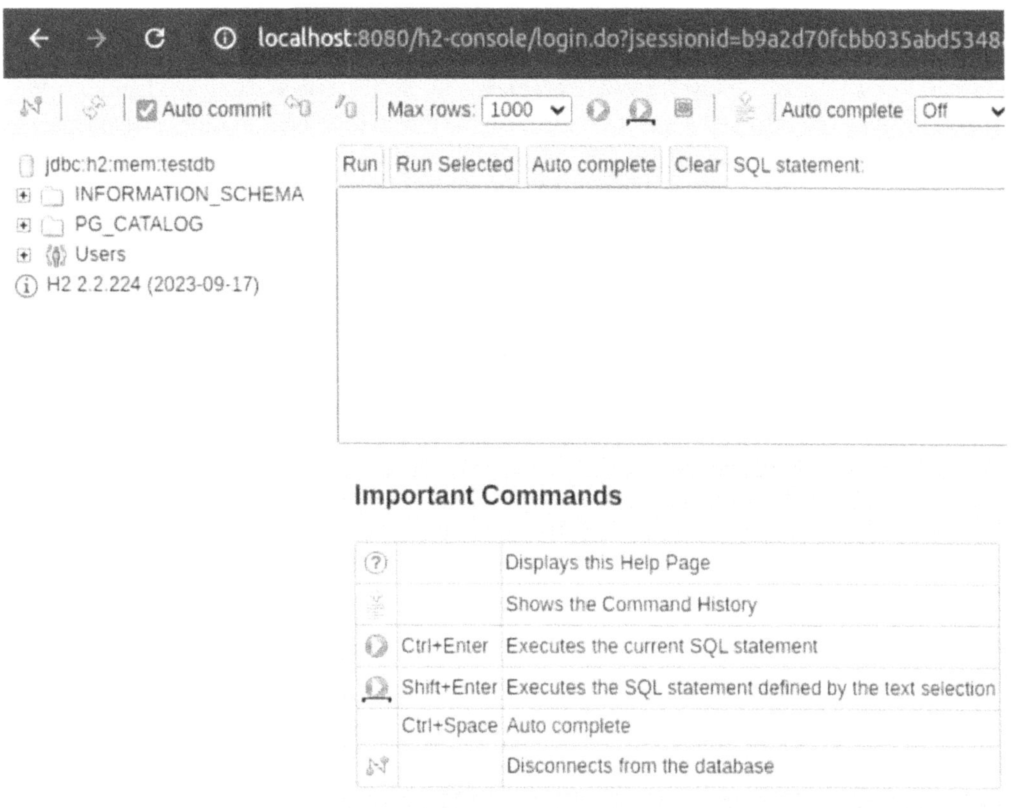

Figure 7.3: H2 SQL console

This is a full-fledged SQL console, connected to our in-memory H2 database instance provided by Spring Data, which aids with development and fast prototyping. But we do not have any application tables since there is no code written on your persistence layer.

Two other interesting properties that we have set on our application properties are `spring.jpa.hibernate.ddl-auto` and `spring.jpa.show-sql`. The way we set the values of those properties tells Spring to create the database schema if it has not been created already, and to show the SQL commands executed in the console output when starting the application. It will be possible to see that output after declaring our entities in code.

We will connect to our database instance again in a few moments. Let's first add some more code to our server.

Defining entities to be persisted

Spring Data offers a variety of ways for you to program your database access and data handling. We will look at the most important ones and why we should use each. But before choosing what tool to use in order to save or retrieve data from your tables, you will need to define the objects to be persisted. This is the most important part of any Spring API persistence layer implementation. Those objects are called **entities**.

An **entity** is the actual representation of your domain object in the database. Usually, an entity will represent a row in one of your tables (or collections/documents if you are dealing with NoSQL databases).

For this chapter, as you already know, we will delve into several ways to implement the persistence layer for the RentalProperties service. In our example, we will have a one-to-one mapping from our `RentalPropertyDTO` class to a `RentalPropertyEntity` class. This means that whenever we are calling one of our API endpoints, we just want to translate DTOs to entities as simply as we can so you can understand how persistence layers work in Spring Data.

Let's start. The following code is an example of how to implement the `RentalPropertyEntity` class. This is how we declare the class:

```
@Entity
@Table(name = "rental_properties")
@Data
public class RentalProperty {

    @Id
    @Column(updatable = false, nullable = false)
    private UUID id;

    @NotNull(message = "Landlord id is required")
    @Column(nullable = false)
    private UUID landlordID;

    @NotEmpty(message = "Name is required")
    @Column(nullable = false)
    private String name;

    @NotEmpty(message = "Address is required")
    @Column(nullable = false)
    private String address;

    @NotEmpty(message = "City is required")
    @Column(nullable = false)
    private String city;
```

```
    @NotEmpty(message = "Country is required")
    @Column(nullable = false)
    private String country;

    @NotEmpty(message = "Zip code is required")
    @Column(nullable = false)
    private String zipCode;

    @NotNull(message = "Rent is required")
    @Column(nullable = false)
    private Double rent;

    @PrePersist
    protected void onCreate() {
        if (id == null) {
            id = UUID.randomUUID();
        }
    }
}
```

The following observations are important here:

- The `@Entity` annotation tells Spring that this class is going to be used as a representation of a table row.

- The `@Table` annotation helps you name your table. You can set any names you see fit. If you miss this annotation, Spring will use the name of your entity as the name of the corresponding table in the database. It is also possible to specify the schema in which the table resides. But H2 does not support that, so we will implement our rental property persistence layer in the default schema.

- The `@Data` annotation comes from Lombok. That prevents us from having to write getter and setter methods for each entity attribute.

- The `@Id` annotation defines the `id` attribute as the primary key in our table.

- Notice that we are using a series of Spring Validation annotations, such as `@NotEmpty` and `@NotNull` to make sure our entity objects will follow these directives.

- There is a specific Spring Data `@Column` annotation used to ensure our database columns restrictions are respected. With this annotation, it is also possible to configure the name of the column in the database by using the `name` attribute. Whatever value you add to that will make Spring Data match the name you have chosen with the column name in the database. That is useful in order to follow the column name conventions in your company. If you do not use it, Spring Data will consider the column name to be the same as your entity attribute.

- Another key thing in this code is the use of the @PrePersist annotation. It ensures the method is called before Spring Data saves the entity. In this case, we are guaranteeing that the entity will be given a new random UUID, in case it is a new one. This is a simple way to create a generator without having to inject more dependencies into this project.

This is where I have added this entity to the project:

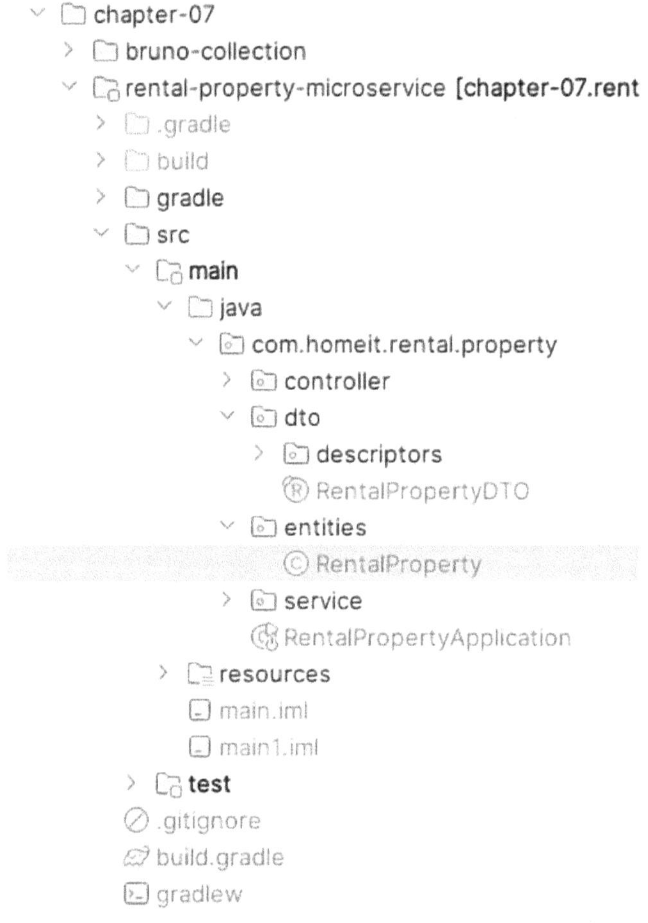

Figure 7.4: RentalProperty entity

Now that we have declared this entity inside our project, if we re-run the Spring application, new logs will appear, demonstrating that Spring Data is capable of creating the database columns that match your entities. This is the output we get:

```
Hibernate: drop table if exists rental_properties cascade
Hibernate: create table rental_properties (rent float(53) not null,
id uuid not null, landlordid uuid not null, address varchar(255) not
```

```
null, city varchar(255) not null, country varchar(255) not null, name
varchar(255) not null, zip_code varchar(255) not null, primary key
(id))
```

As you can see, in this development setup, Spring will always recreate all the tables in our H2 in-memory database. It makes a very fast and valuable local development environment. But, later, when you are connecting to a remote database instance, you will probably want to use a different property value for `spring.jpa.hibernate.ddl-auto`, which is `validate`. The `validate` directive tells Spring to check whether the tables exist and whether the columns are of the same type as the ones you have declared on your entity classes. It makes it very useful for making sure your application is compatible with the database instance you are using.

Now that we know how to declare an entity, let's start writing the code that will persist or retrieve the rows of your database tables. There are different ways to do this, which we will explore now.

The following annotations are also useful for representing data in your columns:

- `@Lob`: Specifies that a persistent property should be stored as a large object

- `@Enumerated`: Specifies that a persistent property should be stored as an enum

- `@Temporal`: Specifies the date/time precision for persistent properties

- `@Transient`: Marks a field to be ignored by JPA and not persisted in the database

Next, we will talk a bit about creating relationships between different entities.

Declaring relationships between entities

These are useful entity annotations if you want to declare relationships between entities in code. I would not advise you to declare classes with these annotations unless you want to make the entity constraints explicit on your API, which is not always advisable:

- `@OneToOne`: Defines a one-to-one relationship between two entities

- `@OneToMany`: Defines a one-to-many relationship between two entities

- `@ManyToOne`: Defines a many-to-one relationship between two entities

- `@ManyToMany`: Defines a many-to-many relationship between two entities

- `@JoinColumn`: Specifies the foreign key column for associations

- `@JoinTable`: Defines a join table for many-to-many relationships

These annotations are a part of the `javax.persistence` package in the Java Persistence API. You can see clear examples of each annotation in the `javax.persistence` javadocs: `https://docs.oracle.com/javaee%2F6%2Fapi%2F%2F/index.html?javax/persistence/JoinColumn.html`.

Using these annotations makes your application a lot more complicated to write and a lot more complex to maintain due to the fact that several different tables are involved in the declarations. Also, your code will not be very easy to read.

Since the pure microservices approach requires the existence of simple APIs to express very simple domain objects, you should not have a lot of entities declared on your microservices, and you also should not have a lot of relationships declared in code. Whenever you need another entity reference in one of your entities, just add the UUID `id` attribute there and make sure your services know how to validate that information. The simpler you get, the faster you can define your APIs and move things to production.

The heavy use of these relationship annotations reveals that your application is becoming a monolith, with a lot of relationships inside a single service, which becomes an anti-pattern. Make sure your services are as simple as possible. IDs are all you will usually need to make sure you can retrieve objects from other systems.

An interesting fact: if your product team adds a lot of features and you find yourself adding a lot of new entities or columns to your database every time you need to release something new, that is probably time for you to jump one abstraction level up and do some refactoring. These are some ideas for you to think about:

- Is it time for you to spin a microservices out from your current one?
- Is it time for you to create a higher abstraction domain object that is capable of storing data for all those use cases without requiring you to change your database that much?

As an example, suppose you are working on a company with a system that has a `car` service and the product team starts to come up with requirements for supporting other kinds of vehicles, and you are forcing your `car` service to support those use cases as well, and new attributes are added to the service. You will face a lot of constraints during development time. Maybe it is time for you and your team to do either of the following:

- Spin off a more general `vehicle` service that is capable of hosting cars and whatever vehicles you have so that your database now has more general tables and column names
- Create other services for dealing with the other vehicle types

Those two ideas are in line with the idea that you should future-proof your architecture once you fully understand the 5-year roadmap that the product team wants to deliver.

Writing aggregated objects as JSON in your columns

If you need nested objects in your entities but you do not feel they deserve their own tables, you can write them as JSON objects in a single column of your table. This is how you should define an entity attribute if you want to send this attribute to your database as JSON in a single column:

```
@Lob
@Convert(converter = JsonAttributeConverter.class) @
Column(columnDefinition = "TEXT")
private Address address;
```

This states that an attribute called `address` will exist as a child object of our entity. But any time we need to write that object to our table or read it from our table, Spring Data will call the converter class and read/write the converted value to the attribute's column.

This is how we write a converter class that takes the `Address` class, serializes it to JSON, and stores it in a column. Then, the converter class can parse the JSON back to an `Address` class when we ask Spring Data to read that class from the table. This is an example of the `Address` object we have just mentioned:

```
public record Address (
    String streetAddress,
    String city,
    String zip,
    String country
){}
```

As you can see, we are using the `record` type since this is a simple class for holding data.

As you can see in the code, the `Address` record is an object that aggregates address data. We will need an `AddressConverter` class that helps Spring Data to read/write this object to the database. This is how it works:

```
@Converter
public class AddressConverter
    implements AttributeConverter<Address, String> {

    private final ObjectMapper objectMapper =
        new ObjectMapper();

    @Override
    public String convertToDatabaseColumn(Address address){
        try {
            return objectMapper
                .writeValueAsString(address);
        } catch (JsonProcessingException e) {
```

```
                throw new IllegalArgumentException
                    ("Error converting Address to JSON string",
                        e);
            }
        }


    @Override
        public Address convertToEntityAttribute(String dbData){
            try {
                return objectMapper
                    .readValue(dbData, Address.class);
            } catch (IOException e) {
                throw new IllegalArgumentException
                    ("Error converting JSON string to Address",
                        e);
            }
        }
    }
}
```

The `Address` class will then help us to simplify our `RentalProperty` class:

```
@Entity
@Table(name = "rental_properties")
@Data
public class RentalProperty {

    @Id
    @Column(updatable = false, nullable = false)
    private UUID id;

    @NotNull(message = "Landlord id is required")
    @Column(nullable = false)
    private UUID landlordID;

    @NotEmpty(message = "Name is required")
    @Column(nullable = false)
    private String name;

    @Lob
    @Convert(converter = AddressConverter.class)
    @Column(columnDefinition = "TEXT")
```

```
    private Address address;

    @NotNull(message = "Rent is required")
    @Column(nullable = false)
    private Double rent;

    @PrePersist
    protected void onCreate() {
        if (id == null) {
            id = UUID.randomUUID();
        }
    }
}
```

When we add `Address` as a child object of the `RentalProperty` class, we can remove other primitive attributes that might even make the original entity a bit dirtier. Now, we have isolated the address data in a single column by making it JSON when saving that data to the `RentalProperty` table.

Notice that, in this last example, we could have tweaked the `Address` `columnDefinition` value to `jsonb` instead of TEXT. There is a good reason for this, as we will see in the next sections.

Other entity lifecycle annotations

Here are other interesting annotations that you can use to trigger methods during your entity's lifecycle. These are important, especially if you have business rules or security systems that should be called if your entities are passing from one stage to the next, or even if you want to troubleshoot your system with some extra logs:

- `@PrePersist`: Invoked before an entity is persisted (inserted into the database) for the first time

- `@PostPersist`: Invoked after an entity has been persisted (inserted into the database)

- `@PreUpdate`: Invoked before an entity is updated in the database

- `@PostUpdate`: Invoked after an entity has been updated in the database

- `@PreRemove`: Invoked before an entity is removed (deleted from the database)

- `@PostRemove`: Invoked after an entity has been removed (deleted from the database)

- `@PostLoad`: Invoked after an entity has been loaded from the `database.Jsonb` type columns

Postgres is a very interesting database. Although it is traditionally a full-fledged SQL database, it has many great features. One of them is the capacity to support JSON objects as a primitive type in a table column. That allows Postgres to provide special JSON queries, which can make a big difference to your data modeling efforts.

In this last example, setting the Address field as a jsonb column in your table allows you to run queries as if your Address field was a document. In fact, whatever JSON object you store in that Address column, you will be able to do special JSON searches in that object. You can add as many new attributes as possible to that object. No problemo. The column will know how to store it if you update your converter class.

The most relevant SQL databases support similar features. Oracle, SQL Server, and MySQL all provide ways for you to store JSON data and query for that data as if that column was a NoSQL document.

Storing child objects as JSON in your entities can greatly reduce the amount of boilerplate code and tables in your application. The decision point is: if the child object can only be accessed from the parent entity, it is then a good candidate for being stored as a JSON column in its parent entity table. This can affect your SQL database choice. Now you have a clean way to make your entities a lot more flexible in your database without making it hard on your SQL scripts, or without needing to write a lot of different tables to store new data.

If you re-run your Spring application with that special JSON twist, this is the SQL output you get when Spring is creating the table:

```
Hibernate: drop table if exists rental_properties cascade
Hibernate: create table rental_properties (rent float(53) not null, id
uuid not null, landlordid uuid not null, name varchar(255) not null,
address jsonb, primary key (id))
```

As you can see, the address attribute is now being declared as a jsonb column, even in the H2 in-memory database. How awesome is that for allowing you to do fast prototyping?

There is just one problem with this approach right now: while using H2 databases, we cannot use the special native JSON search queries. So, we will just use the text type for now. Bear in mind that you can move to special column types when connecting to your real databases.

There is a lot to think about when you model your entities. Let's now go to the code that allows us to retrieve and store those entities.

ORM versus raw SQL in Spring Data

When it comes to writing code to interact with databases, Spring offers two extremes: you can either have fine-grained control over the exact SQL statements being executed for accessing and storing your data or you can let the framework determine the appropriate SQL statements to execute.

The framework that allows Spring to map classes to database queries is called **object-relational mapping (ORM)**. This means that certain packages in Spring can inspect your entity classes and decide how to query them in the configured database. This is also how Spring Data can automatically create your tables if configured to do so.

You might have noticed the word **Hibernate** in the SQL logs. Hibernate is a special package included in Spring Data as a transient dependency. It implements a Java specification called JPA that was designed as a standard for mapping objects to relational databases through a single interface.

Hibernate is an implementation of ORM and can be used to query and store data in our in-memory H2 database.

In the following sections, we will explore various methods to handle data from the entity we have defined. These methods will cover both extremes: manipulating raw SQL queries in Spring Data and using user-friendly Spring Data interfaces that simplify querying and storing data.

Generally, there is a principle to guide your decisions when implementing data access: the easier it is to fetch and store data in Spring Data, the higher the computational cost. This means that if you prioritize speed and high performance, you should opt for raw SQL implementations. If speed is not a major concern, then using the clean and easy-to-use APIs will suffice.

As a rule of thumb, I advise starting with the easiest approach. If you need to fine-tune your application, you can then add implementations that leverage raw SQL queries.

OK. We will start with the easiest repositories to use first (ORM oriented) and then move to the high-performance ones.

JpaRepository – your go-to SQL interface in Spring Data

In the next sections, we will dive into the most important and easy-to-use SQL interfaces in Spring. We will explore their strengths and weaknesses and implement most of our rental property service.

Using JpaRepository as an ORM-enabled repository

The easiest way by far to retrieve and save data from your database SQL tables is by extending the `JpaRepository` interface in Spring. You do not need to even write any methods if you do not want to. That is the power of Spring Data.

Take a look at this example:

```
public interface RentalPropertyJpaRepository
    extends JpaRepository<RentalProperty, UUID> {
}
```

This interface does a lot. Let's see how it works by creating a new implementation for our `RentalPropertyService` interface. If you remember, our first implementation class, `RentalPropertyServiceImpl`, was coded using a simple internal `HashMap`, which worked as a very rudimentary persistence layer.

Let's now create a class called `RentalPropertyServiceJpaImpl`, which now injects the repository we have just created. The class declaration goes as follows:

```
@Service
public class RentalPropertyServiceJpaImpl implements
RentalPropertyService{

    private RentalPropertyJpaRepository jpaRepository;

    public RentalPropertyServiceJpaImpl
        (RentalPropertyJpaRepository jpaRepository) {
        this.jpaRepository = jpaRepository;
    }

    // ... RentalPropertyService method implementation
    // goes here
}
```

Interesting, right? The class should be tagged with the `@Service` annotation, which tells Spring to inject this `impl` class as a Spring Bean whenever another Spring Bean tries to inject the `RentalPropertyService` interface.

Wait, we have already written the first `RentalPropertyServiceImpl` class. Now Spring will have two options to choose from, and my `RentalPropertyController` class will receive just one of them.

How does Spring know which implementation class to inject in the `RentalPropertyController` class?

Well... it does not know. You must tell Spring which implementation class to inject. Before doing this, let's implement the rest of the `RentalPropertyServiceJpaImpl` class so that you understand how to use `JpaRepository`.

Take a look at the method signatures that we need to fully implement from the `RentalPropertyService` interface:

```
public interface RentalPropertyService {
List<RentalPropertyDTO> getAllProperties();

Optional<RentalPropertyDTO> get(UUID id);

RentalPropertyDTO create(RentalPropertyDTO property);
```

```
Optional<RentalPropertyDTO>
    update(UUID id, RentalPropertyDTO updatedProperty);

Optional<RentalPropertyDTO>
    updateSomeFields(UUID id,
    RentalPropertyDTO partialUpdate);

Optional<RentalPropertyDTO> delete(UUID id);

List<RentalPropertyDTO> search(String name,
    String address, String city,
    String country, String zipCode);
}
```

As you can see, all these methods of the `RentalPropertyService` class are returning or receiving the `RentalPropertyDTO` class. But the repository will work with the `RentalProperty` class we have just created, which received the `@Entity` annotation.

Using Lombok to translate DTO to entity classes and vice versa

As we saw in our universal Spring implementation diagram (*Figure 7.1*), the *Persistence* vertical layer works with entity classes, while the *Remote Access* layer works with **Data Transfer Object (DTO)** classes. That means all service classes should translate entities to DTOs when retrieving information from the database and translate DTOs to entity classes when saving data to our database.

Because of that, we need to prepare at least two utility methods. There are other ways to map from DTOs to entities and vice versa, but I like not having to include another dependency in our project. Having more dependencies means that your service could face vulnerabilities and become obsolete faster.

By using the Lombok dependency, it is possible to reduce a bit of the code needed to build those translators. First, let's add the `@Builder` annotation to `RentalPropertyDTO` class, the `RentalProperty` entity class, and the `Address` class since it is a child attribute of the `RentalProperty` entity class. This is how the `RentalProperty` entity class will be annotated:

```
@Entity
@Table(name = "rental_properties")
@Data
@Builder // This is our lombok Builder annotation
@NoArgsConstructor
@AllArgsConstructor
public class RentalProperty { ... }
```

And because of the `@Builder` annotation and the `JpaRepository` we will use, we also need to include a default constructor and an all-arguments constructor. This is why we added `@NoArgsConstructor` and `@AllArgsConstructor` to the class as well.

And this is how the `Address` class will be declared. Just add the `@Builder` annotation to the record class:

```
@Builder
public record Address ( /* our attributes are here*/ )
```

Finally, let's add the same `@Builder` annotation to our `RentalPropertyDTO` record class:

```
@Builder
public record RentalPropertyDTO ( ... ){}
```

With those two classes tagged with `@Builder`, let's now create a `RentalPropertyUtil` class to convert from one class to another. We will go in a very simple way, by declaring a `RentalPropertyConverter` class with two methods. The first one will convert a DTO object to an entity object:

```
public static RentalProperty toEntity(RentalPropertyDTO dto) {
    return RentalProperty.builder()
        .rent(dto.rent())
        .id(dto.id())
        .name(dto.name())
        .landlordID(dto.landlordID())
        .address(Address.builder()
            .zip(dto.zipCode())
            .city(dto.city())
            .streetAddress(dto.address())
            .country(dto.country())
            .build())
        .build();
}
```

The second one will convert an entity object to a DTO object:

```
public static RentalPropertyDTO toDTO(RentalProperty entity) {
    return RentalPropertyDTO.builder()
        .address(entity.getAddress().streetAddress())
        .name(entity.getName())
        .rent(entity.getRent())
        .city(entity.getAddress().city())
```

```
        .landlordID(entity.getLandlordID())
        .id(entity.getId())
        .country(entity.getAddress().country())
        .zipCode(entity.getAddress().zip())
        .build();
}
```

As you can see, both static methods can be freely imported into any `RentalPropertyService` implementation class. Let's use it in our `RentalPRopertyServiceJpaImpl` class.

This is how we return a rental property from an ID:

```
@Override
public Optional<RentalPropertyDTO> get(UUID id) {
    return jpaRepository.findById(id)
        .map(RentalPropertyConverter::toDTO);
}
```

This is how we create a property:

```
@Override
public RentalPropertyDTO create(RentalPropertyDTO property) {
    return RentalPropertyConverter.toDTO(
        jpaRepository.save(
            RentalPropertyConverter.toEntity(property)));
}
```

You can see how the full `RentalPropertyServiceJpaImpl` is created by visiting the class in the book's GitHub repository (`https://github.com/PacktPublishing/Spring-System-Design-in-Practice/blob/main/chapter 07/rental-property-microservice/src/main/java/com/homeit/rental/property/service/RentalPropertyServiceJpaImpl.java`).

As you can see, all these methods in our `RentalPropertyJpaRepository` class come for free. These and several other resources are available for you when using `JpaRepository`.

JpaRepository class hierarchy made simple

`JpaRepository` is a powerful interface because it extends some other important Spring Data repositories. Here is the inheritance hierarchy:

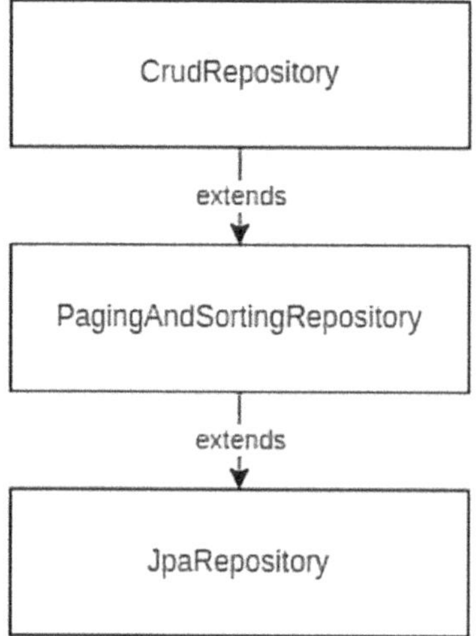

Figure 7.5: JpaRepository class hierarchy

These three interfaces are so rich. Here is a list of the methods you get when using `JpaRepository`. The following ones belong to the `CrudRepository` interface:

- `save(T entity)`: Save an entity
- `saveAll(Iterable<T> entities)`: Save multiple entities
- `findById(ID id)`: Find an entity by its ID
- `existsById(ID id)`: Check whether an entity exists by its ID
- `findAll()`: Find all entities
- `findAllById(Iterable<ID> ids)`: Find all entities by their IDs
- `count()`: Count all entities
- `deleteById(ID id)`: Delete an entity by its ID
- `delete(T entity)`: Delete an entity
- `deleteAll(Iterable<? extends T> entities)`: Delete multiple entities
- `deleteAll()`: Delete all entities

You get some very useful methods from the `PagingAndSortingRepository` interface. These are methods that help you to retrieve subsets of your data – for example, when trying to list all resources from your endpoint (in other words, when firing a GET HTTP request to the `/rental-properties` URI).

If you have to retrieve thousands of objects from your database, you should use these methods from your `JpaRepository` services when listing all resources. Otherwise, you will risk using all of your microservice's available memory, which can crash your service, due to the excessive amount of objects. Here are the methods I am talking about (we will look at an example of how to use them in a few moments:

- `findAll(Sort sort)`: Find all entities with sorting

- `findAll(Pageable pageable)`: Find all entities with pagination

The methods we will see next are useful if you want to operate on lots of objects at once:

- `saveAndFlush(T entity)`: Save an object and immediately commit the change to a database.

- `SaveAllAndFlush(Iterable<T> entities)`: Same as before, but sends all entities before commiting the data to your database.

- `DeleteAllInBatch(...)`: Delete all objects by firing delete requests with lots of IDs at once. This makes the deletion of lots of objects much faster since they run in a single operation in the database.

- `findAll(Example<S> example)`: Find objects in the database by looking at a sample object. All objects that match the non-null example's attributes will be returned.

But what if we want to create very specific queries with special conditions? In the next section, we will learn how to create that by declaring new methods to your JpaRepository interface extension.

Customizing database queries using JpaRepository

Another interesting thing you can do with `JpaRepository` is add methods on your JPA interface extension for creating custom SQL queries. These methods are written using a special syntax that Spring knows how to find in execution time and will provide the proper implementation for you.

Here are some examples I have added to our `RentalPropertyJpaRepository` interface so that you can understand how it works:

```java
public interface RentalPropertyJpaRepository
    extends JpaRepository<RentalProperty, UUID> {

    // Find all properties by landlord ID
    List<RentalProperty> findByLandlordID(
```

```
        UUID landlordID);

    // Find properties by rent less than a specified amount
    List<RentalProperty> findByRentLessThan(
        Double maxRent);
    // Find properties by landlord ID, city, and rent range
    List<RentalProperty> findByLandlordIDAndAddress_
CityAndRentBetween(
        UUID landlordID, String city,
        Double minRent, Double maxRent);
}
```

As you can see, there are a lot of possibilities. Even the `Address` object attributes can be used to create your custom queries on top of the `JpaRepository`. That opens a lot of choices for you to make the best out of using your Spring `JpaRepository` interface.

Here is a quick fact: the best IDEs, such as IntelliJ, will help you to write those custom queries by providing code completion tools. When I am writing a new custom method in my `RentalPropertyJpaRepository`, this is what I see in IntelliJ as I type:

```
List<RentalProperty> findByLandlordIDAAndName(UUID landlordID);

                            ⌐ And
    // Find propertie       ⌐ AndAddress
    List<RentalProper       ⌐ AndId
                            ⌐ NameContaining
    // Find propertie       ⌐ NameBetween
    List<RentalProper
```

Figure 7.6: IntelliJ JpaRepository code completion feature

This makes writing new custom queries a breeze.

Using JPQL to create custom queries

These are some other examples of custom queries you can create on top of Spring JpaRepository by using the `@Query` annotation, which gives you access to the JPQL declarative language:

```
// Custom query to find properties by rent range
@Query("SELECT rp FROM RentalProperty rp WHERE rp.rent BETWEEN
:minRent AND :maxRent")
List<RentalProperty> findByRentRange(@Param("minRent") Double minRent,
@Param("maxRent") Double maxRent);

// Custom query to find properties by name
// and sort by rent ascending
```

```
@Query("SELECT rp FROM RentalProperty rp WHERE rp.name LIKE
%:namePart% ORDER BY rp.rent ASC")
List<RentalProperty> findByNameAndSortByRent(@Param("namePart") String
namePart);
```

As you can see, Spring supports a declarative language that is similar to SQL but deals with objects directly. You can use it if you feel that creating a clearer SQL-type syntax is your way of doing things. I won't spend a lot of time discussing JPQL due to space constraints. This subject deserves a lot of chapters to be covered comprehensively. If you want to go deep into this subject, start with the official documentation: `https://docs.oracle.com/cd/E29542_01/apirefs.1111/e13946/ejb3_langref.html`.

> **A note about the performance and scope of your microservices**
>
> When using custom queries in Spring Data JPA, remember that they are not infallible. Complex queries can challenge your database, especially if they involve large tables with non-indexed columns, resulting in long query execution times. It is crucial to consider how your database is structured, including its size, indexes, column types, necessary operations, and relationships between tables.
>
> For example, if your `RentalProperty` entity has a relationship with the `Landlord` entity (using the `@ManyToOne` annotation), you could create a custom query that performs a join operation between the `RentalProperty` and `Landlord` tables. However, such relationships can complicate your microservices architecture. It might be undesirable for a `RentalProperties` microservice to have access to all landlord data. If `Landlord` is stored together with other users in the system, giving the `RentalProperties` microservice access to the entire user set can lead to unnecessary exposure of data.
>
> It's essential to avoid overcomplicating your data model with these features. Just because Spring Data JPA makes it easy to create custom queries doesn't mean you should always use them. The key is two-fold: avoid the temptation and understand the non-functional and functional requirements of your application. Analyze how your data is organized, determine the best flow for the user experience, and tune your database to handle low-performance queries more efficiently.

Understanding other limitations of JpaRepository

Please also note that in the `RentalServiceJpaImpl` class, we do not support searches since this interface is not optimal for creating search queries. This is the implementation of the search method. We are basically throwing an `UnsupportedOperationException`:

```
@Override
public List<RentalPropertyDTO> search(
        String name, String address,
        String city, String country, String zipCode) {
    throw new UnsupportedOperationException(
```

```
        "This service implementation does not support searches." +
        " Please, use another service implementation instead.");
}
```

We will create a service for implementing the search feature in a bit.

Dealing with a very high volume of data and requests

Another critical part of developing APIs with Spring or any other systems, as we saw a couple of sections ago, is to use paging mechanisms when you know the resource you are querying for has a very high volume of objects.

Imagine a user visits our start-up HomeIt website and decides to list all properties in an entire US state, such as California. When the website audience starts to grow, with potentially millions of search requests each day, how would we make sure the GET request does not entirely blow up our server?

You want your services to be successful and scalable, right? When you have millions of users doing a lot of expensive things on your website, knowing what to do to guarantee access to the information as quickly as possible will be key to keeping your users.

Here are a few optimizations you can do to make sure your website queries will scale:

- **Indexing**: Ensure that key search queries are running on indexed fields in your database. Properly declared column indexes will maximize the efficiency of your searches.

- **Caching**: Create a cache for the most frequently run queries to store the results in memory, enabling fast query responses. For example, when querying for all California rental properties, cache the results of the first 20 pages. Since most users will not go beyond even 10 pages, this approach will serve the majority of users quickly.

- **Database sharding**: Consider creating a separate `RentalProperty` database for each US state to distribute the load. Keeping your microservices data model simple allows greater flexibility in optimizing non-functional requirements. You could have one service implementation per state, for example, and your microservice could store data based on the state being saved.

- **Load balancing**: Even with sharding, some states may still experience heavy load. In such cases, create read replicas of your database to distribute the query load across multiple database instances.

- **Further query optimizations**: Collaborate with a skilled DBA to find ways to optimize database queries. A professional DBA can provide valuable insights and techniques for query optimization.

- **Removing abstraction levels**: `JpaRepository` may not be suitable for performance-critical queries due to the overhead of ORM mapping. Instead, use `JdbcTemplate` repositories to execute raw SQL commands directly, bypassing ORM mapping costs.

- **Asynchronous processing**: Utilize reactive processing to handle multiple concurrent tasks efficiently. Asynchronous processing will be introduced in future chapters.

- **Denormalization**: Optimizing your tables by replicating some relationship data in a single table, rather than running joins across multiple tables, can significantly reduce computational costs and speed up queries.

- **Materialized views**: Pre-compute and store results of high-volume queries in temporary tables that can be refreshed periodically. While this approach may not provide the most up-to-date results, the recency gap can be acceptable depending on your use case and non-functional requirements.

- **Radically remove constraints**: You might want to relieve your database tables from constraints such as foreign keys or data format validations, such as nullable versus non-nullable columns. Some of these constraints can be added to your microservice as new code so that it only gets activated under certain conditions.

- **Move totally or partially to NoSQL databases**: Moving to other kinds of databases on your service implementations can also speed up your queries a lot. There are all sorts of optimized databases that you can tap into, depending on your use case. I have seen implementations with Cassandra that supported more than 15,000 data retrieval requests per second. That is a lot of data retrieval! Another great example is Neo4J, which speeds up any search on a graph (compared to traditional SQL databases) since the relationships are not computed during runtime for `join` commands. If you need to provide graph searches, this is probably the kind of optimization you want.

On top of this, Spring Data provides pageable queries in the `JpaRepository` interface. Let's see how it works to optimize our searches.

Retrieving paged results in Spring JpaRepository

Now that we have talked about ways to improve database query performance, let's create a way to reduce the pressure of your API on your database.

Traditionally, when firing a GET request to our `/rental-properties` resource, we should return the list of all objects that are contained in your microservice. Well, the general idea simply does not work that well if we have thousands of properties to retrieve at the same time, for multiple reasons. One of them is, of course, it will kill your microservice resources (RAM memory, for example) if you have a high volume of objects. But even if you had the hardware resources, it would not be practical from the user's perspective, since it is unable to handle so many objects at the same time. From a usability standpoint, your system becomes useless if your user cannot deal in a very practical way with the data you are presenting.

This is where we can implement a solution that will seek to create a GET `/rental-properties` endpoint that can return result pages instead of just a whole bunch of unmanageable objects.

First, we need to make a small adjustment to our `RentalPropertyService` interface. We will add the following method to retrieve a page of properties:

```
Page<RentalPropertyDTO> getPagedProperties(
    int page, int size);
```

As you can see, it is possible to tell which page should be returned and the size of that page. Now, in the `RentalPropertyServiceJpaImpl` class, let's add a meaningful implementation of a method that can retrieve rental properties with pagination features:

```
@Override
public Page<RentalPropertyDTO> getPagedProperties(
    int page, int size) {

    final PageRequest pageable =
        PageRequest.of(page, size);

    return PageableExecutionUtils.getPage(jpaRepository
        .findAll(pageable)
        .getContent().stream()
        .map(RentalPropertyConverter::toDTO)
        .toList(), pageable, jpaRepository::count);
}
```

As you can see, this implementation makes use of the `findAll()` method from the `JpaRepository` interface. That will fetch a list of the `RentalProperty` entities we have in the database, all contained in a `Page` object. We then transform that result page into a page that contains the DTOs. This is all we need from `JpaRepository` in Spring Data to make sure we are returning data in chunks for our API users.

Because this method is declared at the `RentalService` interface level, we will also have to implement a non-supported exception in the `RentalServiceImpl` class:

```
@Override
public Page<RentalPropertyDTO> getPagedProperties(
    int page, int size) {
    throw new UnsupportedOperationException(
        "cannot retrieve a paged result " +
        "with this implementation");
}
```

This is just to ensure our project is correctly compiled. I do not want to use the implementation in the `RentalPropertyServiceImpl` class, only the one in `RentalPropertyServiceJpaImpl`.

In our `RentalPropertyController` class, we need to implement a call to our `RentalPropertyService` interface:

```
@GetMapping(produces = "application/json")
public ResponseEntity<Page<RentalPropertyDTO>>
    getAllProperties(
        @RequestParam(defaultValue = "0") int page,
        @RequestParam(defaultValue = "10") int size
) {
    return ResponseEntity.ok()
        .body(rentalPropertyService
          .getPagedProperties(page, size));
}
```

As you can see, it is fairly simple to add a paginated endpoint. You can then fire GET requests to `http://localhost:8080/api/v1/rental-properties` and specify how many elements should be included in the page, and which page should be retrieved. We will look at that shortly, as we still have one simple thing to fix in our sample project.

Using multiple service implementations on your application

Now that we have properly coded the `RentalPropertyServiceJpaImpl` class, which is a service that implements `RentalPropertyService` and uses `JpaRepository` behind the scenes to connect to your database, let's use this new implementation class on our `RentalPropertyController` class.

Remember: in Spring's framework philosophy, a service implementation should always inject another interface, and Spring should look for the implementation classes automatically.

Here is a fact that demonstrates this. In our code, `RentalPropertyServiceJpaImpl` injects `RentalPropertyJpaRepository`, which is just an interface that extends `JpaRepository`. Spring is able to provide the `JpaRepository` implementation for you at runtime. In fact, the class that implements `JpaRepository` is called `SimpleJpaRepository`. It is totally possible to find that class source and learn how Spring Data works behind the scenes. This is all done for you by using the Spring Beans management we talked about in the previous chapters.

Now, we have the following situation. `RentalPropertyService` has two implementation classes:

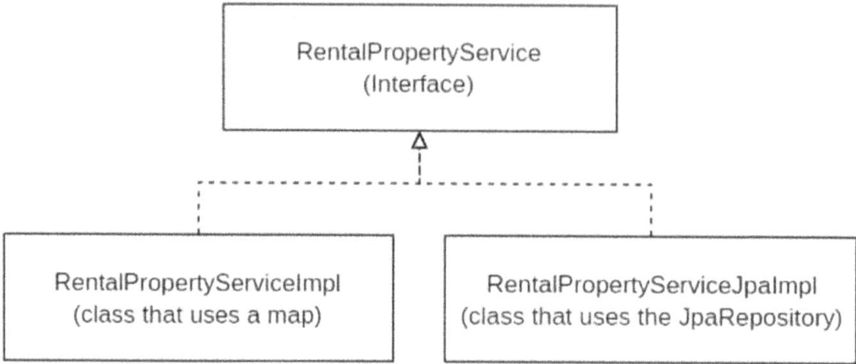

Figure 7.7: A service interface with two implementations

Our `RentalPropertyController` class, on the other hand, injected a reference for the `RentalPropertyService` interface, remember? Here is a recap. This is the code of the V1 API:

```
public class RentalPropertyController {

    private final RentalPropertyService
        rentalPropertyService;
// ... other existing code
}
```

And this is the code of the V2 API:

```
public class RentalPropertyControllerV2 {

    private final RentalPropertyService
        rentalPropertyService;
    private final RentalPropertyHyperMediaUtils
        rentalPropertyHyperMediaUtils;
// ... other existing code
}
```

As we stated before, Spring will try to find the implementation class for that interface. What will happen when we run this code?

The answer is: we cannot run this code since we have not made it clear to Spring which implementation should be used as a bean for the `RentalPropertiesService` interface references in both classes. Since we have now made our bean injection ambiguous, we need to use some special syntax to specify which implementations Spring should use, and where.

Here is the output of the error we get if we try to run the RentalProperties API without changing the way we declare our beans:

```
Parameter 0 of constructor in [...].controller.
RentalPropertyController required a single bean, but 2 were found:
- rentalPropertyServiceImpl: defined in file [.../
RentalPropertyServiceImpl.class]
- rentalPropertyServiceJpaImpl: defined in file [.../
RentalPropertyServiceJpaImpl.class]
This may be due to missing parameter name information
```

Now, this project is just composed of some classes with different approaches for the *Service* layer. We could just delete the `RentalPropertyServiceImpl` class, right? After all, this is an implementation that uses an in-memory HashMap. All should be good once we delete it.

But what if we need multiple beans that implement the same service interface in different ways? That will make sense in the following sections, as we implement other ways to access our database (and we will implement the search feature).

Using @Qualifier to inject multiple bean implementations for the same service

It is not uncommon to need two implementations of the same service interfaces in big Spring projects, especially if you are optimizing your implementation or changing how things work behind the scenes. Here, we will inject two references for the same `RentalPropertyService` interface, but one of the implementations is the old one, the one that uses the hashmap as a repository. The other implementation will use the SQL database as a repository. We will create other implementations in a few minutes.

The key to injecting different implementations for the same service lies in the `@Qualifier` annotation, which goes in a few places:

- In the service implementation classes themselves so that we give a name to our Spring bean

- In the constructor of the class that will inject the beans

This is how we declare the `@Qualifier` annotation on top of our `RentalProperty` implementation classes:

```
@Service
@Qualifier("hashMapRentalPropertyService")
public class RentalPropertyServiceImpl
```

```
        implements RentalPropertyService {
// ... other service code
}
@Service
@Qualifier("jpaRentalPropertyService")
public class RentalPropertyServiceJpaImpl implements
RentalPropertyService{
// ... other service code
}
```

As you can see, now we have added two names or aliases for the conflicting service implementation classes.

The next step is to declare those beans with their respective qualifiers in the constructor of the class you want to use your beans:

```
@RestController
@RequestMapping("/api/v1/rental-properties")
@Validated
public class RentalPropertyController {

    private final RentalPropertyService
        mapRentalPropertyService;

    private final RentalPropertyService
        jpaRentalPropertyService;

    public RentalPropertyController(
        @Qualifier("hashMapRentalPropertyService")
            RentalPropertyService mapRentalPropertyService,
        @Qualifier("jpaRentalPropertyService")
            RentalPropertyService jpaRentalPropertyService)
    {
        this.mapRentalPropertyService =
            mapRentalPropertyService;
        this.jpaRentalPropertyService =
            jpaRentalPropertyService;
    }
// ... other code
}
```

And this is the V2 implementation:

```
@RestController
@RequestMapping("/api/v2/rental-properties")
```

```
@Validated
public class RentalPropertyControllerV2 {

    private final RentalPropertyHyperMediaUtils
        rentalPropertyHyperMediaUtils;
    private final RentalPropertyService
        mapRentalPropertyService;
    private final RentalPropertyService
        jpaRentalPropertyService;

    public RentalPropertyControllerV2(
        @Qualifier("hashMapRentalPropertyService")
            RentalPropertyService mapRentalPropertyService,
        @Qualifier("jpaRentalPropertyService")
            RentalPropertyService jpaRentalPropertyService,
        RentalPropertyHyperMediaUtils
            rentalPropertyHyperMediaUtils)
    {
        this.rentalPropertyHyperMediaUtils =
            rentalPropertyHyperMediaUtils;
        this.mapRentalPropertyService =
            mapRentalPropertyService;
        this.jpaRentalPropertyService =
            jpaRentalPropertyService;
    }
```

With those changes, it is now possible to reference the services you want on both controllers. I basically switched my implementation in both controllers to use `jpaRentalPropertyService` from now on. You can see the fully implemented classes in the GitHub repository.

Now, the question that I would like to invite you to think about is: how does the `JpaRepository` interface do its magic? What other services does its implementation rely on?

`JpaRepository` is implemented by a class called `SimpleJpaRepository`, which in turn injects a bean named `EntityManager`, which is a low-level interface that allows you to have fine-grained control over your objects. You can just see the code for all those classes using your favorite IDE (I recommend IntelliJ for navigating Spring code with ease).

If `JpaRepository` is too high level, what about the underlying `EntityManager` interface? Let's see how it works.

How does EntityManager work?

`EntityManager` is a core interface in JPA that manages the lifecycle of entities within a persistence context. It provides an abstraction for performing **Create**, **Read**, **Update**, and **Delete** (**CRUD**) operations and facilitates the interaction between the application and the database.

`EntityManager` is responsible for ensuring that the state of entities is synchronized with the underlying database. It provides fine-grained control over transactions, caching, and query execution, making it essential for advanced data access operations in JPA-based applications.

Here is a list of important methods implemented by the `EntityManager` bean, which you can inject wherever you want in your applications:

- `persist(Object entity)`: Persists a new entity instance into the database
- `merge(Object entity)`: Updates an existing object in the database
- `remove(Object entity)`: Removes an entity instance from the database
- `find(Class<T> entityClass, Object primaryKey)`: Finds an entity by its primary key
- `createQuery(String qlString)`: Creates a JPQL query to retrieve entities based on specified criteria
- `createNamedQuery(String name)`: Creates a named query defined in the entity class
- `createNativeQuery(String sqlString)`: Creates a native SQL query for database-specific operations
- `getTransaction()`: Retrieves the `EntityTransaction` object to manage transactions manually
- `flush()`: Forces pushing all persistence changes to the underlying database
- `clear()`: Clears the persistence context, detaching all managed entities.
- `detach(Object entity)`: Detaches an entity from the persistence context
- `refresh(Object entity)`: Refreshes the state of the entity from the database
- `getCriteriaBuilder()`: Obtains an instance of `CriteriaBuilder` for creating criteria queries

The `EntityManager` service has an important feature that tracks the changes you make to your object and synchronizes them automatically in the database. That happens if you change your objects inside the context of a transaction, which we are going to see in the next section.

Working with transactions in Spring Data

A **transaction**, as you probably know, is the context in which a sequence of changes to a database counts as just one atomic operation, meaning they cannot be sent separately to your database and cannot be interrupted by concurrent operations, in general. They are executed in one batch, and only after the final result is calculated are they all considered executed and the results available for other concurrent queries.

There are two main ways to manage a transaction using Spring Data.

Using the @Transactional annotation in a method

You can declare whatever methods you want in your classes to be considered transactions. Basically, tag the desired method with the `@Transactional` annotation, and everything that is enclosed by the method will be considered a part of a transactional context.

Here is a simple example. This makes the `update` method of `RentalServiceJpaImpl` a full transaction:

```java
@Override
@Transactional
public Optional<RentalPropertyDTO> update(UUID id,
    RentalPropertyDTO updatedProperty) {

    if(jpaRepository.existsById(id)) {
        return Optional.ofNullable(
            RentalPropertyConverter.toDTO(
                jpaRepository.save(RentalPropertyConverter
                    .toEntity(updatedProperty))));
    }

    return Optional.empty();
}
```

Again, if you have several updates to execute on your database and you want to guarantee that all of those operations are executed in the same step for data consistency reasons, you probably want all of those operations to be transactional. Just move all of them to a single service method and declare the method to be `@Transactional`.

There are several important parameters for the `@Transactional` annotation that allow you to explore the nuances of transaction management. You can look in the Spring docs to see the variants. Let's see the other way of declaring a transaction in Spring Data.

Managing transactions by using the EntityManager bean

Since the `EntityManager` bean is one of the core beans for managing database connections and queries at a low level, you can inject it into any service by using the `@PersistenceContext` annotation on your beans, and if you use that annotation, it is possible to use the `@Transactional` annotation on your methods as well to define which ones should be considered a part of a single transaction.

You can also manually manage a transaction using the `EntityManager` bean. Just use the following resources:

- Inject the `EntityManagerFactory` class into your service

- Create the `EntityManager` reference using the factory, whenever you need a transaction to start

The following methods are a part of the `EntityManager` interface:

- `getTransaction().begin()`: Starts a transaction

- `getTransaction().commit()`: Commits a transaction to the database, finalizing it

- `getTransaction().rollback()`: Rolls back the transaction (great to use if you find an error during the execution of the instructions, such as an exception or some business logic that tells you the transaction should be aborted)

It is as simple as that. Let's see how that is done. Remember, we need to use `@Qualifier` here as well to identify this implementation:

```
@Service
@Qualifier("entityManagerRentalPropertyService")
public class RentalPropertyServiceEntityManagerImpl
    implements RentalPropertyService{

    private EntityManagerFactory entityManagerFactory;

    public RentalPropertyServiceEntityManagerImpl
        (EntityManagerFactory entityManagerFactory) {
        this.entityManagerFactory = entityManagerFactory;
    }
// ... other methods
}
```

This is how we inject the `EntityManagerFactory` into your bean when manually managing transactions.

This is a method by which we use manual transaction handling with an `EntityManager` bean:

```
@Override
public Optional<RentalPropertyDTO> delete(UUID id) {
    EntityManager entityManager =
        entityManagerFactory
            .createEntityManager();
    EntityTransaction transaction =
        entityManager.getTransaction();

    RentalPropertyDTO dto;
    try {
        transaction.begin();

        RentalProperty property =
            entityManager.find(RentalProperty.class, id);

        dto = RentalPropertyConverter.toDTO(property);
        entityManager.remove(property);
        transaction.commit();

    } catch (Exception e) {
        if (transaction.isActive()) {
            transaction.rollback();
        }
        throw e;
    } finally {
        entityManager.close();
    }

    return Optional.ofNullable(dto);
}
```

The important highlights are as follows:

- We are creating a new `EntityManager` reference using the factory

- Then, we create the transaction and commit it or roll it back, depending on the results we get from the database operation

- Finally, we need to close the `entityManager` instance

This is how you can easily move down to a finer-grained control of your transactions. I have used this very successfully to make the speed of a legacy batch processor 100 times faster (no kidding) just because other developers did not do a proper job of analyzing how the batch service was recording data, managing the connections, and tracking the commit times. I also implemented an ACID transaction in place, which guaranteed the data integrity.

Now, let's go over another important subject. What if you need to run raw SQL queries on your database? When high performance is a must, you can use the `JdbcTemplate` repository, which we'll see in the next section.

Using NamedParameterJdbcTemplate to run raw SQL queries

`JdbcTemplate` is a core component of the Spring Framework's JDBC module that is designed to simplify database interactions by providing a high-level abstraction over the standard JDBC API. This feature eliminates much of the boilerplate code required for managing connections, executing queries, and handling exceptions.

It provides convenient methods for common database operations such as querying, updating, and batch processing, which allows you to focus on business logic rather than the intricacies of JDBC.

Although allowing very low-level control over your SQL queries, it imposes a high risk to your service if you do not use it wisely: it can actually create a window for SQL injection, which is a security flaw in which an attacker does not send the data you expect, but instead sends whatever SQL commands they want so that your queries will just run arbitrary code.

Because `JdbcTemplate` is so risky to use, I recommend using the `NamedParameterJdbcTemplate` bean instead. The only meaningful change from `JdbcTemplate` is that Spring will take care of guaranteeing that the query input is regular data, not a random SQL-injected query.

`NamedParameterJdbcTemplate` and `JdbcTemplate` should both be used when you need a straightforward, efficient, and lightweight solution for interacting with relational databases in a Spring application. Both are particularly useful in scenarios where JPA/Hibernate might be overkill, such as simple CRUD operations, batch processing, or when working with legacy databases.

JdbcTemplate is ideal for applications that require precise control over SQL queries and transactions without the overhead of an ORM framework. It provides flexibility, performance, and simplicity, making it the preferred choice for developers who need to execute custom SQL and manage database interactions programmatically.

As an example, I have created another implementation for `RentalPropertyService`, which now uses `NamedParameterJdbcTemplate` as a repository. This time, the only method I will implement is the `search()` method. All the other ones will throw an `UnsupportedOperationException` because they are all implemented in the `RentalPropertyServiceJpaImpl` bean.

Here is an example of the search method in `RentalPropertyServiceJdbcImpl`. This is how I inject the `NamedParameterJdbcTemplate` repository (I am also using `@Qualifier` to identify this implementation):

```
@Service
@Qualifier("jdbcRentalPropertyService")
public class RentalPropertyServiceJdbcImpl implements
RentalPropertyService{

    private final NamedParameterJdbcTemplate jdbcTemplate;

    public RentalPropertyServiceJdbcImpl(
        NamedParameterJdbcTemplate jdbcTemplate) {
            this.jdbcTemplate = jdbcTemplate;
    }
    // .... other methods
}
```

This is the search method implementation:

```
@Override
public List<RentalPropertyDTO> search(String name, String address,
String city, String country, String zipCode) {
    StringBuilder sql = new StringBuilder("SELECT * FROM rental_
properties WHERE 1=1");
    MapSqlParameterSource params =
        new MapSqlParameterSource();

    if (StringUtils.hasText(name)) {
        sql.append(" AND name LIKE :name");
        params.addValue("name", "%" + name + "%");
    }
    if (StringUtils.hasText(address)) {
        sql.append(" AND address LIKE :address");
        params.addValue("address", "%" + address + "%");
    }
    if (StringUtils.hasText(city)) {
        sql.append(" AND address LIKE :city");
        params.addValue("city", "%" + city + "%");
    }
    if (StringUtils.hasText(country)) {
        sql.append(" AND address LIKE :country");
        params.addValue("country", "%" + country + "%");
    }
```

```
if (StringUtils.hasText(zipCode)) {
    sql.append(" AND address LIKE :zipCode");
    params.addValue("zipCode", "%" + zipCode + "%");
}


return jdbcTemplate.query(
    sql.toString(), params, rentalPropertyRowMapper);
}
```

As you can see, I am using a simple `LIKE` operator to find out parts of the actual text in my `Address` column. That is because the H2 implementation does not support native Postgres `jsonb` fields. When you move to a real database, you can use the `->>` operator or whatever other JSON-specific search operators your database supports. `JdbcTemplate` and `NamedParameterJdbcTemplate` are both classes that help you to go native when interfacing with your database. But, again, this should be used with caution, since it removes the possibility of a transparent, painless database migration in the future. It is up to you, your team, and the company to decide how native or low-level you should go. If you really need to optimize your code, do that only in the methods that need to be improved.

Here's some background info: the text search features in Postgres make high-performance queries, queries that are almost as performant as the Elasticsearch database queries. But you could really drive home your design if you wanted to keep two different microservices, one of them for allowing full-text search, using Elasticsearch. You could set your system design in such a way that whatever changes happen on your microservice that keeps the registration of the rental properties, the search microservice would be notified and then would update its own version of that rental property data. We will see some of that when we talk about event-driven architecture.

Referencing all the implementations we have done so far

Now, let's use all these implementations in our V1 `RentalPropertyController`:

```
@RestController
@RequestMapping("/api/v1/rental-properties")
@Validated
public class RentalPropertyController {

    private final RentalPropertyService
        jpaRentalPropertyService;

    private final RentalPropertyService
        jdbcRentalPropertyService;

    private final RentalPropertyService
        entityManagerRentalPropertyService;
```

```
    public RentalPropertyController(
        @Qualifier("jpaRentalPropertyService")
            RentalPropertyService jpaRentalPropertyService,

        @Qualifier("jdbcRentalPropertyService")
            RentalPropertyService
                jdbcRentalPropertyService,

        @Qualifier("entityManagerRentalPropertyService")
            RentalPropertyService
                entityManagerRentalPropertyService) {

        this.jpaRentalPropertyService =
            jpaRentalPropertyService;

        this.jdbcRentalPropertyService =
            jdbcRentalPropertyService;

        this.entityManagerRentalPropertyService =
            entityManagerRentalPropertyService;
    }

// ... other code
}
```

This is where we used the `EntityManager` implementation:

```
@DeleteMapping("/{id}")
public ResponseEntity<Void> deleteProperty(@PathVariable UUID id) {
    return entityManagerRentalPropertyService
        .delete(id)
        .map(opt ->
            ResponseEntity.noContent()
                .<Void>build())
        .orElse(ResponseEntity
            .status(HttpStatus.NOT_FOUND).build());
}
```

This is where we used the JDBC implementation:

```
@GetMapping(
    value = "/search",
    produces = "application/json")
public ResponseEntity<List<RentalPropertyDTO>> searchProperties(
```

```
    @RequestParam(required = false) String name,
    @RequestParam(required = false) String address,
    @RequestParam(required = false) String city,
    @RequestParam(required = false) String country,
    @RequestParam(required = false) String zipCode) {

return ResponseEntity.ok(
    jdbcRentalPropertyService.search(
        name, address, city, country, zipCode));
}
```

After all this refactoring, there are a few interesting things we can extract from creating interface implementations in Spring:

- First, we can mix and match different implementations for the same interface in the same microservice.

- By mixing and matching implementations, you can optimize your microservices as you go. Start small, in an unoptimized way, then improve your application by including optimized implementations for your service interfaces. That works for data, but it also works in other contexts. For example, if you feel your microservice is becoming a lot bigger than it should, you can export the implementation of some services to another microservice. Then, include a new implementation for that service interface in the old microservice, which delegates a remote call to the new microservice.

- With the use of the @Qualifier annotation, it is possible to never touch the implementation classes directly when using them – you just deal with the service interface, whatever implementation you are injecting. That means your code will always comply with your original service interfaces. This is an awesome way of guaranteeing your contracts. Plus, if your service interface changes, the Java compiler will require you to update all the implementation classes, which makes things much more consistent.

- Your interface implementations do not need to support all the methods from the service interfaces. It is OK to leave some methods unsupported so that you can just deliver the methods you want to optimize in the new implementations.

- We have just seen a way to support all kinds of connectivity types to your database in the same application. And you do not even need to care about the real database connection. How cool is that?

- When it is time to deploy your application to real environments, we will just add configuration files so that they override our default options and new connections are made to other database instances without you having to touch the code. We will see how that is done as we proceed in the next chapters.

- For the most part, your class can connect to any SQL database. If you move from Postgres to Oracle, you only need to rewrite the `/search` endpoint implementation, since it's the only one in which you want to use specific, optimized, database-native syntax. Think about how great this is for upgrading your infrastructure in the future.

- Some developers will ask "why are you leaving blunt `OperationNotSupported` exceptions on your service implementations? You can use a fallback strategy that proxies the calls to other implementations, right?" That is possible, but if you do that, you might confuse other developers. It won't be as apparent when your implementation does not support a method. I'd rather have an outright exception being thrown so the lack of support is clear to everyone.

OK, now that we have seen a lot of flexible ways to deal with your SQL data, let's test it all, shall we?

Testing your applications with data integration

This is where having a clear integrated test suite will help you a lot. The automated tests we have written in previous chapters will not change too much. We basically need to add a properties file to our `test` folder so that it follows the same H2 strategy and creates an in-memory database for you to query against:

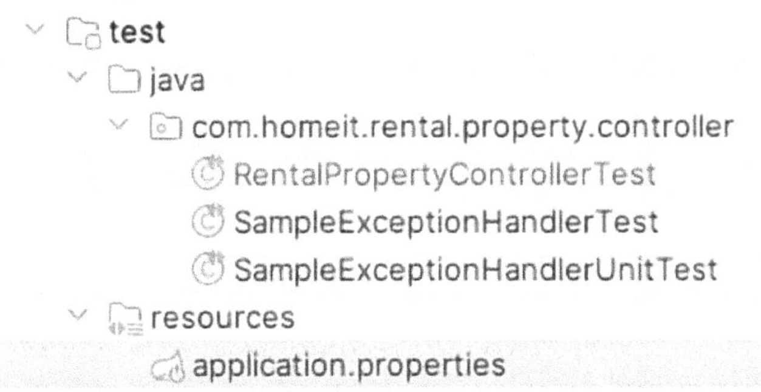

Figure 7.8: Location of the application.properties config file

Here is the content of the `application.properties` file:

```
## H2 Database configuration in PostgreSQL mode
spring.datasource.url=jdbc:h2:mem:testdb;DB_CLOSE_DELAY=-
1;MODE=PostgreSQL
spring.datasource.driverClassName=org.h2.Driver
spring.datasource.username=sampleuser
spring.datasource.password=samplepass
spring.jpa.database-platform=org.hibernate.dialect.H2Dialect
spring.h2.console.enabled=true
```

```
spring.h2.console.path=/h2-console
spring.jpa.hibernate.ddl-auto=create
spring.jpa.show-sql=true
```

Here is the code that changed in the `RentalPropertyControllerTest` class (`https://github.com/PacktPublishing/Spring-System-Design-in-Practice/blob/main/chapter-07/rental-property-microservice/src/test/java/com/homeit/rental/property/controller/RentalPropertyControllerTest.java`):

```
@Test
void testGetAllProperties() throws Exception {
    mockMvc.perform(
        get("/api/v1/rental-properties?page=1&size=2")
        .contentType("application/json"))
        .andExpect(status().isOk())
        .andExpect(jsonPath("$.pageable.pageNumber").value(1))
        .andExpect(jsonPath("$.content[*].name").exists())
        .andExpect(jsonPath("$.pageable.pageSize").value(2))
    ;
}
```

The `testGetAllProperties()` method will now look for pages, one at a time. The JSON returned is actually a bit more complex as it fetches page metadata as well, not just the original object. You might consider making the paged endpoint a part of another version of your API since this change could break HTTP clients that expect the older format.

You just need to run the `gradle test` command to make sure your microservice is correctly communicating with your database. You can see the final implementation of our test classes on GitHub (`https://github.com/PacktPublishing/Spring-System-Design-in-Practice/tree/main/chapter-07/rental-property-microservice/src/test/java/com/homeit/rental/property/controller`).

And, of course, we can also test the H2 database. If we run our service with the `gradle bootRun` command, you will be able to connect to your H2 database and see the exact tables and types that have been created. You will have a full SQL console, connected to your H2 in-memory database. That helps with a lot of triaging issues. This is what happens when you connect to `http://localhost:8080/h2-console` with `sampleuser/samplepass`:

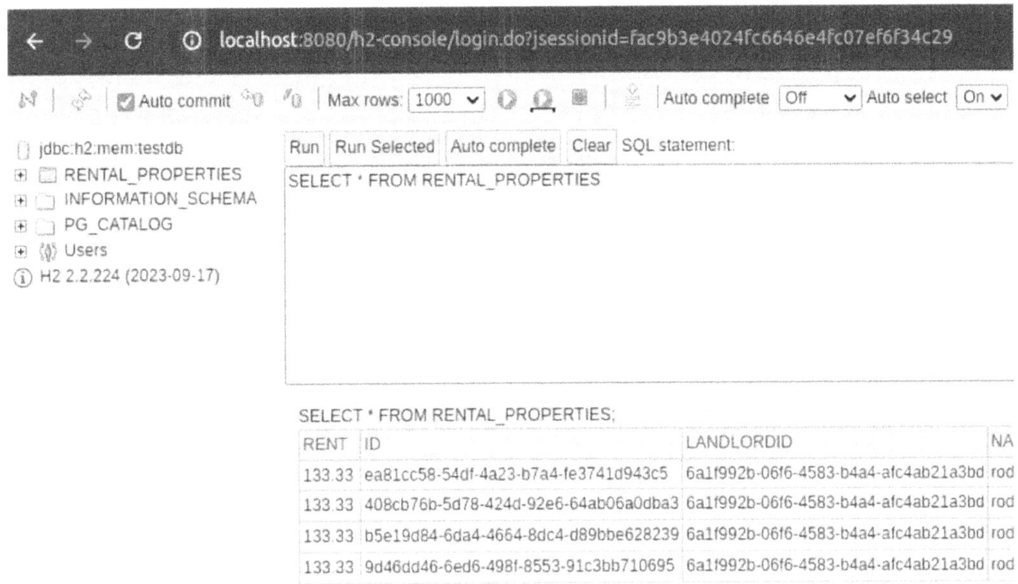

Figure 7.9: Running an H2 SQL query

There are also great ways to test pre-made datasets. We will see that in future chapters, as we proceed with more sophisticated use cases and interactions between microservices.

Summary

In this chapter, we have seen the way to handle data on your services. Although the examples here were all tied to SQL databases, Spring Data provides similar approaches for all major databases. We will look at non-SQL implementations as well throughout the book. But, in essence, the basic template will be found in the extensions for other databases: you need to add the dependency for supporting the other database, then look for which repository types you have available. Some repositories will be more high-level, providing a lot of stuff out-of-the-box for you to use (just as `JpaRepository` did). Other repositories will provide more low-level options for you to have finer control over the way you interact with your database.

In the next chapter, we will switch gears to talk more about security issues and how to properly implement access control to your application. That is it for this chapter. See you in *Chapter 8*!

Get This Book's PDF Version and Exclusive Extras

Scan the QR code (or go to `packtpub.com/unlock`). Search for this book by name, confirm the edition, and then follow the steps on the page.

Note: Keep your invoice handly. Purchase made directly from packt don't require one.

Part 3: Security, Performance, and Scalability

Building a service is just the beginning. This part explores how to secure applications using Spring Security and OAuth 2.0, optimize communication between microservices, and ensure high performance at scale. We'll also introduce event-driven architectures and NoSQL databases to help services react asynchronously to changing data.

This part has the following chapters:

- *Chapter 8, Securing Services with Spring Security and OAuth 2.0*
- *Chapter 9, High-Performance and Secure Communication Between Spring Services*
- *Chapter 10, Building Asynchronous, Event-Driven Systems with NoSQL Databases*

8

Securing Services with Spring Security and OAuth 2.0

Welcome to *Chapter 8*! In this chapter, we will discuss important aspects of user authentication and authorization. There is a world of things we could do in Spring to secure our services, but we will take just a key approach here that is widely used today: the combination of OAuth 2.0 and JWT tokens.

Here are the topics we'll cover:

- Understanding the security areas in your application
- What is OAuth 2.0 and why use it?
- Understanding how JWT tokens work
- Different architectures for validating tokens
- Implementing HomeIt security

We will start by taking a strategic view of the possible vulnerabilities a typical microservice architecture brings. Then, we will proceed by discussing OAuth 2.0 and different ways of providing authentication and authorization. We will also dive deep into the structure of JWTs and how signatures are made. Finally, we will implement these concepts by writing a sample authorization server and adding features to our **Rental Properties** service for validating JWT tokens in an interesting way.

Are you ready? Let's go!

Understanding the security areas in your application

The first thing we need to do to create secure services is to understand the big picture and the main vulnerability spots. Since this book is mostly about creating microservice architectures, let's first understand the microservice landscape itself. The following diagram illustrates it:

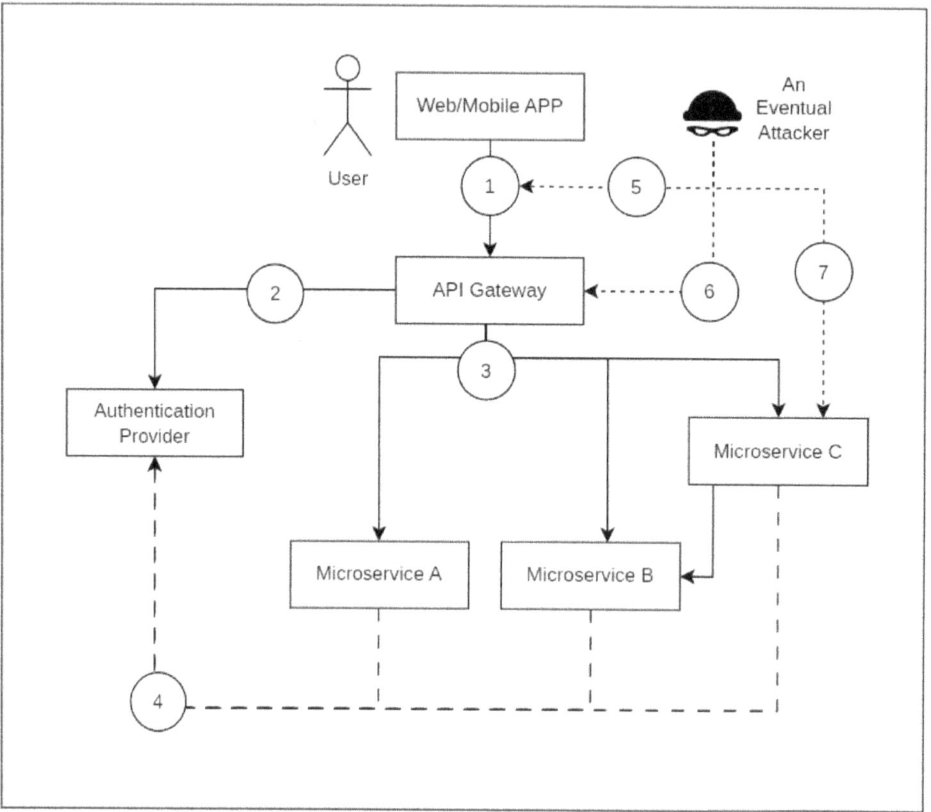

Figure 8.1: Microservice architecture

This diagram simplifies most of the microservice architectures today. The numbers in the diagram represent the following:

1. The user will almost always interact with a client app (it could be through a mobile app or a browser), and the app, in turn, will interact with what we call an API gateway. The API gateway is the entry point for interacting with other microservices.

2. The client app will start the app session by authenticating the user through a service called the **authentication provider (auth provider)**. There are numerous ways of implementing an auth provider, which we will see shortly. A successful authentication process will produce a string that we call the **JWT security token**, which we will see in detail shortly.

3. Once the user is authenticated, every request to one of the microservices will be secured by the JWT token. In other words, every time the client app needs to use some of the app microservices, it needs to send the security token in an HTTP header, along with the request data (payload, headers, URLs, etc.). The API gateway will also forward the token to the microservices.

4. Upon receiving a request, all microservices must receive a token and be able to go back to the auth provider to ask whether the security token is still valid. That will make sure the user is authenticated. Also, the microservice needs to assert that the user is authorized to perform the current request. A regular user (let's say a tenant, in the HomeIt system) might try to perform an admin-level operation, for example, trying to delete a landlord user, which should not be allowed, even if the user is correctly authenticated. The security token can also inform the microservices about the user access levels.

5. An eventual attacker could try to spy on the user's connection. To prevent such attacks, we need to make sure every connection from an app to the API gateway is performed through an HTTPS tunnel. That means all data will be encrypted, and only the client app and the servers will be able to unencrypt it.

6. The attacker could try to perform requests to the API gateway on behalf of the user, which means the system needs to be prepared to filter out such requests, by using **Cross-Site Request Forgery** (**CSRF**) and **Cross-Origin Resource Sharing** (**CORS**) configurations that mitigate those attempts.

7. The attacker might try to access the data stored in the service itself, such as local filesystems and databases. In that case, it is important to implement encryption for data at rest, so that if the attacker can access the server by a terminal, for example, it is still not possible to understand the data, due to strong encryption mechanisms.

Next, let's discover how to secure our application with the use of the OAuth 2.0 standard.

What is OAuth 2.0 and why use it?

You might have heard of OAuth 2.0 before, and there is a lot of material available online about it, but it can be cumbersome and confusing to developers, so I will explain it in very simple terms here. In essence, this is a powerful standard for user authentication and authorization on your applications. **OAuth** stands for **Open Authorization**. It is an authorization architecture and standard fully defined in the RFC-6749 of the **Internet Engineering Task Force** (**IETF**) organization. The RFCs are documents specifying how different internet standards should work; IETF is the community in charge of maintaining those documents today. Our example will be compliant with version 2.0 of the OAuth specification.

The OAuth 2.0 specification is especially important for allowing one system to access resources in another system. The following scenarios are good examples of OAuth 2.0-enabled applications.

Use case 1 – system A accesses system B-owned resources

Imagine you create an app that can access documents hosted on a user's own Google Drive, on the user's behalf. That requires your app to forward the user to a special Google URL where they will be able to log in to their Google account and give the app permission to access their documents. Then, the user will be sent back to your app, which can now access the user's personal documents stored in a Google Drive folder.

The following diagram illustrates this scenario. The numbers dictate the order of the flows:

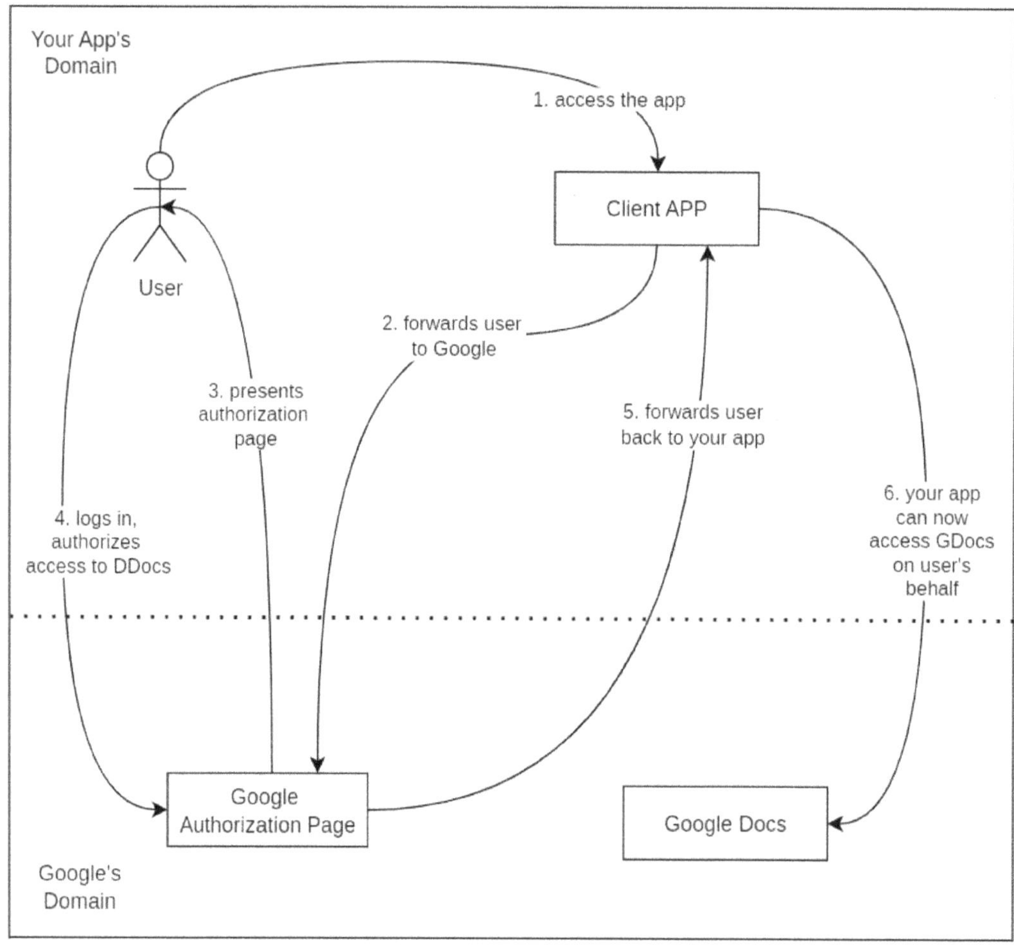

Figure 8.2 – OAuth 2.0 cross-domain authentication

The way it works is Google authorizes your application through the app's own credentials (which we call the client ID and client secret credentials), then authorizes the user login and forwards a special token to your application that your app can use in every request to retrieve data from Google Docs itself.

This is a powerful pattern that leads to a lot of interesting use cases. One of them is to allow registering a new user in system A by having the user authorize themself on system B. In other words, we could register a new user in our HomeIt system by basically requiring the user to authenticate themself on Google's website.

The second case for OAuth 2.0 is simpler.

Use case 2 – system A accesses its own resources

Take a look at the following systems flow diagram. This adds more detail on how the tokens and authorizations flow from one service to the other:

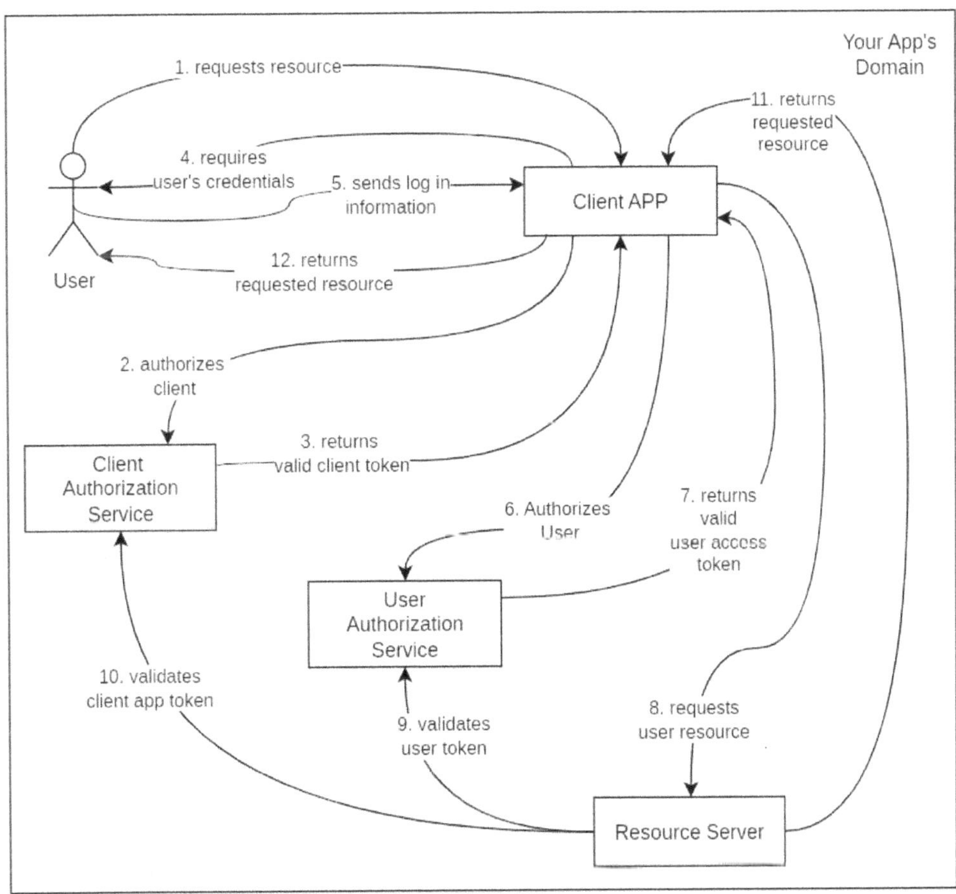

Figure 8.3 – OAuth authentication

It is good to highlight that in OAuth 2.0, both your client application and your users will have to properly validate their own credentials. In total, we might have two sets of tokens. Existing systems today implement this pattern with some slight variations, such as the following:

- Discarding the need for a client application token, but still requiring the client ID and secret, along with the user credentials (username and password). That combination will collapse the client authorization service and the user authorization service together, which is not always a good idea since the client ID and secret validation should not be coupled with the user's own credentials.

- Entirely discarding the client ID and secret, and just using the user/password credentials to generate the user token to access your application resources.

Although I was able to find a lot of applications by different companies that are not in line with OAuth 2.0 standards (you would be surprised by how many can be found), it is not advisable to omit steps in your application, for various security reasons.

On another note, in our first example including Google authorization (*Figure 8.2*), the user and client authorization services are omitted from our diagram. But they are still present in our Google system implementation. You will always need to provide your app ID and secret to interact with Google authentication. I removed them from the first diagram so that it would be easier to grasp the flow.

Let's now discover what types of services OAuth 2.0 proposes in an authentication/authorization system.

Basic service types in OAuth 2.0

According to the OAuth 2.0 specification, there are some critical system functions that need to be in place for us to have enough security in an authentication system. Without these, some important functions could be missed and your application will be more vulnerable to malicious attacks.

The OAuth specification proposes the following service types:

- **Resource owner**: The system that has ownership of the resources you need to access. In the first example, Google is the owner of the documents you need to access. The end user is also considered a resource owner, as they are the sole proprietor and have the right to say when the document can be accessed (this is why they usually hold a user credential, such as a password or an authorization token). In the second example, your application is the resource owner.

- **Authorization servers**: These services are responsible for issuing access tokens that tell your application that your user has successfully authenticated themselves.

- **Client application**: This is the application used to allow users to log in and interact with your resource services. It is important to distinguish your clients because OAuth 2.0 will only permit login attempts from authorized client applications.

- **Resource providers**: These are one or more services that provide important business domain objects to your customers. In other words, any API that implements critical product requirements is considered a resource provider. For instance, think about our Rental Property API. This is a valuable resource that should only be accessible through the proper security filters (a valid client token and a user token).

Now, many of these providers are offered in enterprise vendors and open source projects. Let's see how they fit into our overall picture.

Industry-grade authorization providers

There are quite a few offerings in the industry that will allow you to integrate ready-to-use identity providers with your Spring application and microservices. Some of these are Keycloak, Auth0, Okta, Amazon Cognito, and Google Identity Platform. They come with a lot of strengths and weaknesses.

In this chapter, though, we will implement a sample authorization mechanism by solely using Spring Security. You can replace the authorization provider here with whatever other providers you might want in the future. Remember, the key to Spring services is to design interfaces in such a way that you can just replace the implementations with whatever new services and infrastructure you want.

Understanding how JWTs work

The OAuth 2.0 standard does not enforce any kind of security token implementation. Because of that, it is up to you, as an architect, to choose how to create and validate tokens.

There are many ways of implementing security tokens, such as JWT, PASETO, macaroons, CBOR Web Tokens, and Hawk. Because JWT is the most used, we will use it in this chapter. But bear in mind that you can find other token specifications on the web, should you desire to switch from JWT (you can google the ones I just mentioned).

The other token specifications have different ways of implementing flows, which we won't be able to cover here. But in general, they try to address the authorization challenges with different assumptions. In this chapter, we will cover most of the criticisms of JWT as well, so don't worry, we will be able to see how to use JWT properly. Since this is a well-established standard and the Spring implementation is exceptionally reliable and battle-tested, let's follow the JWT token specs in this chapter.

JWT refers to a token created out of a JSON structure that reveals specific data about authenticated users. This standard was defined by the RFC-7519 of the IETF organization. You can read the full specification here: `https://datatracker.ietf.org/doc/html/rfc7519`.

A JWT token is essentially a string containing three parts separated by a dot, like this:

AAAAAAAAAAAAA.BBBBBBBBBBBBB.CCCCCCCCCCCC

| HEADER | PAYLOAD | SIGNATURE |

Figure 8.4 – JWT token structure

The first thing you should know is that each part is a Base64-encoded JSON string. Next, let's see an explanation of each section of the token.

The JWT header

The first section of a JWT token is the header, which contains the type of token and the encryption signing algorithm that was used. Here is an example:

```
{
  "alg": "HS256",
  "typ": "JWT"
}
```

To create the first part of the token, we apply Base64 encoding, which turns this sample header into the following string:

```
eyAiYWxnIjogIkhTMjU2IiwgInR5cCI6ICJKV1QiIH0g
```

The JWT payload

The second section of a JWT token is what we call the payload, or the additional application data. The data is usually about the user and the token generation itself. It is also called a claim, referring to some permission this token claims the user has.

Here is an example of a JWT payload:

```
{
  "iss": https://auth.homeit.com,       // who generated the jwt
  "sub": "user123",                     // the user id
  "exp": 1716242622,                    // token expiration
  "iat": 1616239022,                    // token generation time
  "name": "John Doe",                   // user name
  "email": john.doe@example.com,        // user email
  "groups": [                           // groups user belongs to
    "tenant"
  ],
  "permissions": {                      // set of permissions
```

```
  "rental_search": [           // service name
    "read"                     // access level
  ],
  "user_info": [
    "read",
    "write"
  ]
}
```

This payload converted to Base64 will look as follows:


```
eyAKCiAgImlzcyI6IGh0dHBzOi8vYXV0aC5ob21laXQuY29tLCAvLyB0aGUgaXNzdWVyIA
oKICAic3ViIjogInVzZXIxMjMiLCAgICAgICAgICAgIC8vIHRoZSB1c2VyIGlkIAo
KICAiZXhwIjogMTcxNjI0MjYyMiwgICAgICAgICAgIC8vIHRva2VuIGV4cGlyYXRp
24gCgogICJpYXQiOiAxNjE2MjM5MDIyLCAgICAgICAgICAgLy8gdG9rZW4gZ2VuZX
JhdGlvbiB0aW1lIAoKICAibmFtZSI6ICJKb2huIERvZSIsICAgICAgICAgIC8vIHVz
ZXIgbmFtZSAKCiAgImVtYWlsIjogam9obi5kb2VAZXhhbXBsZS5jb20sICAvLyB1c2Vy
IGVtYWlsIAoKICAiZ3JvdXBzIjogWyAgICAgICAgICAgICAgIC8vIGdyb3Vwcy
B1c2VyIGJlbG9uZ3MgdG8gCgogICAgInRlbmFudCIgCgogIF0sIAoKICAicGVybWlzc2l
vbnMiOiB7ICAgICAgICAgICAgIC8vIHN1dCBvZiBwZXJtaXNzaW9ucyAKCiAgICA
icmVudGFsX3NlYXJjaCI6IFsgICAgICAgICAgICAgICAgLy8gc2VydmljZSBuYW1l
IAoKICAgICAgInJlYWQiICAgICAgICAgICAgICAgICAgICAgICAgICAvLyBhY2Nlc3
MgbGV2ZWwgCgogICAgXSwgCgogICAgInVzZXJfaW5mbyI6IFsgCgogICAgICAicmVhZCIs
IAoKICAgICAgIndyaXRlIiAKCiAgICBdIAoKfSA=
```


The JWT signature

The third section of a JWT token ensures the integrity and authenticity of the token. It is created by signing the Base64-encoded header and payload with a secret key, using a strong cryptographic algorithm such as HS256 or RSA.

The signature allows your authorization service to verify that the token has not been tampered with and that it was issued by a trusted source. The algorithm and secret key (or private key) are crucial for the security of the JWT, as they guarantee that only the issuer (your authorization service) can generate a valid signature.

This process is essential for your authorization server to confirm that a given JWT was securely generated and is still valid.

There are a few different types of secure algorithms you can use. Here are some options:

- **HS256, HS384, or HS512**: These three algorithms are similar. They use a secret key that is used for both signing and verifying the signature. HS512 provides the highest security level. The number specifies the size of the signature, in bytes. The bigger the number, the more secure the signature is. This can be used when your authorization service generates and verifies tokens.

- **RS256, RS384, and RS512**: These three algorithms use a private key for signing signatures and a public key for verifying signatures. They can be used when you need different services to verify your JWT signatures, and you do not want to export the secret key to other servers. Again, RS512 provides the highest security level.

- **ES256, ES384, and ES512**: This is similar to RS256, which requires private and public keys to sign and verify your token, respectively. It is generally more secure than the RS algorithms, and the signature size is considerably smaller.

To sign your JWT, you will need to do the following operation:

```
Signature = SignAlgo(
            Base64(HEADER).
            Base64(PAYLOAD),
            Secret/PrivateKey)
```

This means you need to convert both your header and the payload to Base64 encoding. They are appended with a dot, and that string is passed through your chosen signature algorithm, by adding the secret or private key as the input.

Here is the final result of a JWT signature section:

```
t5fW4uC-g_0j8smuCV9WbdHZZmDWdaaj7Mu9WqmxNqEOOdDUSuGTo8U8S5t8fZCHtvMR5C
NZXj5-VxW_q5ueAw
```

This is the end result of this JWT:

```
eyJhbGciOiJIUzUxMiIsInR5cCI6IkpXVCJ9.eyJpc3MiOiJodHRwczovL2F1dGguaG9t
ZW10LmNvbSIsInN1YiI6InVzZXIxMjMiLCJleHAiOjE3MTYyNDI2MjIsImlhdCI6MTYx
NjIzOTAyMiwibmFtZSI6IkpvaG4gRG9lIiwiZW1haWwiOiJqb2huLmRvZUBleGFtcGx1
LmNvbSIsImdyb3VwcyI6WyJ0ZW5hbnQiXSwicGVybWlzc21vbnMiOnsicmVudGFsX3N1
YXJjaCI6WyJyZWFkIl0sInVzZXJfaW5mby6WyJyZWFkIiwid3JpdGUiXX19.t5fW4uC-
g_0j8smuCV9WbdHZZmDWdaaj7Mu9WqmxNqEOOdDUSuGTo8U8S5t8fZCHtvMR5CNZXj5-
VxW_q5ueAw
```

The dots separate the three sections: header, payload, and signature.

There are some different approaches you can use to validate your tokens. Let's see some variations now.

Different architectures for validating tokens

When thinking about how to validate your tokens, you need to take into consideration performance factors versus security guarantees. There is not a 100% secure system, so you need to understand where the flaws are in your architecture and plan to remediate them, in case an attacker is able to get unauthorized access.

These are some of the possibilities for creating and validating your tokens:

- **Centralized authorization service creates tokens**: All other services consult back to check token validity with the authorization service itself. This creates an overhead for validating the tokens, since an extra network request is made every time a microservice is called. Those extra network calls mean your authorization service has to deal with a very high number of requests, which puts a lot of load pressure on it. Higher security is enforced every step of the way, though.

- **Centralized authorization service creates token**: Verification happens only once per user request, upon receiving the request in the API gateway, regardless of the number of microservices reached. This reduces the load over the authorization service, since other microservices won't need to call the authorization service again. But it also leaves the door open to an attacker, where they can fire a forged request to a service that is not verifying the token, only trusting the result of the verification made somewhere else.

- **Centralized authorization service creates a token with private keys**: Other services validate requests with a public key. This takes the burden off the authorization service and allows other services to validate the tokens themselves. But now you need to deal with a distributed set of public keys.

- **Client asks for a new token on every request**: This also puts a lot of load pressure on your authorization service, but the added benefit is that a token has a shorter life, meaning an attacker that steals the token will not be able to reuse it.

This is just a head start so that you can produce your own token generation/validation ideas.

The following drawbacks apply in general to using JWTs:

- If an attacker manages to get access to your keys, you need a solid strategy for quickly revoking the keys in all involved services. That basically means every customer will be forced to log in again.

- If a token gets compromised, you should have a way of revoking that token. If your authorization service puts the valid tokens in a database, that means you can mark the token as invalid. But bear in mind that you do not need to store valid tokens in a database. The signing process (only your authorization service is supposedly able to create the token) and the token expiration time guarantee that the token is valid. If you are not storing the valid tokens, you should at least have a blacklisted tokens database. Make sure your verification process checks that database in case you want to revoke a token.

- The longer your clients can use the token, the more it will be vulnerable to attacks. Make sure your expiration is not so long that you could have an attacker using stolen tokens for days. It all depends on your use case (GitHub allows creating tokens that last forever). Just bear in mind the security risk involved and choose your expiration dates wisely.

OK, that is all we need to cover to understand JWT and all its trade-offs. Let's now move on to implementing OAuth 2.0 authentication with JWTs in Spring.

Implementing HomeIt security

When dealing with security requirements at an application level, you should probably use the Spring Security dependency to fill all the requirements we just discussed. This project has a lot of important configurations that help create a more secure set of microservices.

Although there are several ways to use Spring Security on your application, I will show you here a common system design pattern for creating services that allow you to do the following:

- Create user login data and store user passwords securely

- Store additional personal information, such as first/last name and birth date

- Authenticate users so that they can use your services

- Make sure users are assigned to roles that are used as filters to authorize actions on your system

- Validate and authorize each request that reaches every microservice

Are you ready?

This is a sample use case we could have in our system. See the sequence diagram here:

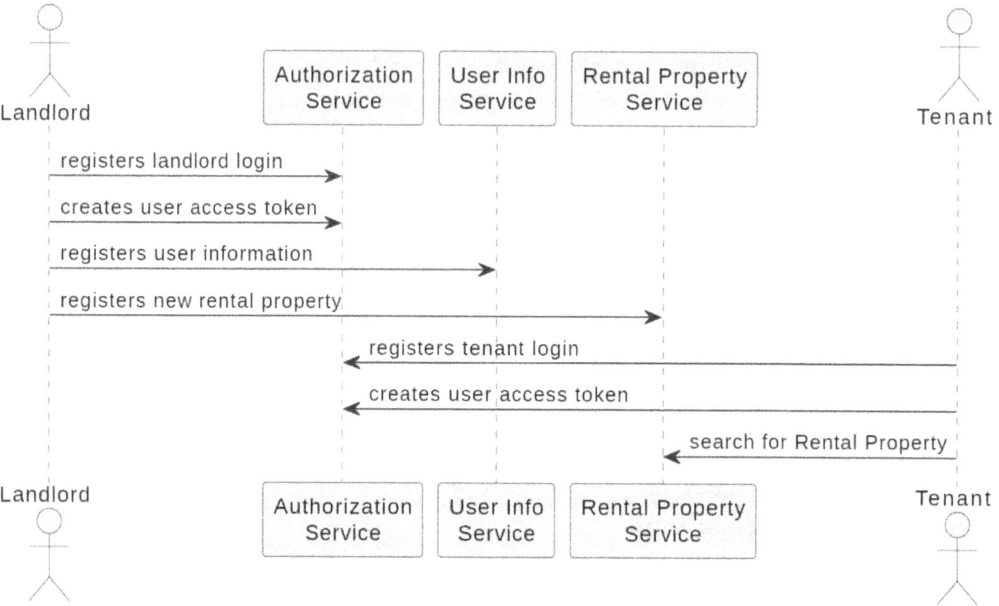

Figure 8.5 – HomeIt sample login implementation

We will work with the following assumptions:

- The system will validate token signatures using an asymmetric key. A private key will be used to create tokens, and a public key will be used to validate the token signatures.

- The authorization service will store user login credentials and create tokens using the private key.

- The other services (**User Info** and **Rental Properties**) will validate tokens locally.

- The client ID and secret will be validated every time a new user is created or an access token is generated.

With this design comes the following weak spots and vulnerabilities:

- Once a resource service (**User Info** or **Rental Properties**) receives a JWT token, it will not validate the actual existence of a user on a database. The resource services will trust that the user credentials (login and password) were actually validated by the authorization service.

- If a hacker gets your private key in the authorization server, they will be able to just recreate JWTs with whatever credentials they want. They will be able to access whatever other microservices you have. That brings a lot of potential risks, so if you get attacked, you need to manually rotate your public and private keys and restart all services – every user will have their tokens unauthorized.

- One more vulnerability will be introduced in the resource server implementation, to illustrate how authorization systems can be tricky to implement.

We will not be able to implement the **User Info** service in this chapter, but you will be able to implement it by yourself, once you see how the **Rental Properties** service is changed to validate a token. OK, now it's time to jump into the code.

At the beginning of the chapter, I showed you a design that uses an API gateway as the entry point. API gateways will be explored in future chapters. We will keep things simple, where possible, so that we can see a thorough example of a login system using Spring Security with the OAuth 2.0 model and JWT tokens.

The first thing to do is to implement the authorization server.

Creating your project

So, we start by generating the app using the Spring Initializr website. As seen in *Chapter 5* (in the *Using Spring Initializr* section), once you generate your app using Spring Initializr and choose Springboot 3.3.1, your `build.gradle` file will start with this:

```
plugins {
    id 'java'
    id 'org.springframework.boot' version '3.3.1'
    id 'io.spring.dependency-management' version '1.1.5'
}
```

This is the list of dependencies we will use:

```
dependencies {
    implementation 'org.springframework.boot:spring-boot-starter'
    implementation 'org.springframework.boot:spring-boot-starter-web'
    implementation 'org.springframework.boot:spring-boot-starter-data-
jpa'
    implementation 'com.h2database:h2'
    implementation 'org.springframework.boot:spring-boot-starter-
security'
    implementation 'org.springframework.security:spring-security-
oauth2-authorization-server'


    compileOnly 'org.projectlombok:lombok:1.18.32'
    annotationProcessor 'org.projectlombok:lombok:1.18.32'

    testImplementation 'org.springframework.boot:spring-boot-starter-
test'
    testCompileOnly 'org.projectlombok:lombok:1.18.32'
    testAnnotationProcessor 'org.projectlombok:lombok:1.18.32'
    testRuntimeOnly 'org.junit.platform:junit-platform-launcher'
}
```

Notice that we are using many of the dependencies we have been using in the Rental Property microservice. We are also using an H2 dependency, to facilitate an in-memory database connection.

The new dependencies are the following:

- Spring-boot-starter-security, which provides the basic filters infrastructure

- The Spring Security OAuth 2.0 authorization server

The full `build.gradle` file can be found here: `https://github.com/PacktPublishing/Spring-System-Design-in-Practice/blob/main/chapter-08/authprovider/build.gradle`.

Creating your security configuration class

For Spring, we need to set our security configuration class as well. Here is how it is written:

```
@Configuration
public class SecurityConfiguration {

    @Bean
    public PasswordEncoder passwordEncoder() {
```

```java
        return new BCryptPasswordEncoder();
    }


    @Bean
    protected DefaultSecurityFilterChain
        configure(HttpSecurity http) throws Exception {
        return http
            .csrf(AbstractHttpConfigurer::disable)
            .cors(AbstractHttpConfigurer::disable)
            .authorizeHttpRequests(auth ->
                auth.requestMatchers(
                    "/users/register",
                    "/users/token").permitAll()
                    .anyRequest().authenticated()
            )
            .sessionManagement(sess -> sess.
    sessionCreationPolicy(SessionCreationPolicy.STATELESS))
            .build();
    }
}
```

`@Configuration` is an important Spring annotation that tells Spring to create a bean out of the annotated class. The `config` beans exist to help you configure your application in numerous ways. In Spring Security, there is usually one security configuration bean whose purpose is to set the security filters.

Spring Security offers an incredible number of ways in which you can configure security in your application. In essence, you are able to choose how to authenticate a user (by looking at any existing database or remote services, for example), and also how to enforce authorization on any method.

In our case, since we are basically interested in creating users and issuing tokens, we are just interested in implementing two methods: `passwordEncoder()` and `configure()`. Both methods are tagged with `@Bean`, which tells Spring that these are factory methods for creating Spring beans. In other words, when instantiating the `SecurityConfig` bean, Spring will also call the two methods in this class, to create a `PasswordEncoder` (returned by `passwordEncoder()` method) and a `DefaultSecurityFilterChain` (returned by the `configure()` endpoint).

The `PasswordEncoder` returned is a class of type `BCryptPasswordEncoder`, which is considered a very customizable encoder with high security standards. In essence, whatever passwords we receive will be hashed by this object, to make sure we are not storing raw-text passwords in our database.

The filter chain returned by the `configure()` method will basically tell Spring how to enforce security across your client call life cycle and which endpoints to make public, as well as which to make private. If you do not explicitly configure access controls for an endpoint in your Spring Security configuration class, Spring will make it inaccessible to clients, no matter which credentials they use. In this case, Spring will pass an `HTTPSecurity` bean created behind the curtains to the `configure()` method. Then, we first disable CSRF and CORS filters (we allow any website and domain to use our services), and during the `authorizeHttpRequests()` method call, we are saying that the `/users/register` and `/users/token` endpoints can be called by anyone (`permitAll()`), while any other endpoint should be used by authenticated users only (since we do not have any other endpoints in this service, it does not really matter).

Last but not least, we set this service to be `STATELESS`. This means it does not persist session objects to track user state while the user is logged in. In this design, you will only use your JWT tokens to identify your users across services. Having `STATELESS` services means that every microservice is responsible for handling its own objects and user states instead of relying on the user login objects. Let's add a few words about what a session cookie is and why we are not using it in our design.

Session cookies are, in essence, a way to track the user state across the use of your website. They work like this:

1. The cookie itself, which is a string that your microservice creates and returns in the header of your HTTP response. You can create this string in any way you want – for instance, as a UUID or even a JWT token.

2. To set a new session, once the user is authenticated, you can return your cookie in the headers of your HTTP response using the `set-cookie` header.

3. Once the browser receives the `set-cookie` header, it is already programmed to store that cookie and hand it back in all future requests to your service, by adding it to the cookie header.

4. Your service can validate cookies by extracting them from the cookie header, in the request.

5. Once you have a session cookie going, you can use it to correlate the cookie session with an object that you persist on the server side, while the session is valid. For example, in an e-commerce site, you can store the cart items in your user session object. That is a common use case for cookies.

6. If you are using cookies, and you have a microservice architecture, you will need to evaluate which services should have access to the cookie session, and how you will provide access to it. Some common architectures will basically make session cookies available through the use of in-memory object databases, such as Memcached or Redis. You can also use other services, such as DynamoDB, Cassandra, or any fast database from which you can retrieve the session object.

7. Accessing a user session object from different services is quite an expensive task and requires special consideration and care, due to race conditions and simultaneous access from different services. As microservices have their own databases and entities, nowadays session objects are used less and less. We usually work with stateless sessions and the bearer token. That means each microservice only knows about its own state and can access some other remote microservices. Still, you need to invest some thought in avoiding race conditions, due to the distributed nature of microservice architectures.

So, in a nutshell, we are not using session cookies here because, in our architecture, different microservices are not sharing critical data with other microservices. So, we can rely on stateless services and the JWT token alone. Also, we do not want to create unnecessary race conditions that might end up producing bugs in our app.

These are the most important things you should know about session cookies. Now, let's understand the role of the authorization provider in your architecture.

Implementing the authorization provider domain

In this sample implementation, the authorization provider's responsibility is to keep a database of valid user credentials that allow for creating users, validating their existence, checking their password, and generating a valid JWT token, once the user authenticates themself.

Because of that, we need the following essential classes and services:

- `UserRepository`, for storing users

- `UserEntity`, for representing user credentials that will be persisted

- `UserService`, a JWT service that creates the tokens

- `ClientService`, which validates our client app ID and app secret (remember, your app should validate its own credentials)

- `ScopeService`, which produces the access scope from a user type

- `UserController`, which provides a REST interface with two endpoints: `/users/register` and `/users/token`, for creating a user and creating a token from the user credentials, respectively

Let's take a look at those classes in detail. The compiled code in this section can be found here: `https://github.com/PacktPublishing/Spring-System-Design-in-Practice/tree/main/chapter-08/authprovider/src/main/java/com/homeit/authprovider`.

The UserEntity and UserRepository classes

Let's start by finding out how users are created and stored in our database. Here is the `UserEntity` for representing user credentials that will be persisted:

```
@Entity
@Table(name = "users", uniqueConstraints = @
UniqueConstraint(columnNames = "email"))
@Data
@NoArgsConstructor
@AllArgsConstructor
public class UserEntity {

    @Id
    private UUID id;

    @Column(unique = true, nullable = false)
    private String email;
    private String password;
    private String userType;
}
```

Our `UserEntity` contains an email address (the login), an ID (which is the actual primary key that we will use to correlate the user in other services), the password, and the user type (tenant or landlord, in our example).

When you are writing such a service, avoid the temptation to use the user email as the user ID across your microservices. That will create a mess in your services if your users decide to change their emails. Believe it or not, I have seen big companies face huge challenges in their authentication systems due to the fact that the user email was chosen as the user ID in their systems. Do not repeat this mistake!

As you will notice, I have suggested an architecture in which we have another `UserInfo` microservice. The User Info service would be responsible for persisting other important user data (address, birth date, ID, etc.). That keeps the critical login information isolated from what we call **Personally Identifiable Information (PII)**, which helps to identify the user. PII deserves a different treatment altogether (privacy is a very critical non-functional requirement in any system nowadays, with so many heavy regulations about how companies are allowed to use or expose user data).

Here is the `UserRepository` class:

```
public interface UserRepository extends
    JpaRepository<UserEntity, UUID> {

    Optional<UserEntity> findByEmail(String email);
}
```

The user service

In our authorization provider, we have a `UserService` interface, responsible for creating user logins and checking for their existence. Here's the interface and its methods:

```
public interface UserService {
    Optional<UserDTO> createUser(
        String email, String password, String userType);
    Optional<UserDTO> findByEmail(String email);
    boolean validateUser(String email, String password);
}
```

Of course, we have also included the `UserInterfaceImpl` class, which implements our interface. It injects two important beans: `UserRepository` and `PasswordEncoder`. Here is the declaration:

```
@Service
public class UserServiceImpl implements UserService {

    private final UserRepository userRepository;
    private final PasswordEncoder passwordEncoder;

    public UserServiceImpl(UserRepository userRepository,
        PasswordEncoder passwordEncoder) {
        this.userRepository = userRepository;
        this.passwordEncoder = passwordEncoder;
    }
```

As you may remember, `PasswordEncoder` is a bean created in our `SecurityConfiguration` class, with a `@Bean` annotated method. Before instantiating `UserServiceImpl`, the Spring Framework will instantiate `PasswordEncoder` by calling that method from our `SecurityConfiguration` bean, then inject it here.

Here is how we create a user in this service implementation:

```
@Override
public Optional<UserDTO> createUser(String email,
    String password, String userType) {

    if(!userRepository.findByEmail(email).isEmpty()) {
        return Optional.empty(); // email already used
    }

    return Optional.of(userRepository.save(
```

```
new UserEntity(UUID.randomUUID(),
    email, passwordEncoder.encode(password),
        userType)))
    .map(UserConverter::fromUserEntity);
}
```

This method will reject the user creation if the user password is already in use. Returning an empty `Optional` in case the password is already used is not quite the best option because it is unclear what happened during the user creation. But that is not a big problem in this implementation.

Also, it is important to notice the use of the `passwordEncoder` service. We provide a raw password, and the encoder will create a hash string that will be stored in the database, using bcrypt. That increases security by not exposing all user passwords as raw text in the database.

Here is how we validate the existing user:

```
@Override
public boolean validateUser(String email, String password) {
    return userRepository.findByEmail(email)
        .map(user ->
            passwordEncoder
                .matches(password,user.getPassword()))
        .orElse(false);
}
```

Easy enough, right? We provide the email and password, then we find the user by email and create the hash from the raw password, comparing it with the hash we stored in the database. If both hashes are equal, that means the user provided the right password.

Finally, here is how we find a user by email:

```
public Optional<UserDTO> findByEmail(String email) {
    return userRepository.findByEmail(email)
        .map(UserConverter::fromUserEntity);
}
```

The client service

We also provide a client service, which is a very simple implementation in our example. Here is the interface:

```
public interface ClientService {
    boolean validateClient(String clientId,
        String clientSecret);
}
```

Here is the implementation class:

```
@Service
public class ClientServiceImpl implements ClientService{

    private final String clientId =
        "4ca8f880-0bee-4c24-88ce-3402fe7e37f0";

    private final String clientSecret =
        "b08cee2b-e79f-472b-a0b9-b210465c8bf3";

    @Override
    public boolean validateClient(String clientId,
        String clientSecret) {
        return this.clientId.equals(clientId)
            && this.clientSecret.equals(clientSecret);
    }
}
```

Since the focus in this chapter is on creating and validating JWTs in a distributed way, I have basically provided a hardcoded implementation for the client ID and secret validation. There are numerous ways to improve this implementation. I have seen big companies implementing client validation in the following ways:

- Adding valid client app IDs and secrets to external configuration files and loading them in a map, using a `@Configuration` annotated bean class. That bean will provide a map of client IDs to client secrets, allowing us to compare the strings.

- Creating API gateway apps in the cloud, then attributing client IDs and secrets to those API gateways. The API gateways themselves have out-of-the-box features to even generate client tokens.

- API products, such as Twilio, Google Maps, Facebook, and PayPal, will offer you a service in which you can create a set of credentials for the application you want to integrate with their services. Of course, those API products provide an implementation in which the client ID and secret are generated on demand and persisted on a database.

Here are other ways to do client validation:

- You could extend this service to also create a client token before trying to create the user token. The authorization service would be able to create the user only if a valid client token were used. The other services should also be able to validate the client token.

- You can use other ready-to-go services, such as Keycloak, to create client IDs and secrets.

There are countless other ways; these are just some options to get you started.

The scope service

As previously mentioned, the scope service will provide the JWT scope tokens from the user type. Here is the sample interface:

```
public interface ScopeService {
    String findScope(String userType);
}
```

Here is the sample implementation:

```
@Service
public class ScopeServiceImpl implements ScopeService{
    @Override
    public String findScope(String userType) {
        if("tenant".equals(userType)) {
            return "rental_properties:read";
        }

        if("landlord".equals(userType)) {
        return
          "rental_properties:read rental_properties:write";
        }

        return null;
    }
}
```

As you can notice, this is also a hardcoded implementation just to get you started. Essentially, if the user is of the `tenant` type, they get access to the **Rental Properties** service. They have read permission to this service. If the user is a landlord, they will have both read and write permissions. This means that landlords are able to add their own properties, whereas tenants can only search for properties and read property details.

Here are some ways to improve this implementation:

- You could change the implementation of the scope service and have it configured on an external configuration file, which allows you to have different access scopes configured in each deployment environment (we will see how to use external config files in the future).

- You could change the implementation of the scope service and add a scope entity and scope repository, as well as endpoints to the auth provider. That would allow you to use an API endpoint to set which access scope strings should be mapped for each user type.

- You could create a remote scope microservice that, given a user type, will return the access scope string. In that microservice, you are able to configure different user types and their scope access strings as you see fit, by persisting your configurations on a separate config file or even on a database.

- There could be a way of overriding the default return of the scope service and assigning the scopes directly to the user. So, when generating a token, instead of trying to extract the access scope directly from the user types, the scopes would be extracting the user ID itself. This could be implemented in very different ways, such as in the scope service itself or in another microservice. I would not recommend adding this feature to the user entity in the auth provider, because it adds too much responsibility to this service.

- The scope could not only create service access permissions but also generate user roles in the system, so that you could add restrictions based on roles, not just on service operation permissions.

With these key services defined, let's understand the role of the JWT service itself, which actually creates tokens.

The JWT service

Finally, let's check how we create the tokens. Here is the JWT service interface:

```
public interface JWTService {
    TokenResponse getJWTToken(
        TokenRequest tokenRequest,
        String scope, String userId);
}
```

First, I want to show you a method for generating an asymmetric key pair:

```
private static KeyPair generateRsaKey() {
    try {
        KeyPairGenerator keyPairGenerator =
            KeyPairGenerator.getInstance("RSA");
        keyPairGenerator.initialize(2048);

        KeyPair keyPair =
            keyPairGenerator.generateKeyPair();

        // Encode the keys to Base64 strings
        String privateKeyString =
            Base64.getEncoder().encodeToString(
                keyPair.getPrivate().getEncoded());

        String publicKeyString =
```

```
        Base64.getEncoder().encodeToString(
            keyPair.getPublic().getEncoded());

        // Print the keys
        System.out.println("Private Key: " +
            privateKeyString);

        System.out.println("Public Key: " +
            publicKeyString);

        return keyPair;

    } catch (Exception ex) {
        throw new IllegalStateException(ex);
    }
}
```

I have used this method as a source for creating the pair I use in this implementation, but you can also use any online generator of your choice. The advantage of knowing how to generate this pair in JavaScript is that you could create a separate microservice just for creating an asymmetric pair for each token request. That would make your services much more secure, since every token request would be backed up by a new set of public and private keys at runtime. But that also adds some more latency, due to the fact that all microservices would need to retrieve the public key from the key microservice. As always, it is all about trade-offs.

This is how you load a pair of static keys:

```
private static KeyPair loadRsaKey() {

    // Decode the Base64 encoded strings
    byte[] privateKeyBytes = Base64.getDecoder()
        .decode("your base 64 encoded private key here");

    byte[] publicKeyBytes = Base64.getDecoder()
        .decode("your base 64 encoded public key here");

    // Generate PrivateKey from decoded bytes
    PKCS8EncodedKeySpec privateKeySpec =
        new PKCS8EncodedKeySpec(privateKeyBytes);

    KeyFactory keyFactory = null;

    try {
        keyFactory = KeyFactory.getInstance("RSA");
```

```
    } catch (NoSuchAlgorithmException e) {
        throw new RuntimeException(e);
    }

    PrivateKey privateKey = null;
    try {
        privateKey =
            keyFactory.generatePrivate(privateKeySpec);
    } catch (InvalidKeySpecException e) {
        throw new RuntimeException(e);
    }

    // Generate PublicKey from decoded bytes
    X509EncodedKeySpec publicKeySpec =
        new X509EncodedKeySpec(publicKeyBytes);

    PublicKey publicKey = null;
    try {
        publicKey =
            keyFactory.generatePublic(publicKeySpec);
    } catch (InvalidKeySpecException e) {
        throw new RuntimeException(e);
    }

    // Create and return the KeyPair
    return new KeyPair(publicKey, privateKey);
}
```

In this code, I hardcoded the public and private keys, but you could add them to an external config file as well, or even to a database.

Lastly, this is how we generate the JWT token:

```
@Override
public TokenResponse getJWTToken(TokenRequest tokenRequest,
    String scope, String userId) {

    try {
        KeyPair keyPair = loadRsaKey();
        RSAPublicKey publicKey = (RSAPublicKey)
            keyPair.getPublic();
        PrivateKey privateKey = keyPair.getPrivate();

        Date issueTime = new Date();
```

```
Date expiry = new Date(
    System.currentTimeMillis() + 3600000);

JWTClaimsSet claimsSet = new JWTClaimsSet.Builder()
        .subject(userId)
        .issueTime(issueTime)
        .claim("scope", scope)
        .expirationTime(expiry) // 1 hour
        .build();

String keyId =
    "fab38aa6-d05b-4ab8-b045-8362b90acfdf";

SignedJWT signedJWT = new SignedJWT(
    new JWSHeader.Builder(JWSAlgorithm.RS256)
        .keyID(keyId).build(),claimsSet);

signedJWT.sign(new RSASSASigner(privateKey));

String jwtToken = signedJWT.serialize();
return new TokenResponse(
    jwtToken, "Bearer", "3600", scope );

} catch (Exception e) {
    throw new RuntimeException(
        "Error creating token",e);
    }
}
```

This method expects a `TokenRequest`, which is implemented as follows:

```
public record TokenRequest (String grant_type,
                            String username,
                            String password,
                            String client_id,
                            String client_secret){}
```

As you can notice, the `getJWTToken()` method also expects the user ID.

You can see in this code that the expiration date is calculated in 3,600,000 milliseconds after the current time, which translates to 60 minutes. As mentioned before, depending on your use case, you can set the duration in any way you want. It could be for an entire year if you want. There are some cases in which an entire year for token expiration could make sense, such as read-only tokens for low-value information.

The key ID is another interesting thing. In this implementation, I just added a static ID, but if you had an external microservice just for generating keys, you would be able to return the key ID here. Hence, when a microservice receives your JWT token, you would be able to retrieve the key ID and request the public key from your keys microservice.

`TokenResponse` is actually an implementation from the authorization service code. Here it is:

```
public record TokenResponse(
        String access_token,
        String token_type,
        String expires_in,
        String scope
){}
```

That is all there is to JWT generation.

The UserController class

In order to create our `UserController` class – the entry point for both registering a user and creating a valid, signed token – this is the opening:

```
@RestController
@RequestMapping("/users")
public class UserController {

    private final UserService userService;
    private final ClientService clientService;
    private final JWTService jwtService;
    private final ScopeService scopeService;

    public UserController(UserService userService,
        ClientService clientService, JWTService jwtService,
        ScopeService scopeService) {
        this.userService = userService;
        this.clientService = clientService;
        this.jwtService = jwtService;
        this.scopeService = scopeService;
    }
```

In other words, we inject four services: `UserService`, `ClientService`, `JWTService`, and `ScopeService`.

Next, let's check how to register a user:

```java
@PostMapping("/register")
public ResponseEntity<UserDTO> registerUser(
    @RequestBody UserDTO userDto) {

    return userService.createUser(
        userDto.email(), userDto.password(),
        userDto.user_type())
    .map(ResponseEntity::ok)
    .orElse(ResponseEntity.badRequest().build());
}
```

Creating a user is a very simple task. If the creation is not successful, we return 400 – bad request. That means something was not correct in the user creation. In this implementation, I do not want to add too much information to the clients, since this could lead to potential vulnerabilities. Considering security, if you return too many details, hackers can make use of them.

This is how I have implemented the endpoint for creating a signed JWT token:

```java
@PostMapping(
        value = "/token",
        produces = "application/json",
        consumes = "application/json")
public ResponseEntity<TokenResponse>
    createToken(@RequestBody TokenRequest tokenRequest) {

    if(!"password".equals(tokenRequest.grant_type())) {
        return
            ResponseEntity.status(
                HttpStatus.UNAUTHORIZED).build();
    }

    if(!clientService.validateClient(
        tokenRequest.client_id(),
        tokenRequest.client_secret())) {

        return ResponseEntity.status(
            HttpStatus.UNAUTHORIZED).build();
    }

    if(!userService.validateUser(
        tokenRequest.username(),
```

```
        tokenRequest.password()))  {

        return ResponseEntity.status(
            HttpStatus.UNAUTHORIZED).build();
    }

    UserDTO foundUser =
        userService.findByEmail(
            tokenRequest.username()).get();

    return ResponseEntity.ok(
        jwtService.getJWTToken(tokenRequest,
            scopeService.findScope(
                foundUser.user_type()),
                foundUser.id())));
}
```

As you can see, I wrote four different security tests and all of them should return an UNAUTHORIZED HTTP status code (401) if something goes wrong. Again, we do not want to give too much detail, as hackers could use those details to guide themselves while trying to exploit your service.

The configuration file

Last but not least, I have added an external configuration file to this implementation, which is located in the resources folder and is named application.yml – Spring just "knows" how to read the file from that place and set as config variables in your application:

```yaml
spring:
  application:
    name: authprovider
  datasource:
    url: jdbc:h2:mem:testdb
    driverClassName: org.h2.Driver
    username: sa
    password: password
  h2:
    console: true
    enabled: true
  jpa:
    hibernate:
      ddl-auto: update
    show-sql: true
```

```
server:
  port: 8081
```

I set the server port as `8081`, to not clash with the `RentalProperties` service, which already uses port `8080`.

Using the service

When running this Spring application on my local machine, these are two requests I can make:

- **Creating a user**: By using curl, I can send the following request:

```
curl --request POST \
  --url http://localhost:8081/users/register \
  -H 'Content-Type: application/json' \
  --data '{
    "email": user@example.com,
    "password": "userpass",
    "user_type": "tenant"
}' -vvvvv
```

  This is the response I get:

```
{
    "id": "10a66b7f-134f-437f-a58f-ad15447c05a0",
    "email": user@example.com,
    "password": null,
    "user_type": "tenant"
}
```

  The password will be null, of course, since it would be unsafe to send the password once more through the network.

- **Creating a JWT token**: This is the body of the request. We basically state that we are authenticating the user through the password grant type, and provide the username, password, client ID, and secret:

```
{
    "grant_type": "password",
    "username": user@example.com,
    "password": "userpass",
    "client_id": "4ca8f880-0bee-4c24-88ce-3402fe7e37f0",
    "client_secret": "b08cee2b-e79f-472b-a0b9-b210465c8bf3"
}
```

This is the answer we get back from our server:

```
{
    "access_token":
"eyJraWQiOiJmYWIzOGFhNi1kMDViLTRhYjgtYjA0NS04MzYyYjkwYWNmZGYiLCJ
hbGciOiJSUzI1NiJ9.
eyJzdWIiOiIxMGE2NmI3Zi0xMzRmLTQzN2YtYTU4Zi1hZDE1NDQ3YzA1YTAiLCJ
leHAiOjE3MjA1OTAzODcsImlhdCI6MTcyMDU4Njc4Nywic2NvcGUiOiJyZW50YW
xfcHJvcGVydGllczpyZWFkIn0.CTWh7bG9WZaXRxOj0hQ-
lRzLi6nCXpGPBBPD8ipXnaUOKBCqYMGK_
iImj5zjr3epM68wfu3bzVYwTF_TMPcRktGS3n1e7iJOsrDePO_
eanQo7ZEzGHpOPjGHq9TnRsSZiyNYT9OJXtTrzKBYrXwhn5t2Idd6VcQJJp9ti
TUIPxQePgEt1yI8LV13puNFnjP_DJi7n33x9ZR3E1tqfgiDISGo-mGjXnwy_r_
GwUZOoMsWGIjMGT6v42XqhvxywaMZv1rf4iWFDGOb-2Q_1SQ-GUm_
XM3Yn2uKd76DtGoMpUlPQmjNT9ZZiro9Aiq2psPr6NpYCkgQZ9fOMGvD7QYaHg",
    "token_type": "Bearer",
    "expires_in": "3600",
    "scope": "rental_properties:read"
}
```

OK, this is it for the authorization service. Let's jump now to the changes added to the **Rental Properties** service, so it can validate our JWTs.

Adding Spring Security to the Rental Properties service

In order to add security configurations to the **Rental Properties** service, these are the steps we need to go through:

1. Add the Spring Security dependencies.
2. Set the configuration files.
3. Set the security configuration class.
4. Add annotations to protected endpoints.

Let's go over each of these in detail in the next few subsections.

Adding the Spring Security dependencies

In the dependencies section of the `build.gradle` file, add these libraries:

```
implementation 'org.springframework.boot:spring-boot-starter-security'
implementation 'org.springframework.boot:spring-boot-starter-oauth2-
resource-server'
```

As you know, the `starter-security` dependency provides the basic security filter infrastructure, and the OAuth 2.0 resource server dependency will help us secure our endpoints with the right JWT validation.

Setting the configuration files

To use the resource server built-in JWT validation feature from the OAuth 2.0 resource server dependency, we need to create an `application.properties` file in our rental properties resource folder and add the following entries:

```
spring.application.name=Rental-Property-App
spring.security.oauth2.resourceserver.jwt.public-key-
location=classpath:public.key
```

You may remember that both auth providers used a YAML file instead of the `.properties` we are using here. Spring supports both file types for externalizing configurations.

As you can see, the OAuth 2.0 resource server dependency provides a default configuration for acquiring the public key. Since we are using the classpath, we just need to add the public key as a file inside the resource folder as well, with our Base64-encoded public key in it. This is the location of both the `application.properties` and `public.key` files:

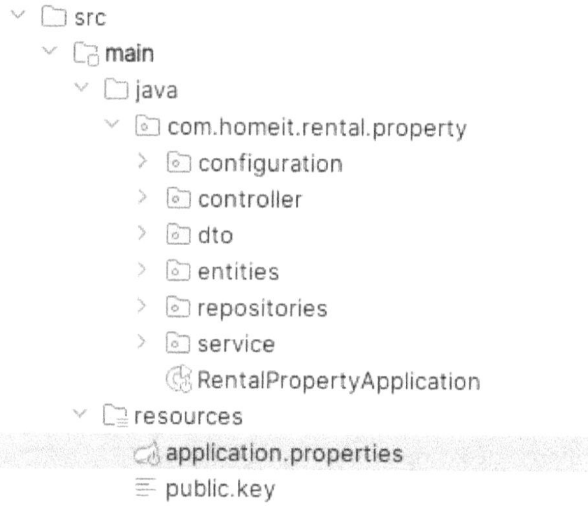

Figure 8.6: Configuration files location

Now, let's implement the security configuration object, which is an important Spring bean on your authorization service.

Setting the security configuration class

This is how we configure Spring Security in the **Rental Properties** service. Here's the class declaration:

```
@Configuration
@EnableWebSecurity
```

```
@EnableMethodSecurity
public class SecurityConfig {

    protected DefaultSecurityFilterChain
        configure(HttpSecurity http) throws Exception {

        http.csrf(AbstractHttpConfigurer::disable)
        .sessionManagement(
            httpSecuritySessionManagementConfigurer ->
                httpSecuritySessionManagementConfigurer
                    .sessionCreationPolicy(
                        SessionCreationPolicy.STATELESS));

        http.authorizeHttpRequests(
        authorizeRequests ->
            authorizeRequests.anyRequest()
                .authenticated())
    .oauth2ResourceServer(oauth2ResourceServer ->
        oauth2ResourceServer.jwt(jwt ->
            jwt.jwtAuthenticationConverter(new
                JwtAuthenticationConverter())));
        return http.build();
    }
}
```

By declaring the annotations at the class level, we are saying Spring Security should provide method-level and Spring Web security features. This config class should be annotated with `@Configuration`, so that Spring knows that this is a bean class and should be instantiated in the application start.

Next, we disable CSRF security, agreeing to let any domain call our API. We also set this service as a stateless microservice. Finally, we declare that any request should be authenticated. Through the OAuth 2.0 resource server dependency, we are also saying that the JWTs sent through the bearer token will be converted to an Authentication object.

As Spring Security provides many different ways of authenticating a user, you need to provide information on your security config class as to how the users should be authenticated. In our case, we are just declaring that JWTs should be considered proof of authentication. The magic with this dependency is that, since we have already provided the public key in our configuration files, the dependency will use that to validate our token signature. This is all provided out of the box.

Now, this alone will make Spring validate the signatures of the JWT tokens in your resource servers. Now, if you are generating different key pairs for each token (this is not a common scenario, since the computational cost is pretty high to do it), you can provide a new `JWTDecoder` implementation class that would retrieve the key from the key ID contained in the JWT token.

Another interesting thing: if you want to see how the OAuth 2.0 resource server dependency works under the hood, you can look at the source code of the `NimbusJWTDecoder` class. The `decode()` method is the one that provides that implementation. If you are using IntelliJ or another good IDE, you can even download the source code and documentation, then add a breakpoint to the `decode()` method and see the JWT decoder working in real time. It is possible to inspect all variables and methods.

Adding annotations to protected endpoints

Now that we have validated our JWT, we need to make sure the user is authorized to use the endpoints. Remember, if the user is a landlord, we want them to be able to access all rental property edition endpoints, as well as endpoints that just read properties. If the user is a tenant, they should be able to just retrieve rental properties, and not edit them.

The main change I added to our `RentalProperties` service is in the `RentalPropertyController` class. Here, are two examples of the changes made:

```
@PostMapping(
    consumes = "application/json",
    produces = "application/json")
@PreAuthorize(
    "hasAuthority('SCOPE_rental_properties:write')")
public ResponseEntity<RentalPropertyDTO> createProperty(
    @Valid @RequestBody RentalPropertyDTO property) {

    RentalPropertyDTO createdRentalProperty
            = jpaRentalPropertyService.create(property);

    return ResponseEntity.status(HttpStatus.CREATED)
        .body(createdRentalProperty);
}
```

In this endpoint, we basically added a `@PreAuthorize` annotation with the use of the **Spring Expression Language (SpEL)**. In this case, we are requiring that the user has the power to write a rental property.

This other endpoint is the one that allows us to retrieve a property:

```
@GetMapping(
    value = "/{id}",
    produces = "application/json")
@PreAuthorize("hasAuthority('SCOPE_rental_properties:read')")
public ResponseEntity<RentalPropertyDTO> getPropertyById(
    @PathVariable UUID id) {
    return jpaRentalPropertyService.get(id)
        .map(ResponseEntity::ok)
```

```
        .orElse(ResponseEntity.status(HttpStatus.NOT_FOUND)
            .body(null));
}
```

In this case, we have used the same `PreAuthorize` annotation to make sure the user has the read property.

Bear in mind that the scopes created in our authorization server should match the ones we are requiring here. The format is `<service>:<accesslevel>`. The `SCOPE_` prefix is a default string that the OAuth 2.0 dependency adds to your parsed JWT.

Also, you are able to use `@PreAuthorize` in any method from any service – not just on endpoints. This can bring great security customization to your resource servers.

Here are two other formats, among many, that you can use on your method-level validations:

- `@PreAuthorize("hasRole('ROLE_ADMIN')")`

- `@PreAuthorize("hasRole('ROLE_ADMIN') and hasAuthority('SCOPE_ write:rental-properties')")`

If you are interested in method-level permissions like that, Spring Security has a lot of options, including custom permissions you can create yourself.

Also, these other annotations can be used in case you want more flexibility on how to leverage these security restrictions:

- `@Secured`: Simpler role-based access control

- `@RolesAllowed`: Another annotation for role-based access control

- `@PostAuthorize`: Post-execution authorization checks

- `@PreFilter` and `@PostFilter`: Allow you to filter any object collections based on a security directive (for instance, only return rental properties that belong to a user)

Now, let's implement a very important aspect of your system's security, which is to restrict the access rights to the owners of the objects only.

Adding ownership security restrictions

Imagine a hacker acquires a token by registering as a landlord on your website, then decides to forge a request to delete a rental property added by another landlord. With the current implementation, your rental service will validate the JWT and the delete endpoint will allow the request to be processed, right? After all, the JWT is legit, and landlords have the ability to delete a rental property. With the current implementation, we could even have a landlord trying to create a rental property on another landlord's account. You must be very careful about this kind of stuff. For instance, we could have a landlord trying to reconfigure another landlord's bank account so that they can receive payment from contracts that do not belong to them.

These sample implementations do not enforce ownership. So, for example, to ensure a landlord is only allowed to delete their own rental properties, you can basically inject a special Spring Security bean called an Authentication object in the controller endpoint you want to enforce this restriction for. Take this example:

```java
@DeleteMapping("/{id}")
@PreAuthorize(
    "hasAuthority('SCOPE_rental_properties:write')")
public ResponseEntity<Void> deleteProperty(
    @PathVariable UUID id, Authentication authentication)
        throws ParseException {

    Jwt jwt = (Jwt) authentication.getPrincipal();
    String userId = jwt.getClaim("sub");
    return entityManagerRentalPropertyService
        .delete(id,userId)
        .map(opt ->
            ResponseEntity.noContent()
                .<Void>build())
        .orElse(ResponseEntity
            .status(HttpStatus.NOT_FOUND).build());
}
```

But where does this Authentication object come from? In Spring Security, all authorized requests will produce an Authentication object behind the curtains, after the security filters approve the request. This interface is built out from whatever authentication mechanism you used, and it's basically an object representing the authenticated user, with whatever important data is available. Another example is this: you can configure Spring Security to provide a login form and look for your user details in your company's existing database. Once the user is authenticated with those special providers, an Authentication object is instantiated and attached to a session cookie, and it is provided on each request; you can just inject it. But that is a completely different Spring Security configuration that is beyond the scope of this scope.

As you can notice, the Authentication object in our implementation will basically be an instance of a JWT token object, which was the authentication mechanism used, and we can retrieve the user ID from the Subject claim. Remember how we set the user ID as the token subject in our authorization service? Here is why.

I have also changed the `RentalPropertyService` interface to support a `userId` argument as the granted user in the `delete()` method. Also, I added a change to the implementation of `entityManagerRentalPropertyService`. See the following lines, in which we ensure the deletion is only processed if the owner of the rental property is requesting it:

```java
@Override
public Optional<RentalPropertyDTO>
    delete(UUID id, String userId) {

    EntityManager entityManager =
        entityManagerFactory.createEntityManager();
    EntityTransaction transaction =
        entityManager.getTransaction();

    RentalPropertyDTO dto;
    try {
        transaction.begin();
        RentalProperty property = entityManager
            .find(RentalProperty.class, id);

        if (!property.getLandlordID()
            .toString().equals(userId)) {
            transaction.rollback();
            return Optional.empty();
        }

        dto = RentalPropertyConverter.toDTO(property);
        entityManager.remove(property);
        transaction.commit();
    } catch (Exception e) {
        if (transaction.isActive()) {
            transaction.rollback();
        }
        throw e;
    } finally {
        entityManager.close();
    }

    return Optional.ofNullable(dto);
}
```

Essentially, if the property does not belong to the authenticated user, it will be impossible to delete it. Also, the system will consider the property to be "not found."

OK, this last topic took us further into securing our apps using Spring Security.

Implementing and using refresh tokens

Another important aspect of OAuth 2.0 authentication is what we call refresh tokens. A refresh token is a second token used to re-generate the user token, in case the first token expires. There are some considerations required when using refresh tokens.

First, the refresh token is especially important if you do not want your user to input their username and password again once the main token expires – which might be valid if your user token has an especially short duration. But that bears a controversial question: why should a user token be short-lived?

Let's say we are working on a banking mobile app. You do not want the JWT token to live for more than two minutes under user inactivity, right? In that case, it might make sense to create a very short-lived token (let's say, an expiry time of one minute) and a refresh token (it could have an eight-hour expiry time). If your user has used the app in the last 60 seconds, you can use the refresh token to renew the main token. If the user spends more than one minute without using it, your app can revoke both tokens and the app will sign the user out. That is probably a good way of renewing the access and keeping security constraints very tight.

The problem with very long-lived refresh tokens is that they could be used by an attacker to get access to a valid user token without the need for the user credentials (login and password).

In most cases, you just need a regular user token. Let's say that, in HomeIt, we set our expiry date to one entire week. The user could just stay logged in and would occasionally be required to sign in again. In this case, you can also use refresh tokens to avoid a jarring user experience. The token might expire right when the user is doing an important operation, for example, and they're required to log in again. You need to evaluate the volume of events where that happens to users, in order to decide whether you need a refresh token or not. Again, this just means balancing trade-offs.

Consider another important aspect of refresh tokens. You might make refresh tokens JWT tokens as well, with a different scope. Since the refresh token is only used to renew the user token, the scope does not need to include other operations in the system, only the access to a specific endpoint that allows generating a user token out from a refresh token. And the only place that validates the refresh token, of course, is the authorization server itself.

When programming the refresh token, you will want to receive the same request payload as you sent with the creation of the original token for the first time, but this time the grant type is `refresh_token`. Take this example:

```
{
    "grant_type":"refresh_token",
    "refresh_token":"YOUR_REFRESH_TOKEN",
    "client_id":"YOUR_CLIENT_ID",
    "client_secret":"YOUR_CLIENT_SECRET"
}
```

Whenever you generate a new user token, you can also re-generate the refresh token. This is a sample payload you can use in all your token creation response payloads:

```
{
    "access_token":"NEW_ACCESS_TOKEN",
    "token_type":"Bearer",
    "expires_in":3600,
    "refresh_token":"NEW_REFRESH_TOKEN"
}
```

That's all! Let's go ahead and wrap this chapter up now.

Summary

In this chapter, we discussed many important security aspects of a Spring application, and more specifically, diverse ways in which you can write OAuth 2.0-enabled implementations. We learned how JWT tokens work, and how tokens can be signed and verified in a very secure way without the need for multiple applications to connect over and over again to the authorization services. As you can imagine, there are a multitude of ways to implement OAuth 2.0 flows, and it all comes back to how your company is doing it. When joining a new Spring project, make sure to ask how the tokens are generated and validated. You now have a lot of conceptual and practical understanding to consider which security trade-offs your architecture is taking. You will also be able to ask powerful questions such as the following:

- If an attacker manages to find our signature keys and secrets, how can we rotate with minimum effort?

- Why do we use the current token with the current expiry date?

- Do we need refresh tokens? Why?

And that's it! In the next chapter, we will investigate how to make communication happen between services. We will also explore how to test our apps now that we want different services to work well together. See you there!

Get This Book's PDF Version and Exclusive Extras

Scan the QR code (or go to `packtpub.com/unlock`). Search for this book by name, confirm the edition, and then follow the steps on the page.

Note: Keep your invoice handly. Purchase made directly from packt don't require one.

High-Performance Secure Communication Between Spring Services

Welcome to *Chapter 9*! This is quite an intense chapter in which we are going to delve into three key topics for creating your Spring microservice architecture.

In this chapter, we will expand on how to implement Spring APIs, but this time with very high performance, using Spring WebFlux. We will also talk about how to have your services communicate with each other, and make it happen in a more secure way. Here's a breakdown of our topics:

- Service communication made easy

- Adding more security to HomeIt authentication

- Writing a high-performance service with Spring WebFlux

- Connecting services with API requests

- Writing API integration tests with RestAssured

Since we are connecting services in an intricate way now, it is imperative that we go beyond just unit tests and isolated API tests. In this chapter, you will learn how to use a powerful tool called RestAssured that will run requests through your whole set of services, to make sure they can work together. Are you excited? I know I am. Let's go!

Technical requirements

For this chapter, you will be required to refer to the code in our Git repository. All the code for *Chapter 9* is here: `https://github.com/PacktPublishing/Spring-System-Design-in-Practice/tree/main/chapter-09`.

Service communication made easy

If we are developing microservices, it is a given fact that each service will need to communicate with other services. If we are developing RESTful services, that means one service should be able to send `api http` requests to other services.

In Spring, there are three main ways to communicate through REST APIs:

- **RestTemplate**: This is the basic HTTP client used by many applications. It makes it quite easy to fire any HTTP request and convert the JSON response back to **Data Transfer Objects (DTOs)**.

- **Feign client**: This is a client that allows us to declare HTTP requests with annotations in Java interfaces directly. This allows seamless integration with Spring Cloud, which makes service discovery easier.

- **WebClient**: This is a non-blocking HTTP client, and it is a part of **WebFlux** dependency. If you need very high throughput, you should use this one.

Next, let's look at examples of how services can communicate with each other. We will be using the **HomeIt** project as the playground to build that inter-service communication. In this chapter, we will show you how to use `RestTemplate` to fire the API requests. The use of the Feign client and `WebClient` will come in *Chapter 12* when we talk about adding optimizations to our code.

Adding more security to HomeIt authentication

Suppose you want to protect your application from a token breach. That is a case where a malicious user interacts with your app with a valid token, to exploit some vulnerability in your system. It could be a stolen token, a client app takeover, or any other way in which tokens could be used to give hackers access to a forbidden set of functions in your system.

In such circumstances, it is always great to have a way to revoke a token. In our HomeIt system, we will develop what we call the **Revoke Token Service**. That service will possess just two endpoints: one will be a `POST` request for revoking a token, and the other endpoint will implement a `GET` method, so we know if any given token is revoked.

The Revoke Token service will be consumed in our app by the **Rental Property Service**, during **Spring Security token validation**. In that way, it will be possible for your microservices to always check whether a token is in good condition, or whether it was manually revoked by you or automatically revoked by other microservices.

The following diagram explains what we will implement here:

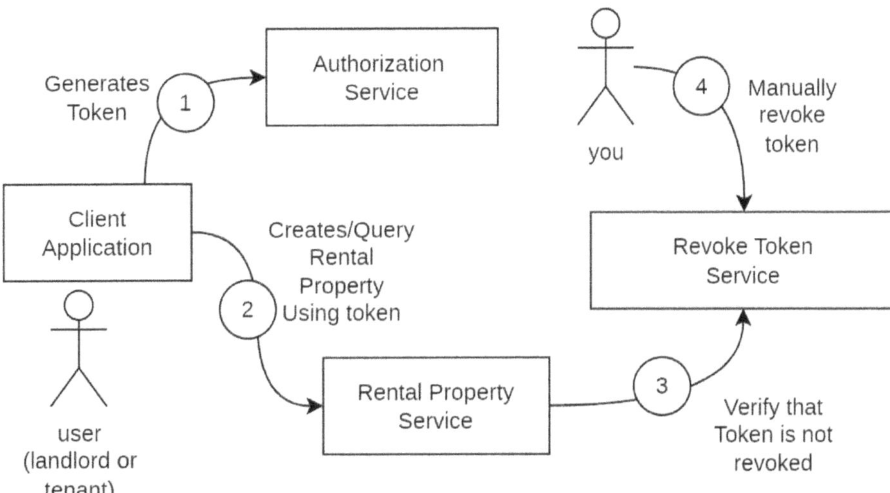

Figure 9.1: The Homelt authentication flow

To make sure all services can work in sync, we will create a test suite that simulates our users and their client applications, allowing us to run end-to-end tests that fully cover a portion of our user journey. This includes interactions between a landlord and a tenant with our backend system. To achieve this, we will use a tool called `RestAssured`.

What is RestAssured?

RestAssured is not actually a part of the Spring ecosystem, but it is very useful. It makes it extremely easy to write REST API calls, which we can then check to ensure they work correctly.

Because all services should work together and communicate with each other seamlessly, we call this testing suite an **integrated test**. That contrasts with unit tests, in which we test single classes in an isolated manner using mock objects. It is also different from testing a single microservice in isolation with the `@SpringBootTest` annotation. And because we are trying to simulate entire system use, we can also call it an end-to-end test.

The client application will be used by landlords and tenants to generate their user credentials and access tokens, so they can create and retrieve rental properties in our system. Across this path, we will ensure the responses are good enough and allow us to fully implement the conversation between services.

It is especially important to mention that we will add some functionality to the Rental Property Service, in such a way that every time one of its endpoints is called, instead of just verifying the JWT signature, it can also fire an API request to the Revoke Token Service to verify that the token is not revoked. That is important since the Rental Property Service cannot by itself decide/distinguish whether the user token was or should be revoked or not.

Another important thing to consider for a microservice such as Revoke Token is this: when your application has a security filter for revoking access tokens in real time, every microservice should call the Revoke Token Service to make sure the token is still valid. Because of that, the Revoke Token Service might suffer from a heavy load and will receive thousands of simultaneous requests if you have too many services. To make sure the Revoke Token service can handle the requests more appropriately, we will write this service with Spring WebFlux – so that you understand how to create non-blocking services that can scale much better than Spring Web.

Okay, let's get down to business.

Writing a high-performance service with WebFlux

The first thing we need to do to write a Spring Web Flux microservice is, of course, to generate the app using the **Spring Initializr** website (`https://start.spring.io/`). In this example, I am generating a barebones application with the following options:

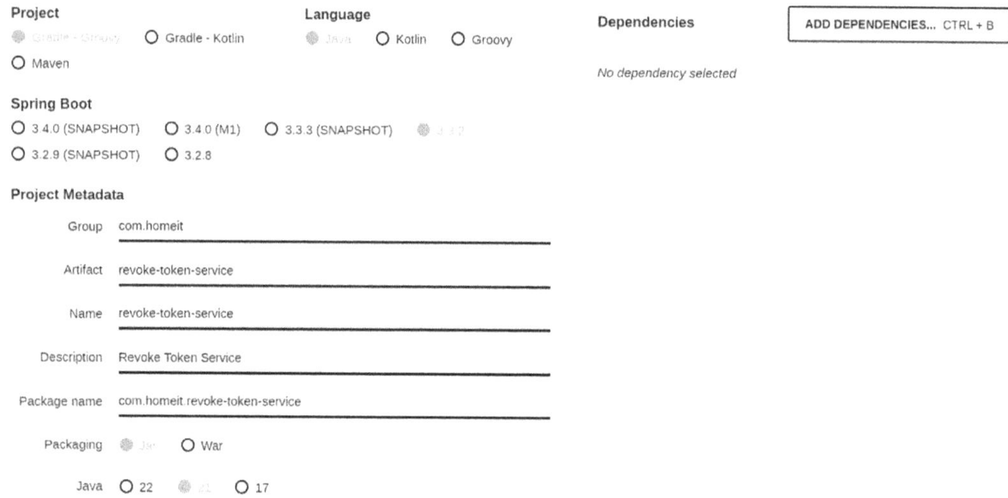

Figure 9.2: Creating the Revoke token with Spring Initializr

You do not need to select a dependency on this screen. Once you click on **Generate** and download your app, just add the following dependencies to the `build.gradle` file in the `dependencies` section:

```
dependencies {
    implementation 'org.springframework.boot:spring-boot-starter-
webflux'
    implementation 'org.springframework.boot:spring-boot-starter-data-
r2dbc'
    implementation 'io.r2dbc:r2dbc-h2'
    implementation 'org.springframework.boot:spring-boot-starter-
security'
    implementation 'org.springframework.security:spring-security-
config'
    implementation 'org.springframework.security:spring-security-web'
}
```

The `starter-webflux` dependency will guarantee that the service is blazing fast compared to serving requests with Spring Web.

The `starter-data-r2dbc` dependency will guarantee that your database connection also supports non-blocking operations.

To recap, a non-blocking operation (also called a reactive operation) allows your Java thread to remain free while an I/O task (such as a database query, network request, or file access) is in progress. When such a task is initiated, the thread doesn't wait idly; instead, it becomes available to handle other tasks. Once the I/O operation completes, the original task is resumed, assigned to a thread, and continues processing as usual.

On top of the WebFlux and R2DBC dependencies, we are adding Spring Security dependencies, so that our Revoke Token Service can deal with authentication, as usual. You do not want this service to be accessible without proper credentials.

Looking at the Revoke Token Service folder structure

The Revoke Token Service is very simple, as it just supports two endpoints: one for revoking the token and another for checking whether a given token is revoked.

The whole microservice can be seen in our project repository, here: `https://github.com/PacktPublishing/Spring-System-Design-in-Practice/tree/main/chapter-09/revoke-token-service`

Now, please take a few seconds to look at the project structure:

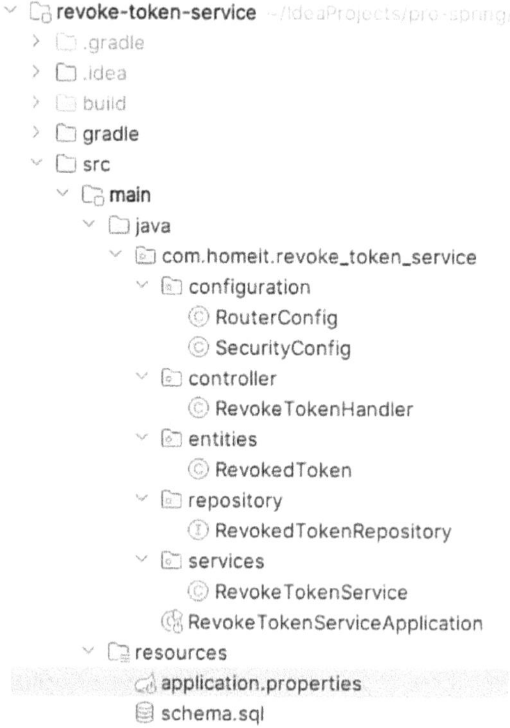

Figure 9.3: The Revoke Token Service properties file location

The first thing we are going to do is to set the properties file in the next subsection.

Writing the Revoke Token Service properties file

We will create a file called `application.properties`, in the `resources` folder, as you saw in *Figure 9.3*.

The following lines should be added to the properties file:

```
spring.application.name=revoke-token-service
spring.r2dbc.url=r2dbc:h2:mem:///revokedtokendb
spring.r2dbc.username = sa
spring.r2dbc.password = password
spring.h2.console.enabled = true
spring.sql.init.mode = always
logging.level.org.springframework.data.r2dbc.core=DEBUG
logging.level.io.r2dbc.h2=DEBUG
server.port=8082
```

These lines will ensure the following:

- The in-memory database connection is created

- You can see every SQL query that is happening in the service at runtime

- The server is instantiated at port 8082, since the other services are already being exposed at ports 8080 and 8081

Writing the database schema file

The R2DBC dependency does not work like Spring Data, in the sense that you need to create the database schema in a different way. In this case, we are adding a schema file in the `resources` folder, such that Spring can take that schema file to write the database tables if they do not exist. Here it is:

```
CREATE TABLE revoked_tokens (
    REVOKED VARCHAR(1024) PRIMARY KEY
);
```

The Revoke Token Service database is simple: we just need one table and one column to store the revoked tokens.

Writing the Revoke Token Service persistence layer

Please look at how simple it is to write an `Entity` class to store our revoked tokens:

```
@Table("revoked_tokens")
public class RevokedToken {

    private String revoked;

    public RevokedToken(String revoked) {
        this.revoked = revoked;
    }

    public String getRevoked() {
        return revoked;
    }

    public void setRevoked(String token) {
        this.revoked = token;
    }
}
```

As you can see, the RevokedToken class is a very simple entity class that has just one attribute, called revoked, which represents our revoked token.

The @Table annotation defines the name of the table itself, the schema for which was defined in the schema file.

Next, take a quick look at our repository interface:

```
public interface RevokedTokenRepository extends
    ReactiveCrudRepository<RevokedToken, String> {
        Mono<RevokedToken> getByRevoked(String token);
}
```

As you can see, we just need a custom method for querying the revoked token from the database. Since the schema defines the revoked column as the primary key, that query will result in a very fast search.

Bear in mind, for a second, that this repository class extends the ReactiveCrudRepository interface. What that does is give you access to a different return type for your queries. This is key to understanding reactive versus blocking services.

Reactive versus blocking services

When you write blocking services, you always call functions that return the actual object you are expecting to handle. So far, every time you do a database call using Spring Data, what you get back from the method call is the actual database Entity object. That means the code needs to wait for the entire database I/O operation to give you that object. In Java terms, that normally means your thread is basically stalled, waiting for your return type. That is what gives you a lot less performance, even if you use the virtual threads feature. It will be faster than the standard thread handling but less performative than reactive operations, which are non-blocking—in other words, it does not occupy your thread indefinitely.

When dealing with reactive programming, you will find two types of return objects that you have to carry across your execution stack:

- Mono<T>: This means your return type will be delivered in the future, whenever the I/O operations are resolved. When working with a Mono object, your return type (i.e., your database object) is encapsulated inside the Mono interface.

- Flux<T>: This means your return type is a series of objects of type T that will be delivered in the future when the I/O operations are resolved. Think about this as a stream of objects.

In both cases, when working with Mono<T> of Flux<T> interfaces, you will be able to handle the return objects by working with a functional programming style. What does that mean? It basically means you will use the type of syntax that resembles the Java Stream API. We will see some examples of that and we will explain more about what it implies for your API runtime execution.

Writing the Revoke Token service class

The `Service` class now can be written, and it will access the repository both to save and to query for the revoked token:

```
@Service
public class RevokeTokenService {

    private final RevokedTokenRepository repository;

    public RevokeTokenService(
        RevokedTokenRepository repository) {
        this.repository = repository;
    }
    public Mono<RevokedToken> revokeToken(String token) {
        return repository.save(new RevokedToken(token));
    }

    public Mono<RevokedToken>
        getRevokedToken(String token){
        return repository.getByRevoked(token);
    }
}
```

As you can see, both methods just deal with a `Mono<RevokedToken>` object, meaning you will be able to return a `Mono` – a function that will return the `RevokedToken` object, whenever the database can retrieve it for you.

Notice that you need to avoid resolving the `Mono<T>` or `Flux<T>` anywhere in your entire application. Your work is basically to chain methods in a functional way, and return those execution pipelines in your controllers, so that the Spring WebFlux dependency itself can resolve and schedule the pipelines, and also pause them, as the I/O operations start and return data. By returning those pipelines to your controller, you ensure that your code is non-blocking and reactive.

You have methods for extracting objects from the `Mono` and `Flux` interfaces immediately. But that means you risk your code becoming more complex and even blocking at some points.

Spring WebFlux is the type of dependency that deserves a whole book since it is a very important project that allows you to write high-performing services. In this chapter, we will basically show you a very quick intro, so that you can understand the concept.

Let's write the controller now. In the WebFlux language, we say we will write the `Handler` class.

Writing a reactive endpoint Handler class

This is how you write a `Handler` class that can deal with your requests and call your service class:

```
@Component
public class RevokeTokenHandler {

    private final RevokeTokenService revokeTokenService;

    public RevokeTokenHandler(
        RevokeTokenService revokeTokenService) {
        this.revokeTokenService = revokeTokenService;
    }

    public Mono<ServerResponse> revokeToken(
        ServerRequest request) {

        String token = request
            .queryParam("token").orElse("");

        return revokeTokenService
            .revokeToken(token)
            .flatMap(revokedToken ->
                ServerResponse.status(201)
                    .contentType(
                        MediaType.APPLICATION_JSON)
                    .bodyValue(revokedToken))
            .switchIfEmpty(
                ServerResponse.badRequest().build())
            .onErrorResume(error ->
                ServerResponse.badRequest().build());
    }

    public Mono<ServerResponse> isTokenRevoked(
        ServerRequest request) {

        String token = request
            .queryParam("token").orElse("");

        return revokeTokenService.getRevokedToken(token)
            .flatMap(revokedToken ->
                ServerResponse.ok()
                    .contentType(
                        MediaType.APPLICATION_JSON)
```

```
            .bodyValue(
                revokedToken.getRevoked()))
        .switchIfEmpty(
            ServerResponse.noContent().build());
    }
}
```

This is an example in which you can see the entire WebFlux writing style. In the `revokeToken()` method, you would extract the token parameter from the request object your HTTP client has sent you. You would then call the `revokeToken` service, which would return a `Mono<RevokedToken>` object. From that object, you would write a reactive pipeline, which matches the functional programming style as we write it in the Java Streams API way. The `flatMap()` method would extract the `RevokedToken` object from your `Mono` interface and then turn it into a `ServerResponse.io()` object. We are saying we want to return our `RevokedToken` object as JSON.

You might have noticed that, so far, I have not included a translation from our `RevokedToken` entity object to any DTOs. That is because the Revoke Token Service is fairly simple, so we can make it even simpler by breaking a rule here. If this service becomes more complex and with fairly complicated business rules, you should definitely refactor it to include DTOs and translation processes, so that you can isolate your database object implementation from your network JSON object implementation.

Still in the `revokeToken()` method, if any error occurs – for example, if we try to revoke the same token twice, we will simply return bad request HTTP code, with no details. You might want to extend this service to match some other particular use case. I am just giving you a barebones implementation so that you can understand the WebFlux implementation concept itself.

The `isTokenRevoked()` method is very similar to `revokeToken()`. But instead of trying to revoke a token, you are basically asking the service to return the token if it is revoked. If the token is not present in the database, you will get an empty `Mono`, which will then return a `204 - no content` HTTP return code. That means your token is not revoked.

Next, we will show you how to assign the URI endpoints.

Writing the RouterConfig and resource addresses

This is how you finally use your handlers to create endpoints in Spring WebFlux – see the following code:

```
@Configuration
public class RouterConfig {

    @Bean
    public RouterFunction<ServerResponse>
        route(RevokeTokenHandler handler) {

        return RouterFunctions
```

```
                .route(RequestPredicates.POST(
                    "/api/revoke-tokens"),
                    handler::revokeToken)
                .andRoute(RequestPredicates.GET(
                    "/api/revoke-tokens"),
                    handler::isTokenRevoked);
        }
    }
```

As you will notice, the `RouterConfig` class is the equivalent of the `controller` class in a Spring Web project. But instead of writing several methods, one for each URL and endpoint, you will write a `route()` method that injects your `handler` class instance as a Spring bean. You will annotate this `route()` method with the `@Bean` annotation, meaning Spring Boot will call this method at the beginning of the application lifecycle, in order to instantiate the `RouterFunctions` Spring bean.

The `RouterFunctions` implementation you see in the `route()` method is what actually defines your endpoints. You can pass the method references from your `handler` class to the `route()` and `addRoute()` methods so that you can define which URLs should be handled by which handler methods.

Last but not least, we need to write the security config file, so that requests to your Revoke Token Service are secured by a specific application ID and secret you can configure.

Writing a customized Basic authorization filter

Here's an example of how we should write the Spring Security filter in a way that includes App ID and secret validation for every endpoint in a single place. That is in contrast to what we did in the `RentalProperty` service, in which the controller methods validated the ID and secret directly:

```
@Configuration
@EnableWebFluxSecurity
public class SecurityConfig {

    private static final String APP_ID = "myAppId";
    private static final String APP_SECRET = "mySecret";

    @Bean
    public SecurityWebFilterChain
        securityWebFilterChain(ServerHttpSecurity http) {
        return http
            .authorizeExchange(spec ->
                spec.anyExchange().authenticated())
            .httpBasic(authConfigurer ->
```

```
            authConfigurer.authenticationManager(
                authentication -> {
                    String principal =
                        authentication.getName();
                    String credentials = authentication
                        .getCredentials().toString();
                    if (APP_ID.equals(principal) &&
                        APP_SECRET.equals(
                            credentials)){

                        Authentication auth = new
                UsernamePasswordAuthenticationToken(
                            principal, credentials,
                            Collections.emptyList());

                        return Mono.just(auth);
                    } else {
                        return Mono.empty();
                        // Returning an empty Mono
                        // if authentication fails
                    }
                }))
            .csrf(ServerHttpSecurity.CsrfSpec::disable)
            .build();
    }
}
```

To consume the methods in the Revoke Token Service, you should fire a request with a basic `auth` header. That means concatenating the app ID and secret as the user and password, in base 64 encoding.

Now, your Revoke Token microservice is entirely ready to go, built on top of Spring WebFlux. If you are interested in writing very high-performing services, you can see more about WebFlux in the *Hands-On Reactive Programming in Spring 5* book, from Packt Publishing: `https://www.packtpub.com/en-us/product/hands-on-reactive-programming-in-spring-5-9781787284951`.

We can now make some changes to the rental properties service, so that each time you fire a request to it, the Rental Properties service will also query the Revoke Token Service to check whether the token is still valid – that is in addition to validating the JWT token signature itself.

Let's see that in action next.

Connecting services with API requests

We will now move on to implement a simple security filter in the Rental Properties service that will send an HTTP request to our new Revoke Token Service. For that, we will use the `RestTemplate` Spring bean, which is included as a dependency from the Rental Properties service:

```java
@Service
public class RestTemplateRevokedTokenService {

    private final RestTemplate restTemplate;

    public RestTemplateRevokeTokenService(
        RestTemplate restTemplate) {
        this.restTemplate = restTemplate;
    }

    public boolean isTokenRevoked(String token) {
      String url =
        "http://localhost:8082/api/revoke-tokens?token="
            + token;

        // Create headers and add them to the request
        HttpHeaders headers = new HttpHeaders();
        headers.set("Authorization",
            "Basic bXlBcHBJZDpteVNlY3JldA==");
            // this is a base64 encoded version
            // of the string "myAppId:mySecret",
            // which is the id and secret expected
            // by the Revoke Token Service

        HttpEntity<String> entity =
            new HttpEntity<>(headers);

        // Use exchange to send the request with headers
        ResponseEntity<String> response =
            restTemplate.exchange(url,
                HttpMethod.GET, entity, String.class);

        if (response.getStatusCode().value() == 204) {
            return false;
        }

        if (response.getStatusCode().value() == 200) {
```

```
        return
            Objects.requireNonNull(response.getBody())
            .contains(token);
    }

    return true;
    }
}
```

As you can see, this class is a Spring bean that expects to have the `RestTemplate` interface injected. That means we have to provide an `@Bean` annotated factory method, which is provided by a new `RestTemplateConfiguration` class you can see here:

```
@Configuration
public class RestTemplateConfiguration {
    @Bean
    public RestTemplate restTemplate() {
        return new RestTemplate();
    }
}
```

Once created by Spring, the `RestTemplate` bean will be used across the entire application. It is designed to be thread-safe, which means different calls to the same bean do not share data or HTTP connections. `RestTemplate` will manage a pool of connections for you, which means you can do concurrent calls with no risks of overriding memory areas from other calls.

Coming back to the `RestTemplateTokenService` class, as you can see, we have created a single method, `isTokenRevoked()`, which fires a request to `RevokedTokenService`. It includes an authorization header with a basic credential encoded in base 64. That is our application ID and secret. This is just to illustrate another way to authenticate your calls in other services.

We are also parsing the response object to a string, but we could parse it to whatever objects you want, given that you can map the JSON object to that other class. You can write your DTOs and parse the response objects to DTOs directly.

Plus, we are doing a very simple test. If our response is `204`, that means the token is not revoked. If the response is `200`, we test to see whether the token we sent is included in the response. That is the final test that asserts that our token is actually revoked.

That is, in essence, how you write an HTTP request to another service. That's very easy, right? Let's now include this service in the `RentalPropertyService` token validation flow, using Spring Security.

Adding security filters to your authentication flow

Spring Security has a concept that we call the **Security Filter Chain**. That means you can write as many security filters as you want for your application, and you can chain them using the HTTP security `config` class.

First, we will write a simple security filter that will be called once per request:

```java
public class TokenRevocationFilter
    extends OncePerRequestFilter {

    private final RestTemplateRevokedTokenService
        revokeTokenService;

    public TokenRevocationFilter(
        RestTemplateRevokedTokenService
            revokeTokenService) {
        this.revokeTokenService = revokeTokenService;
    }

    @Override
    protected void doFilterInternal(
        HttpServletRequest request,
        HttpServletResponse response,
        FilterChain filterChain)
            throws ServletException, IOException {

        // Extract token from the Authorization header
        String authorizationHeader = request
            .getHeader("Authorization");

        if (authorizationHeader != null &&
            authorizationHeader.startsWith("Bearer ")) {

            String token =
                authorizationHeader.substring(7);

            // Validate the token against
            // the revocation service

            if (revokeTokenService.isTokenRevoked(token)) {
                // If the token is revoked, return 403
                // Forbidden
```

```
            response.sendError(
                HttpServletResponse.SC_FORBIDDEN,
                "Token is revoked");
            return;
        }
    }
    // Continue the filter chain
    filterChain.doFilter(request, response);
}}
```

As you can see, this service injects the `RestTemplateRevokedTokenService` Spring bean, so that it can fire the request to the remote server. Another important thing is the `TokenRevocationFilter` class extends `OncePerRequestFilter` – as the name suggests, it will be activated exactly one time for each HTTP client request. Your customized filter will be called every time there is an incoming request. The `doFilterInternal()` method is what we need to implement for the filter to allow or forbid a request. If you forget that, your request will not be processed by the rest of the filter chain.

A customized filter brings you the responsibility for some critical things, such as the need to manually continue the filter chain execution after applying your tests. Within the filter, you are free to play with the request and the response object. We basically extracted the authorization header and found the actual JWT token to send to the Revoke Token Service. Finally, if the filter detects that the request should not be allowed (in this example, by detecting that the token is revoked), you can set the error in the response object, just like we did in the sample code.

Now, let's see how we need to change the `SecurityConfig` class to add this custom filter:

```
@Configuration
@EnableWebSecurity
@EnableMethodSecurity
public class SecurityConfig {

    private final RestTemplateRevokedTokenService
        restTemplateRevokedTokenService;

    public SecurityConfig(
        RestTemplateRevokedTokenService
            revokeTokenService) {

        this.restTemplateRevokedTokenService =
            revokeTokenService;
    }

    @Bean
```

```java
protected DefaultSecurityFilterChain
    configure(HttpSecurity http) throws Exception {

    return http.csrf(AbstractHttpConfigurer::disable)
    .sessionManagement(session ->
        session.sessionCreationPolicy(
        SessionCreationPolicy.STATELESS))
    .authorizeHttpRequests(auth ->
        auth.anyRequest().authenticated())
    .oauth2ResourceServer(oauth2 -> oauth2
        .jwt(jwt -> jwt.jwtAuthenticationConverter(
            new JwtAuthenticationConverter())))
    .addFilterBefore(
        new TokenRevocationFilter(
            restTemplateRevokedTokenService),

            BearerTokenAuthenticationFilter.class )
    .build();
    }
}
```

You can see that this is our filter chain, and we basically added the custom filter after adding the jwtAuthenticationConverter filter. This will now ensure that we call the Token Revoke service every time a user request arrives. Having a stronger verification like that can be very useful, but it costs a lot of extra requests to the Revoke Token service. Since the Revoke Token Service is a reactive service made with WebFlux, it can handle more requests than a simple Spring Web service. We can also improve performance here by caching the responses from the Revoke Token Service so that subsequent calls in a short period of time do not need to fire requests to the Revoke Token Service. We will see that in *Chapter 12* when we will see how to optimize your architecture.

Okay, so everything is in place and RentalPropertiesService can communicate with RevokeTokenService. Next, let's create a test suite that is able to verify that the entire user flow is working between services.

Writing API integration tests with RestAssured

The Rest Assured project is not actually a part of the Spring ecosystem, but it makes it very easy to write API tests that verify that different services can work together. In this chapter, we will create a new project in our repo that runs a test case in which a landlord creates a rental property and a tenant looks at the rental property details.

Creating the project structure

To create the project structure, you can use the Spring Initializr website and download a default project with no extra dependencies. Then, you can delete all classes from the Java `src` folder. Your resulting directory structure will be this one:

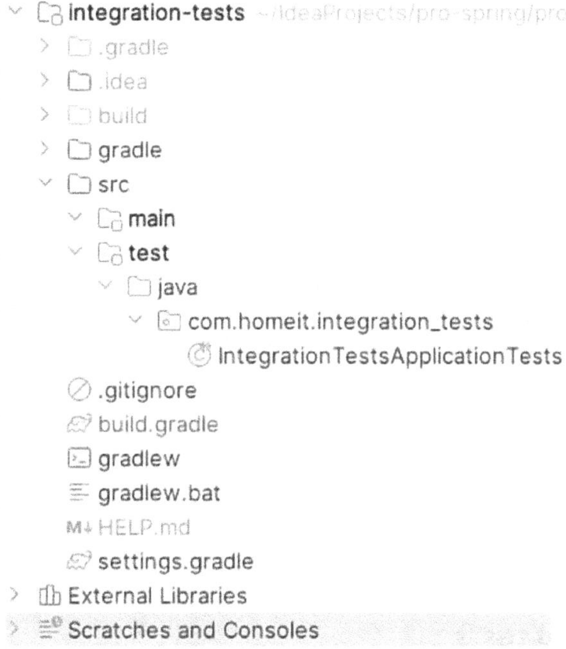

Figure 9.4: The integration test project structure

This is really all you need to create your integration tests. Next, let's declare some dependencies.

Declaring dependencies

Let's now look at the `build.gradle` file, in which we declare the important dependencies:

```
plugins {
    id 'java'
}


group = 'com.homeit'
version = '0.0.1-SNAPSHOT'


java {
    toolchain {
```

```
        languageVersion = JavaLanguageVersion.of(21)
    }
}

repositories {
    mavenCentral()
}

dependencies {
    testImplementation 'com.fasterxml.jackson.core:jackson-
databind:2.17.2'
    testImplementation 'io.rest-assured:rest-assured:5.3.0'
    testImplementation 'org.junit.jupiter:junit-jupiter:5.8.2'
}

tasks.named('test') {
    useJUnitPlatform()
}
```

As you will notice, the only dependencies we are using here are `jackson-databind`, `rest-assured`, and `junit-jupiter`. Those three dependencies will help us to fire our requests to our services, parse the answers, and verify them to make sure they are the expected ones.

With that, let's now see the actual test class.

Writing the actual tests

The only test method we have here is the one called `endToEndFlow()`. That is because this method will contain the whole process in which the following occurs:

- Two users are created: a landlord and a tenant

- Both users have their access tokens created

- The landlord creates a sample property

- The tenant is able to retrieve the sample property

- The tenant tries to create a property but fails

- We verify that the landlord token is not revoked in the Revoke Token Service

- We then revoke the landlord token

- The landlord tries to create a property but fails because their token is now revoked

Here is the full implementation. The first method is basically a sequence of calls to test methods in the right order. These methods will fire requests and verify the responses using `RestAssured` classes:

```
@Test
void endToEndFlow() {
    CreatedUser createdLandlord =
        createUserAndToken("landlord");

    CreatedUser createdTenant =
        createUserAndToken("tenant");

    CreatedProperty createdProperty =
        landlordCreatesProperty(createdLandlord);

    tenantRetrievesProperty(
        createdProperty.createdPropertyResponse(),
        createdTenant.userTokenResponse());

    tenantFailsAtCreatingProperty(createdTenant);

    verifyLandlordTokenIsNotRevoked(
        createdLandlord.userAccessToken());

    revokeLandlordToken(createdLandlord.userAccessToken());

    landlordFailsAtCreatingProperty(
        createdLandlord.userId(),
        createdLandlord.userAccessToken());
}
```

Okay, this is the way I like to organize end-to-end tests. Since they are very dense, with a lot of test cases whose results depend on each other in just one test flow, it is just good practice to separate test cases into different methods. This makes the class easier to read and understand.

Now, let's see how we create a landlord user – the first method in our end-to-end test:

```
private CreatedUser createUserAndToken(String userType) {
    // First request to localhost:8081
    RestAssured.baseURI = "http://localhost/users";
    RestAssured.port = 8081;
    System.out.println("===== CREATES USER OF TYPE: "
        + userType);

    ExtractableResponse<Response> createdUserResponse =
```

```
        createUser(userType);

    ExtractableResponse<Response> userTokenResponse =
        createToken(createdUserResponse.path("email"));

    return new CreatedUser(createdUserResponse,
        userTokenResponse);
}
```

Here is where we start to see RestAssured in action. We use baseURI and the port to specify the target address for our first request. The ExtractableResponse class helps to handle the server response by using JSON path queries – we can identify the fields in our request by using the path() method. We created the CreatedUser record class just to store the values we will use later.

The createUser() and createToken() methods are used in sequence to create the landlord user and a valid JWT access token so that the landlord can query the Rental Properties service later.

The CreatedUser record is fairly simple:

```
private record CreatedUser(
    ExtractableResponse<Response> userIdResponse,
    ExtractableResponse<Response> userTokenResponse) {

    String userAccessToken() {
        return userTokenResponse.path("access_token");
    }
    String userId() {
        return userIdResponse.path("id");
    }
}
```

The userAccessToken() and userId() utility methods were made to facilitate extracting the values from the JSON response we receive from the authorization service.

Making the actual requests using RestAssured

Now, let's see how the actual requests are made using RestAssured. Here is the createUser() method implementation:

```
private ExtractableResponse<Response> createUser(
    String userType) {

    return given()
            .contentType("application/json")
            .body(userPayload(userType)).
```

```
when()
    .log().all()
    .post("/register").
then()
    .log().all()
    .body("id", notNullValue())
    .body("email", endsWith("user@example.com"))
    .body("user_type", equalTo(userType))
    .extract();
}
```

This is a brief sample of how we create a request and validate its return using `RestAssured`. It follows the same structure for test cases we learned about in *Chapter 6*: `given`, `when`, `then`. In this implementation, we are saying that we want to fire a request with a `contentType` header of the `"application/json"` value, and we set the body to be the content returned from the `userPayload()` method – we will look at that in a bit.

We then proceed to the `when()` directive, in which we set `RestAssured` to log all relevant information and execute a POST HTTP method request to the `"/register"` endpoint. Remember, we set the target URI and the port in the method that called the `createUser()` method.

After firing the request, we proceed with verifying that the response contains the content we expect. In this case, we are also logging the response, and we make sure that the body contains the ID of the user (a non-null value), the email ends with a specific suffix, and the user type is the same one we provided to this method. Finally, we return the value extracted from the response.

Let's look at the `userPayload()` method implementation now:

```
private static Map<String, String> userPayload(
    String userType) {

    return Map.of("email",
        new Date().getTime() + "_user@example.com",
        "password", "userpass",
        "user_type", userType);
}
```

The `userPayload()` method basically creates a map of keys/values. That map is transparently used by `RestAssured` to create the payload. Because we will create different users, it is good to dynamically generate the email in this utility method.

The `createsLandlord()` method also contains another utility method called `createToken()`. Let's see how it is implemented:

```java
private ExtractableResponse<Response> createToken(
    String email) {

    return given()
            .contentType("application/json")
            .body(tokenPayload(email, "userpass")).
        when()
            .log().all()
            .post("/token").
        then()
            .log().all()
            .body("access_token", notNullValue())
            .body("token_type", equalTo("Bearer"))
            .body("expires_in", equalTo("3600"))
            .extract();
}
```

As you can see, this is just another `RestAssured` request with the `given-when-then` structure. This time, we are setting the POST URI to `"/token"`, as this is the token controller address in our authorization service. In the `then()` section, we are verifying that the `"access_token"` field is being returned in the response with a non-null value as well as `"token_type"` and the expiration date for the token.

Similarly, the rest of our end-to-end test flow is composed of several `RestAssured` calls to other services and subsequent verification of the results. Here is the code for the `revokeToken()` method, used to revoke the landlord token and make sure they cannot register new properties:

```java
private ExtractableResponse<Response> revokeToken(
        String token) {

    return given()
        .header("Authorization",
            "Basic bXlBcHBJZDpteVNlY3JldA==")
        .when()
            .log().all()
            .post("/api/revoke-tokens?token="+token).
        then()
            .log().all()
            .body("revoked", equalTo(token))
            .extract();
}
```

In this method, we are sending an `Authorization` header, which basically comprises the `"myAppId:mySecret"` string, parsed with `Base64` encoding. This implementation calls the Revoke Token Service using the `"/API/revoke-tokens"` URI, parsing the token as a query parameter. Also, we verify that the response contains the `"revoked"` attribute, and it contains the original token we revoked.

This is the essence of how you write an end-to-end API integration test. Of course, to have it working, we need to make sure all services are running. Then, it is possible to execute this test suite by running the following command:

```
> gradle test
```

That will trigger the end-to-end flow up to its completion. If you want to look at the entire code of our end-to-end test flow, it is in the *Chapter 9* code in the GitHub repo, as stated in the *Technical requirements* section at the beginning of this chapter.

Summary

In this chapter, we have learned many interesting things about the following:

- How to create a high-performance Spring WebFlux service that is capable of handling a lot of parallel requests

- How to create extra security filters in Spring Security configurations and how to chain them to harden your application security

- How to get your services communicating with each other, through the use of a `RestTemplate` Spring bean

- How to implement full end-to-end microservice integration tests that verify a specific set of services that depend on each other are working properly together

In the next chapter, we will continue looking at inter-service communication. But this time, we will learn how to implement it in an event-driven way. See you there!

Get This Book's PDF Version and Exclusive Extras

Scan the QR code (or go to `packtpub.com/unlock`). Search for this book by name, confirm the edition, and then follow the steps on the page.

Note: Keep your invoice handly. Purchase made directly from packt don't require one.

10

Building Asynchronous, Event-Driven Systems With NoSQL Databases

Welcome to *Chapter 10*! I feel really excited about this chapter, as we are jumping to completely different topics using Spring Framework.

In this chapter, we will start by exposing some critical issues with RESTful APIs and how integrating different systems could lead to a massive amount of code that is hard to maintain. Then, we will present the alternative of event-driven architectures to de-couple services.

Here are the main topics covered in this chapter:

- A maintainability issue with RESTful APIs
- Introducing event-driven architectures
- Using Kafka in event-driven services
- Using MongoDB for NoSQL persistency
- Our event-driven HomeIt
- Building our rental proposal service publishers
- Building our rental properties service subscribers
- Extending our end-to-end tests

Alongside the main topic, which is event-driven architecture, we will also explore some more nuances of writing asynchronous systems using WebFlux, as well as how to incorporate MongoDB, the most widely used NoSQL database. I hope this chapter really opens your eyes to the power of event-driven systems. Let's go!

Technical requirements

The entire code base for this chapter can be found at `https://github.com/PacktPublishing/ Spring-System-Design-in-Practice/tree/main/chapter-10`.

A maintainability issue with RESTful APIs

The REST standard is generally a great tool for developing software. It offers a concise way for mapping your entities in endpoints, and to standardize essential operations, such as listing, creating, updating, and deleting objects. It's no wonder it took the world by storm as the default method for building web services.

Although powerful, there is still a very critical pain point in this great standard. That is the problem of **strongly/heavily coupled services**.

What is heavy coupling?

To understand what I mean by *strongly coupled services*, consider the following scenario: suppose that in our HomeIt startup, we had a rental proposal service, the role of which is to make sure that the rental transaction occurs smoothly between tenants and landlords.

Suppose the rental proposal service only holds information about the state of a current rental negotiation and this service needs to communicate with other services while the negotiation happens.

Suppose we also have other services that depend on the rental proposal service, such as the following:

- **Rental properties service**: This service, the code samples for which are already provided at `https://github.com/PacktPublishing/Spring-System-Design-in-Practice/tree/main/chapter-10/rental-property-microservice`, needs to know the current state of the negotiation so that it can track whether a property is available for rentals or not.

- **Messaging service**: This service will fire messages to the related users if the state of a rental proposal changes. When someone makes an offer or counteroffer, or approves or rejects an offer, the messaging service is the one that will send the actual message to the landlord or tenant.

- **Payment service**: This service will track whether it is time to charge the customer or not. That is, once an offer has been accepted by the landlord or the tenant, this service starts the process of requesting the actual payment from the tenant.

Now, let's try to coordinate the three services by only using RESTful API endpoints, all from the rental proposal service API. That is, once a rental negotiation changes its state, that service will have to fire API requests to the three other services. This is illustrated in *Figure 10.1*:

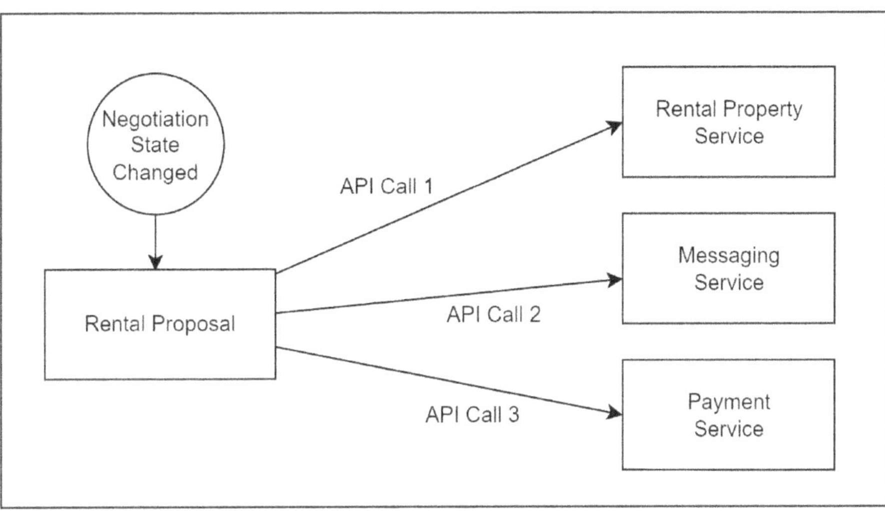

Figure 10.1 – An example of RESTful API communication

Now, based on *Figure 10.1* we can conclude that every time a negotiation state changes, we need to check whether the API calls are being correctly fired to the other APIs. What this means is that every time we add new negotiation states or new API services, we need to evaluate whether we are going to write or change every single API call in the rental proposal service.

That is interesting, as it makes the rental proposal service the single service responsible for orchestrating every other service. That might be OK for orchestrating three or four services but once the service number in your microservice cloud grows, this might make things a lot more complicated to manage and maintain.

As more services are integrated with each other over time, the amount of code can grow exponentially if we are exclusively using REST APIs to express the connection between services. Also, when we use only RESTful APIs to connect services, that means every service needs to have knowledge about other service domains. That is what we mean by **heavy coupling**. If you add four more services to the right side of *Figure 10.1*, that means your rental proposal service is forced to have some code referring to the other new services.

Now, let's explore the implications of the topology proposed here and how different programming decisions could create unmaintainable software.

How service coupling makes code harder to maintain

Heavy coupling goes as follows: as the number of connected services grows, the harder it is to make those services work separately and independently. In our example, by always using RESTful APIs, since the rental proposal service would contain explicit code that fires requests to the rental property service, messaging service, payment Service, and others, it is just a lot more code to read and edit when making changes.

Among the most critical decisions you will have to make in your life as a software architect is choosing how to connect systems.

Knowing how to model system integrations is a complex matter, so I will list some key variables and questions at play when designing them:

- How many system integrations will there be in your microservice architecture? The more systems are connected, the bigger the amount of code you must deal with, and the harder it will be to maintain when you change something.

- Which systems provide the more stable interfaces compared with others? Suppose that the messaging service APIs keep changing from month to month, so every service that uses the messaging service must be kept up to date with the changes. You will require new code in other services very often as the messaging service evolves.

- Do your services depend on the response from other services to continue their operations? For instance, if you write the rental proposal service such that it must use the messaging service response to decide how to continue its operation, that makes the rental proposal service more complex to write. It also makes it harder to recover from failures in the messaging service. Believe me, every service will fail at some point.

Due to those three key points, here is some critical guidance when writing systems.

Create well-established domain boundaries

Avoid having specific knowledge from one service written in another service. That keeps your code *cleaner*, in the sense that different services will have well-isolated domains.

For instance, ideally, the messaging service should not know anything about rental properties or rental proposal objects. It should just know about *messages*.

Write stable interfaces

As much as you are able to, design your services in a way that will not require changes to their interface (endpoints) in the future. Releasing the *flavor of the month* endpoint throughout the entire year will require adding new code to other services in the future just because you changed your original service. You should instead create a few endpoints that represent the essence of the domain your service is dealing with and stop changing them after they are released.

For example, in the messaging service, instead of writing endpoints for SMS, email, WhatsApp channels, and so on, write a single endpoint that is abstract enough to be used to implement communication with whatever platforms your company uses. The way you implement that endpoint will allow your product team to decide where the messages should be sent. That prevents a lot of headaches and saves development time and company money in the future.

Develop response independency

Make your services work independently from the other services you need communication with. Doing this shows that you know how to isolate matters and facilitates consistency throughout your microservice cloud. This also makes it easier to recover from failure as well.

Here is another example: it might be enticing to write the rental proposal service in a way that it waits for the result of an API call to the payment service so that you can define the status of a proposal. However, doing that will create a data consistency risk because if your rental proposal API is unable to call the payments service, or if the payments service processing breaks during a call, you will have a big problem at hand! It will be impossible to determine the status of a rental proposal, and that will leave you with eventual financial losses – especially when you achieve high business volume.

Know your highest-order business service

This is an especially important consideration that can save millions in development efforts for the company you are working with, and we do not see this advice in a lot of places. When writing your microservices, evaluate whether you really need business-related rules in each one of them.

In our case, a messaging service should not know anything about the state of the proposals. The payment service should also not know about rental properties. Rental properties should also not know about the proposals. Cross-domain knowledge should not matter on a service.

Plus, this is a special case of the domain boundary principle: you need to determine which service should contain the core of your business rules. You should design or identify which service represents the highest-order business rules. In other words, although every service participates in your system and helps to drive revenue, which service(s) will be responsible for containing the business rules that really drive the core value you are providing to your customers?

Let me explain it through our example: in the HomeIt system, we are all about renting properties, so the critical service for driving the rental relationships is the rental proposal service. That means your highest-level business rules must be contained in the rental proposal service, and this service is the highest-value service in your architecture. Since the rental proposal service represents the thing of the highest value to your company (the rentals themselves), you should never ever spread logic that should be in the highest value service in other services.

In the HomeIt example, failing to identify the highest-order business service usually involves writing a lot of `if-else` statements for rental property statuses in a lot of different services. If you find that the messaging service, the payment service, and the rental properties service are all trying to implement logic based on the current status of a proposal, that means we have failed at isolating the logic of higher value in just one or a few services.

Why is this important? It's because if you get rental proposal logic spread over different services, every time the business wants to add new logic, use cases, products, and flows, you will have to change a lot of services and add new `if-else` statements everywhere. Your code will not scale, and you will impose a cost of millions to change and adapt to the market on your company. Your code will become non-scalable, slow, and very costly to maintain. Developers will not be happy about it; you will increase turnover. Usually, companies take a long time to discover that this is an architecture issue – if they ever do.

Therefore, make sure you have just one or a few services that hold critical business rules.

Identify the services orchestrator

If you write your services in a way that the endpoints are general and flexible enough, that means you will have the opportunity to orchestrate them the way you want. You could define when messages will be sent via WhatsApp, email, or anything else. You will be able to define whether the charge is supposed to be done on a credit card or bank transfer more easily. If you write your services endpoint such that the parameters describe the behavior you want, instead of writing one endpoint for each kind of behavior, it will be possible to create configuration objects that will define the way your system flow will work. You will have a lot more power to scale and speed up your development.

Think about this: depending on the status of a rental proposal, the other services will behave in diverse ways. Now, let's suppose you have more than one type of rental proposal flow. Suppose that for different countries, you have some special states that should be represented in the rental proposal objects. You might think about ways in which your proposal service – or a helper service – acts as an orchestrator for how other services should behave.

How would that work in real life? If you know that you should have different flows for the rental proposal that change behavior in other services, that means creating a new proposal in your API might take some parameters to inform how other systems should behave.

Maybe you want a specific rental proposal flow that only works with credit cards, or through WhatsApp communication? That might require you to add some special parameters to drive that behavior, when creating your new Rental Proposal object.

As you can see, this principle is a violation of the Domain Boundary I stated earlier. It adds to one of the services some cross-domain information to inform other systems how to behave. It turns out that this exception to the Domain Boundary rule works beautifully if you want to make your service more flexible. By implementing cross-domain parameters in one of your higher order business services, you will be able to twist the system flows in any ways you want. This could drive a lot of speed on your development.

De-Coupling Calls

By looking at our first picture, you will certainly deduce that, if we are using REST API calls only, the Proposal Service will have one extra call to each service that it communicates to. That means 10 services require 10 API calls and so on.

De-coupling calls means we should strive to reduce the number of calls we make for other services, and this is where the event-driven architecture shines. By using what we call *topics* or *queues*, with the response-independency principle, we can have the rental proposal service basically connected to an intermediary service that has the responsibility of forwarding messages to other services that are interested in knowing about updates in the rental proposal service.

We will explore how it works in the next section.

Introducing event-driven architectures

Now you know: if we only have REST APIs, that means each service we need to connect to represents a new call we need to write, specifically to that service. In contrast, when using the event-driven approach, we eliminate the need to write specific API calls to each service our microservice communicates to.

How does that work? Instead of allowing services to communicate directly with each other through the API calls, we will add an intermediary service that represents a queue of messages. That service receives update notifications from the service that originates the call and forwards the notifications to every other service interested in those notifications.

Let's look at the following figure:

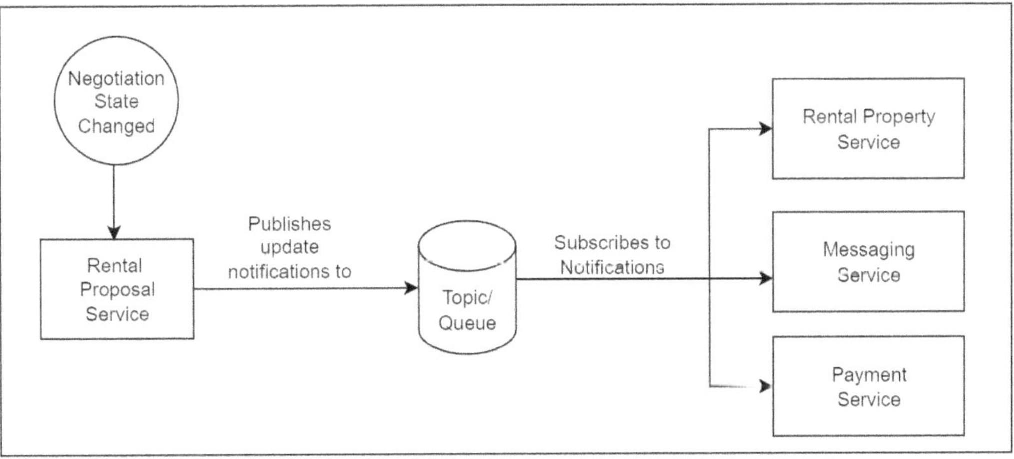

Figure 10.2 – An example of event-driven communication

In this model, we have included an intermediary service that tracks every update event that happens in the rental proposal service. Once the rental proposal state changes, a single notification is fired from the rental proposal service to the *topic* or *queue*, as we call it. Then, other systems can subscribe to those notifications. Whenever a new message is fired, every service that subscribes to the notifications receives a copy of the notification.

This means that the rental proposal service does not know which services are being triggered once the proposal state changes at all. It just knows how to tell the microservice cloud a single thing: *Hey, I have updated myself. Please tell everybody who is interested.*

Hence, every service that should react to those changes should be a subscriber of the topic itself. This bears several advantages:

- You can include new services in your architecture without requiring changes to the proposal service.

- The amount of code in the proposal service is greatly reduced, as you never need to write specific calls to every service.

- Given that your system can send the messages to the messages topic/queue, it does not need to wait for the other services to respond. This means that the systems will work asynchronously, which has the potential to bring a lot of speed to your system.

- With topics, by adding as many subscribers as you want, you have a mechanism that helps to decouple your services, making the domains potentially more isolated from each other (this will be discussed from the next section onward).

- You can choose the policy you want to implement for publishing and consuming messages. Do you want to mark messages as *read* as soon as the subscribers pull them, or do you want the subscribers to mark the messages as *read only* after they finish processing them?

Now, with this system design, let's discuss how to design the messages themselves. However, first, let's talk a bit more about the difference between queues and topics.

What is the difference between a queue and a topic?

A *queue* is a messaging model wherein messages are sent to a specific destination and consumed by a single consumer. In a queue, messages are typically processed in the order in which they arrive (first-in, first-out), and each message is removed from the queue once consumed. This setup ensures that each message is handled by only one receiver, making it ideal for tasks that require point-to-point communication.

A *topic*, on the other hand, is mostly like a queue, except that it can be subscribed to by different groups. With a queue, you will usually have just one consumer. On a topic, though, you might have multiple systems consuming it. So, we can safely say that a queue is a single destination channel, whereas a topic is possibly a multiple-destination channel.

Now, let's discuss why we use one over the other. Choosing between a queue and a topic depends on your application's communication needs:

- Use a queue when you want each message to be processed by only one consumer. This is suitable for load balancing tasks, work distribution, throttling requests (to deal with peak request volumes), or when tasks should not be duplicated across multiple consumers.

- Use a topic when you need publish-subscribe functionality, whereby messages are broadcasted to multiple subscribers, which handles the messages differently between each other. This is ideal for event notifications, updates, or any scenario wherein multiple systems need to react differently to the same message, and each subscriber tracks the message's consumption from the other subscribers.

Now that we know the key difference between queues and topics, let's discuss different ways in which you could decide to structure your messages. There's a lot to discuss here, so you will be surprised as to how the message design itself can be flexible and different among systems and companies.

How should your notification messages look?

When deciding what information should be contained in your notification messages, there are a few structure types to consider. Let's take a look.

The message format

You can really format your messages with any format you want. For starters, I would advise you to just choose the JSON format, since it is already familiar. You can also choose the **Protocol Buffers** or **Avro** formats, both of which are geared toward higher performance, but are less readable. Neither one will be covered in this book.

Thin versus fat messages

When thinking about how much data you should provide in your messages, it is important to consider how big the message will be – in other words, how *fat* or *thin* your messages should be. There is no right or wrong answer; however, you should definitely think about the implications so you can understand what the best approach would be for your use case and company.

Thin messages

One of the ways you can build your notification system is by providing messages that hold very little information. For example, we could create a message that contains the object ID and the status that you moved your object to. You can even program only the ID of the object and a second attribute saying whether the message was created, updated, or deleted. Although thin events are very simple to implement and will usually move faster in the queues and topics, the subscriber systems will have to query the original object from your API to check its content and decide what to do. This also has the advantage of allowing the subscriber API to check the current status of the object.

An example in HomeIt would be to send a message to the subscriber systems that just states the ID of the proposal and its current status, such as the following:

```
{
    "proposal_id": "74cfd995-358e-4854",
    "status": "ACCEPTED"
}
```

Fat messages

You might want to provide more data on your notification messages. That is, instead of just sending two attributes with the modified object ID and maybe a changed status, you might want to provide more information, or even the entire object in the queue or topic. That means the subscriber systems will not have to query the original object as much.

We are going to see a fat messaging approach for our rental proposal service in a few pages. Here is a quick example of adding more data to your notification:

```
{
     "proposal_id": "74cfd995-358e-4854",
     "status": "REJECTED",
     "message": "Sorry, I cannot accept this deal",
     "landlord_id": "2d913fd0-431a-4ee5-9d27",
     "tenant_id": "b33b250e-9208-4ad9-8c78",
     "author_id": "2d913fd0-431a-4ee5-9d27"
}
```

As you can see, in the preceding example, we added the tenant ID, the landlord ID, a message, the proposal ID, and the status to which the proposal was moved. That means subscriber systems have less necessity of pulling the original object from the API, which can help reduce the load in the proposal service.

Given the circumstances, you should define whether you would prefer a heavier load on your message topics or on your original API. Bear in mind that if you need your subscribers to fetch data from the original API, that means writing an HTTP GET call to your subscriber services, which increases the coupling and makes it more difficult to update the publisher service in the future.

Beware of higher-order domain spilling

In a sense, both approaches – fat and thin messages – mean that your subscriber systems need to know your publisher domain even a tiny bit. Since it relies on the updated object from the publisher system to decide what to do, it means subscribers need to implement logic that is attached to the modified object domain. I call that **domain spilling**. Similar to how spilling some coffee on your shirt is undesirable, you do not want a stain from a domain in a service that does not deal with that domain.

For instance, in HomeIt, upon receiving a notification that the rental proposal status has changed, your payments service will have to reason around the rental proposal status to define what its next step is. That means the developer in the payment service needs to know the rental proposal domain, even at a superficial level. Doing that means you are moving business rules from a higher-order domain (the rental proposal domain, which is at the core value from HomeIt, as we explained before) to a lower-order domain (the payment system is critical for receiving money, but it is not a core service that allows orchestrating actions from tenants and landlords while negotiating the rental proposal). The payment system enables the exchange of money, which is a critical function. However, it is not a core system to the HomeIt business, which means it should bear as little logic about the higher-order rental proposal domain as possible.

Moving the cross-domain knowledge to the publisher system

As I said, domain spilling is generally undesirable when your lower-order domain services have business rules that are related to higher-order domains. So, if you do not want the subscriber systems to depend on business rules from higher-order domain services, you can move a bit of the logic from the lower-order domains to the higher-order ones.

Think about it this way: as we have established, the most important business function you have is sequencing and orchestrating the interaction between tenants and landlords. It means that, depending on the result of that interaction, you want that service to inform other services about how they should behave.

From the proposal service, you want to specify what messages should go to your participants and how they should be delivered. You will also want to inform the payment service about how much money is to be collected and how. You will also want to inform the rental property service if a specific property number is unavailable, such that your proposal service can tolerate some more knowledge about other services. That is, the service that orchestrates your business can offer some known parameters for other services.

How would that be done? Well, there are two options. One is to add some configuration attributes to your core proposal service so that, depending on how you want other services to behave, the proposal object can hold some different parameters for the other services such that when those services are activated, they might receive their well-known parameters directly instead of trying to derive their own behavior based on the proposal states. That has the drawback of using your rental proposal object to store data from other domains, which might still not be too desirable.

Another way of configuring how other services should behave is creating a separate configuration service. That is, any time a rental proposal is created, a configuration object is created and stored in that configuration service. The rental proposal flow will update the configuration object to orchestrate the other systems depending on your user input. This means that when other systems receive notifications about the original rental proposal, they can query the configuration service and extract their known parameters in order to discover how they should behave. Alternatively, we could configure your queues and topics in other ways, as we are going to see next.

Business versus entity-driven events

When creating a queue or topic for sending notifications, you should decide whether you want the events on that topic to be defined around your entities, general user journeys, or business events. When discussing thin versus fat messages, the examples we gave were centered on creating our events based on the status of the rental proposal object. That means that the event is designed to reflect the current status of an entity.

In contrast, you could define events based on your user journey. We could name the events based on some action that just happened. For instance, we could create the following event names: `RENTAL_PROPOSAL_OPENED`, `OFFER_SENT`, `OFFER_REJECTED`, `OFFER_CANCELLED`, and `OFFER_APPROVED`. When you create your events around the business story, it might make more sense for the consumers. You know exactly where the users are in their journey.

Destination versus source topics

Another crucial decision you should make is whether the topic you are creating refers to the objects in the service that is emitting the events, or the object in a specific service that is receiving that event. This might be especially useful in cases where a topic is connected to a subscriber service, and that service is interested in its own events. You might want to create this topic just because you can afford to have asynchronous operations, and that might be more productive. The publisher service does not depend on the subscriber service results, so you might just prepare a topic that allows the publisher to send messages that refer entirely to the destination service (the subscriber).

Of course, in our HomeIt example, the topic we designed is a source topic, since the topic was created just to publish changes in the rental proposal objects themselves. The publisher is notifying the subscribers about the changes in the publisher domain.

A good example of a destination topic is this: suppose you have a reporting service that expects to receive some very specific events that only the reporting service itself understands. Those events help the reporting service to track rental proposals in general, ultimately to create business reports. The rental proposal service publisher could produce events exclusively for the reporting service, tailored to the input the reporting service needs. Then, the rental proposal service would be able to notify the reporting service when a rental proposal was created or accepted or a proposal was paid. Telling the story of the proposal itself (created, accepted, paid) puts more focus on the business side, so we say those events are *business-driven*. That is, when sending an event, we will be focused on what happened to the business itself, not on sharing everything about the rental proposal entity object, which is more of a technical aspect of our API. It is important for reporting services to understand the user journey, as well as the business side itself. It is not as important to know the state of the rental proposal data object over time. There is a slight but serious difference between both options, and understanding whether you need to focus on a data object or a business use case might help a lot to facilitate the development.

Shared versus non-shared topics

When considering new topics and queues on your architecture, you should define whether you want to use a single topic to be used by many different systems, just a few systems, or just one system. In our HomeIt example, we created one topic that supports events just for the rental proposal service. However, maybe we want to use that same topic to support events for other services as well. Suppose we want the payment service to publish the results of the financial transactions in that topic. We would have the same topic flowing events from two different systems. If you want to keep things more separate, you can create a different topic just to flow notifications about payments.

Of course, there are pros and cons to each choice. If you decide to have multiple topics, each of which works just for a single service, prepare to be able to manage a lot of different topics if your architecture grows a lot. On the other hand, when you have a single topic that can receive events from multiple services, you will require all subscribers to just ignore messages from systems if they are not interested.

Single versus multi-tenant topics

A tenant, in this context, does not refer to the person locating the rental property, but to a company that might use your entire service to host their own business. Take HubSpot and Salesforce, for instance. Their systems are used by different companies to host their own operations. Each company will create accounts for every one of their users. We say that HubSpot and Salesforce are multi-tenant. They are able to host the operations from multiple companies.

So, when designing your topics, you need to decide important things in regard to being single-tenant or multi-tenant. First, does your company work like HomeIt, in that we are a single company that allows landlords and home tenants to do business with each other? Or does your system operate more like HubSpot, allowing different companies to implement their operations on your website?

If your architecture is single-tenant, every topic you have will be single-tenant, but one topic will flow data from different users. If your architecture is multi-tenant, you might choose to create topics for each one of your tenants – so that one company does not see events from any others. You can also go multi-tenant with topics that flow events from multiple companies.

When you allow your topics to flow data from multiple users or companies, you need to make sure that they cannot see events and notifications from other services. Even UUIDs from an entity ID cannot be seen by some actor that does not own that object. Leaking object IDs to someone who does not own the topic opens an attack window, and you don't want that.

Input versus output topics

When your topic is used to carry over the result of an operation, we say it is an output topic. When the topic is used to carry the input to another service, we say it is an input topic.

You might want to create services that have their own input and output topics. For instance, if you have a service that takes a long time to do some processing – let's say three hours – you cannot support that with a RESTful API. You will need to make that operation asynchronous. So, create your service with two topics: an input topic and an output topic. Any time you want to trigger the service, just publish an input message in the input topic. Then, once that service finishes its process, it publishes the result as an event in the output topic. Interested services can fetch that resulting notification to continue their operations.

In HomeIt, we could create a media processor service that handles movie files and pictures. We could set up two topics for that service: one that informs the files to be processed, where they are stored, and how they should be processed, and another that returns the resulting media and where it is stored.

Unidirectional versus bidirectional topics

Another option for designing our topics is determining whether they are used to flow messages in just one direction or in two directions.

We have set up our HomeIt rental proposal topic in a unidirectional way. That means every event flows from the rental proposal service to the subscriber services. It flows in one direction only. In contrast, if we allow the payments service to publish messages to the same topic and the rental proposal service now has a subscriber just to listen to that message specifically, then we would have made this topic a multi-directional topic because the messages will flow from and to the rental proposal service as well.

Multi-directional topics are generally a bad pattern since different systems would have to know which messages to discard and which ones to handle. That might lead to a lot of useless processing and could even break systems with unsupported messages. However, it might be useful when you are doing quick proofs of concept, for example. If you just want to see things happening, then speed is important.

Dead letter topics

What will you do when your services fail to process a message? This is what we use dead letter topics for. These are specialized topics that handle messages that cannot be delivered or processed successfully after multiple attempts.

When a message continually fails due to issues like processing errors, invalid data formats, or exceeding its **time-to-live** (**TTL**), it is redirected from its original topic to the dead letter topic. This mechanism isolates problematic messages from the main flow, preventing them from causing repeated processing failures or clogging the system.

By segregating these undeliverable messages, you can analyze and address the underlying issues without disrupting the overall messaging infrastructure.

Dead letter topics enhance system reliability and maintainability by allowing for the separate handling of faulty messages, facilitating debugging and compliance auditing, and ensuring that the messaging system continues to operate smoothly despite individual message failures.

These are the main variables you can use to design your queues/topics. Topic or queue management is an essential part of the work you should do when designing your system. It is very important to account for failures in such systems as well.

Now, let's learn how to use one of the most widely used systems for building event-driven architectures: Apache Kafka.

Using Kafka in event-driven services

Kafka is an open source distributed event streaming platform used for building real-time data pipelines and applications. It efficiently handles large volumes of data by publishing and subscribing to streams of records in a fault-tolerant manner. Kafka was originally developed by engineers at LinkedIn to address the company's need for processing massive real-time data feeds. It was open sourced in 2011 and later became an Apache Software Foundation project.

In this book, we will not be able to explore how to maintain a Kafka cluster in production – that is a matter for entire books. Instead, we will present you with a quick setup so that you can connect your Spring services.

Not, let's start by learning about some core concepts related to Kafka. They are key in every company you will work on.

Kafka main concepts

To use Kafka, we will need to understand the following concepts: topics, subscribers/consumers, consumer groups, and partitions. When you understand these core concepts, you will easily know how to do basic system designs using this powerful system:

- Topics in Kafka form a database whose sole purpose is to allow streaming messages from producers to consumers.

- Subscribers (or consumers) are applications that read and process messages from Kafka topics. They subscribe to specific topics based on their data requirements. Consumers can work individually or as part of a consumer group.

- Consumer groups are collections of consumers that coordinate to read messages from topics collectively. They are crucial because they enable scalability and fault tolerance in message consumption. By distributing the workload among multiple consumers in a group, Kafka ensures that each message is processed by only one consumer within the group, preventing duplicate processing and allowing for efficient load balancing.

- Partitions are a fundamental component of Kafka topics. Each topic is divided into multiple partitions, which are ordered sequences of messages. Partitions allow Kafka to scale horizontally by distributing data across different brokers (servers) in a cluster. This distribution enables the parallel processing of messages and improves the system's throughput. Importantly, within each partition, messages are stored and consumed in the exact order they were produced, preserving message order on a per-partition basis. However, Kafka does not guarantee ordering across different partitions within the same topic.

Look at *Figure 10.3* to understand how these elements work together:

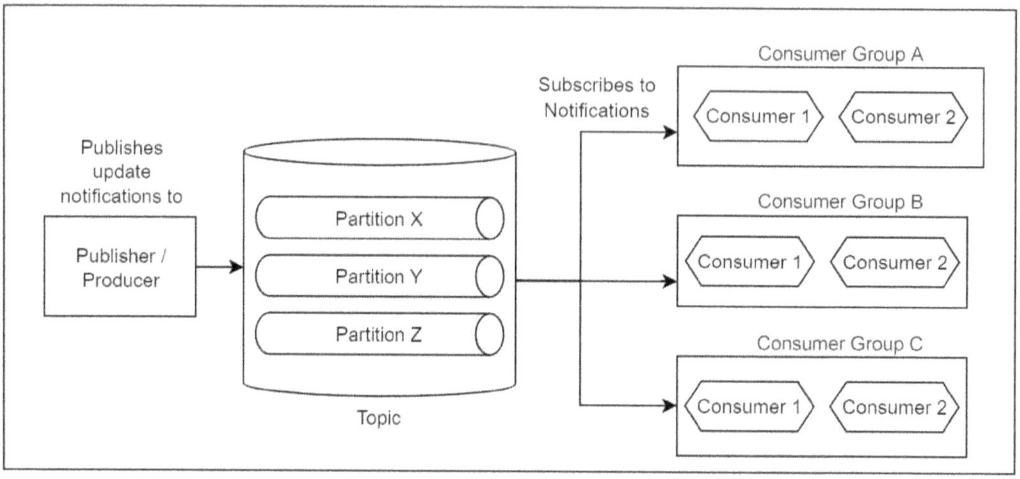

Consumer Group A

Subscribes to Notifications

Consumer 1   Consumer 2

Publishes update notifications to

Publisher / Producer

Partition X

Partition Y

Partition Z

Topic

Consumer Group B

Consumer 1   Consumer 2

Consumer Group C

Consumer 1   Consumer 2

Figure 10.3 – Kafka topology: publishers, partitions, consumer groups, and consumers

From the diagram, you can see the difference between partitions inside a topic, consumers (also called subscribers), and publishers and producers.

Now, let's learn to run a Kafka topic in the simplest way so you can move to implementing a POC for this chapter. Companies in general will usually have topics already available for you to work with.

Installing Kafka on a Linux machine

The services we will implement in this chapter use Kafka as the event infrastructure. To use it, you need to set up a dev instance with the following steps:

1. Download Kafka at `https://kafka.apache.org/downloads`.

    You can use the latest version. Just download the binary package and extract it to a separate home directory, such as `/kafka`.

2. Run the dev instance.

    To run your `kafka` dev instance, you will need to run these two commands:

    *   Here's the ZooKeeper command:

        ```
        cd ~/kafka/<your-kafka-extracted-directory>
        ./bin/zookeeper-server-start.sh config/zookeeper.properties`
        ```

Here's the Kafka command:

```
cd ~/kafka/<your-kafka-extracted-directory>
./bin/kafka-server-start.sh config/server.properties
```

Running these two commands will get you a `kafka` dev instance online, which is enough for this Spring service to connect and create the topic.

3. Connect a console consumer group so that you can see the produced events.

    Run the following command in order to create a separate consumer in your terminal:

    ```
    cd ~/kafka/<your-kafka-extracted-directory>
    ./bin/kafka-console-consumer.sh --bootstrap-server
    localhost:9092 --topic proposal-topic --group console-consumer-
    group --from-beginning
    ```

    This will ensure that every event published to `proposal-topic` can be subscribed to in the console. It makes it easier for you to see the events being produced in real time.

These instructions will get you an independent Kafka instance that you should manually start – consider it a dev environment that you can quickly put online to do your development. So, it does not prepare your Kafka instance to serve streams in production.

OK, so that completes the basics of Kafka. Since Kafka is also considered a specialized NoSQL database, let's also learn how to run and use a MongoDB instance in this chapter, so we can store our API entities in it and have a feel of different NoSQL applications.

Using MongoDB for NoSQL persistency

To build our rental proposal service and make it event-driven, we are also choosing the MongoDB NoSQL database as our persistence layer. Kafka is also a kind of NoSQL database with the purpose of streaming events between services. So, let's make this chapter all about the NoSQL persistence layers.

Here is how you can set up a development environment `MongoDB` instance that will allow you to quickly connect our rental proposal service.

> **Important note**
>
> These instructions work on Ubuntu Linux. We will not have too much time to explore the Windows configuration here. However, it is the same approach in general, with the exception that running the tools will require you to use different executable files. Or, you might want to use Windows WSL, which creates a full-fledged Ubuntu environment. Then you will be able to run these commands as they are.

Let's start:

1. Download the MongoDB binary from the MongoDB download page:

   ```
   https://www.mongodb.com/try/download/community
   ```

   If you want to keep it simple, download the **tarball** and extract it in a local directory.

   If you intend to create a test database for development purposes, feel free to use your own home directory. For instance, you can download your tarball straight to your ~/mongodb database.

2. Extract the latest version of mongodb to your test directory, then create another directory for your actual database files. For instance, I created the following directory to host any test databases I might need:

   ```
   ~/mongodb/mongodbs
   ```

3. Inside the mongodbs database, create one directory for hosting the proposal service database, which I called proposaldb:

   ```
   ~/mongodb/mongodbs/proposaldb
   ```

4. Inside this database, create the following directories:

   ```
   cd ~/mondodb/mongodbs/proposaldb
   mkdir -p data/db
   mkdir log
   ```

   With those two directories, it is possible to start your mongodb instance with the following command:

   ```
   cd ~/mongodb
   ./mongodb-linux-x86_64-ubuntu2204-7.0.14/bin/mongod --dbpath
   mongodbs/proposaldb/data/db --logpath mongodbs/proposaldb/log/
   mongodb.log --fork
   ```

   That command will work as long as you have downloaded and extracted mongodb to your home directory.

5. This command runs mongod, which is the Mongo server daemon. To make sure it is running, just use the following command now:

   ```
   ps aux | grep mongod
   ```

   If you get an output such as the following, it means your instance is running correctly:

   ```
   rodrigo@rodrigo-desktop:~/mongodb$ ps aux | grep mongod
   rodrigo     15992  0.6  0.7 559832 126904
   ?           Sl    20:30   0:11 mongodb-linux-x86_64-
   ubuntu2204-7.0.14/bin/mongod --dbpath mongodbs/proposaldb/data/
   db --logpath mongodbs/proposaldb/log/mongodb.log --fork
   ```

6.　Now, you need a client app to connect to `mongodb`. Make sure to download **Mongodb Shell** from the official MongoDB website:

7.　`https://www.mongodb.com/try/download/shell`

Once you download and extract it to a separate directory on your home `dir`, you will be able to use it with the following command:

```
cd ~/mongodb
./mongosh-2.3.1-linux-x64/bin/mongosh
```

This command will automatically connect `mongo shell` to your local Mongo daemon.

8.　Here are some important and essential commands for you to know how to navigate your database:

```
show dbs # show your databases
use <dbname> # use or create a new database
show collections # show your document collections inside a
database (your tables, basically)
db.myCollection.find() # show all documents in a collection
named myCollection
```

9.　To shut down your `mongodb` server, try the following commands:

```
use admin # this will use your admin database
db.shutdownServer() # this will kill your mongodb process
```

If you manually shut down your `mongodb` server and restart it with the same command line stated before, the same database will be used again, thus keeping your saved data intact.

That is how you can set up your `MongoDB` instance. Now, let's see some details for our rental proposal service.

Our event-driven sample in HomeIt

Just to illustrate how to connect publishers and subscribers using Spring Framework, imagine this: we will create the rental proposal service, which registers the interaction between landlords and tenants while negotiating the rental agreements.

Every rental proposal is an object that keeps the landlord ID, rental property ID, and tenant ID, as well as a collection of *rounds*, which keep the prices each party is trying to negotiate.

The way we will use event-driven implementation here is as follows: we want the rental properties service to inform the tenants if a property has received many proposals recently. We created a points system that we called the *score*. The more proposals a property receives, the higher the score is. So, every time a landlord or a tenant communicates by means of a rental property round – to make an offer or a counteroffer or to reject or approve a proposal – we will increase that rental property score by one.

In essence, every time there is a new negotiation round happening, the rental proposal service will store the rental proposal data in our MongoDB database. Then, it will fire an event to a Kafka topic. Plus, in the rental property service, we will implement a very simple Kafka subscriber that can be notified about a rental proposal round. When a round occurs and the notification arrives, there will be a service in charge of updating the score of the property that received the proposal round.

Here is how we are modeling the `RentalProposal` entity in the rental proposal service:

```java
@Document
public record RentalProposal(
    @Id
    String id,
    String tenantId,
    String landlordId,
    String propertyId,
    List<Round> rounds,
    String status // OPEN, NEGOTIATING, ACCEPTED,
                  // REJECTED, CANCELLED
    ){

    public RentalProposalDTO toDTO() {
        return new RentalProposalDTO(
            this.id, this.tenantId, this.landlordId,
            this.propertyId, this.rounds(), this.status );
    }
}
```

As you can see, creating an entity to be saved in MongoDB basically requires you to use the @Document annotation, from the MongoDB dependency (we will see which dependency to declare in a few minutes).

Also, here is how we are defining the Round entity:

```java
public record Round (
    String roundId,
    String status, // OPEN, OFFER, COUNTER_OFFER, APPROVED,
                   // REJECTED, CANCELLED
    String authorId,
    Double value,
    String message) {

    // Getters and Setters
}
```

That means that a `RentalProperty` object can hold as many rounds as is required to make the entire negotiation happen.

Also, here are the `RentalProposalStates` and `RoundStates` enum classes, which help us to maintain the actual stage in which we are in a negotiation:

```
public enum RentalProposalStates {
    OPEN,
    NEGOTIATING,
    ACCEPTED,
    REJECTED,
    CANCELLED
}
public enum RoundStates {
    OPEN,
    OFFER,
    COUNTER_OFFER,
    APPROVAL,
    REJECTION,
    CANCELLATION
}
```

So, once the `Round` move from one state to the next one, the `RentalProposal` objects also resolve to new, more general statuses.

Now, let's see how the rest of the service is created.

Building our rental proposal service publishers

As I have stated before, the rental proposal service is very important: it will be used in HomeIT to register the interaction between a tenant and a landlord while negotiating the terms of the rental agreement.

We will not have the time to explore it entirely, so I will add some key data about this service. You can take your time to read about the entire service at `https://github.com/PacktPublishing/Spring-System-Design-in-Practice/tree/main/chapter-10/rental-proposal-service`.

Combining WebFlux, MongoDB, and Kafka in Spring Services

Since we want to make this service asynchronous and robust, we will create it using WebFlux. Plus, we will use a bit of the Spring Web style while declaring the controller interfaces.

So, here is how we have declared our dependencies – mixing Spring Web, Kafka, MongoDB, and WebFlux dependencies. This is present in the `dependencies` section of our `build.gradle` file:

```
implementation 'org.springframework.boot:spring-boot-starter-webflux'
implementation 'org.springframework.boot:spring-boot-starter-data-
mongodb-reactive'
implementation 'org.springframework.kafka:spring-kafka'
implementation 'com.fasterxml.jackson.core:jackson-databind'
```

Since we will be using JSON objects to send and receive notifications from our Kafka topics, we also had to include the `jackson-databind` dependency.

Now, let's see a quick example of how to write the actual endpoints in our controllers. Here is how we create a new `RentalProposal` and add a `Round` to a `Proposal`. They are both declared in the `RentalProposalController` class:

```java
@PostMapping()
public Mono<RentalProposalDTO> createProposal(
    @RequestBody RentalProposalDTO rentalProposalDTO) {
    return service.createProposal(rentalProposalDTO);
}


@PostMapping("/{proposalId}/rounds")
public Mono<ResponseEntity<RentalProposalDTO>> addRound(
    @PathVariable String proposalId,
    @RequestBody Round round) {

    return service.addRound(proposalId, round)
        .map(ResponseEntity::ok)
        .switchIfEmpty(
            Mono.just(ResponseEntity.notFound().build()));
}
```

We can see that this time, we are mixing the Spring Web endpoint declaration with WebFlux. They can work together in a seamless way. For the `addRound()` method, if we provide the ID of a proposal that does not exist, we just return a `404 (NOT_FOUND)` HTTP code.

Let's take a quick look at how to save the rental proposal entity data to the database, in the `Service` layer. Here's how we have defined our `Service` interface:

```java
@Service
public interface RentalProposalService {
    Mono<RentalProposalDTO> createProposal(RentalProposalDTO
newRentalProposal);
```

```
Mono<RentalProposalDTO> addRound(String proposalId, Round round);

Flux<RentalProposalDTO> getProposals();

Mono<RentalProposalDTO> deleteProposal(String proposalId);

Mono<RentalProposalDTO> getProposal(String proposalId);
}
```

Here is how we declare the service implementation (the `RentalProposalServiceImpl` class):

```
@Service
public class RentalProposalServiceImpl implements
RentalProposalService {

    private final RentalProposalRepository repository;
    private final KafkaTemplate<String,
        RentalProposalEvent> kafkaTemplate;

    public RentalProposalServiceImpl(
        RentalProposalRepository repository,
        KafkaTemplate<String, RentalProposalEvent>
            kafkaTemplate) {
        this.repository = repository;
        this.kafkaTemplate = kafkaTemplate;
}
}
```

As you can see, we are injecting two important Spring Beans here: `RentalProposalRepository` and the `KafkaTemplate` interface.

`RentalProposalRepository` is a basic Mongo Repository extension, which we can see here:

```
public interface RentalProposalRepository extends
    ReactiveMongoRepository<RentalProposal, String> {}
```

It is important to note that, since we are using Spring WebFlux here, we need to use `ReactiveMongoRepository`. It means that our operations in MongoDB will be processed asynchronously. That makes the entire `WebFlux` async pipeline work correctly.

Since we do not need any custom methods (as we saw in *Chapter 7*), we can just leave this interface as is. We are saving `RentalProposal` objects using MongoDB, the ID is a string, and that's it.

In `RentalProposalServiceImpl`, we can also see that we are injecting the `KafkaTemplate` interface, which comes directly from the Kafka dependency itself. It allows us to publish our events to Kafka topics. To use that interface, we need to specify the key type (a string; it serves when we want to order the messages and distribute them among partitions) and the object that will flow through that topic. In our case, we have chosen to publish `RentalProposalEvent`, which we can see here:

```
public record RentalProposalEvent(
        String proposalId,
        String roundId,
        String propertyId,
        String roundType) {
}
```

As we can see, when saving a new `Proposal` or `Round`, we will publish `RentalProposalEvent` so that the `RentalProperties` service can subscribe to the notifications and update the score in `RentalProperty` that lives in the `RentalProperties` database. In that way, other customers will see whether a property has a high score – meaning that there are a lot of people trying to negotiate for that property. `RentalProposalEvent` contains the proposal ID, the ID of the round that was published inside the rental proposal, the property ID that is referenced in the proposal, and the `roundType` attribute, indicating whether it was an offer, a counteroffer, an approval, a rejection, and so on.

Here is how we create a proposal and how we emit the Round at the `Service` layer:

```
public Mono<RentalProposalDTO> createProposal(
    RentalProposalDTO newRentalProposal) {

    Round firstRound = new Round(UUID.randomUUID().toString(),
        RoundStates.OPEN.toString(),
        newRentalProposal.tenantId(),
        null,
        null);
    List<Round> rounds = List.of(firstRound);

    return repository.save(new RentalProposal(
        UUID.randomUUID().toString(),
        newRentalProposal.tenantId(),
        newRentalProposal.landlordId(),
        newRentalProposal.propertyId(),
        rounds,
        RentalProposalStates.OPEN.toString()))
        .flatMap( proposal ->
            Mono.fromFuture(
                kafkaTemplate.send("proposal-topic",
                    new RentalProposalEvent(
                        proposal.id(),
                        firstRound.roundId(),
```

```
                            proposal.propertyId(),
                            firstRound.status())))
                .thenApply(result -> proposal)))
        .map(RentalProposal::toDTO);
}
```

As you can see, when creating a new `RentalProposal`, we create a new Round with the OPEN state and add it to the new `RentalProposal`, then save it in the mongodb repository.

When we receive the result from the `repository.save()` operation, it is time to finally publish our event. This is how we tell other systems about the newly created `RentalProposal` object. As you can see, we need to name the topic, then create the event we are sending. Finally, we map the result to a DTO that we will return in our controller method.

Similarly, this is how we save a new Round to the `RentalProposal` object:

```
public Mono<RentalProposalDTO> addRound(
    String proposalId, Round round) {

    return repository.findById(proposalId)
        .flatMap(proposal -> {
            RentalProposal p = new RentalProposal(
                    proposal.id(),
                    proposal.tenantId(),
                    proposal.landlordId(),
                    proposal.propertyId(),
                    allRounds(round, proposal),
                    newProposalStatusFromRound(round)
            );
            return repository.save(p);
        })
        .flatMap(proposal ->
            Mono.fromFuture(
                kafkaTemplate.send("proposal-topic",
                new RentalProposalEvent(
                    proposalId,
                    round.roundId(),
                    proposal.propertyId(),
                    round.status())))
            .thenApply(result -> proposal)))
        .map(RentalProposal::toDTO);
}
```

This is also very easy to understand. We provide the proposal ID, referencing the proposal to which we want to add the new negotiation round, and the actual Round object, which we saw earlier.

After saving the new Round object, we can also publish the update to our Kafka proposal topic, then parse the original RentalProposal object to a DTO that we will return in our controller class.

That is basically it for the publisher class. There are two moments in which we will notify other systems that something has changed here.

Now, in order to allow this system to connect to our Kafka topic, we need to see how the actual application.properties file is built:

```
spring.application.name=rental-proposal-service
server.port=8084
spring.kafka.bootstrap-servers=localhost:9092
spring.kafka.producer.key-serializer=org.apache.kafka.common.
serialization.StringSerializer
spring.kafka.producer.value-serializer=org.springframework.kafka.
support.serializer.JsonSerializer
```

As you can see, we are defining port 8084 for this service, then we define localhost:9092 as the default Kafka server port, and finally, we indicate which classes we will use to serialize our messages and keys.

Streaming object collections with WebFlux

Another thing important to notice is that, when using WebFlux, we can rely on streaming objects from your server to your client. Instead of using pagination, we can use Flux objects to stream objects without needing the whole collection to be available in memory.

This is very interesting, as it gives us the power for our HTTP clients to consume these objects little by little. Here is an example of how we can stream data using the Flux interface:

```
@GetMapping
public Mono<ResponseEntity<Flux<RentalProposalDTO>>>
    getProposals() {

    return Mono.just(ResponseEntity.ok(
        service.getProposals()))
        .switchIfEmpty(
            Mono.just(ResponseEntity.notFound().build()));
}
```

This is probably confusing but let me break it down for you. The service.getProposals() method will basically query the database and return a stream of objects that will be available little by little, as our client HTTP browser requests them.

In this implementation, we are wrapping our Flux stream of `RentalProposalDTO` with a `ResponseEntity` object. However, since we cannot resolve `ResponseObject` immediately, we wrap it around a `Mono` object.

So, in the return of the controller, we provide a `Mono` object that will return a `ResponseEntity` object. `ResponseEntity`, which is a single object containing the HTTP return status code, will in turn contain a `Flux` that allows our client requests to stream objects, little by little, directly from the database.

Interesting, isn't it? You will be able to see the entire flow by visiting the code from our application.

Bear in mind, however, that your HTTP client should support at least version 1.1 to be able to stream objects, and HTTP 2.0 if you need optimized streaming with multiple channels. Other than that, you can control how you are retrieving data in your client app. The best way to use it would be twofold:

- If your client application is a backend system, you should use WebFlux and other async processing tools so it can stream the objects with an asynchronous pipeline, just as we are doing in the rental proposal service.

- If your client application is a frontend app, you can fetch new objects as your customer requests more objects. You can build effects that are similar to the Facebook message stream, which fetches a few new objects as the user scrolls down, for example.

That's all. There is a lot to say about streaming architectures as well, and I have tried to provide you with some very simple and powerful examples here. Now, let's see the other side of the equation in our microservice architecture: the changes we will make in the `RentalProperties` service to subscribe to the rental proposal updates.

Building our rental properties service consumers

As we stated before, the rental properties service is interested in whatever negotiations are happening in our rental proposal service. That way, every time a new offer is made on a rental property, the rental properties service will be able to increase that property's score.

The change is pretty easy. Here is how we define a consumer service that listens to the message updates:

```
@Service
public class ProposalConsumerService {
    private final ScoreService scoreService;
    private final ObjectMapper objectMapper
        = new ObjectMapper();

    public ProposalConsumerService(
        @Qualifier("jdbcRentalPropertyService")
        ScoreService scoreService) {
```

```
        this.scoreService = scoreService;
    }


    @KafkaListener(topics = "proposal-topic",
        groupId = "rental-properties-proposal-group")
    public void consume(String message)
        throws JsonProcessingException {

        RentalProposalEvent event = objectMapper.readValue(
            message, RentalProposalEvent.class);

        scoreService.addScore(
            UUID.fromString(event.propertyId()));

        System.out.println("Consumed message: " + event);
    }
}
```

As you can see, to reach the messages, we need to convert the `RentalProposalEvent` JSON back from a string by using the `ObjectMapper` class. It is pretty easy, we just declare the @ `KafkaListener` annotation. Its parameters are the topic name and the consumer group the listener belongs to. The consumer group is especially important when you want to stream events to different services. Each service should have its own consumer group. Also, when you are scaling your services – let's say, adding more copies of the rental properties service in the runtime – the Kafka topic will detect that there are multiple consumers inside the same consumer group and the messages will be distributed evenly among them.

Well, once you receive your message as a string and de-serialize it back to `RentalProposalEvent`, we call the score service `addScore()` method. The implementation is as follows:

```
@Override
public void addScore(UUID propertyId) {
    StringBuilder sql = new StringBuilder("UPDATE rental_properties
SET score = score + 1 WHERE id=:propertyId");

    MapSqlParameterSource params = new MapSqlParameterSource();
    params.addValue("propertyId", propertyId);

    int rowsAffected = jdbcTemplate.update(
        sql.toString(), params);

    if (rowsAffected > 0) {
        System.out.println(
        "Score updated successfully for property: " +
```

```
            propertyId);
    } else {
        System.out.println(
        "No property found with ID: " + propertyId);
    }
}
```

That's all. We are basically using a JDBC Template to run a customized SQL query and update a single property score. Of course, we had to add the `score` attribute to our `RentalProperty` class so that it is possible to use the update query. We have also adjusted the DTO classes and the endpoints so that the `score` attribute is present whenever we fetch `RentalProperty` data in our rental properties service.

That's all! You can see the entire resulting implementation of our rental properties service at `https://github.com/PacktPublishing/Spring-System-Design-in-Practice/tree/main/chapter-10/rental-property-microservice`.

Extending our end-to-end tests

Of course, now that we have the new rental proposal service, we want to know whether it is working properly. The best way we could do that is to add new calls to our end-to-end or integration tests project.

Due to page constraints, we will not be able to show every single new line of code in our integration tests. However, here is just a small sample of the new lines we added to our integration tests project:

```
scoreIs(0, createdProperty, createdTenant);

CreatedProposal proposal =
    tenantCreatesProposal(createdTenant,
        createdLandlord, createdProperty);

tenantMakesFirstOffer(createdProperty, createdTenant, proposal);

tenantRetrievesProperty(
    createdProperty.createdPropertyResponse(),
    createdTenant.userTokenResponse());

scoreIs(2, createdProperty, createdTenant);

landlordRejectsOffer(createdProperty,
    createdLandlord, proposal);

tenantMakesCounterOffer(createdTenant,
    createdProperty, proposal);
```

```
landlordMakesCounterOffer(createdLandlord,
    createdProperty, proposal);

scoreIs(5, createdProperty, createdTenant);

tenantAcceptsOffer(createdTenant, createdProperty, proposal);
scoreIs(6, createdProperty, createdTenant);
```

As you can see, I have provided a method for testing the score of a `RentalProperty` – it fetches the rental property from our properties service and makes sure the expected score is found. We also have new methods to simulate the negotiation. Our tenant will make the first offer, then the landlord rejects it, then the tenant proceeds with a counteroffer, and the landlord does another counteroffer... Finally, the tenant accepts the offer. Every time along the way, we test the rental property score to make sure the `RentalProperty` service is updating the score according to the last negotiation rounds.

You can see and run the entire end-to-end tests at `https://github.com/PacktPublishing/ Spring-System-Design-in-Practice/tree/main/chapter-10/integration- tests`.

Summary

In this chapter, we discussed a lot of great things about event-driven architecture. We learned how to design topics and service topologies, and a series of variables you can choose from in order to make your topics well-organized according to your company and product requirements.

We also included a few pages demonstrating how to create a service using Spring Web, Spring WebFlux, and MongoDB as a NoSQL persistence layer. I hope this can spark some creativity in your service designs.

This has been a fun chapter! I hope you had a great learning experience here. In the next chapter, we will organize our services in a better way so we can learn how to prepare it in a self-organizing cloud architecture using Spring Cloud.

Get This Book's PDF Version and Exclusive Extras

Scan the QR code (or go to `packtpub.com/unlock`). Search for this book by name, confirm the edition, and then follow the steps on the page.

Note: Keep your invoice handly. Purchase made directly from packt don't require one.

Part 4: Orchestrating Resilient Services

Now, we'll take everything we've built and prepare it for real-world deployment. This part covers launching microservices in a cloud environment, optimizing them for resilience, and structuring configurations to handle failures gracefully. We'll also dive into advanced techniques for making microservices fault-tolerant and self-healing.

This part has the following chapters:

11

Launching Your Self-Organizing Microservice Cloud

Welcome to *Chapter 11*! So far, we have created services with a prototypical approach. We have not cared too much about how they are instantiated or how they find each other. We also have not bothered about how they are producing logs. That was because we wanted to provide the most fun and important parts first.

Now, you have the key tools and techniques to develop systems with Spring. You know how Spring beans work and how to write APIs using Spring Web and WebFlux. We have seen examples of how to manage data with SQL and NoSQL examples. We have also learned how to test our systems in several ways and how to write event-driven systems.

That was a lot! Now, let's prepare our architecture to be released in production. To deploy your system, we need to deal with other important things, such as the following subjects that we are going to cover in this chapter:

- How to better structure your service logs

- How to organize your property files for different environments

- Setting up your services using Spring Cloud infrastructure

These three key points will set you up for success in orchestrating your cloud infrastructure using native Spring tools. It will become fairly easy to manage your cloud configurations, for your microservices to find each other, and to expose a unified API to your clients. Plus, you will also be able to hide the endpoints you don't want to go public. Are you ready? Let's go!

Technical requirements

You can use the reference code for *Chapter 11* contained in our GitHub repository: `https://github.com/PacktPublishing/Spring-System-Design-in-Practice/tree/main/chapter-11`.

How to produce your service logs

To write your service prototypes quickly to begin with, it is OK to write logs by using the simple `System.out.println()` method. But to make sure your services can report operations in a more clear and structured way in production and other test environments, you will need to write your logs in a distinct way that allows you to choose how much detail will be exposed in each environment.

It is really important to write your logs properly. Forgetting this crucial step is something that even seasoned developers do regularly, and it creates difficulties in troubleshooting. Great logs will make it quite easy to find the root cause of systemic problems. If you want to make your life a lot easier as a developer, make sure you implement the logging standards we will see in the next sections.

What are the existing log levels?

In general, when writing logs using tools such as Log4J or Logback (both of which are supported by Spring), you will be able to declare log **levels** – that is, your messages will have a specific meaning.

These levels categorize the purpose and severity of each log entry, making it easier to interpret and prioritize them during analysis.

These are the common log levels we regularly use, regardless of the tool we use to create the logs:

- **TRACE**: This is the finest-grained information, typically used for diagnosing specific issues by tracing program execution at a very detailed level. It is rarely enabled in production due to the high volume of output. I like to use it during development when I am testing my apps locally, as it sometimes helps me to not use debug features in my IDE.

- **DEBUG**: This is detailed information on the flow through the system. It is also used for debugging purposes during development and test validation. Sometimes, we will want to enable it during troubleshooting in production to understand the application's behavior. Beware that debug and trace logs can be very verbose, which can cause problems in triaging logs in production, when you have a high volume. It could also create a lot of unnecessary storage costs.

- **INFO**: This highlights the progress of the application at a high level. It is generally enabled in production to log significant events such as startup, shutdown, or configuration changes. Avoid using info logs for high-volume operations, since most successful operations will produce the same logs and will become meaningless.

- **WARN**: These are potentially harmful or unexpected situations that are not necessarily errors but may require attention. It indicates issues that do not prevent the application from functioning but might need investigation. I like to use warn logs when dealing with operations that happen in high volume. By omitting info logs and only issuing warn logs in high-volume operations, we can just see the logs when things get odd or unexpected. Then it becomes meaningful for troubleshooting.

- **ERROR**: This informs about events that might still allow the application to continue running but indicate a failure in a specific operation. It is used to log exceptions or errors that are handled but signify a problem. It is good to highlight the difference between error and warn logs. A warn log means you do not have an error but only an unexpected situation, such as a client sending a request in the wrong way and your application answering with a 400 (bad request) response. A bad request response is not an error per se, but since your application is not supposed to receive malformed requests in a well-configured environment, it is good to look at warn messages to check that your system is behaving the way it should.

- **FATAL**: These are severe error events that will make the application abort. It indicates critical failures that require immediate attention, such as system outages or data corruption.

With these log levels, you will be able to tell the severity of the output in your console. Now, let's learn how to actually write the logs using Spring's natively supported tools.

How to write logs in Spring

The two Java log tools/frameworks I like to use the most in Spring services are Log4J and Logback. They contain similar features and allow logs to be formatted in interesting ways, so we will pick the most common way to use Log4J here (Logback is an alternative framework, but we don't have enough space in the book to show you how to use it). We can create a log service instance for any class by annotating the class with @Slf4j. That will use Log4J framework to create a `log` object that can be referenced from anywhere in that class instance. Here's an example:

```
@RestControllerAdvice
@Slf4j
public class SampleExceptionHandler {

    @ExceptionHandler(RuntimeException.class)
    public ResponseEntity<ProblemDetail>
        handleGenericException(RuntimeException ex) {

        log.error("exception: ", ex);

        ProblemDetail problemDetail =
            ProblemDetail.forStatus(
                HttpStatus.INTERNAL_SERVER_ERROR);

        problemDetail.setTitle(
            "Customized Internal Server Error");
        problemDetail.setDetail(
            "An unexpected error occurred: "
                    + ex.getMessage());
        problemDetail.setInstance(
```

```
        URI.create(
            "/api/v1/rental-properties/error"));
    problemDetail.setProperty("timestamp",
        LocalDateTime.now().toString());

    log.debug("The resulting error object: {}",
        problemDetail);

    return new ResponseEntity<>(problemDetail,
        HttpStatus.INTERNAL_SERVER_ERROR);
    }
    // ... the rest of the code goes here
}
```

In this class, we are saying that the first issued log is at the ERROR level and the second one is at the DEBUG level. These are two different detail levels that you will want to be mindful of when running your application. Debug logs are normally used when you need to know the key variable values and the flow details from the logs so that you know your program is running correctly. Error logs are used when you do not need details about the program's normal execution, just the exception details – in essence, instructions that did not behave as expected, which means your software is broken at some level.

Now, you need to specify which log level you want to be active when you are running an application. You can specify that in the properties file. Here are three examples from our rental properties microservice properties file:

```
# Enable INFO logs for your entire application
logging.level.root=INFO


#Enable DEBUG logs for one of your classes
logging.level.com.homeit.rental.property.controller.
SampleExceptionHandler=DEBUG


# Enable DEBUG logs for Spring Web packages logging.level.org.
springframework.web=DEBUG logging.level.org.springframework.web.
servlet=DEBUG
```

In the first example, we are saying that we just want logs starting from the INFO level (the root log). That means that when you are running the service, the application will not produce logs from levels below INFO (DEBUG and TRACE), but it will still produce logs for levels higher than INFO (WARN, ERROR, and FATAL).

As you can see, it is very important to choose the level at which you want your application to produce logs, so always keep a log level hierarchy in mind.

In the second example, we can see that we have set up the logs for a specific class (`SampleExceptionHandler`). This means, only for the `SampleExceptionHandler` class, that your application will produce logs from the `DEBUG` level and below (which includes `INFO`, `WARN`, `ERROR`, and `FATAL`).

Specifying which log levels to produce for specific classes allows you to focus on the details of the parts of your application you want to investigate or monitor more closely. If you set your log level to `DEBUG` for your whole application, it might become impossible to monitor all messages.

It is also possible to turn on more detailed logs for Spring-specific packages. That is what we did in the third example. Since the root logger configuration targets only your application classes, you will have to explicitly turn on `DEBUG` or `TRACE` logs for Spring-specific classes and packages when you want to understand what is happening inside the Spring Framework. It is quite useful to turn on logs for Spring classes sometimes, and you will be able to see how the Spring native classes behave over time. One example is that you might find it useful to turn on `TRACE` or `DEBUG` logs for your `RestTemplate` beans. Then, you will be able to look at the HTTP requests logs in much finer detail.

Understanding your log output

Once you have set up your logs, you will get different output in your application console. As you run and test your application, you might find it useful to play with different levels a bit so that you understand which ones you will need in different environments. Here is an example of a log we get in the console:

```
2024-10-07T09:26:25.749-03:00 ERROR 464821 --- [rental-property-
microservice] [nio-9601-exec-1] c.h.r.p.c.SampleExceptionHandler:
exception:
java.lang.RuntimeException: This was a sample
unhandled runtime exception at com.homeit.rental.
property.controller.RentalPropertyController.
runtimeExceptionSample(RentalPropertyController.java:150)

...
```

As you can see, the log you produce will have a default date format and severity level (`ERROR`, `TRACE`, `DEBUG`, `INFO`, etc). It will also emit the class name, as well as any text we have added. Of course, your personalized text should match the log level you desire. An `INFO` log will usually produce success messages in the console, just to let the team know that the execution is going on as expected. A `DEBUG` log will have variable details to make it easier to assert that the code is running as expected and the key variables hold the expected data. An `ERROR` log should come with the stack trace and key variable values to make it easier to identify where the error occurred and why.

Compared to the first log example, logs produced at the `DEBUG` level will come out a bit differently, as in the following:

```
2024-10-07T09:26:25.752-03:00 DEBUG 464821 --- [rental-property-
microservice] [nio-9601-exec-1] c.h.r.p.c.SampleExceptionHandler:
The resulting error object: ProblemDetail[type='about:blank',
```

```
title='Customized Internal Server Error', status=500, detail='An
unexpected error occurred: This was a sample unhandled runtime
exception', instance='/api/v1/rental-properties/error',
properties='{timestamp=2024-10-07T09:26:25.752887017}']
```

As you can see, the main difference between both logs is the level, as mentioned above. As we change from the `log.error()` method to the `log.info()` method, we can see the levels printed when you're running the application. Again, in this case, when you set your log levels to `INFO` and don't define `DEBUG` logs for your classes, that means every `log.debug()` call will produce no output in your console.

That is pretty much it for an introduction on how to better structure your logs. Now, let's talk about how to structure your application properties.

How to organize your property files

Besides organizing our logs, we also need to correctly inform our services about the important values we want them to use during runtime. For instance, in our HomeIt example, at the startup time of the `RentalProperties` service, we probably want to tell it the name of the topic we want it to read events from, or the address and port of important services the `RentalProperties` service is connecting to, such as the database address and credentials.

These are called **service properties**, and there are two types of properties:

- The ones that are required by Spring dependencies to define their behavior

- The ones that you will require in your application to define the behavior of your code

There are two important reasons why you would want to set some variables using service properties:

- Because you want to make it easier to change those values when you launch the same service in different environments.

- Because you want to hide values that should be secret, such as credentials. You don't want to have passwords hardcoded in your services.

There is not too much to say about what a service property is. Its basic function is to inform your service about important configuration values that should be used at execution time.

Now that we have explained the *what*, we will show some examples of *how* you can inject property values into your application. But first, let's learn the different ways to declare properties in Spring.

Writing your properties files

In general, your file should always be created inside your project folder, in the `src/main/resources` folder. Depending on the format chosen to write your properties, the file name will be different.

Let's start by looking at the regular `application.properties` format, and then we'll look at YAML format.

Writing an application.properties file

An `application.properties` file is in a simple format in which you can set one application property per line, and the name of the property is separated by a dot. The property value is separated from the property name by an equals sign. Here is an example, showing a slice of the properties we are using in our `RentalProperties` service:

```
spring.application.name=rental-property-microservice
server.port=8085
spring.kafka.bootstrap-servers=localhost:9092
spring.kafka.consumer.group-id=proposal-group
spring.kafka.consumer.auto-offset-reset=earliest
```

As you can see, the properties are organized in a hierarchy. Every Spring Kafka dependency property will have the prefix `spring.kafka`, which makes it easier to see which dependencies are using each property you declare.

You can see the entire file here: `https://github.com/PacktPublishing/Spring-System-Design-in-Practice/blob/main/chapter-11/rental-property-microservice/src/main/resources/application.properties`.

YAML properties file

A YAML property file has a different format:

- First, the file should always be named with the `.yml` extension, by convention – therefore, it should be named `application.yml`

- Second, the properties prefixes all have their own lines, and the child values are nested with two spaces indentations

Here is an example from the `AuthorizationProvider` service. Just like the `application.properties` file in the `RentalProperties` service, the `application.yml` property is also located in the `src/main/resources` folder of your project:

```
spring:
  application:
    name: authprovider
  datasource:
    url: jdbc:h2:mem:testdb
    driverClassName: org.h2.Driver
    username: sa
    password: password
```

Again, this example is just a slice of the complete set of properties used in the `Authorization` service. You can see the entire properties file here: `https://github.com/PacktPublishing/Spring-System-Design-in-Practice/blob/main/chapter-11/authprovider/src/main/resources/application.yml`.

Overriding a property file when starting the packaged application

After you package your application in a JAR file, there are a number of ways to override your properties file so that you do not need to edit the JAR file itself. These methods are useful when you are packaging your app with some development properties file, then you want to override these environment properties with properties from the actual environment you will work with (in production, for example).

Let's look at five methods in the following subsections.

Adding a new properties file in the same directory from your application

Place an `application.properties` or `application.yml` file in the same directory where your JAR file is located:

```
rental-properties-microservice.jar
application.properties
```

When the application starts, Spring Boot looks for external configuration files outside the JAR file first. By adding a properties file in the same directory, you can override the properties packaged within the JAR file.

Adding the properties file to the /config directory

Create a `config` directory in the same location as your JAR file and place your `application.properties` or `application.yml` file inside this directory:

```
yourapp.jar
config/
    application.properties
```

Spring Boot automatically checks the `/config` subdirectory for configuration files. Properties defined here will override those inside the JAR file.

Overriding a property value using the command line

Pass properties directly as command-line arguments when running your application:

```
java -jar yourapp.jar --server.port=8081
```

Command-line arguments have the highest precedence in Spring Boot's property hierarchy. This means they will override properties set in both external files and those packaged within the JAR.

If you declare your property using `-D`, that means you will inject the property into the JVM environment:

```
java -Dserver.port=8082 -jar yourapp.jar
```

In this example, you are just overriding one property, the server port.

Defining a new properties file at the command line

Create a new `application.properties` or `application.yml` file with the configurations you want and place it in a directory of your choice. Then you can use the `--spring.config.location` option to specify the path to your custom properties file when running your JAR:

```
java -jar yourapp.jar --spring.config.location=file:/path/to/your/
custom.properties
```

Hardcoding your properties

Another way to set properties in your Spring application is to write them in your code. In our `RentalProperties` service, we already did this. We wrote properties in our `RentalPropertiesApplication` class like so:

```java
private static void virtualThreads(SpringApplication app){
    app.setDefaultProperties(
        Map.of("spring.threads.virtual.enabled", "true"));
}
```

Now that you know a few essential ways to declare your service properties, let's move to some other tactics you can use to set properties on your Spring services.

Setting property values using environment variables

In Spring Boot applications, you can also set property values using your operational system environment variables. Let's see two ways to define property values using environment variables.

Overriding properties with environment variables

Environment variables can override properties defined in your application's configuration files. When your application starts, Spring Boot checks for environment variables that match property names and uses their values to override the properties you have defined within property files or from hardcoded properties in your Spring service (the ones you saw in the previous examples). To declare your properties with operating system environment variables, you will replace the dot that separates the properties words with an underscore.

Here is an example of defining the server port in a Linux environment. You should remember that, originally, declaring a server port in a properties file requires you to write `server.port`. Now, we just replace the dot with an underscore. This command can be used on your Linux console to declare your server property using a system variable:

```
export SERVER_PORT=8081
```

Here is an example of defining the server port in a Windows environment:

```
set SERVER_PORT=8081
```

With that, whenever you start any Spring application, because Spring Web will, by default, try to read the `server.port` property from your configuration, it will read the server port from the environment variable and override property files.

Property values order of precedence

When you combine different ways of declaring property values, some will override the others. Here is the order of precedence– that is, which property value sources will override the others:

- Command-line arguments override all other property sources
- Java system properties come next in precedence
- Environment variables override properties in files
- External configuration files override packaged ones
- Packaged configuration files are used if no external properties are provided
- Default properties are the last resort (including properties declared directly in your code)

This is how you can organize your way into declaring property values. But wait, there's more. In the next section, let's see how to pre-package different property files for different environments. This is what we call the Spring profiles.

Creating property files per deployment environment

Suppose your application needs to be deployed in a development environment, then deployed into a staging environment for final tests and quality assurance, before being moved to production. That is a very common scenario in the industry. In that case, wouldn't it be nice to have a different set of property values already defined for each one of those environments? By using Spring Profiles, you can prepare one `.property` or `.yml` file for each environment.

Let's say you want your application to run on different server ports depending on the environment:

- Development (dev): Run on port 8081

- Staging (stg): Run on port 8082

- Production (prod): Run on port 8080

Here's how you can set this up using Spring Profiles. First, create profile-specific property files. In your `src/main/resources` directory, create separate property files for each environment:

- `application-dev.properties`

- `application-stg.properties`

- `application-prod.properties`

In each property file, declare your `server.port` with different values. When you run your application, you can specify which profile to activate, and Spring Boot will automatically load the corresponding properties file. For example, this is how you load the dev property file:

```
java -jar yourapp.jar --spring.profiles.active=dev
```

That means your service will load `application-dev.properties` along with the default `application.properties` file. The dev environment file will override the default property file with whatever properties you have declared in it. By declaring an active profile, Spring will try to load the file named `application-{profile}.properties` on top of your default properties file.

Reading properties from environment variables

Your property values can also reference environment variables. For example, when declaring the `server.port` property for your Spring application, you are allowed to use the following syntax so that you can extract the value of the environment variable to your property file:

```
server.port=${RENTAL_PROPERTIES_SERVER_PORT}
```

This means your `server.port` value will be the same value as the `RENTAL_PROPERTIES_SERVER_PORT` environment variable.

Injecting environment variables is very important when you want to hide secrets, such as passwords for important services. Storing those values in environment variables means you do not need to write them directly in your properties files. And because they are not in the properties files, you can safely guard those files using Git.

OK, this explains everything you need to know to declare properties in your services. Now, how can you actually inject one of those properties into your Spring applications? That's what we will learn in the next section.

Injecting properties in your services

If you need to inject an environment variable into your Spring application, just use the following syntax on your services. In this example, we are changing the `Proposal` service in the `RentalProposalServiceImpl` class so that we can declare the name of the `kafka` topic in our property file:

```
@Value("${rental.proposal.topic.name:sample-name}")
private String topicName;
```

This is how we can declare the property in the `application.properties` file:

```
rental.proposal.topic.name=proposal-topic
```

This wraps up how you can structure your application property values. To summarize, you can do the following:

- Write separate property files in different formats (`properties` or `.yml` files)
- Write specific property files for different execution profiles (useful for providing value to different environments)
- Set the property files to be used when starting the application
- Set the property values in the command line for starting your Spring application
- Set the property files directly in your code
- Use your operating system to store property file values that Spring will detect at startup time
- Inject your own property files in your Spring services

With that, we can go to the next topic, where we see how we can use Spring Cloud to launch services in a self-organizing way.

Setting up your services using Spring Cloud

Spring Cloud is a set of tools in Spring that helps you launch your services with a series of features that allow you to simplify your connections. By using Spring Cloud, you are able to do things such as the following:

- Create a configuration service that will host the config files for all your microservices
- Create a discovery service that will help your services to connect to one another automatically, regardless of the IP and ports used by each service
- Scale your microservices to multiple copies and have them working behind load balancers automatically

- Map all your services in a single API gateway in such a way that your clients can reach any of your microservices by just hitting one IP and one port

Let's see how this works by first looking at the Spring Cloud topology. We will use our HomeIt example to illustrate how the Spring Cloud topology is built.

Understanding the Spring Cloud topology

The following diagram lays out how the Spring Cloud components fit into the architecture we have built so far for HomeIt:

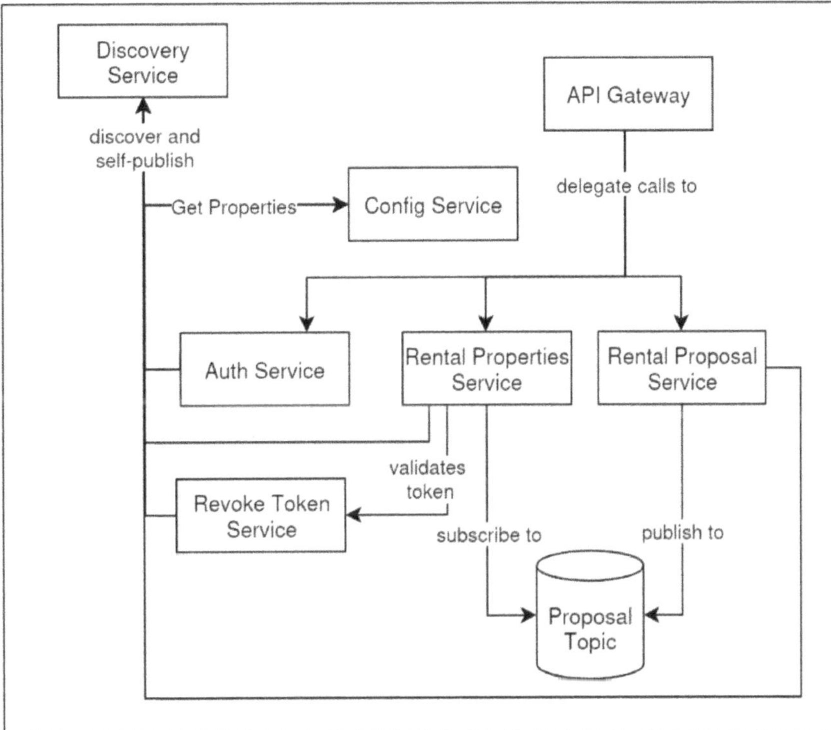

Figure 11.1: HomeIt Spring Cloud topology

The following observations apply:

- First, the API gateway is a special Spring Cloud service we are going to write that will allow our clients to consume just one IP and port in order to reach any service in your cloud. That will mean you don't have to force your clients to have addresses for every service copy. Also, the API gateway will automatically load-balance the calls to your services if you create several copies for each one. That helps to scale your app horizontally (when you need to create multiple copies of the same service to handle more throughput).

- Second, the Config service is a special Spring Cloud service that allows you to expose a config repository so that any of your services will be able to load configurations from the Config service directly. The Config service enables retrieving property files from different mediums. In our example, we will expose the configuration files using GitHub as a central repository, which is ideal when we want to version our property files. When starting up, the Config service will basically clone your Git configuration repository and make the files available to other services.

- Third, the Discovery service (also called the Eureka service) allows every service on your cloud to find every other service. It serves the following purposes:

  - It allows all the services in your architecture to publish their own instances and say which IP they are running on and which HTTP port they are listening to.

  - As the Discovery service will know every other service on your cloud, as well as its IP and port, it can inform every other service where to find any available service. That means all your services will be able to find each other automatically when you use the special Spring Cloud configurations that we will see in the next sections.

  - Because every service will read its own configurations from your Spring Cloud Config service, you will have a much easier time setting specific configurations for your services in different environments that you might have to use.

As you can see, your Spring Cloud environment will take care of connecting all the services to each other in whatever environment you need to launch your services in.

In the next sections, we will learn how to write these special services and how to change our current services to enjoy the benefits of a self-configuring cloud environment.

Launching the Discovery service

The Discovery service, also known as the Eureka service, is a very simple microservice that helps you to map every other service in your cloud. It was originally created by Netflix for their own use, but later, the company decided to make it open source. Due to its obvious benefits, it was incorporated into the Spring Cloud set of services.

There is no need to configure extra dependencies to create your Discovery service. You just create a sample service using the Spring Initializr. Then, extract the project content to your hard drive and set your `build.gradle` file to the following:

```
plugins {
    id 'java'
    id 'org.springframework.boot' version '3.3.4'
    id 'io.spring.dependency-management' version '1.1.6'
}

group = 'com.homeit'
```

```
version = '0.0.1-SNAPSHOT'

java {
    toolchain {
        languageVersion = JavaLanguageVersion.of(21)
    }
}

dependencyManagement {
    imports {
        mavenBom "org.springframework.cloud:spring-cloud-
dependencies:2023.0.3"
    }
}

repositories {
    mavenCentral()
}

dependencies {
    implementation 'org.springframework.boot:spring-boot-starter'
    implementation 'org.springframework.cloud:spring-cloud-starter-
netflix-eureka-server'
    implementation 'org.springframework.boot:spring-boot-starter-
actuator'

    testImplementation 'org.springframework.boot:spring-boot-starter-
test'
    testRuntimeOnly 'org.junit.platform:junit-platform-launcher'
}

tasks.named('test') {
    useJUnitPlatform()
}
```

In the code block, the dependencyManagement section downloads the correct version of any Spring Cloud dependencies you might have so that you don't need to set the version in every dependency.

The key dependency here is netflix-eureka. This is the one that automatically adds some REST endpoints to your service that allow the Discovery service to receive registration requests from other services, and that allows other services to discover registered services. The registered services are kept in an in-memory database by default.

These are the key properties of the Eureka service in the HomeIt architecture:

```
spring.application.name=eureka-server

server.port=8761
eureka.client.register-with-eureka=false
eureka.client.fetch-registry=false
```

As you can see, we are setting the name of the service and the default port, and finally, we have two key options: `register-with-eureka`, which tells the service to not try to register itself in another Eureka service, and `fetch-registry`, which is currently setting the Eureka service to not fetch registry data from other Eureka services. These options are useful when doing standalone Eureka service configurations.

Also, in order to have your application running the Eureka services, you will need to add a special annotation to your main application class. Here's an example:

```
@SpringBootApplication
@EnableEurekaServer
public class EurekaServerApplication {

  public static void main(String[] args) {
    SpringApplication.run(EurekaServerApplication.class, args);
  }
}
```

By doing that, you will be able to run the Eureka service. It runs on standalone mode, which means you will have just one Eureka service instance available for your cloud. The downside is that if your Eureka service stops, all the other services won't be kept up to date with their peer service addresses. If any of your services change, Eureka will not be there to update your cloud services about that change.

Standalone mode can be a bit risky, so we need to add multiple instances of the Eureka service. If you want to have high availability with multiple Eureka service instances, you need to define what other Eureka service instances are available in all your service instances. You will list all the Eureka service instances that are available by using the `defaultZone` configuration on your service properties (including all Eureka instances). Also, you will have to set the `fetch-registry` and `register-with-eureka` options to `true` in your Eureka services as well.

Here is an example of how one Eureka service can query other services:

```
eureka.client.register-with-eureka=false
eureka.client.fetch-registry=false
eureka.client.service-url.defaultZone=http://localhost:8761/
eureka/,http://localhost:8762/eureka/
```

And that's it for our Discovery service. You can see the full implementation of an Eureka service here: `https://github.com/PacktPublishing/Spring-System-Design-in-Practice/tree/main/chapter-11/eureka-server`. Next, let's see how to run the Config service, which allows your microservices to download property files from a central place.

Launching the Config service

The Config service allows you to have a centralized location from which your microservices can download their property files. We have seen that managing your property files is a very important part of making your microservices work in many different environments. So, instead of having distributed property files and deciding how each service should discover them on a case-by-case basis, why not have a single location from which all your services can just query their properties at startup time?

Making this design uniform all across your microservices is the purpose of a Config service. This is how to build one.

Building a Spring Cloud Config service

To create a Spring Cloud Config service, Go to the Spring Initializr website and create a basic Spring application. You can add whatever application and package name you want. Then, this is what your `build.gradle` file should look like:

```
plugins {
    id 'java'
    id 'org.springframework.boot' version '3.3.4'
    id 'io.spring.dependency-management' version '1.1.6'
}

group = 'com.homeit'
version = '0.0.1-SNAPSHOT'

java {
    toolchain {
        languageVersion = JavaLanguageVersion.of(21)
    }
}

dependencyManagement {
    imports {
        mavenBom "org.springframework.cloud:spring-cloud-
dependencies:2023.0.3"
    }
```

```
}

repositories {
   mavenCentral()
}

dependencies {
   implementation 'org.springframework.boot:spring-boot-starter'
   implementation 'org.springframework.cloud:spring-cloud-config-
server'
   implementation 'org.springframework.cloud:spring-cloud-starter-
netflix-eureka-client'

   testImplementation 'org.springframework.boot:spring-boot-starter-
test'
   testRuntimeOnly 'org.junit.platform:junit-platform-launcher'
}

tasks.named('test') {
   useJUnitPlatform()
}
```

In the `plugins` section, I have set the version and dependency management to a specific version number.

In the `dependencyManagement` section, I have set the `imports` directive, in which we specify what BOM file to use. Those directives help with writing the `dependencies` section, as you won't need to write the version number for your Spring dependencies. If you don't have those dependency management guides in your build file, you will need to know exactly which version you should use for each Spring dependency.

In the `dependencies` section, we have these important dependencies:

- The Spring Cloud Config Server dependency, which adds everything you need in this microservice to serve configuration files effortlessly.

- The Spring Cloud Starter Netflix Eureka Client, which gets your Config Server to automatically register itself in the Eureka service. This allows your microservices to automatically know where to find the Config service.

Now that we have added the dependencies to our Config service, let's learn how to set its properties, which is a critical step to make it work.

Setting the Spring Config Server properties

Because there are quite a few important properties that should go on a Spring Config server, let's break down the properties file and add a few different sections in order to make it easier to understand.

Setting basic application properties and GitHub access

Just like in the Eureka service, a full Config Server is actually pretty simple to write, as you do not need to add extra classes and services to your code. Once you have set up the dependencies in your `build.gradle` file, this is the default property file we are going to use for the HomeIt Config Server:

```
spring.application.name=config-server
server.port=8888
spring.cloud.config.server.git.uri=https://github.com/rsantiago/
professional-spring-system-design-patterns.git
spring.cloud.config.server.git.username=${GIT_USER}
spring.cloud.config.server.git.password=${GIT_KEY}
spring.cloud.config.server.git.searchPaths=config-repo/
```

As you can see, I am setting the port to `8888`, then setting up the Git repository where I want to get the configuration files from. I am also setting the username and password to two environment variables (I am using the GitHub developer token as the password). Plus I am telling Spring that, once it clones the repository, the configuration files lie in the `config-repo/` directory.

Those were all the property values we needed for setting up the Git configuration and the basic service properties, such as the application name and the server port. Let's now look at the properties used by the Eureka clients so that your Config Server knows how to publish itself to your Eureka service, and also so that it knows how to get other service addresses from the Eureka registry.

Setting the Eureka properties

The following properties are related to the Eureka service. It will help your Config Service to connect to your Spring Cloud environment:

```
eureka.client.service-url.defaultZone=http://localhost:8761/eureka/
eureka.client.register-with-eureka=true
eureka.client.fetch-registry=true
eureka.instance.prefer-ip-address=true
```

Here, I am telling my Config Server that the Eureka service can be found at port 8761 and that this config server should register itself in Eureka. This server will fetch the registered servers from Eureka and will prefer to use the IP addresses to reach other servers.

Setting the right log levels for transparency

Knowing what is happening with your Config service is crucial for troubleshooting your Spring Cloud environment. So, let's see some other important options in the properties file for our HomeIt Config Server that will produce logs that say what is happening in your Config Server:

```
logging.level.org.springframework.cloud.config.server.
environment=DEBUG
logging.level.org.eclipse.jgit=DEBUG
logging.level.org.springframework.web=DEBUG
logging.level.org.springframework.cloud.config.server=DEBUG
```

After setting up the Eureka properties, in this section, I am setting the log levels I want for the Config service so that I know what is happening when the server is running.

As you can see, I am first setting the logs to the DEBUG level in the following parts:

- The JGit dependency, which deals with connecting to the configured GitHub repository (the JGit dependency is automatically and implicitly imported when you use the Spring Cloud Config Server dependency).

- The Spring Web dependency and the Cloud Config server dependency as well. This allows me to understand what is happening under the hood when my config server starts and when other microservices try to download their property files, respectively.

And this is pretty much it for your Config service. Let's see the last step, which is to create your main application class that will run the Configuration service.

Writing the application class

In order for the Config Service to work properly, you need a simple application class that goes something like this:

```
@SpringBootApplication
@EnableConfigServer
@EnableDiscoveryClient
public class ConfigServerApplication {
  public static void main(String[] args) {
    SpringApplication.run(ConfigServerApplication.class, args);
  }
}
```

You need just two extra annotations:

- `@EnableConfigServer` will ensure that Spring injects everything you need for your Config Server to run properly, allowing other services to query for their own configuration files.

- `@EnableDiscoveryClient` will ensure this Config Server registers itself in the Eureka service. Remember, Eureka needs to know where the services are so that they can connect to each other effortlessly. We will see how that happens in the *Integrating your services with Spring Cloud* section.

If you want to see the full code for this config service, just follow this link: `https://github.com/PacktPublishing/Spring-System-Design-in-Practice/tree/main/chapter-11/config-server`.

Next, let's see an example of how you can structure your property files in your Git repository.

Setting up your property files on a Git repository

To make sure your applications can download property files from different environments, let's use the Spring Profiles feature. I have created four different property files for each service: a default property file and three different files for hypothetical environments: dev, stg, and prod.

Here's a list of the files I created. As you can see, there are four files prefixed with the `rental-property-microservice` string. That means these are the four property files for the rental property microservice we wrote in our HomeIt project – one for each environment (the default file, then dev, stg, and prod):

```
authprovider-dev.properties
authprovider-prod.properties
authprovider.properties
authprovider-stg.properties
rental-property-microservice-dev.properties
rental-property-microservice-prod.properties
rental-property-microservice.properties
rental-property-microservice-stg.properties
rental-proposal-service-dev.properties
rental-proposal-service-prod.properties
rental-proposal-service.properties
rental-proposal-service-stg.properties
revoke-token-service-dev.properties
revoke-token-service-prod.properties
revoke-token-service.properties
revoke-token-service-stg.properties
```

All these files can be seen in the repository for the project `https://github.com/PacktPublishing/Spring-System-Design-in-Practice/tree/main/config-repo`.

Also, I have created the files in a very simple way, just to illustrate how to change properties from one environment to another. Here is an example for the rental properties microservice in prod:

```
server.port=9801
```

As you can see, I am only changing the port number in each property file. In the real world, the Rental Property service property file would have a lot of different properties in each environment, depending on external services you would like to use, for example. In general, dev, stg, and prod would provide the same external services but in different URLs (think about database connections, for instance).

Your property filename in the Config Server repository must start with the server name you set in the default property file of your project. In the case of the Rental property service, we have set this value in the `application.properties` file:

```
spring.application.name=rental-property-microservice
```

This means that whatever profile I run the Rental Property service with, once I configure this service to integrate with my Spring Cloud environment, it will try to fetch property files starting with the `rental-properties-microservice` prefix. That is crucial for ensuring you get the right configuration.

Next, let's see how we should program our own services for them to integrate automatically with Spring Cloud.

Integrating your services with Spring Cloud

To fully integrate your services with Spring Cloud, there are three requirements:

- Prepare your server to register itself to a Eureka service

- Prepare your server to fetch property files from a Spring Cloud Config Server

- Get your server to discover other services automatically

To implement those three requirements, we will go through five steps in total. In the following sections, these are the steps we will follow. Let's adapt the Rental Properties service adapted to this environment. You can adapt these steps to integrate other services into a Spring Cloud environment.

Adding necessary Spring Cloud dependencies

First, add these dependencies to your `build.gradle` file:

```
implementation 'org.springframework.cloud:spring-cloud-starter-
netflix-eureka-client'
implementation 'org.springframework.cloud:spring-cloud-starter-config'
```

The first dependency will ensure your service connects to a Eureka service, while the second will ensure your service downloads the config files from a Config Server.

Setting your service properties

In order to force your microservice to download configurations from a Config Service and to connect to Eureka, the following properties need to be added to your default properties file:

```
eureka.client.service-url.defaultZone=http://localhost:8761/eureka/
spring.config.import=configserver:
```

Remember that our Eureka service is set up to work on port 8761 and that the `spring.config.import` option is telling your microservice to look for a config server in Eureka. Because we have added the started config dependency, Spring will do all it needs to download the configuration from the Config Server – this all comes out of the box with Spring Cloud architecture.

Configuring your application class

To make sure your microservice integrates with the Eureka service, you will need to add the following annotation to your application class:

```
@SpringBootApplication
@EnableDiscoveryClient
public class RentalPropertyApplication {
    // the rest of the code goes here...
}
```

With the properties and annotations set in this section and in the last two sections, your microapp will register itself with your Eureka service. Then, it will try to fetch the configuration file from the Config server. Remember, your config server is also configured to register itself with the Eureka service.

`@EnableDiscoveryClient` will set your application to connect to your Eureka service, but it can only know how to connect to it because you have set up the dependencies and the properties in the right way.

Choosing what property file your microservice will use

OK, but how can we set up our Rental Properties application class to download the prod properties file, for example? That's easy: just make sure you are setting the right Spring Profile at startup time. Then, get your microservice JAR file and run the following command:

```
java -jar rental-property-microservice.jar --spring.profiles.
active=prod
```

This command will make our Rental Properties microservice look for the `rental-property-microservice-prod.properties` file in the Config Server.

Calling other services with self-discovery

What about connecting to other services? When you integrate your application into a Spring Cloud architecture, it is possible to connect to another service using `RestTemplate` by doing two things.

First, declare your `RestTemplate` bean factory with a special annotation:

```
@Configuration
public class RestTemplateConfiguration {
    @Bean
    @LoadBalanced
    public RestTemplate restTemplate() {
        return new RestTemplate();
    }
}
```

By using the `@LoadBalanced` annotation, Spring Cloud will ensure two things:

- First, that your application uses the registry that Eureka provides. That means your application will be able to know the IP and port of your other microservices by just using the names of the other microservices declared in their own properties file.

- Second, Spring Cloud will ensure that if you have multiple copies of the same services running on your Spring Cloud environment, the calling service alternates between different target service instances when calling another microservice. This is what we call **load balancing**. In other words, the service starting the HTTP calls will distribute the calls, or the load, between different copies of the same destination services.

This is an important aspect of the discovery service in Spring Cloud. If you run multiple copies of the same services and they are configured to use the Eureka service, Eureka will keep a list of all existing instances in different IPs and ports. In other words, if you run the Proposal service multiple times from different IPs and ports, your Eureka service will know every instance. And every time a service tries to call the Rental Property service, the load-balanced `RestTemplate` will receive a list of those different instances and will distribute the calls evenly. Keep this in mind when you're thinking about scaling your services to deal with more traffic.

Here is the second thing to do to allow your Spring services to automatically discover other services in your cloud environment. Let's see how the Rental Property service is able to call another server. We need to declare the `url` parameter using just the name of the destination service. Plus, since we have programmed the Rental Properties service to query the Revoke Token service to discover if the token is still valid, we set the call to automatically discover the address of the Revoke Token service. This is what the code will look like:

```
public boolean isTokenRevoked(String token) {
    String url = "http://revoke-token-service/api/revoke-
```

```
tokens?token=" + token;

    // the rest of the code goes here
}
```

Remember, this is the code in the `RestTemplateRevokedTokenService` class. Before the Spring Cloud configuration, we needed to set the location and port of the destination service. But since we are now using Eureka as a discovery service, by just referring to your destination service using the name of your target server set in the properties file, Spring Cloud will make sure Eureka informs your calling server where the destination service will be located. This is incredible and useful! That makes your cloud self-configuring in every environment that you launch it.

These are the most important things you need to do in every one of your services. If you want to see how this is set up for all the services we have built so far, the final code for our servers is here:

- Eureka: `https://github.com/PacktPublishing/Spring-System-Design-in-Practice/tree/main/chapter-11/eureka-server`

- Config Server: `https://github.com/PacktPublishing/Spring-System-Design-in-Practice/tree/main/chapter-11/config-server`

- Rental Properties service: `https://github.com/PacktPublishing/Spring-System-Design-in-Practice/tree/main/chapter-11/rental-property-microservice`

- Rental Proposal service: `https://github.com/PacktPublishing/Spring-System-Design-in-Practice/tree/main/chapter-11/rental-proposal-service`

- Authorization provider: `https://github.com/PacktPublishing/Spring-System-Design-in-Practice/tree/main/chapter-11/authprovider`

We have gone very far! At this point, your microservice cloud is able to serve configuration files remotely and discover other services automatically. Now, let's discuss how to serve all your service requests from a single location: a Spring API gateway.

Launching the API Gateway service

If you have done everything we've discussed so far, the following situation is true: your services are launching and discovering each other automatically, and your configuration files are all centralized in one place. That's cool, but there is one problem still to be solved: if an external HTTP client were supposed to consume these services, they would have to either find out the microservice IPs and ports by querying the Eureka service or we would need another way to make the external client know where to find your servers.

Enter the Spring Cloud Gateway. Instead of forcing your external clients to know how to query the Eureka server, the Spring Cloud Gateway allows you to centralize all your endpoints in a single service by setting up a façade server. In our HomeIt cloud, this means our frontend would be able to create users and tokens, create and query properties, and create and query proposals using a single IP and port, with different endpoints.

The way to configure the Spring Cloud Gateway is to follow these steps:

1. Create a simple Spring application in Spring Initializr.

2. Add the dependencies needed by the gateway.

3. Configure the endpoints using the properties file.

Let's see how that happens with our HomeIt example.

Create a simple Spring application in Spring Initializr with the right dependencies

By now, you know how to create a simple app with Spring Initializr. So, go there and create one without any special dependencies.

Next, set your `build.gradle` file to the following:

```
plugins {
    id 'java'
    id 'org.springframework.boot' version '3.3.4'
    id 'io.spring.dependency-management' version '1.1.6'
}

group = 'com.homeit'
version = '0.0.1-SNAPSHOT'

java {
    toolchain {
        languageVersion = JavaLanguageVersion.of(21)
    }
}

dependencyManagement {
    imports {
        mavenBom "org.springframework.cloud:spring-cloud-
dependencies:2023.0.3"
    }
}
```

```
repositories {
    mavenCentral()
}

dependencies {
    implementation 'org.springframework.boot:spring-boot-starter'
    implementation 'org.springframework.cloud:spring-cloud-starter-
gateway'
    implementation 'org.springframework.cloud:spring-cloud-starter-
netflix-eureka-client'
    testImplementation 'org.springframework.boot:spring-boot-starter-
test'
    testRuntimeOnly 'org.junit.platform:junit-platform-launcher'
}

tasks.named('test') {
    useJUnitPlatform()
}
```

By setting the Eureka client dependency, your API gateway will connect to your Eureka service, and every service you run will be made available to your API gateway.

Next, let's set the application class to enable the discovery client services by adding the @ EnableDiscoveryClient annotation:

```
@SpringBootApplication
@EnableDiscoveryClient
public class ApiGatewayApplication {

  public static void main(String[] args) {
    SpringApplication.run(ApiGatewayApplication.class, args);
  }
}
```

Easy enough, right? Setting up the application is quite simple. Now, we need to configure the API gateway.

Configure the endpoints using the API gateway service properties file

In order to create our API gateway endpoints, we need to declare them in our .yml property file. There is no need to write a lot of code. This is the start of the application.yml file:

```
spring:
  application:
    name: api-gateway
  cloud:
    gateway:
```

```
discovery:
  locator:
    enabled: true
    lower-case-service-id: true
```

This informs Spring Cloud that this application is called `api-gateway`, that the gateway service will be activated to discover the other services in the cloud, and that every service query should be handled by parsing service names to lowercase.

Now, this is what we need to declare the endpoints we want in this API gateway. It is all done within the configuration file. Notice the spaces, which have been left intentionally, as all these routes are children of the `spring.cloud.gateway` property in the properties hierarchy:

```
routes:
  - id: authprovider
    uri: lb://authprovider
    predicates:
      - Path=/auth/**
    filters:
      - StripPrefix=1
  - id: revoketoken
    uri: lb://revoke-token-service
    predicates:
      - Path=/revoke/**
    filters:
      - StripPrefix=1
  - id: rentalproposal
    uri: lb://rental-proposal-service
    predicates:
      - Path=/proposals/**
  - id: rentalproperties
    uri: lb://rental-property-microservice
    predicates:
      - Path=/properties/**
    filters:
      - StripPrefix=1
```

These configurations create API gateway endpoints for all the important services we have so far. Let's take just one of the defined paths to understand its pieces:

```
  - id: rentalproperties
    uri: lb://rental-property-microservice
    predicates:
      - Path=/properties/**
```

```
filters:
  - StripPrefix=1
```

Now, let's see what each attribute means.

Spring API gateway configuration attributes

The `id` attribute helps to create a name for an API gateway endpoint. It generally means we are setting an endpoint for one of our services. In the HomeIt context, we are talking about creating an API gateway endpoint for providing external clients access to the Rental Properties service.

The `uri` attribute means the service location inside the Eureka registry. Here, we are declaring that we want load-balanced access to the service named `rental-property-microservice` (remember, this is the name of the service we have set up in the default `application.properties` file in the Rental Properties service).

Note that by **load balanced**, we mean that every call to our API gateway that is destined to the Rental Properties service will be distributed across every running instance of the Rental Properties service that registers itself in our Eureka service. That is a lot to take, so read it again to make sure you understand what it means. Spring Cloud is an architecture that makes a lot of things automatically!

The `predicates` section tells us that whenever a request comes to the API gateway and the URI has the `/properties/` prefix, the API gateway will forward that request to the Rental Properties service that was discovered in the Eureka registry.

The `filters` section tells us that when we forward a request to the Rental Properties service, we will strip away the `/properties/` prefix by using the `StripPrefix=1` directive. In other words, we strip away one level of the root URL in every request before forwarding it to the destination service.

That means, in practice, that other applications will have to call the API gateway in `http://{api-gateway:port}/properties/api/v1/rental-properties` so that the gateway can strip away the `properties` portion of the URI and forward the request to `http://{rental-properties-microservice:port}/api/v1/rental-properties`.

That was `rentalproperties`, but as you can see in this collection of endpoints, we have also declared endpoints for all important services in our HomeIt architecture, including `authprovider`, `revokentoken`, and `rentalproposal` too. How interesting is that?

Now, let's see the other parts of our `application.yml` file:

```
logging:
  level:
    com.homeit.logs.GlobalFilterLogs: DEBUG
    org.springframework.cloud.gateway: DEBUG
    org.springframework.http.server.reactive: DEBUG
    reactor.netty.http.server: DEBUG
```

We have set these log levels to make sure we can see everything that is happening when the API gateway receives a call and forwards it to other servers. It will produce debug logs for our GlobalFilter logs (we will see these in a bit), and it will also produce debug logs for the API Gateway dependency, the Reactive Server dependency, and the HTTP server dependency as well.

Let's look at the last properties:

```
server:
  port: 8080

eureka:
  client:
    service-url:
      defaultZone: http://localhost:8761/eureka/
```

As you can see, we are setting our API gateway to serve requests at port 8080, and the service URL for eureka to port 8761 in localhost. This means that whatever requests at `http://localhost:8080/` `{whatever-uri}` hit our API gateway configurations, if the prefixes match any of the filters we created, the API gateway will know how to forward that request to one of our services.

With that, you have set up your API gateway. Now, we need to improve the transparency of our logs, so we will add a global filter class that will let you know everything important about every request your API gateway receives.

Setting transparent logs in your Spring API gateway

Because we need more transparency to check whether our API gateway works properly, I have created a class called `GlobalFilterLogs`. It means that all the calls the API gateway receives will produce logs with every bit of information in that HTTP request. Let's look at the implementation:

```
@Component
public class GlobalFilterLogs
    implements GlobalFilter, Ordered {

    private static final Logger logger = LoggerFactory
        .getLogger(GlobalFilterLogs.class);

    @Override
    public Mono<Void> filter(ServerWebExchange exchange,
  org.springframework.cloud.gateway.filter.GatewayFilterChain  chain) {

        // Log the request path and headers
        logger.info("Incoming request: {} {}",
            exchange.getRequest().getMethod(),
            exchange.getRequest().getURI());

        exchange.getRequest().getHeaders()
```

```
    .forEach((name, values) -> {
        values.forEach(value -> logger.debug(
            "Request Header: {}={}", name, value));
    });

return chain.filter(exchange)
    .then(Mono.fromRunnable(() -> {

    // Log the response status code and headers
    logger.info("Outgoing response: {}",
        exchange.getResponse().getStatusCode());

    exchange.getResponse().getHeaders()
        .forEach((name, values) -> {
            values.forEach(value -> logger.debug(
            "Response Header: {}={}", name, value));
        });
    }));
}


@Override
public int getOrder() {
  return -1; // Ensure this filter is applied first
}
}
```

This neat code piece will inject a class in our API gateway cycle that will log all handled request and response objects to our console at the debug level. This makes it transparent that we are making requests in the right way to our destination services.

This is what we needed to set up our API gateway properly. Let's test the entire Spring Cloud environment.

Hitting the API gateway with our integration tests

Now that we have configured our Spring Cloud environment, how do we test it completely?

First, we need to know how to make it all available for our external clients. To make sure all the servers are connecting with each other in the right way, this is the order in which you need to run your services:

1. The Eureka service needs to be started before everything else.

2. The Config service needs to be started next.

3. Then your API gateway can be started.

4. Finally, you can start your own services.

Your services will then register and query the Eureka service registry, and hence they will be able to fetch the config files from the Config Server. Also, the API gateway will discover your services automatically since the Eureka service updates the other clients.

Understanding these steps and the order in which you should start them is crucial for making your Spring Cloud work. Here are a few other interesting facts about Spring Cloud that you must have in mind:

- If one of your service instances is down, Eureka will update its own registry automatically in just a few seconds, and all Eureka clients will know that a service instance is down.

- When a new service instance is up, its Eureka clients will inform the Eureka service, which will in turn inform all other servers that a new instance of a service is online.

  These two first bullets mean that you can spin new service instances up or kill instances, and all your other services will know about it. They will figure out on their own which instances are alive over time.

- If your Eureka service is down, the other services will try to connect to one another by using the last information they have about their peer services.

- Once your Eureka service is up again, it will automatically gather information about other services and refresh itself.

- The API gateway will be updated over time as new instances are down or up, and because it also uses load balancers, it can distribute calls to servers dynamically as the IPs and ports change over time for different servers.

These features make Spring Cloud very powerful and resilient. We are going to explore other important Spring Cloud features in the next chapter.

Now, we still need to make some adjustments in our integration tests, to make sure they are calling our HomeIt service by using the API gateway we have set up. Since I wanted our integration tests to hit the API gateway directly, I have made the following changes to our code:

- Every request address was changed to `localhost:8080` because I am running these services on my local computer, but it could be in any IP in which you will run your API gateway.

- All requests were changed to add the prefix we created in our API gateway. Before the change, we were calling our individual services directly, so the URL of the service was a bit different. For instance, for the Rental Properties service, we would have the URL `/api/v1/rental-properties`, and in the API gateway, we expect to receive the prefix `/properties/` in the URL. If we try to call our services without fixing the prefix to the one accepted by our API gateway, you will get a series of 404 responses.

You can see the full implementation of our integration tests here (insert the repository's URL here). This version of the integration tests will create users, tokens, properties, and proposals by directly accessing our API gateway without knowing where the other services lie behind the curtains. It is simply superb that we can hide those details from our clients and make our cloud services much simpler.

And that is how we create a full Spring Cloud architecture, allowing your services to be self-configurable and discoverable.

Summary

In this chapter, we have discussed how to organize our services to properly run in different environments. We started by looking at how to structure our logs and how to activate/deactivate log levels. We have also learned how to organize our properties with very different strategies that allow us to adapt to different environments, purposes, and circumstances. Finally, we have set up our services by using the Spring Cloud framework, which provides very high configurability, load balancing, discoverability, and resilience to our microservice cloud. We have learned that by using an API gateway, we can simplify external access to different services in whatever IPs and ports are available. Plus, we have updated our integration tests to ensure we can do end-to-end tests directly by connecting to the API gateway.

In the next chapters, we will learn how to optimize this architecture further so that we can have faster services that can recover from failure. I hope to see you there!

Get This Book's PDF Version and Exclusive Extras

Scan the QR code (or go to `packtpub.com/unlock`). Search for this book by name, confirm the edition, and then follow the steps on the page.

Note: Keep your invoice handly. Purchase made directly from packt don't require one.

12

Optimizing Your Services

Welcome to our last chapter! This book was a wild ride going through several different Spring Framework patterns. In this chapter, we will look at what could go wrong with services—because it is not always a happy world, right? Dealing with systems means we will see many severe issues—including in production. This chapter is meant to soften the blow. That is, it is meant to help you to prepare your system to be more resilient, fault-tolerant, and optimized.

We will cover the following topics in this chapter:

- Setting the right performance expectations for your projects
- Using caching to speed up access to critical data
- Recovering from failures with dead letter queues
- Real-time service monitoring with Spring Actuator
- Handling faulty services with Resilience4j
- Preventing race conditions with a SQL trick
- Recovering from failures using an audit job
- Dealing with a surge of requests by using throttling

In this chapter, you will be presented with a series of strategies for handling pitfalls in your systems. OK, let's get down to it!

Technical requirements

In order to go through these examples, you will need access to the chapter-12 folder of our sample code repository: https://github.com/PacktPublishing/Spring-System-Design-in-Practice/tree/main/chapter-12.

More specifically, you can find the new code sample in the implementation of the **Rental Properties** service: `https://github.com/PacktPublishing/Spring-System-Design-in-Practice/tree/main/chapter-12/rental-property-microservice`.

Setting the right performance expectations for your project

When you write software, you pour a part of your heart into the code. You spend a lot of time imagining great ideas to write. It turns out that a lot of our best ideas are faulty and buggy, which could be hard to accept. Because of that, software is also an emotional rollercoaster of sorts. The following principles may help you to deal with those emotions and expectations.

Failures are unavoidable

Bugs, errors, malfunctioning, outages, network errors, hardware failures—these are all expected in software architecture and completely unavoidable in anyone's microservices. It is simply impossible for developers to deal with so many variables. I often say to my teams that the internet is a complete miracle. Can you imagine how many data structures and systems need to be perfectly aligned—in software and hardware—so that this incredible environment can freely distribute information throughout the world? Dealing with systems is a nightmare sometimes, so we need to just be at peace with the fact that software is risky. When you build something, it does not matter how much attention and quality assurance you bring to the table—something is going to break; something is going to be offline unexpectedly.

When your system grows, the chance of something going wrong grows more and more. So, the first thing you should keep in mind about performance improvement and troubleshooting is this: you will need to do it at some point.

Launch early, optimize later

The second thing I like to think about software optimization is this: since there are countless ways to improve your engineering, do not try to launch the perfect system from scratch—else, you will never launch it and will spend a lot of money on optimizations that never see production.

Optimizations take time and eat up your company's money, so you should only optimize against clear issues you are likely to face in production. If you know that your system will need to serve 20,000 requests per second, then create your system to handle that from the very first version. But if you know the first version of your system will be released to barely 1,000 users in the first month, just launch it without support for thousands of requests per second. Having that mindset will allow you to apply your company resources with efficacy. Being able to ship things, instead of delaying deliveries for a utopian perfection, will make you stand out among developers.

Key bottlenecks that can slow things down

Performance bottlenecks in software can occur in various key areas. Take *Figure 12.1* as an example. That is a very simplified version of our current architecture. Each component represents something that can break. Let's take a look:

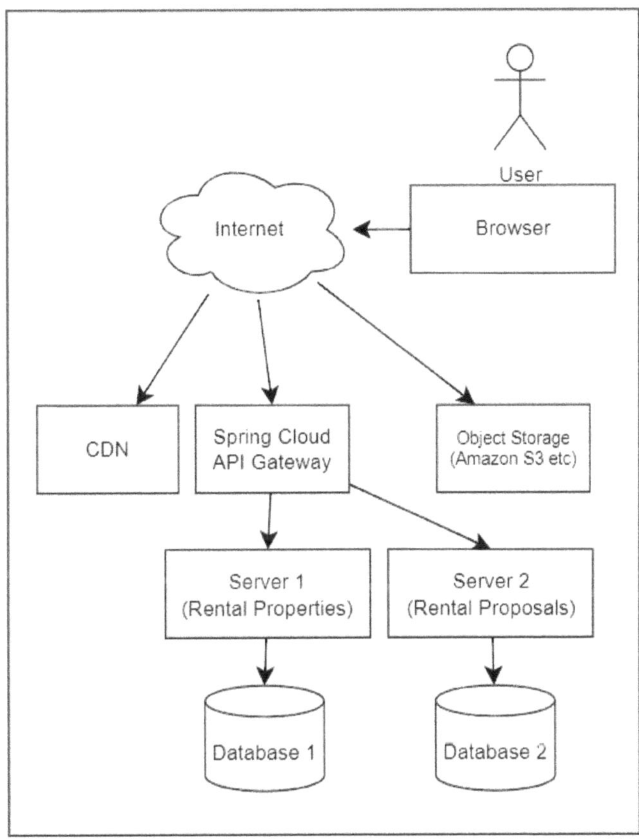

Figure 12.1 – A sample internet architecture

In the browser, rendering heavy pages or inefficient scripts can slow down interactions or break network calls. A CDN might introduce latency if improperly configured. An API gateway can become a bottleneck if overloaded. Object storage access may be slow due to network or even local hardware constraints. A poorly optimized microservice can consume excessive CPU or memory. Network issues can affect data flow between services, especially in containers. Slow hard disks and network filesystems can delay data retrieval. Inefficient databases can lead to sluggish queries, impacting overall performance. Finally, if you design your software in the wrong way—which we usually discover once our systems are being used in the real world—you will learn that your system is using its resources in a suboptimal manner.

The best way to figure out issues in your system is to break your architecture down into its components and overall network topology and then test each component separately. For example, if your users are experiencing a long latency time for a request, you need to check that each hop in this network is working adequately until you find the step that is taking a long time to finish. Maybe it is the database query or your microservice algorithm. You will have to figure it out by investigating each small step.

Eliminate single points of failure

Another thing to take into account when optimizing systems is this: as much as possible, you should eliminate what we call "single points of failure"—which means any individual component, service, or dependency that, if it fails, would cause the entire system or a critical part of it to stop working.

That usually means you should have service copies running in parallel. If one of the copies fails, the others can take over and continue the work.

This is a critical step in software engineering. Make sure you do not have systems running in standalone mode.

Distributed transactions going wrong

Monolithic architecture has a clear advantage in transactions, compared to microservices. Since the entire system is connected to just one database, any new transaction you create with several changes in different tables can be wrapped inside a single database transaction. The database infrastructure guarantees that, if a single operation fails in the transaction, every other operation will be rolled back, and your system data will be left untouched and consistent.

With microservices, you need to think differently. Since a single-user operation can span across different servers, if something goes wrong in one of the services affected, other services can be left in the wrong state. That requires a special way of thinking. In general, each of your services needs to have very clear states and messaging systems. So, if something goes wrong in one service, you can recover messages from other services and roll back the transactions that took place in other systems.

There are countless ways of solving distributed transaction errors; since we are approaching the end of the book, we don't have enough space to discuss and demonstrate them here. But bear in mind that if one of the services fails in the chain of the execution of a distributed transaction, it must provide events so that other servers can roll back their part of the transaction.

Prepare your services for concurrent requests

Another critical aspect of service optimization is the good old concurrency issue. In our HomeIt system, for instance, we have not created any safeguards to prevent the same landlord from accepting two or more proposals from different people. That will lead to a very basic concurrency issue. I left that hole open so we could discuss it further. Even if we have created a service to mark which properties are already rented, a landlord with bad intentions could try to accept two contracts at the same time.

It is key to put features in place to prevent people from using resources concurrently in a way that they should not be allowed to.

These topics introduce and summarize the kinds of issues we deal with when thinking about optimization, performance, and failures. We will spend the rest of the chapter looking at several strategies to prevent failures and optimize our strategy.

Using caching to speed up access to critical data

Caching is an interesting topic that is easy to explain but sometimes hard to get right in practice. Suppose that on HomeIt, you start to see a lot of users looking for properties, and then you decide that you do not want the database to be engaged every time the endpoint for retrieving the property by ID is used. After all, firing a request to the database is a costly I/O operation, and properties do not change too much over time anyway after the owner registers its basic data.

In that case, you might decide that, when receiving a call to get properties by ID, your **Rental Properties** service should query a caching system before reaching for the database—that usually means putting an in-memory database, such as Redis or Memcached, before the database operation.

We are not going to cover how to install or configure a different Redis instance here, as this is a topic for an entire book itself. You can use this official how-to page to learn how to install Redis on your machine:

`https://redis.io/docs/latest/operate/oss_and_stack/install/install-redis/`

Let's just look at how to configure Redis inside Spring Boot. You will need an already-running Redis instance:

1. First, we are going to add these two dependencies to the `build.gradle` file:

    ```
    implementation 'org.springframework.boot:spring-boot-starter-
    cache'
    implementation 'org.springframework.boot:spring-boot-starter-
    data-redis'
    ```

2. Then, we create a `Configuration` class that will tell the Spring Framework to start the caching service:

```
@Configuration
@EnableCaching
public class CacheConfig {
}
```

If you are using an external Redis server, just add these properties to your project. In our sample code, I just added it but commented, so you can just use it if you want on your project:

```
spring.cache.type=redis
spring.data.redis.host=localhost
spring.data.redis.port=6379
```

Now that we have the dependency, the configuration bean class, and the properties included in our project, we can just add the caching declaration to the service classes we want. In this case, I will add a cache to the `RentalPropertiesServiceImpl` class, as I want the getter by ID to return properties from the cache. Here is the code:

```
@Override
@Cacheable(value = "properties", key = "#id")
public Optional<RentalPropertyDTO> get(UUID id) {
    return Optional.ofNullable(rentalProperties.get(id));
}
```

What does this `@Cacheable` annotation do? It creates an in-memory collection of properties. When we first hit the rental properties GET endpoint with the id A, for instance, the caching system won't find the property inside its collection. Therefore, it will query the database and, besides returning the property, it will cache it so the next call will not require a query to a database, but just an in-memory scan of the cached properties.

Here's an interesting language point: when our cache is able to return an object we are requesting, we say we have a "cache hit." When our object is not yet cached and we need to go to the database, we say we have a "cache miss." These are universal terms that you will hear people use.

Now, here is an important thing. When you have a cached object, you need to make sure it gets renewed if that object gets updated in the database. In other words, you need to "evict" the object from the cache, whenever that object is being updated in your system. This is how we do it:

```
@Override
@CacheEvict(value = "properties", key = "#id")
public Optional<RentalPropertyDTO> update(
        UUID id,
        RentalPropertyDTO updatedProperty) {
```

```
    // implementation goes here
}
```

By adding the @CacheEvict annotation to your code, it is possible to instruct the caching system to always remove the property with the ID you are currently updating in the database. In that way, the next time someone tries to get the property using the same ID, you will have a cache miss and the new version will be cached again.

Simple enough, right? Now, let's move on to the next topic: dead letter queues.

Recovering from failures with dead letter queues

In our HomeIt system, we created a very simple messaging system, such that our **Rental Properties** service can update a property that has ongoing negotiations. That is a very simple service that just updates the service with a new number, and the message itself is pretty simple. So, no room for mistakes, right? Right?!

Well, what happens if, for some reason, someone changes the rental proposal code and introduces a different message structure by accident? Or what if you have a service that has a complex notification object, and it gets changed in some way, such as by an error coming from a system it depends on? That would mean the consumers of that malformed message might face an issue while parsing the data.

To handle malformed messages in your system, you can create one or more dead letter queues. That means you can create one or more topics that will serve as alarm queues—once you try to parse the notification from other systems, any error in handling the notification can be forwarded to a dead letter topic.

You can pretty much have a system to consume dead letter messages, or you can set up some alarm systems to trigger email messages if your dead letter topic grows to a certain point. Dead letter queues help you to have visibility of malformed messages on your architecture.

Since you already know how to create topics, I am going to just leave this idea here without a code sample, so that we can cover more optimization ideas in this chapter.

Real-time service monitoring with Spring Actuator

As you may have noticed, we added the Spring Actuator dependency to some of our services in this book project, but we didn't get a chance to really explain what it was about.

OK, here is the kicker: Spring Actuator is a dependency that provides some important infrastructure functions to make it easier for you to monitor your services. These endpoints can be leveraged by other systems to create dashboards and monitor the readiness and aliveness of your services.

For example, if you are using Kubernetes to deploy your applications, you can use the health endpoint to check whether your service instances are still online. Once the health endpoint stops responding, Kubernetes will remove that instance and spin up a new one to replace the failing service.

Here is a list of useful endpoints from Spring Actuator:

- **Health monitoring**: Check whether the app is running (`/actuator/health`)
- **Performance metrics**: View CPU, memory, and request stats (`/actuator/metrics`)
- **Environment inspection**: See config properties and system variables (`/actuator/env`)
- **Logging management**: Change log levels at runtime (`/actuator/loggers`)
- **Endpoint mapping**: List all API routes (`/actuator/mappings`)
- **Thread and memory analysis**: Get thread and heap dumps (`/actuator/threaddump` and `/actuator/heapdump`)
- **Security auditing**: Track login events (`/actuator/auditevents`)
- **Scheduled task monitoring**: View active scheduled tasks (`/actuator/scheduledtasks`)

If we spin up our API gateway server, here is where you will find these endpoints:

```
http://localhost:8080/actuator/health
```

You will be able to enable the actuator endpoints by adding the dependency to your services, just as we did with the API gateway. Just go to your `build.gradle` file and add the following line to your dependencies section:

```
implementation 'org.springframework.boot:spring-boot-starter-actuator'
```

With this, any service you run will have the same set of endpoints. Here's an interesting thing: as I am using the IntelliJ IDE to write these services, I can use its native integration with the Actuator endpoints. Here is a screenshot of what you will get by accessing this feature:

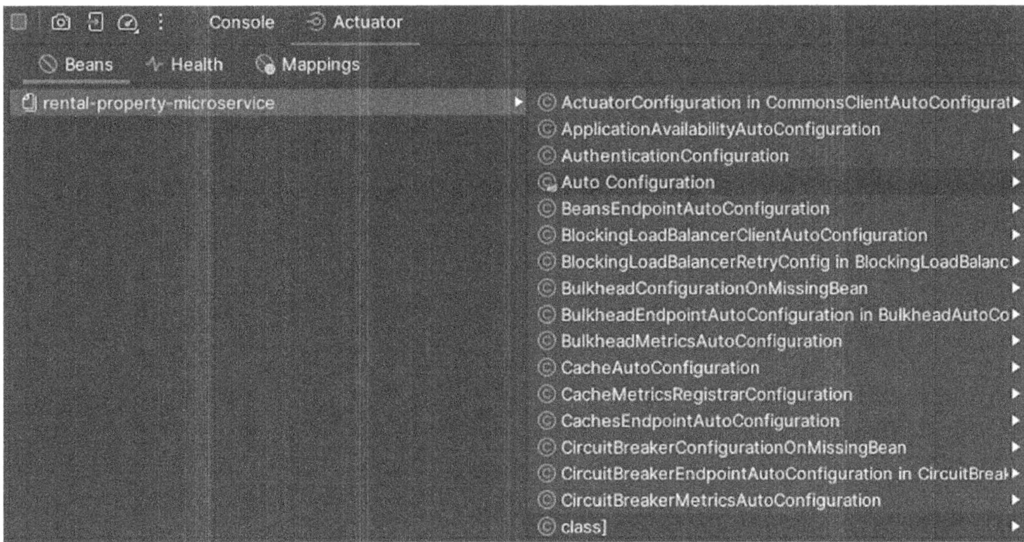

Figure 12.2 – IntelliJ Actuator interface

Other IDEs will provide you with similar other useful features and integrations. In this screenshot, you can see every bean on your running service. You are also able to just navigate through a lot of other vital information at runtime.

All right, Actuator makes it a lot easier to understand what is happening with your service. Let's now see how we can integrate logs from different services, using the Circuit Breaker pattern.

Handling faulty services with Resilience4j

If one of your services stops responding to another service, you can implement policies to determine what the caller will do. You can use Resilience4j in Spring to define those policies.

Resilience4j helps you to define a different behavior for your application in the face of or to avoid making your services faulty—you can choose alternate behavior when a call fails, or maximum thresholds for receiving calls from other services. You can instruct your service to automatically retry a failed call. There are a lot of interesting things you can do to get systems back to normal.

The first thing we will look at is how to use Resilience4j to switch a service behavior in the face of a failure in another service. We call this pattern the Circuit Breaker.

Using the Circuit Breaker pattern

Let's think about the HomeIt company. You know that the **Rental Properties** service now depends on the **Revoke Token** service, to discover if a token was made invalid by an admin. But what if the **Revoke Token** service is down? How is our application supposed to behave in that case? By now, if the **Rental Properties** service is unable to call the **Revoke Token** service, it will basically be unable to validate a token.

So, in order to make our architecture a bit more resilient, let's suppose we want to adopt the following policy: if the **Revoke Token** service is down, we will just consider all tokens valid. This policy is important so that we don't completely remove the user's ability to use the website.

OK, here is how to do it. First, we need to add the following dependency to our **Rental Properties** service, in the dependencies section:

```
implementation 'io.github.resilience4j:resilience4j-spring-boot3'
implementation 'org.springframework.boot:spring-boot-starter-aop'
```

Once your dependency is added, you can configure the Circuit Breaker with the following directives.

First, for HomeIt's **Rental Properties** service, we will add the following annotation to the `RestTemplateRevokeTokenService.isTokenRevoked()` method:

```
@CircuitBreaker(name = "revokeTokenCircuitBreaker", fallbackMethod =
"revokeTokenServiceOutage")
//@Cacheable(value = "token", key = "#token")
public boolean isTokenRevoked(String token) {
    // the rest of the code does not change
}
```

As you may notice, we need to set a name for our Circuit Breaker, and also the name of the fallback method, in case the **Revoke Token** service is unavailable. Here is the implementation of the fallback method. I implemented it right in the `RestTemplateRevokeTokenService` class itself:

```
private boolean revokeTokenServiceOutage(Exception ex) {
    log.error("Revoke Token service is out! " +
            "All tokens are considered not revoked until " +
            "revoke service is back", ex);
    return false;
    // no tokens are considered revoked
    // while revoke service is down
}
```

Also, you will need to add the following configs to your `application.properties`:

```
# circuit breaker configs
resilience4j.circuitbreaker.instances.revokeTokenCircuitBreaker.
failureRateThreshold=50
resilience4j.circuitbreaker.instances.revokeTokenCircuitBreaker.slow-
call-rate-threshold=50
resilience4j.circuitbreaker.instances.revokeTokenCircuitBreaker.slow-
call-duration-threshold=2s

resilience4j.circuitbreaker.instances.revokeTokenCircuitBreaker.wait-
duration-in-open-state=5s
resilience4j.circuitbreaker.instances.revokeTokenCircuitBreaker.
permittedNumberOfCallsInHalfOpenState=3
resilience4j.circuitbreaker.instances.revokeTokenCircuitBreaker.
slidingWindowSize=10
resilience4j.circuitbreaker.instances.revokeTokenCircuitBreaker.
minimumNumberOfCalls=5
```

Here is a quick explanation of the configurations:

- `FailureRateThreshold`: The percentage of failures through which the system will recognize that there is an ongoing failure. In this case, if 50% of our calls to the **Revoke Token** service fail, the circuit opens and the fallback method will be used to replace the default implementation that tries to reach the remote server. The fallback methods are those that will implement the policy you want to have in the absence of a remote server. In our case, we will consider the token to be valid by default if the remote **Revoke Token** service is down.

- `slow-call-rate-threshold`: The circuit opens if more than 50% of the calls are considered slow

- `slow-call-duration-threshold`: What should be considered a "slow call"—in this case, a two-second call to another server will be considered a slow call

- `wait-duration-in-open-state`: When the circuit opens, this is the time it takes to operate with the fallback before triggering another request to test the faulty service again

- `permittedNumberOfCallsInHalfOpenState`: The number of calls that will be fired when the Circuit Breaker is half open and tries again to reach for the remote, faulty service

- `SlidingWindowSize`: The number of last X calls the Circuit Breaker will monitor to measure whether the circuit is open or closed

- `MinimumNumberOfCalls`: The minimum number of calls that need to happen before the Circuit Breaker starts to really measure efficiency

With that, any time the **Revoke Token** service goes offline, the Circuit Breaker will open and a default implementation of the `isTokenRevoked()` method will be fired. All tokens will be considered valid.

OK, this summarizes the main points of the Circuit Breaker pattern. Let's see the next pattern, Rate Limiting.

Using the Rate Limiting pattern

Rate limiting a service means making other services unable to call your service more than X times in a given period. That is important to protect your service from excessive calls, which could lead to it completely breaking down and going offline.

To use rate limiting in Resilience4j, use the following annotation as an example:

```
@RateLimiter(name = "revokeTokenServiceRateLimiter", fallbackMethod =
"rateLimitFallback")
public boolean isTokenRevoked(String token) {
    // your service implementation goes here
}
```

In this case, you also need to set the fallback method, which goes pretty much however you want—you could just return a default answer (making the token valid, in our HomeIt example), or return a default error to the caller (that could be a troubling idea for our example, if you think that an excessive number of real users would be stopped from successfully accessing your website).

As you did with the Circuit Breaker usage, you will also need to parameterize how you want the rate limiter to play on your application. See the HomeIt example here:

```
# rate limiting
resilience4j.ratelimiter.instances.revokeTokenServiceRateLimiter.
limit-for-period=100
resilience4j.ratelimiter.instances.revokeTokenServiceRateLimiter.
limit-refresh-period=1s
```

In this case, we are taking only two parameters: the number of calls we want our application to support and the time we want to refresh the counter. In this example, we say that our service should not run more than 100 times per second.

Note that we always give a name while declaring the annotation. That name is then written in the configuration file. Every time we use one of the Resilience4j annotations, we call it an "instance" of Resilience4Jj Therefore, we can declare different policies for every service you want to protect with Resilience4j. This allows us to get pretty flexible and specific, and we can tailor our resilience strategies for each different situation.

Another important Resilience4j strategy is Retry. Let's see it in detail.

Using Retry in Resilience4J

Sometimes, services fail due to transient circumstances. Maybe a momentary network issue happened and your call to another service was lost. Or maybe some overload made your service stop responding for a few seconds. In busy, high-volume architectures, that might happen occasionally. Now, since this did not make your service go entirely offline, it basically means the next time you call it, it will be able to respond. What we should do then is be able to retry the request. That is easy with Resilience4J. Just use the `@Retry` annotation. And, of course, you need to set a name for that specific instance. See the following:

```
@Retry(name = "revokeTokenServiceRetry")
public boolean isTokenRevoked(String token) {
      // your service implementation goes here
}
```

A key difference between the `@Retry` annotation and others from Resilience4j is that you don't need to declare a fallback method. After all, you are just asking the system to retry the same method if something goes wrong.

In order to set the actual policy for this `@Retry` instance, we can use the following declaration on our `application.properties`:

```
# retry config
resilience4j.retry.instances.revokeTokenServiceRetry.max-attempts=3
resilience4j.retry.instances.revokeTokenServiceRetry.wait-duration=2s
```

In this case, we say that Resilience4j should run the same method up to three times, waiting two seconds between each retry. That might not be a useful setting for your own application; it is just an example. You should always think about your use case. For example, if you think your app could answer in half a second again, or even less, you should just set the time in ms—500 ms, for example.

OK, let's see the Bulkhead pattern now.

Using the Bulkhead pattern

This one seems a bit similar to the Rate Limiting pattern. But instead of setting how many requests you can take per period of time, you will choose how many parallel requests you can serve at the same time in your application. This is particularly useful to prevent actual memory crashes if you notice that on some occasions, your server gets heavily loaded because of multiple threads being opened to serve requests in parallel. If you do not have access to more memory in your service instance, implementing Bulkhead will prevent your service from completely crashing.

Here is how you use the @Bulkhead annotation:

```
@Bulkhead(name = "revokeTokenBulkhead", fallbackMethod =
"bulkheadFallback")
public boolean isTokenRevoked(String token) {
    // your service implementation goes here
}
```

As you can see, you will set a name to this Bulkhead instance, and you should also define a method that will be executed in case you don't have more threads to open.

Here is an example of how to parameterize the Bulkhead on your `application.properties` file:

```
# bulk head
resilience4j.bulkhead.instances.revokeTokenBulkhead.max-concurrent-
calls=50
resilience4j.bulkhead.instances.revokeTokenBulkhead.max-wait-
duration=50s
```

The `max-concurrent-calls` parameter defines the maximum number of threads you want the application to use. `max-wait-duration` means the maximum amount of time calls will wait for their turn. In this example, we are saying we will serve up to 50 calls at a time, and the maximum wait duration will be 3 seconds. So, if more than 50 calls happen at the same time, the excessive ones will wait up to three seconds to be processed. If more than three seconds pass, the Bulkhead will throw an exception for each request that is waiting in the queue.

OK, this summarizes a handful of useful annotations for Resilience4j. Be aware if you use more than one at the same time in the same method, you will want to test it thoroughly to see whether it works.

Now, let's talk a bit about concurrency.

Preventing race conditions with a SQL trick

In our HomeIt system, imagine a scenario where two tenants attempt to accept a rental proposal for the same property at the exact same time. How can we prevent both agreements from being finalized simultaneously? And how do we decide which tenant actually secures the rental?

Why microservice-level solutions won't work

You might consider handling this at the microservice level using synchronized blocks, semaphores, or distributed locks. However, if your system runs multiple instances of the same service, they won't always be aware of each other. This means that two users could still accept the rental proposal at the same time—leading to a classic race condition.

The problem worsens if accepting an agreement involves multiple services (e.g., payments, contract signing, or notifications). Now, you're dealing with a distributed transaction, where concurrent requests could trigger inconsistent states across services.

Some argue that you should create a dedicated locking microservice to control access. The first user to acquire the lock in that service would proceed with the rental process. But what happens when your system scales? If you horizontally scale your lock service, you may introduce new synchronization issues across multiple instances.

A simple and effective solution – database locks

Instead of relying on microservices, you can let your database handle concurrency. With a simple atomic SQL update, you can ensure that only one user successfully locks the rental. This approach is safe and scalable and does not depend on distributed services.

SQL query – acquiring a lock for a rental property

This query updates the rental status only if the home is not already rented:

```
UPDATE rental_properties
SET rented = TRUE, tenant_id = <tenant_id>
WHERE property_id = <property_id> AND rented = FALSE
RETURNING *;
```

You can basically see the entire updated row with the RETURNING directive. If you have a row, that means the user succeeded in acquiring the property rental. With that, you are able to safely move on with further steps without the risk of other users closing the same deal concurrently.

Some developers might suggest using a stored procedure to enforce this logic. However, stored procedures are database-dependent, making it harder to switch between databases in the future. They also add complexity to your system by introducing logic at the database level, making debugging and maintaining business rules more difficult. By using a simple atomic SQL statement, you keep the logic at the application level, making your system more flexible and easier to scale.

OK, that prevents us from a lot of concurrency trouble in a simple and effective way. Now, let's talk about how to recover from some failures.

Recovering from failures by using an audit job

In our HomeIt system, processing a rental contract involves sending requests to multiple systems—making it a **distributed transaction**. But what happens if an error occurs partway through? How do we ensure the system can recover automatically, without requiring manual intervention or troubleshooting?

One of the most effective solutions I've seen is implementing what I call an **audit job**. The idea is simple yet powerful.

Whenever a user accepts a *rental proposal*, we record the exact time of acceptance. This timestamp is stored as part of the proposal data. Additionally, we register the *rental proposal ID as a foreign key* in all downstream services. In other words, a rental proposal is considered *fully processed* only when all required services have recorded data referencing the original agreement. To facilitate tracking, this *proposal ID should be indexed* in every relevant table.

With this setup, we can now implement an *audit job* that runs at regular intervals—say, once per hour for a full day. The job scans rental agreements accepted in the past *24 hours* and verifies that every downstream service has the necessary records. If it detects *missing or incomplete data*, it automatically *retries* the process for that specific service, ensuring that the operation is eventually completed as expected.

Over *24 hours*, each agreement undergoes *24 automated verifications*, significantly reducing the likelihood of unnoticed failures. If you want even *stricter consistency*, you can extend the audit period to a week or even a month, depending on system requirements and performance constraints.

By leveraging an audit job, we create a *self-healing mechanism* that continuously monitors, detects, and corrects inconsistencies—without requiring manual debugging or intervention.

Here's a quick way to implement an audit job in **Spring Boot** using the @Scheduled annotation:

```
@Component
public class RentalAgreementAuditJob {
    @Scheduled(fixedRate = 3600000) // Runs every hour
    public void auditRentalAgreements() {
        // Logic to verify if downstream services have
        // the expected data
        // If missing data is detected,
        // retry processing the rental agreement
    }
}
```

You can use the audit job to produce logs that can be scanned by observability systems so that you can get an immediate grasp of systems that have inconsistent states.

Dealing with a surge of requests by using throttling

There may be situations where your application experiences a sudden surge of requests. Imagine that, in HomeIt, we launch a special campaign offering discounted rates for landlords who register their rental properties on a specific date. The campaign has become so successful that thousands of landlords attempt to register their properties at the exact same time.

How do we prevent our system from becoming overloaded and going offline?

A powerful solution is to use the Throttling pattern, which essentially decouples the time a user sends a request from when the system processes and completes it. Instead of handling all incoming requests immediately, you process them asynchronously, allowing your system to absorb the traffic in a controlled manner.

A simple way to implement this is by placing a Kafka topic (or another message queue system) between the user and the service that handles registrations. The process works as follows:

1. When a landlord submits their registration request, the system immediately acknowledges it and places the request in a Kafka topic. The user receives a quick **Request received** response, preventing slowdowns or failures due to system overload.

2. A separate background worker consumes requests from the topic at a controlled rate, ensuring the registration service processes them without overwhelming the system.

3. As each request is processed, the user receives updates, such as an email or a notification on the website, informing them that their property has been successfully registered.

By using this pattern, the peak load is spread over time, preventing sudden spikes from overwhelming your servers while maintaining a smooth experience for users.

Additionally, you can enhance the user experience by providing status updates. Instead of making users wonder whether their registration was successful, your system can do the following:

- Show a progress indicator on the website

- Send an email or push notification once processing is complete

- Allow users to check their request status via a dashboard

This ensures that even though their request wasn't processed instantly, they always know what's happening, improving trust in your system. This brings us to the end of the chapter. I hope this has been an interesting way of thinking about common issues with your application.

Summary

In this chapter, we provided some critical tips for making your services hit performance, resiliency, and fault tolerance targets, as well as just some good spice on dealing with concurrency.

We started our journey with some principles for you to manage expectations and performance in your services. We then talked about how to use caching to speed up access to data and how to recover from failures in very different ways: by working with dead letter queues, using Spring Actuator to monitor your services, using the amazing Resilience4j to implement retries, Circuit Breaker, and some other great tools for dealing with errors in your services.

We talked about how to handle concurrency by using very simple SQL tricks instead of having distributed services all over the place. We also talked about how to implement audit jobs to verify your system is behaving in a consistent manner when you use distributed transactions, as well as how to prevent your services from just blowing off your memory with the use of an interesting throttling strategy.

I hope this has been helpful. There are countless other ways to make your architecture better, but these tips are very important and ones I wish I had known about when I was starting out.

This concludes the book. I hope to see you on our next journey. Cheers!

Get This Book's PDF Version and Exclusive Extras

Scan the QR code (or go to `packtpub.com/unlock`). Search for this book by name, confirm the edition, and then follow the steps on the page.

Note: Keep your invoice handly. Purchase made directly from packt don't require one.

Epilogue

This book has been a true marathon. It was written over a period of a year. During this time, I faced a lot of hard changes in my own life. As a software engineering manager, I had releases to work on with my team. We also carried out a huge re-architecture at my current company. Also, I bought a new house and sold my previous one. My wife went through a major surgery that took her weeks to recover. I spent a month visiting my family in Rio de Janeiro and had some family members come to live with us.

Can you imagine writing an entire 500-page book under those circumstances? It was quite a marathon! But here we are, and this chapter was all about adversities in systems and several strategies to deal with them. Talking about difficulties!

I truly hope you have enjoyed reading this book as much as I have enjoyed writing it. It was also a self-discovery process. With this last chapter, I hope you are now able to realize your vision as a great Spring Framework architect. May your systems recover easily from failures!

13

Unlock Your Exclusive Benefits

Your copy of this book includes the following exclusive benefit:

- Next-gen Packt Reader
- DRM-free PDF/ePub downloads

Follow the guide below to unlock them. The process takes only a few minutes and needs to be completed once.

Unlock this Book's Free Benefits in 3 Easy Steps

Step 1

Keep your purchase invoice ready for *Step 3*. If you have a physical copy, scan it using your phone and save it as a PDF, JPG, or PNG.

For more help on finding your invoice, visit `https://www.packtpub.com/unlock-benefits/help`.

> **Note**
>
> If you bought this book directly from Packt, no invoice is required. After *Step 2*, you can access your exclusive content right away.

Step 2

Scan the QR code or go to `packtpub.com/unlock`.

On the page that opens (similar to *Figure 13.1* on desktop), search for this book by name and select the correct edition.

Figure 13.1: Packt unlock landing page on desktop

Step 3

After selecting your book, sign in to your Packt account or create one for free. Then upload your invoice (PDF, PNG, or JPG, up to 10 MB). Follow the on-screen instructions to finish the process.

Need help?

If you get stuck and need help, visit `https://www.packtpub.com/unlock-benefits/help` for a detailed FAQ on how to find your invoices and more. This QR code will take you to the help page.

Note

If you are still facing issues, reach out to `customercare@packt.com`.

Index

Symbols

`packtpub.com`

Subscribe to our online digital library for full access to over 7,000 books and videos, as well as industry leading tools to help you plan your personal development and advance your career. For more information, please visit our website.

Why subscribe?

- Spend less time learning and more time coding with practical eBooks and Videos from over 4,000 industry professionals
- Improve your learning with Skill Plans built especially for you
- Get a free eBook or video every month
- Fully searchable for easy access to vital information
- Copy and paste, print, and bookmark content

At `www.packtpub.com`, you can also read a collection of free technical articles, sign up for a range of free newsletters, and receive exclusive discounts and offers on Packt books and eBooks.

Other Books You May Enjoy

If you enjoyed this book, you may be interested in these other books by Packt:

React Key Concepts, Second Edition

Maximilian Schwarzmüller

ISBN: 978-1-83620-227-1

- Build modern, user-friendly, and reactive web apps
- Create components and utilize props to pass data between them
- Handle events, perform state updates, and manage conditional content
- Add styles dynamically and conditionally for modern user interfaces
- Use advanced state management techniques such as React's Context API
- Utilize React Router to render different pages for different URLs
- Understand key best practices and optimization opportunities
- Learn about React Server Components and Server Actions

Microservices with Spring Boot 3 and Spring Cloud, Third Edition

Magnus Larsson

ISBN: 978-1-80512-869-4

- Build reactive microservices using Spring Boot
- Develop resilient and scalable microservices using Spring Cloud
- Use OAuth 2.1/OIDC and Spring Security to protect public APIs
- Implement Docker to bridge the gap between development, testing, and production
- Deploy and manage microservices with Kubernetes
- Apply Istio for improved security, observability, and traffic management
- Write and run automated microservice tests with JUnit, test containers, Gradle, and bash
- Use Spring AOT and GraalVM to native compile the microservices
- Use Micrometer Tracing for distributed tracing

Packt is searching for authors like you

If you're interested in becoming an author for Packt, please visit `authors.packtpub.com` and apply today. We have worked with thousands of developers and tech professionals, just like you, to help them share their insight with the global tech community. You can make a general application, apply for a specific hot topic that we are recruiting an author for, or submit your own idea.

Share your thoughts

Now you've finished *Spring System Design in Practice*, we'd love to hear your thoughts! Scan the QR code below to go straight to the Amazon review page for this book and share your feedback or leave a review on the site that you purchased it from.

`https://packt.link/r/1803249013`

Your review is important to us and the tech community and will help us make sure we're delivering excellent quality content.